# Air Power in the Age of Prim

MW00811317

Since the end of the Cold War, the United States and other major powers have wielded their air forces against much weaker state and nonstate actors. In this age of primacy, air wars have been contests between unequals and have been characterized by asymmetries of power, interest, and technology. This volume examines ten contemporary wars where air power played a major and at times decisive role. Its chapters explore the evolving use of unmanned aircraft against global terrorist organizations as well as more conventional air conflicts in Bosnia, Kosovo, Afghanistan, Iraq, Lebanon, Libya, Yemen, Syria, and against ISIS. Air superiority could be assumed in this unique and brief period where the international system was largely absent great power competition. However, the reliable and unchallenged employment of a spectrum of manned and unmanned technologies permitted in the age of primacy may not prove effective in future conflicts.

PHIL M. HAUN, is a retired US Air Force colonel and decorated A–10 pilot with combat tours over Bosnia, Kosovo, Afghanistan, and Iraq. His previous books are *Lectures of the Air Corps Tactical School* (2019) and *Coercion, Survival, and War: Why Weak States Resist the United States* (2015). He is the Dean of Academics at the US Naval War College.

COLIN F. JACKSON, held the position of Deputy Assistant Secretary of Defense for Afghanistan, Pakistan, and Central Asia (2017–2019). He has published in *International Security*, *Journal of Strategic Studies*, and *Political Science Quarterly*. He is the Chair of the Strategic and Operational Research Department at the US Naval War College.

TIMOTHY P. SCHULTZ, is a retired US Air Force colonel and formerly the Dean of the USAF's School of Advanced Air and Space Studies and a U-2 high–altitude reconnaissance pilot. He is also the author of *The Problem with Pilots: How Physicians, Engineers, and Airpower Enthusiasts Redefined Flight* (2018). He is the Associate Dean of Academics at the US Naval War College.

# Air Power in the Age of Primacy

*Air Warfare since the Cold War*

*Edited by*

## Phil M. Haun
*US Naval War College*

## Colin F. Jackson
*US Naval War College*

## Timothy P. Schultz
*US Naval War College*

CAMBRIDGE
UNIVERSITY PRESS

# CAMBRIDGE
## UNIVERSITY PRESS

University Printing House, Cambridge CB2 8BS, United Kingdom

One Liberty Plaza, 20th Floor, New York, NY 10006, USA

477 Williamstown Road, Port Melbourne, VIC 3207, Australia

314–321, 3rd Floor, Plot 3, Splendor Forum, Jasola District Centre, New Delhi – 110025, India

103 Penang Road, #05–06/07, Visioncrest Commercial, Singapore 238467

Cambridge University Press is part of the University of Cambridge.

It furthers the University's mission by disseminating knowledge in the pursuit of education, learning, and research at the highest international levels of excellence.

www.cambridge.org
Information on this title: www.cambridge.org/9781108839228
DOI: 10.1017/9781108985024

First published 2022

*A catalogue record for this publication is available from the British Library.*

*Library of Congress Cataloging-in-Publication Data*
Names: Haun, Phil M., 1964– editor. | Schultz, Timothy Paul, 1966– editor. | Jackson, Colin, 1970– editor.
Title: Air power in the age of primacy : air warfare since the Cold War / edited by Phil Haun, US Naval War College; Colin Jackson, US Naval War College; Tim Schultz, US Naval War College.
Other titles: Air warfare since the Cold War
Description: Cambridge, United Kingdom ; New York, NY : Cambridge University Press, 2021. | Includes index.
Identifiers: LCCN 2021031085 | ISBN 9781108839228 (hardback) | ISBN 9781108984751 (paperback) | ISBN 9781108985024 (ebook)
Subjects: LCSH: Air power. | Air warfare – History – 20th century. | Air warfare – History – 21st century. | Drone aircraft. | Air warfare – Forecasting. | BISAC: POLITICAL SCIENCE / International Relations / General | POLITICAL SCIENCE / International Relations / General
Classification: LCC UG630 .A37 2021 | DDC 358.4/03–dc23
LC record available at https://lccn.loc.gov/2021031085

ISBN 978-1-108-83922-8 Hardback
ISBN 978-1-108-98475-1 Paperback

# Contents

# Figures

# Tables

# Contributors

NICHOLAS BLANCHETTE is a PhD student in political science at the Massachusetts Institute of Technology, where he researches nuclear security, military effectiveness, and coercion. He holds an MPhil in international relations awarded with distinction from the University of Oxford.

NIMROD HAGILADI is a lecturer at the Command and Staff College, Israel Defense Force (IDF), and a member of the Center for Military Studies in the IDF. Nimrod specializes in social and military Israeli history and received his PhD from the Hebrew University of Jerusalem. He was a postdoctoral fellow at the Taub Center for Israel Studies, New York University; a teaching fellow at the Hebrew University; and taught in the Israeli Air Force (IAF) Flight Course, Ben Gurion University. He served as an F-16 navigator in the Israeli Air Force.

PHIL M. HAUN is professor and Dean of Academics at the US Naval War College. He is the author of *Lectures of the Air Corps Tactical School and American Strategic Bombing in World War II* (Kentucky, 2019), *Coercion, Survival, and War: Why Weak States Resist the United States* (Stanford, 2015), and coeditor of *A-10s over Kosovo* (Air University, 2003). He received his PhD in political science from MIT and is a retired US Air Force colonel and A-10 pilot with multiple combat tours.

THOMAS ALEXANDER HUGHES is a professor at the School of Advanced Air and Space Studies, Air University, Maxwell Air Force Base, Alabama. He is the author of *Admiral Bill Halsey: A Naval Life* (Harvard, 2016) and *Overlord: General Pete Quesada and the Triumph of Tactical Air Power in World War II* (Free Press, 1995). His previous appointments include the Ramsey Fellowship at the National Air and Space Museum, The Ohio State University, Bowling Green State University, and the Air War College. He holds a PhD from the

University of Houston and specializes in twentieth-century military history, with a focus on air power.

COLIN F. JACKSON is Chair, Strategic and Operational Research Department, at the Center for Naval Warfare Studies at the US Naval War College. He previously held the position of Deputy Assistant Secretary of Defense for Afghanistan, Pakistan, and Central Asia (2017–19). Colin completed his PhD in political science at MIT and has published in *International Security*, *Journal of Strategic Studies*, and *Political Science Quarterly*. He served four years with the US Army as an armor and cavalry officer and is an intelligence officer in the US Army Reserve.

JAHARA MATISEK is a military professor in the Department of Military and Strategic Studies at the US Air Force Academy in Colorado Springs. He earned his PhD in political science from Northwestern University and has published numerous articles in academic and policy-relevant journals. A US Air Force officer, he flew more than 200 combat sorties in the C-17. Deployed in 2011 to the Combined Air Operations Center in Qatar, he planned and coordinated air operations supporting the Libyan no-fly zone (Operations Odyssey Dawn and Unified Protector).

STEPHEN RENNER holds a PhD from Oxford and is a retired US Air Force colonel. Currently the Director of the Air Force Negotiation Center and formerly professor of Strategy and Security Studies at the School of Advanced Air and Space Studies at Maxwell Air Force Base, Alabama, he is a career A-10 pilot with numerous combat tours. Stephen commanded the 25th Fighter Squadron, Osan Air Force Base, Republic of Korea, and served as Vice Commander of the 355th Fighter Wing, Davis Monthan Air Force Base, Tucson, Arizona. In 2017 he was deployed as the senior airman in northern Iraq during the retaking of Mosul. He is the author of *Broken Wings: The Hungarian Air Force, 1918–45* (Indiana, 2016).

TIMOTHY P. SCHULTZ is an associate professor and Associate Dean of Academics at the US Naval War College. He authored *The Problem with Pilots: How Physicians, Engineers, and Airpower Enthusiasts Redefined Flight* (Johns Hopkins, 2018) and earned his PhD in the history of technology from Duke University. A retired US Air Force colonel and formerly a U-2 high-altitude reconnaissance pilot, Tim served as the Commandant and Dean of the US Air Force's School of Advanced Air and Space Studies at Maxwell Air Force Base, Alabama.

RALPH SHIELD graduated with Highest Distinction as the top graduate from the US Naval War College with an MA in national security and strategic studies, specializing in insurgency and counterterrorism. As a US Navy intelligence officer, he supported airborne surveillance and strike operations over the Balkans, drug interdiction and reconnaissance missions in Latin America, counterpiracy and hostage rescue events off the Horn of Africa, and multiple combat support tours in Afghanistan, most recently as a military advisor to the Afghan National Army. He has published in the *Journal of Strategic Studies* and the *Journal of Slavic Military Studies.*

ANDREW L. STIGLER is an associate professor in the National Security Affairs Department of the US Naval War College. His book *Governing the Military* (Routledge, 2018) explores the requirements and potential problems associated with presidential command of the military. Previously he published "A clear victory for air power: NATO's empty threat to invade Kosovo" in *International Security.* He holds a PhD in political science from Yale University.

HEATHER VENABLE is an associate professor at the Air Command and Staff College, Air University, Maxwell Air Force Base, Alabama. She earned her PhD in history from Duke University and authored *How the Few Became the Proud: Crafting the Marine Corps Mystique, 1874–1918* (Naval Institute Press, 2019). She serves as editor of *The Field Grade Leader* and associate editor of *The Strategy Bridge,* and her recent publications include articles in the *Journal of Military History, Military History Now,* and the *Modern War Institute.*

# Preface

In June 2016, when receiving a briefing on the curriculum of the School of Advanced Air and Space Studies at Maxwell Air Force Base, Alabama, I recognized the need for a book on air warfare since the Cold War. One of the courses, Modern Air Campaigns, interested me. When I asked for the syllabus, the professor blushed as he handed over a thin copy, stating that the readings were not very good. He was right. Scholarship from an air perspective has been lacking in the numerous wars that have taken place in recent years. This volume fills that important gap in the literature by examining wars in an age of primacy where airpower has played a major role.

Given the diverse wars that have transpired over the past three decades, I decided an edited volume would make the most sense and recruited two excellent coeditors and eight brilliant authors, each dedicating themselves to writing a chapter (with Ralph Shield contributing two!). In October 2019 the authors and editors presented their research at a Contemporary Air Wars Workshop at the US Naval War College in Newport, Rhode Island. Caitlin Talmadge, Brendan Green, and Stephen Chiabotti chaired panels for the papers and provided extraordinary advice and recommendations to improve the project. Jane Bresko did a great job organizing the workshop, and Rachael Chaffer took detailed notes. Students from the Foundation of Air Power Theory course at the Naval War College, Chris Roy, Nick Gydesen, Jamie Douglas, Dave Bishop, Rashed Hossain, and Lauren Murphy, provided comments to the chapters. The workshop was made possible by the support of the Center on Irregular Warfare & Armed Groups (CIWAG) and the Naval War College Foundation. Additionally, we are indebted to the Security Studies Program at MIT and the Watson Institute at Brown University for their insightful comments on talks I gave on early drafts of the book.

While working on this manuscript, an important book on the subject was published by Anthony Schinella, *Bombs without Boots: The Limits of Airpower*. Though we did not know Tony personally, his writing had an impact on this work and his unexpected passing is a true loss. On a more personal level, we have been greatly saddened by the untimely passing of Stephen Chiabotti, a mentor, colleague, and friend. Steve dedicated his professional life to teaching those of us who had the honor of knowing him on how to think strategically. This book is dedicated to his memory.

# Abbreviations

A2AD (anti-access/area denial)
AAA (antiaircraft artillery)
ACC (Air Combat Command)
AFCENT (Air Forces Central)
AFRICOM (US Africa Command)
AGM (air-to-ground missile)
AGR (air-to-ground rocket)
AOR (area of responsibility)
APKWS (advanced precision kill weapons system)
AQ (Al-Qaeda)
AQI (Al-Qaeda in Iraq)
AWACS (airborne warning and control system)
BMP (Boyevaya Mashina Pekhoty, infantry fighting vehicle)
C2 (command and control)
CAIFF (Combined Air Interdiction of Fielded Forces)
CAOC (Combined Air Operations Center)
CAP (combat air patrol)
CAS (close air support)
CBU (cluster bomb unit)
CENTCOM (US Central Command)
CIA (Central Intelligence Agency)
CJFLCC (Combined Joint Forces Land Component Command)
CJOC (Combined Joint Operations Center)
CJTF (Combined Joint Task Force)
CJTF-OIR (Combined Joint Task Force–Operation Inherent Resolve)
CTS (Counterterrorism Service)
DJI (Da-Jiang Innovations)
DNI (Director, National Intelligence)
DoD (Department of Defense)
EBO (effects-based operations)
EC (European Community)
EUCOM (European Command)

F3EA (find, fix, finish, exploit, analyze)
FAC (forward air controller)
FEDPOL (Federal Police)
FMV (full-motion video)
GBU (guided-bomb unit)
GCS (ground control station)
GLONASS (global navigation satellite system)
GPS (global positioning system)
HMMWV (high-mobility multipurpose wheeled vehicle)
HVT (high-value terrorist)
IADS (integrated air defense system)
IAF (Israeli Air Force)
ICBM (intercontinental ballistic missile)
ICC (International Criminal Court)
IDF (Israeli Defense Force)
IED (improvised explosive device)
IFAC (Iraqi forward air controller)
INF (Intermediate Range Nuclear Forces Treaty)
IRAM (improvised rocket-assisted munition)
IRGC (Iranian Islamic Revolutionary Guard Corps)
IS (Islamic State)
ISF (Iraqi Security Forces)
ISI (Islamic State in Iraq)
ISIS (Islamic State in Iraq and Syria)
ISIS-K (Islamic State in Iraq and Syria–Khorasan)
ISR (intelligence, surveillance, and reconnaissance)
JDAM (joint direct attack munition)
JN (Jabhat al-Nusra)
JSOC (Joint Special Operations Command)
JSTARS (joint surveillance target attack radar system)
JTAC (joint terminal attack controller)
JTJ (Jamaat al-Tawhid wal-Jihad)
KLA (Kosovo Liberation Army)
LRA (long-range aviation)
LRE (launch and recovery element)
MANPADS (man-portable air defense system)
mIRC (Microsoft, or multiuser, internet relay chat)
MTS (multispectral targeting system)
NATO (North Atlantic Treaty Organization)
NCV (noncombatant casualty cut-off value)
NFZ (no-fly zone)

NSC (National Security Council)
NTC (National Transitional Council)
OAF (Operation Allied Force)
OCO (overseas contingency operations)
OEF (Operation Enduring Freedom)
OIF (Operation Iraqi Freedom)
OIR (Operation Inherent Resolve)
OMG (operational maneuver groups)
OOD (Operation Odyssey Dawn)
OUP (Operation Unified Protector)
PED (processing, exploitation, and dissemination)
PGM (precision-guided munition)
PMF (Popular Mobilization Front)
PSYOP (psychological operation)
R2P (responsibility to protect)
RAF (Royal Air Force)
ROE (rules of engagement)
ROVER (remote-operated video-enhanced receiver)
RPA (remotely piloted aircraft)
RS (reconnaissance squadron)
RSAF (Royal Saudi Air Force)
RSO (remote-split operations)
RuAF (Russian Air Force)
SAM (surface-to-air missile)
SEAD (suppression of enemy air defense)
SLA (South Lebanon Army)
SOF (special operations forces)
SyAAF (Syrian Arab Air Force)
TACP (tactical air control party)
TADS (terrorist attack disruption strikes)
TEA (target engagement authority)
TUAS (tactical unmanned aerial system)
UAE (United Arab Emirates)
UAV (unmanned aerial vehicle)
UN (United Nations)
UNPROFOR (United Nations Protection Force)
UNSCR (United Nations Security Council Resolution)
US (United States)
USAF (United States Air Force)
VBIED (vehicle-borne improvised explosive device)
WWII (World War II)

# 1    Air Power in the Age of Primacy
## Air Warfare since the Cold War

*Phil M. Haun* *

### Introduction

Questions as to the efficacy of the use of violence to achieve a nation's foreign policy goals have long been the subject of debate. Wars are costly with innocents suffering and infrastructure left destroyed, domestic and international order undermined, and the survival of the state and its ruling regime endangered. Given the enormous consequences, war should be a last resort reserved for only those circumstances that imperil the security of a nation or its allies.[1] Yet since the end of the Cold War there has been an age of primacy marked by a series of conflicts for which powerful states, the most conspicuous being the United States, have chosen to go to war over nonvital interests against much weaker state or nonstate actors. In these asymmetric conflicts, the powerful have coerced concessions, imposed regime change, and suppressed the spread of violence through counterterrorism or counterinsurgency operations.[2]

As this book demonstrates, powerful nations have largely succeeded in achieving both their military and political objectives in this age of primacy. They have further taken advantage of asymmetries in technology to wage war from afar, at low risk to their own forces. Though largely achieving the *ex ante* objectives for which these wars were waged, these outcomes have not always translated into broader foreign policy objectives of long-term peace and stability. In Afghanistan and Iraq, US and NATO forces continued to conduct operations that, over time, accrued enormous costs in terms of blood and treasure.[3] In other cases for which troops were not deployed, as in Libya and Yemen, the resulting power

---

* The views expressed by the author do not reflect those of the US government, the Department of Defense, or any of its organizations.
[1] United Nations Charter, "Action with Respect to Threats to the Peace, Breaches of the Peace, and Acts of Aggression," Article 51, Chapter VI.
[2] Phil Haun, *Coercion, Survival, and War: Why Weak States Resist the United States* (Stanford: Stanford University Press, 2015).
[3] Watson Institute, *The Costs of War Project*, https://watson.brown.edu/costsofwar.

vacuums have perpetuated instability and/or civil war. Winning the war has not always meant winning the peace.[4]

This book examines ten contemporary air wars, recent conflicts in which air forces have played a major and, at times, dominant role. For the past three decades, air power has been the military instrument of choice in conflicts pitting the United States, NATO, Israel, a Saudi-led coalition, and Russia against weak opponents with inadequate air defenses. A surplus of aircraft armed with advanced sensors and precision weapons have been able to loiter over enemy territory with impunity and have afforded these dominant powers the luxury of not having to choose a specific strategy, permitting them to conduct multiple air campaigns targeting militaries, militants, and, at times, even civilians.

Contemporary air forces have not been entirely free to do as they please, however. In asymmetric wars, powerful states have largely fought over interests not of vital national concern. To keep the costs of war low, they have therefore been reluctant to deploy ground forces and have limited most air operations to the relative safety of medium altitude. Further, in most, though not all, cases they have placed restrictions on the rules of engagement in order to mitigate collateral damage.

Despite these self-imposed restrictions, air forces have still been relatively unconstrained to employ a variety of strategies that target military forces, political leadership, economic infrastructure, and populations. The effectiveness of these air campaigns has varied significantly, however, depending on the desired military and political objectives and the nature of the targets attacked. Operations against fielded forces have generally worked well when air forces have coordinated with competent, but often proxy, ground forces. Attacks on enemy economies and populations have been utilized less frequently, though they have had a long-term impact when the aim has been to impose costs on opponents. Far less successful have been air strikes against political leaders due to the high fidelity of intelligence required. Leadership strikes remain a popular choice, nonetheless, much as the purchase of lottery tickets for which the costs are low but the wished-for gains immense.

This book examines air wars in the age of primacy through chapter-length studies of the remotely piloted wars against terrorist groups and the wars in Bosnia, Kosovo, Afghanistan, Iraq, Lebanon, Libya, Yemen, Syria, and the Battle of Mosul. The remainder of this chapter provides context with an overview of the evolution of air power theory, presents characteristics of contemporary air warfare and measures of military and

---

[4] Basil Liddell Hart, *Strategy* (New York: Frederick A. Praeger, 1954, reprint 1967), 366–70.

political effectiveness, and then briefly assesses the ten air wars examined in subsequent chapters.

### The Evolution of Air Power Theory

For seven decades, from World War I through the end of the Cold War, the major debates over air power centered on how to gain command of the air and, once obtained, what to target. Prominent early air power theorists from the interwar period, Giulio Douhet, Hugh Trenchard, Billy Mitchell, and later Mitchell's lieutenants at the US Air Corps Tactical School, all argued for an independent air force in peacetime that could seize the initiative at the outset of war by deploying large formations of bombers to gain air superiority and then decisively defeat the enemy.[5]

World War II revealed that gaining command of the air was a task far more challenging than the theorists had anticipated as radar shifted the advantage to the defender as evidenced in the Battle of Britain and the Combined Bomber Offensive. In addition, the ability to locate and hit targets, even those that were the size of small cities, was initially problematic and required the adaptation of tactics, techniques, and procedures, along with the introduction of new technologies to improve navigation and target identification. Finally, even as nations suffered and sustained enormous damage from the air, civilians and economies proved more resilient than airmen had expected. Even though air power did not independently win the war by bombing German cities and factories, it did prove to be critical to the allied victory in Europe by gaining command of the air, interdicting lines of communication, and contributing to the combined arms campaign that defeated the Nazi military.[6]

Meanwhile, US naval, land, and air forces moved across the Pacific in a series of battles which attrited the Japanese air and naval forces. The Americans further decimated the Japanese economy and population through the blockade of shipping and the firebombing of cities. The problem of what to target in Japan was simplified by the wooden

---

[5] Giulio Douhet, *Command of the Air* (Air Force History and Museums Program, 1998) original text 1926; Bernard Brodie, *Strategy in the Missile Age* (Santa Monica: RAND, 1959), 71–106; Hugh Trenchard, "Memo to the Chief of Staff Subcommittee on the War Object of an Air Force," May 2, 1928, in Phil Haun *Lectures of the Air Corps Tactical School and American Strategic Bombing in World War II* (Lexington: University Press of Kentucky, 2019), 11–13, Appendix 1; Harold George, "Air Power and War" 1936; Haun, *Lectures of the Air Corps Tactical School*, Chapter 2.

[6] Tami Biddle, *Rhetoric and Reality in Air Warfare* (Princeton: Princeton University Press, 2002); Richard Overy, *The Bombers and the Bombed: Allied Air War over Europe, 1940–1945* (New York: Penguin Books, 2013); Phillips O'Brien, *How the War Was Won* (Cambridge: Cambridge University Press, 2015); Williamson Murray and Allan Millett, *A War to Be Won: Fighting the Second World War* (Harvard: Harvard University Press, 2000).

construction of its cities, which made the population vulnerable, and by the willingness of the Americans to brutalize the Japanese population so long as it avoided another bloody invasion as had just taken place in Europe. Although the war in the Pacific was a truly joint effort, the manner in which it ended with the atomic bombings of Hiroshima and Nagasaki and the immediate surrender by the Japanese government only fortified the belief of American airmen in the efficacy of strategic bombing.[7]

Following World War II, the US Air Force gained its independence on the promise of strategic bombing and through the 1950s and 1960s constructed an impressive strategic fleet of long-range bombers and, later, intercontinental ballistic missiles (ICBMs) armed with thermo-nuclear warheads.[8] In the Cold War, the United States faced off against the Soviet Union in a nuclear arms race that produced weapons with such destructive potential as to deter another global war.[9] Debate over gaining air superiority appeared less relevant when nuclear armed bombers and missiles could penetrate enemy defenses in sufficient numbers to accomplish their mission. Targeting problems were also solved by the exponential destructiveness of thermonuclear warheads. Further, distinctions between counterforce (military) and countervalue (populations and economies) targets mattered less as the number and potency of these nuclear devices grew unabated. In the face of such vast destructive potential, the primary purpose of strategic forces no longer was to win wars but to demonstrate to the other side the credibility of a second-strike capability in order to prevent wars altogether.[10]

While deterring each other from major conflict, the superpowers nevertheless competed aggressively over ideologies and allies. Competition in Europe solidified between a US-led NATO and a Soviet-dominated Warsaw Pact. While the conflict remained cold on that front, on other continents crises turned violent in civil and regional wars. In Korea, Vietnam, the Middle East, and Afghanistan the superpowers intervened to arm their proxies with the latest in conventional weaponry. In the air

[7] See Murray, *A War to Be Won*; S. C. M. Paine *The Japanese Empire: Grand Strategy from the Meiji Restoration to the Pacific War* (Cambridge: Cambridge University Press, 2017), 161–77.

[8] James Forrestal to President Harry Truman "Functions of the Armed Forces and the Joint Chiefs of Staff" J.C.S. 1478 Series, April 21, 1948, http://cgsc.cdmhost.com/cdm/ref/collection/p4013coll11/id/729; Phillip Meilinger, *Bomber: The Formation and Early Years of Strategic Air Command* (Maxwell Air Force Base: Air University Press, 2012).

[9] David Alan Rosenberg "The Origins of Overkill: Nuclear Weapons and American Strategy, 1945–1960," *International Security* 7:4 (Spring 1983): 3–71.

[10] United States Air Force, *Manual 1–1 Basic Doctrine*, August 14, 1964, Air Force Historical Research Agency K168.13001-1, 1–2; Brodie, *Strategy in the Missile Age*.

domain, this meant the return of aerial warfare with the deployment of the latest jet fighters and, in the 1960s, the introduction of radar- and infrared-guided surface-to-air missiles.[11] Gaining air superiority over the Yalu, Hanoi, and Sinai proved formidable in an environment where only high-performance tactical aircraft (tacair) could survive. Even in Afghanistan, where the Soviets faced an insurgent Mujahideen incapable of operating such advanced weapons, the proliferation of US Stinger missiles, simple shoulder-launched man-portable air defense systems (MANPADS), made Soviet air operations risky. In addition to the battle for air superiority, air forces struggled as their strategic bombing campaigns failed independently to win wars.[12]

In the aftermath of the Vietnam War and the frightening losses of both tacair and mechanized forces suffered by the Israelis in the 1973 Yom Kippur War, the US military turned its attention back to Europe and the problem of a conventional deterrence of the Soviet Red Army. The United States and its allies converged on similar doctrines known as AirLand Battle in the United States and Follow-on Force Attack in NATO. NATO ground forces were to blunt the initial wave of invading Warsaw Pact armies while its air forces simultaneously interdicted the second echelon units, the Red Army's specialized operational maneuver groups (OMGs) designed to exploit breakthroughs in the front lines. The battle for command of the air would rely on technologically sophisticated fighter-interceptors along with specialized suppression of enemy air defense (SEAD) aircraft to neutralize Soviet air defenses, while low-altitude close air support and battlefield air interdiction missions by NATO tacair stalled the Red Army's advance.[13]

In the process of implementing AirLand Battle, new air defense systems were developed by the United States and Soviet Union in the late 1970s, which shifted the offense-defense balance back in favor of the defense. Phased-array radars were coupled with fast and maneuverable

[11] Robert Futrell, *The United States Air Force in Korea 1950–1953* (Washington, DC: Center for Air Force History, 1983); Mark Clodfelter, *The Limits of Air Power: The American Bombing of North Vietnam* (New York: The Free Press, 1989); Chaim Herzog, *The Arab-Israeli Wars: War and Peace in the Middle East from the War of Independence through Lebanon* (New York: Vintage, 1982); The Russian General Staff, *The Soviet-Afghan War; How a Superpower Fought and Lost* (Lawrence: University Press of Kansas, 2002).

[12] Futrell, *The United States Air Force in Korea 1950–1953*; Clodfelter, *The Limits of Air Power*; Phil Haun and Colin Jackson "Breaker of Armies: Air Power in the Easter Offensive and the Myth of Linebacker I and II in the Vietnam War," *International Security* 40:3 (Winter 2015/16): 139–78.

[13] Phil Haun, "Peacetime Military Innovation through Inter-Service Cooperation: The Unique Case of the US Air Force and Battlefield Air Interdiction," *Journal of Strategic Studies* (January 8, 2019): 9–12.

6		*Phil M. Haun*

long-range surface-to-air missiles (SAMs).[14] These SAMs resisted radar
jamming and could engage tacair at low altitude. To counter the Soviet
surface-to-air threat, the United States invested in stealth technology with
radar absorbing and deflecting surfaces to reduce radar signatures on
aircraft. The resultant F-117 stealth fighter-bomber, conventionally
armed with laser-guided bombs, could penetrate enemy integrated air
defenses at night and surgically strike high-value targets. This approach
was a revised version of America's high-altitude daylight precision bombing of World War II.[15]

The Cold War thankfully ended without putting these new weapons
to the test. Close on its heels, however, came the Gulf War in
January 1991. The US-led coalition's decisive victory over Iraq
appeared to justify the substantial investment in technologically sophisticated weaponry. Air superiority was achieved by US fighter suppression of Iraq's air defense systems, while F-117s and cruise missiles
struck targets in Baghdad from the war's onset. In the Gulf War's
aftermath, debate arose as to the most significant contribution made
by air power, whether by the targeting of Iraqi leadership or by the defeat
of the Iraqi military.[16] There was, however, little disagreement as to the
exceptional capabilities of US air forces with their impressive technologies on display for the world.[17]

With the collapse of the Soviet Union and the age of primacy that
followed where the United States remained the sole superpower, there
arose a number of crises in which air power played a significant, and at
times a critical, role. These contemporary wars, however, looked very
different from those of the past, for which the initial concern had been
how to gain command of the air. Further, the question of what to target
had also lessened in importance as air forces no longer had to choose
between targets but now had the capacity to conduct simultaneously
multiple air operations.

---

[14] The United States deployed the Patriot and the Soviets the SA-10 Grumble (S-300).
[15] David Aronstein and Albert Piccirillo, *Have Blue and the F-117A: Evolution of the "Stealth Fighter"* (Reston: American Institute of Aeronautics and Astronautics, 1997).
[16] John Warden, "Enemy as a System," *Air Power Journal* (Spring 1995): 40–55; Robert Pape, *Bombing to Win* (Ithaca: Cornell University Press, 1996); Pape and Warden *Security Studies* debate; John Warden "Success in Modern War: A Response to Robert Pape's Bombing to Win," *Security Studies* 7:2 (Winter 1997–98): 172–90; Robert Pape, "The Air Force Strikes Back: A Reply to Barry Watts and John Warden," *Security Studies* 7:2 (Winter 1997–98): 191–214.
[17] An exception is Daryl Press, "The Myth of Air Power in the Persian Gulf War and the Future of Warfare," *International Security* 26:2 (Fall 2001): 5–44.

## Characteristics of Contemporary Air Warfare

Contemporary air wars are those conflicts since the end of the Cold War in which air power has been relied upon heavily or, as in the case of Kosovo, exclusively. In these conflicts, air forces have been employed in ways quite different from how they were utilized for much of the twentieth century. Wars are no longer waged between great powers as in the World Wars, nor have their proxies been relied upon to test the capabilities and resolve of the other superpower as in the Cold War.

Obtaining air superiority, the prerequisite for effective operations in previous eras, has become a relatively simple task. From medium altitude, even older aircraft have been able to operate freely while vulnerable propeller-driven remotely piloted aircraft (RPA) have proliferated. Further, the large deployment of ground troops has become rare, the invasion of Iraq being the exception. Air forces have instead coordinated their operations with local proxy ground forces. How these air wars differ from those of the past is explained in the next section through their asymmetries in power, interests, and technologies.

*Asymmetries in Power*

The dominant characteristic of contemporary warfare has been the great disparity in capabilities between combatants, whereby dominant powers have fought against much weaker states and nonstate actors. Asymmetry of power in war is not new. In World War II, the United States out-matched the Japanese, and in the Cold War, the superpowers frequently waged asymmetric wars around the globe. What has changed, however, is the balancing behavior of great powers inherent in multipolar and bipolar international systems.[18] In the Cold War, the superpowers indirectly competed against each other by arming proxies in Korea, Vietnam, the Middle East, and Afghanistan. In contemporary wars, third-party inter-vention has been rare, the Russian intervention in Syria being an excep-tion. In the age of primacy, the stronger side has thus enjoyed an even greater military advantage over its adversary than in the past, an imbal-ance particularly evident in the air domain.

---

[18] Robert Art, "Europe Hedges Its Security Bets," in *Balance of Power: Theory and Practice in the 21st Century*, eds. T. V. Paul, J. J. Wirtz, and M. Fortmann (Stanford: Stanford University Press, 2004); Barry Posen, "European Union Security and Defense Policy: Response to Unipolarity?" *Security Studies* 15:2, 149–86; Christopher Lane, "The Unipolar Illusion Revisited: The Coming End of the United States' 'Unipolar Moment,'" *International Security* 31:2 (Fall 2006): 7–41.

*Air Superiority Easily Gained*   Against weak adversaries, dominant states have exploited their asymmetric advantage in air power, making it a significant and sometimes central factor in contemporary warfare. The United States, NATO, Israel, Saudi Arabia, and Russia, all armed with modern, technically sophisticated aircraft, have faced overmatched opponents with grossly inadequate air defenses. As a result, air superiority has been a goal easily obtained. Unlike previous eras in which gaining command of the air was one, if not the most essential, challenge, in contemporary air warfare only at low altitude has the air domain been contested.[19] In the Gulf War, the large conventional war that straddled the Cold and post–Cold War eras, gaining air superiority for the US-led coalition proved an easier task than anticipated. Even Serbia, which had a capable, though dated, integrated air defense system (IADS), chose not to risk its assets, instead husbanding its resources to be able to threaten, though rarely engage, NATO aircraft over Bosnia and Kosovo.

Contemporary air warfare has not seen a recurrence of the historic aerial battles over the Yalu, Hanoi, Sinai, or Golan Heights. With air superiority assumed, a wide range of older aircraft have played significant roles in air-to-ground operations. These "legacy" systems, so derided because of their inability to operate in a high-threat, radar environment, have continued to engage in combat with acceptable levels of risk for the past thirty years. Free from the task of gaining command of the air, airmen have been able to focus instead on how best to leverage that advantage.

Dominant powers have thus been free to choose from a range of air options targeting the enemy's military, leadership, economy, and population. Logic would dictate a prioritization of targets based on which strategy provides the best expected outcome. A selected air campaign should further provide a causal chain that links military objectives to the desired political aims for which the war is fought. In contemporary wars, however, given the vast advantage in air power and abundance of air assets, powerful states have not had to make such difficult strategic choices. Instead, political and military decision makers have been free to conduct multiple, simultaneous air operations, to include those with a low probability of success.

### Asymmetry in Interests

A second characteristic of warfare in an age of primacy is the asymmetry of interests. Weak state and nonstate actors must be concerned with their

---

[19] Barry Posen, "Command of the Commons: The Military Foundation of US Hegemony," *International Security* 28:1 (Summer 2003): 5–46.

very survival when confronting a much more powerful state.[20] By contrast, dominant powers do not risk their survival fighting a much weaker opponent, which, in turn, allows them to go to war over lesser interests.[21] Because of their military advantage, powerful states have the luxury of choosing not only whether to go to war, but also what political objectives they wish to achieve. National interests can be divided into vital, important, and peripheral. Vital interests are core issues of security, prosperity, and identity for which a nation is willing to die. Important interests include an array of issues from economic access to resources and markets to broad security concerns for allies and the stability of the international system. These are reasons for which a state may not be willing to die, at least not in large numbers, but may be willing to kill. Peripheral interests include more minor foreign policy goals such as concerns over humanitarian rights, issues for which a nation may not wish to die or kill, but may be willing to assist others to do so.[22]

Unlike weak states and nonstate actors, in asymmetric wars dominant states are not fighting over vital issues that place the existence of the nation at risk. Because the benefits are relatively low, they have been less willing to choose high-cost strategies, such as brute force invasions and occupations, the notable exception being the conquest of Iraq in 2003. Whereas there have been fewer external constraints to powerful states, there has been greater domestic pressure to keep the costs and risks of war low.

*Limiting Ground Forces*    A preferred method for suppressing the costs of war has been to limit the deployment of a nation's ground troops.[23] Boots on the ground significantly increase expected combat casualties. In asymmetric conflicts over nonvital interests, powerful states may well be willing to employ their air forces, but reluctant to risk their soldiers. In such cases, they have often relied upon local proxies.

Although limiting boots on the ground may diminish the combat losses suffered in war, it can come at a price of reduced combat effectiveness. An ineffectual ground force can degrade air operations in two ways. First, the training and doctrine for attacking fielded forces presumes a deployed army with a functioning air-ground system of communication networks,

---

[20] Phil Haun, *Coercion, Survival, and War*, 12.
[21] Andrew Mack, "Why Big Nations Lose Small Wars," *World Politics* 27 (1975): 181.
[22] Derek Reveron, Nikolas Gvosdev, and John Cloud, eds., *The Oxford Handbook of US National Security* (Oxford: Oxford University Press, 2018), 39.
[23] Anthony Schinella, *Bombs without Boots: The Limits of Airpower* (Washington, DC: Brookings Institution Press, 2017).

liaisons, and forward air controllers.[24] In air campaigns against the enemy's military forces, air power success has largely depended on a capable ground force. Minus a friendly army, air forces struggle on their own.[25]

Second, the absence of a friendly ground force can limit the potential of air power as enemy ground forces are left to focus solely on the air threat. A combination of air and ground threats, on the other hand, places the enemy army on the horns of a dilemma. Does it disperse and conceal to neutralize an air force overhead only to leave itself defenseless to a ground offensive or does it instead concentrate and maneuver against a surface threat only to then be vulnerable to air strikes? This conundrum was presented to Saddam Hussein in 2003, who chose to disperse his armies against the threat of US air power instead of fortifying Iraqi defenses against the ground invasion (see Chapter 6).

*Restrictive Rules of Engagement*   In addition to limiting the risks to soldiers, dominant states also have a heightened sensitivity to air combat losses. Casualty aversion manifests in the imposition of restrictive rules of engagement (ROE) to reduce exposure to airmen. Aircrew are forced to fly at medium altitude, well above the threat of small arms fire, light AAA (antiaircraft artillery), and infrared MANPADS. Although flying above 10,000 feet increases aircraft survivability, it comes at the price of diminished lethality by degrading the ability of airmen to identify and accurately strike targets. This difficulty in visually acquiring targets has led to a reliance on onboard sensors such as targeting pods. Offboard sources of targeting information also come into play such as remotely piloted aircraft (RPAs) or ground forward air controllers. As discussed later, advanced sensors and precision-guided munitions have collectively increased the tactical effectiveness of air forces at medium altitude.

*Collateral Damage*   In contemporary air warfare, rules of engagement (ROE) have further played a critical role in providing directives not only as to what can be attacked but, equally as important, what should not be. Air force leaders, especially those of the United States and NATO allies, in response to domestic and international concerns over humanitarian suffering, have imposed stringent ROE. They practice lawfare, whereby military lawyers provide interpretation as to the legitimacy of target selection. Such legal advice ensures that leaders incorporate the

---

[24] Chairman of the Joint Chiefs of Staff, *Joint Publication 3.09 Close Air Support*, November 25, 2014. https://fas.org/irp/doddir/dod/jp3_09_3.pdf

[25] Christopher Haave and Phil Haun, eds., *A-10s over Kosovo* (Maxwell AFB: Air University Press, 2003).

political and diplomatic risks of collateral damage into their decision making.[26]

Along with the expanded role of legal counsel so, too, has there been an increase in the number of target analysts who specialize in conducting prestrike collateral damage assessments. Intelligence personnel utilize simulation to predict weapon fragmentation patterns in order to estimate the potential for civilian casualties. These risk assessments then factor into a military and/or political leader's decision to place restrictions on the type, timing, and location of targets to be attacked. In addition, the category and size of weapons may be determined not by their anticipated effects against designated targets, but by their ability to limit damage to the immediate area. For example, in 1999 the USAF used laser-guided bombs filled with concrete, instead of explosives, to neutralize air defenses in northern Iraq.[27] More recently in targeting specific individuals, the United States has employed "ninja" styled, small precision-guided weapons substituting sharpened steel blades for explosives, munitions that can take out the passenger in an automobile while leaving the driver unharmed.[28]

In contemporary warfare, the avoidance of collateral damage incidents may well be the most important military objective. In Bosnia, hypersensitivity to the potential diplomatic blowback from civilian casualties led NATO air commander, USAF Lieutenant General Michael Ryan, to approve every strike and weapon employed (see Chapter 3). Ryan's concerns were well founded, as four years later the US bombing of the Chinese embassy in Belgrade placed the entire NATO air campaign in jeopardy.[29]

Weak states and nonstate actors recognize the political and diplomatic fallout to be garnered from collateral damage and take advantage by mixing combatants with civilians much as guerrilla fighters have done for centuries. Alternatively, they may exaggerate civilian suffering as when the Serbians dragged bodies into bomb craters in an effort to influence international reporting following NATO's attack on a convoy of Kosovar

[26] Charles Dunlap, "Law and Military Interventions: Preserving Humanitarian Values in 21st Century Conflicts," The Carr Center, Kennedy School of Government, November 2001. https://people.duke.edu/~pfeaver/dunlap.pdf
[27] Steven Lee Myers, "United States Wields Defter Weapon against Iraq: Concrete Bomb," New York Times, October 7, 1999. https://nytimes.com/1999/10/07/world/us-wields-defter-weapon-against-iraq-concrete-bomb.html
[28] "'Ninja Bomb': Pentagon's New Bladed Missile that Kills Targets without Exploding," The Telegraph, May 9, 2019. https://telegraph.co.uk/news/2019/05/09/pentagon-builds-knife-bomb-kills-targets-without-exploding
[29] Michael Mandelbaum, "A Perfect Failure: NATO's Air War against Yugoslavia," Foreign Affairs 2 (1999).

refugees.[30] In some cases, opponents may even manufacture collateral damage incidents, as when US remotely piloted aircraft filmed ISIS fighters detonating religious sites in Mosul that ISIS then blamed on US air strikes (see Chapter 11).

One concern over civilian casualties is the impact they will likely have on domestic and international support for the war. They can also threaten the unity of a coalition where national interests vary. Coalitions may deal with collateral damage concerns either by granting nations veto power over strikes or by allowing nations to opt out of particular missions. Nations may further place restrictions on the types of weapons their aircraft carry, such as when certain NATO countries would not allow their aircraft to drop cluster bomb units (CBU) in Kosovo.[31]

Amplifying the impact of collateral damage has been the emergence of 24-hour news coverage, the so-called CNN effect, whereby networks repeatedly broadcast reports, including detailed graphic imagery of civilian suffering, into the homes of voters. More recently, the ubiquity of smartphones and social media has made every witness a photographer and a reporter, increasing the proliferation of unfiltered collateral damage content.[32]

This increased media exposure has influenced both domestic and international perception as to the legitimacy and proportionality of air strikes. Of further concern is the political blowback collateral damage may generate among the local population of the area targeted and the extent to which it elicits their support for the insurgent and terrorist groups under attack.[33] All told, the potential for civilian casualties has had a significant effect upon US and NATO air operations in their efforts to reduce the political fallout when air strikes inevitably go astray.

In contemporary warfare, while Western powers have gone to great lengths to avoid civilian casualties, collateral damage has not been as great

---

[30] On April 9, 1991, a USAF F-16 AFAC misidentified a refugee column and repeatedly attacked it until was called off by A-10 AFACs. See Christopher Haave, *A-10s over Kosovo*, 173.

[31] The author was an A-10 forward air controller in Kosovo and selected NATO aircraft to strike targets in part by the weapons their countries allowed them to carry.

[32] Piers Robinson, "The CNN Effect: Can the News Media Drive Foreign Policy?" *Review of International Studies* 25 (1999): 301–9; Steven Livingston, "The CNN Effect Reconsidered (Again): Problematizing ICT and Global Governance in the CNN Effect Research Agenda," *Media, War & Conflict* 4:1 (April 2011): 20–36.

[33] Analysts disagree as to the degree to which blowback from collateral damage generates local, regional, and international support for terrorist and insurgent groups. Aqil Shah, "Do US Drone Strikes Cause Blowback? Evidence from Pakistan and Beyond," *International Security* 42:4 (Spring 2018): 47–84; Ahsan Butt, "ISSF Article Review 108 on Shah. 'Do US Drone Strikes Cause Blowback?'" *H-Diplo* (February 19, 2019). https://networks.h-net.org/node/28443/discussions/3643482/issf-article-review-108-butt-shah-%E2%80%9Cdo-us-drone-strikes-cause

a concern for all air forces. Saudi Arabia and Russia have been less susceptible to domestic and international criticism of their targeting of civilians in Yemen and Syria, respectively (see Chapters 9 and 10). Much as Western powers, however, neither Saudi Arabia nor Russia have deployed significant ground forces to keep costs low and have flown their aircraft at medium altitude in an effort to minimize risk to aircrews. For all contemporary air forces, these goals have been achieved through the use of advanced technologies, a development that comprises the third asymmetry of contemporary air warfare.

### Asymmetry in Technology

Over the past thirty years, three groups of technologies have increased the effectiveness of contemporary air forces at medium altitude with advances in precision strike, persistent operations, and networked warfare. A brief discussion follows, with a more thorough appraisal reserved for Chapter 2.

*Precision Strike*    Precision strike involves two different technologies: guided weapons and advanced sensors. Many believe the introduction of precision-guided munitions (PGMs) by the United States toward the end of the Cold War brought about a revolution in military affairs made evident by the lopsided victory in the Gulf War. Here a high-tech US force decisively defeated a large but technically outmoded Soviet-equipped Iraqi military.[34] The development of PGMs, however, has been more evolutionary in nature as its origins can be traced back to as early as World War II.[35] It was not until the Gulf War, however, that the full impact of PGMs became widely recognized. Not only were PGMs more efficient, allocating a single bomb per target compared to the hundreds of bombs previously required, but their accuracy also appeared to reduce the likelihood of collateral damage.[36]

---

[34] James Kievet and Steven Metz, *The Revolution in Military Affairs: From Theory to Policy* (Army War College: Strategic Studies Institute, 1995). https://ssi.armywarcollege.edu/pubs/display.cfm?pubID=236; John Warden "Success in Modern War: A Response to Robert Pape's Bombing to Win," *Security Studies* 7:2 (Winter 1997/98): 172–90, 178.

[35] Paul Gillespie, *Weapons of Choice: The Development of Precision Guided Weapons* (Tuscaloosa, University of Alabama Press, 2006). The largest improvement came with the introduction of the laser-guided bomb in the Vietnam War. Phil Haun and Colin Jackson, "Breaker of Armies."

[36] Because of their perceived accuracy, air forces may employ PGMs against targets in urban areas where unguided munitions otherwise would not have been employed. Collateral damage estimations assume the PGM guides accurately, designators do not malfunction, and there is no operator error.

Despite the fanfare over smart bombs, only a small percentage (6 percent) of the weapons employed in the Gulf War were guided. Four years later over Bosnia, PGM usage soared to two-thirds (69 percent) of munition totals due to the small number of weapons dropped and the high level of control over each strike. In 1999, PGM employment dipped to 29 percent in Kosovo, though the war did witness a leap in technology with GPS-guided bombs making possible all-weather air strikes. Thereafter, PGM usage by the United States rose steadily to 57 percent in Afghanistan, 68 percent in Iraq, and 100 percent in Libya.[37] Precision weapons are now ubiquitous in contemporary air warfare. Lesser known, but arguably equally as important, have been advancements in electro-optic (TV) and infrared sensors, the onboard targeting pods that can locate and designate targets as well as assess strikes.

The combination of guided weapons and advanced sensors has made medium altitude air operations far more efficient at locating and striking targets than was ever achievable in the past. Yet another technology that has improved the effectiveness of air power has been the development of remotely piloted aircraft (RPAs), an advancement that adds persistence to the characteristics of asymmetry and precision in contemporary air warfare.

*Persistent Operations*    A technology that has matured and proliferated rapidly over the past two decades has been the remotely piloted aircraft (RPA), also known as unmanned aerial vehicles (UAVs) or more colloquially as drones.[38] The history of the operationalization of RPAs by the US Air Force is detailed in Chapter 2. Their ability to loiter for days over uncontested airspace has added an entirely new capability to air warfare. The platform's onboard sensors and precision weapons further enable air strikes against individuals in urban settings with an acceptable level of risk of collateral damage.

In addition to being constantly overhead, the live feed from RPAs streams video back to air operations centers. This real-time intelligence, surveillance, and reconnaissance (ISR) capability, combined with extensive communication networks allows senior military and political leaders an unprecedented level of oversight and control over air combat.[39]

[37] Karl Mueller, ed., *Precision and Purpose: Airpower in the Libyan Civil War* (Santa Monica, CA: RAND, 2015), 4; Michael Mosely, "Operation Iraqi Freedom: By the Numbers." www.comw.org/pda/fulltext/oifcentaf.pdf
[38] Sebastien Roblin, "Don't Just Call Them 'Drones': A Guide to Military Unmanned Systems on Air, Land and Sea," *Forbes*, September 30, 2019. https://forbes.com/sites/sebastienroblin/2019/09/30/dont-just-call-them-drones-a-laypersons-guide-to-military-unmanned-systems-on-air-land-and-sea/#47f6e62c2b00
[39] Mark Bowden, "The Hunt for Geronimo," *Vanity Fair*, October 12, 2012. https://vanityfair.com/news/politics/2012/11/inside-osama-bin-laden-assassination-plot

*Networked Warfare*   A third technology characteristic of contemporary air warfare is the utilization of global communication networks that enable multiple actors to now participate in combat decision making. Whereas command and control once consisted of the two-way interaction between headquarters and deployed units, the proliferation of the internet now allows for pilots, sensor operators, intel analysts, military lawyers, and air and ground commanders to coordinate in near real time. Communication satellites, internet programs such as mIRC (Microsoft, or multiuser, Internet Relay Chat), and streaming ISR video have made networked warfare standard operating procedure for the United States and NATO.

The combination of precision strike, persistent operations, and networked warfare has changed the face of air warfare. Although alluring, such asymmetric advantages are no guarantee of victory. The next section introduces measures of effectiveness for evaluating the success of air power in contemporary wars.

### Air Power Effectiveness

The evaluation of contemporary air power effectiveness includes two measures.[40] First, to what degree did air forces succeed in achieving their military objectives? Second, to what degree did military success lead to achieving the political aims for which the wars were fought, and if so, to what degree did air power contribute to those outcomes?

### Military Effectiveness

The primary measure of military effectiveness is the degree to which an air force achieves its military objectives. Military objectives can range widely. A relatively simple air objective is the establishment of air superiority that then denies an opponent from enacting its preferred strategy. NATO air superiority over Bosnia deterred Bosnian Serb forces from maneuvering against the Croat-Muslim ground offensive. Likewise, US air dominance over Iraq compelled Saddam to disperse and conceal his armies against air attack rather than prepare defenses against a ground invasion. By contrast, a much more challenging objective has been the decapitation

---

[40] Allan R. Millet and Williamson Murray, eds., *Military Effectiveness* (Cambridge: Cambridge University Press, 2010); Stephen Biddle, *Military Power: Explaining Victory and Defeat in Modern Battle* (Princeton: Princeton University Press, 2004); Caitlin Talmadge, *Dictator's Army: Battlefield Effectiveness in Authoritarian Regimes* (Ithaca: Cornell University Press, 2015).

of leadership, a task complicated by the high level of intelligence involved in acquiring the target.

Although the primary measure of military effectiveness lies in the attainment of military objectives, a discussion on the overall capabilities needed to achieve these objectives is also warranted. To compare the military capabilities of different nations, scholars have developed absolute measures of their competence in performing tactics and conducting operations.[41] Tactics involve individual and small unit combat tasks while operations are an expansion of tactics to include the coordination of dissimilar units. Operations range from a single-strike package to the synchronization of all air, land, and naval forces within a combat theater.

For contemporary air power, operational effectiveness involves three aspects: the ability to coordinate within the air domain, to reach back to rear-echelon units, and to synchronize activity across domains. The air forces examined in this book all demonstrate proficiency within the air domain. Aircrews utilize such technologies as GPS navigation, radar, advanced targeting pods, and precision-guided munitions that combine to solve the major challenges of navigation, target identification, and accurate weapons employment, all of which plagued airmen for much of the twentieth century.

The second operational capability allows operators to reach back to ISR analysts, legal advisors, and service liaisons at air operations and intelligence centers. Rear-echelon personnel perform the key tasks of target assessment, ROE interpretation, and collateral damage risk estimation, which enable real-time command and control by military decision makers. Though aircrews have long been able to communicate with headquarters via radio, the proliferation of airborne datalinks, streaming video, and other communications networks integrated globally via satellites and the internet have allowed significant advances in information sharing and distributed decision making. Although all contemporary air forces demonstrate some level of proficiency at networked warfare, the United States and NATO have the most robust capability.

A third operational capability involves synchronization across warfighting domains. For air-to-ground operations this means a formal or informal air-ground system to determine target prioritization, liaisons at operations centers to facilitate communication and coordinate activity, and forward air controllers (FACs) to locate and validate targets and oversee strikes.[42] Having a competent deployed army significantly

---

[41] Talmadge, *Dictator's Army.*
[42] Chairman of the Joint Chiefs of Staff, *Joint Publication 3.09 Close Air Support,* November 25, 2014. https://fas.org/irp/doddir/dod/jp3_09_3.pdf

enhances an air force's ability to attack enemy fielded forces. Friendly armies play a lesser role in targeting leaders, economies, or populations, however. Against terrorist groups, coordination may best be established with intelligence agencies, such as the USAF remotely piloted operations carried out with the Central Intelligence Agency (CIA) (see Chapter 2).

Even when air forces have all of the tactical and operational capabilities just described, they may not necessarily meet with success. It is one thing to be able to hit a fixed target on a bombing range and quite another to engage the enemy in combat. Ultimately, it is the difference between marksmanship and hunting. The quality of training, doctrine, and equipment determines an air force's readiness to perform tactics and operations. In war, however, the environment and the enemy can significantly degrade combat effectiveness. The most capable air force may still struggle as did NATO over Kosovo in 1999, where poor weather and a skilled Serbian army neutralized an otherwise competent air fleet.[43]

Three final comments on military effectiveness are warranted. First, air forces must be able to adapt to the environment and to the enemy. What worked today will not necessarily work tomorrow as the enemy either adapts or dies. To remain effective, air forces must be continuously evolving tactics and operational procedures. Second, measuring military effectiveness is not as simple as counting the number of tanks destroyed.[44] When air power is most lethal, the enemy disperses and conceals its forces. In such cases, few targets may be located and struck, as the enemy abandons its offensive aims and prioritizes its survival. An army that hides instead of fights and deploys decoys instead of combat forces has been degraded, however, despite the fact that few of its forces are attrited. Under certain circumstances such as those previously cited in Bosnia and Iraq, air power overhead that deters an army from fighting below may be sufficient for military success. On other occasions, however, having command of the air alone may be insufficient as in Kosovo, where Serbian soldiers traded their tanks for civilian automobiles and resumed their ethnic cleansing operations.

Third, determining the military effectiveness of air power in a combined arms campaign is particularly challenging as its contribution is linked with that of the ground forces. What impact does air power have on the overall outcome of a battle when tasked with gaining air superiority, interdicting enemy lines of communication, and providing close air support? In the aftermath of a successful ground campaign, military

---

[43] Christopher Haave, *A-10s over Kosovo.*
[44] For a critique of air power based on targets destroyed see Kenneth Pollack, "Air Power in the Six-Day War," *Journal of Strategic Studies* 28:3 (2005): 483–85.

analysts easily overlook the contribution of air power for enemy air strikes that never took place or for enemy forces that never reached the battlefield or were deterred by the air threat from maneuvering altogether. One method for determining the significance of air power under such conditions asks the counterfactual question, "How effective would friendly ground forces likely have been without air power?" In Afghanistan, Libya, and Syria the arrival of US, NATO, and Russian air forces, respectively, fundamentally shifted the military balance of power on the ground. In these cases it is hard to imagine how friendly armies would have been able to take the offensive without the intervention of air power.

In sum, the military effectiveness of air power is measured by its contributions to the military objectives of a war. Success is measured not by tank kills or body counts but by the degree to which one's military objectives are achieved and the enemy's objectives are denied. The next section considers the second measure of effectiveness, that is, whether military success attains the political aims of the war.

### Political Effectiveness

To be politically effective, military success must also secure the objectives for which a war is fought. Most wars end with mixed results whereby not all the desired political goals are achieved. This is particularly true of wars ending in a negotiated settlement as settling implies compromise. The attainment of all the *ex ante* political objectives is, in fact, too high a bar for coding success. The procurement of the core political objective(s) for which the powerful state went to war, therefore, is a more reasonable measure.

Political objectives vary from the relatively minor goal of reaching a permanent ceasefire as in Bosnia and Lebanon to much more ambitious goals of regime change as in Afghanistan, Iraq, and Libya. The political goals chosen affect the air strategy adopted as well as the likelihood of its success. For lesser aims, air power might be used to coerce the opponent to make concessions, as in Bosnia and Kosovo.[45] For greater demands, where the survival of the enemy state and/or leadership is at stake, a combined arms strategy to include a brute force invasion may be required.[46]

As with military effectiveness, measuring the political effectiveness of air power requires an assessment of its impact relative to other factors.

[45] On coercion see Thomas Schelling, *Arms and Influence* (Yale: Yale University Press, 1966); Robert Pape, *Bombing to Win*.
[46] Phil Haun, *Coercion, Survival, and War*, 32–48.

Determining the contribution of air power can be a challenge as a powerful state employs multiple instruments of power in war. For instance, coercive air campaigns are often accompanied by the imposition of economic sanctions and intense diplomatic activity in order to isolate the targeted state or nonstate actor. As previously discussed, a counterfactual method for evaluating the significance of air power would consider how other efforts would have fared absent the air campaign. How likely would economic sanctions and/or diplomacy have achieved the desired political objectives independently?

Finally, in the discussion on political effectiveness it is important to acknowledge that in several contemporary air wars, most notably those in Afghanistan and Iraq, the achievement of both military and political objectives has not led to long-term peace and stability. The US foreign policy decisions to invade Afghanistan and Iraq have been criticized for failing to anticipate the cost of the occupations that followed.[47] These interminable counterinsurgency and counterterrorism operations have required the outsized and lengthy deployment of troops, which have proven far more costly in terms of both blood and treasure than the initial conventional combat that imposed the regime change.[48] Likewise, criticism has been leveled at the foreign policy decision to intervene in Libya with air power alone. Peacekeeping forces were never deployed, and the collapse of Qaddafi's regime led not to greater political freedom but to a failed state.[49]

It is unfair to criticize air power, however, for the foreign policy decision to go to war or for policy mistakes made during and after the war, that is, with two exceptions. First, the allure of air power in the age of primacy with its promise of easy gains at low costs and little risk to soldiers and airmen may influence short-sighted leaders to discount the long-term costs of occupation or the externalities associated with failed

---

[47] Steve Walt, "We Lost the War in Afghanistan. Get over It," *Foreign Policy* (September 11, 2018). https://foreignpolicy.com/2019/09/11/we-lost-the-war-in-afghanistan-get-over-it; Daniel Lewis, "Foreign Policy Failure: America Has Not Learned from Its Wars," *The National Interest* (April 28, 2018). https://nationalinterest.org/blog/the-skeptics/foreign-policy-failure-america-has-not-learned-its-wars-25607

[48] Amy Belasco, *The Cost of Iraq, Afghanistan, and Other Global War on Terrorism Operations since 9/11* (Washington, DC: Congressional Research Service, 2014), 15. https://fas.org/s gp/crs/natsec/RL33110.pdf; US casualties as of September 17, 2019, are 4,432 dead and 31,994 wounded. See US Department of Defense "Casualty Status," https://defense.gov /casualty.pdf. Iraqi casualty counts vary significantly with a minimum of 134,000 combat deaths, and total deaths could reach as high as a quarter of a million. See Neta Crawford, "Civilian Deaths and Injury in the Iraq War, 2003–2013," Watson Institute Costs of War Project. https://watson.brown.edu/costsofwar/costs/human/civilians/iraqi

[49] Alan Kuperman, "Obama's Libya Debacle: How a Well-Meaning Intervention Ended in Failure," *Foreign Policy* (March/April 2015). https://foreignaffairs.com/articles/libya/2019-02-18/obamas-libya-debacle.

states.[50] Under such conditions, air power may generate a moral hazard for myopic political leaders to ignore the full costs of war. Second, an air-only approach, with no boots on the ground, can adversely affect the postwar order. A well-recognized limitation of air power is its inability to control territory. Though air power is good at destroying, it is not good at rebuilding economic, social, and political institutions. Even when air forces partner with local ground forces, the interests of these proxies may diverge in ways that can jeopardize success. For example, differences between the Northern Alliance and the United States over the threat of Al-Qaeda in 2001 allowed its senior leadership to escape Afghanistan and evade capture (see Chapter 5). In Libya, chaos continues long after the fall of Qaddafi's regime due in large part to the unwillingness of rebels to allow in international peacekeepers (see Chapter 8).

## Summary

The remainder of this chapter summarizes the ten contemporary air wars analyzed in this volume. In Chapter 2, Tim Schultz assesses the development of the US remotely piloted air force, which since 2001 has conducted operations against insurgent and terrorist groups in such disparate locations as Afghanistan, Iraq, Libya, Yemen, Syria, and Somalia. Sustained by an increasingly complex and far-reaching manned/unmanned architecture, these air campaigns have targeted irregular military forces and their leaders with a combination of "signature" and "personality" strikes. Signature strikes target low-level operatives who support or conduct terrorist activities, and these strikes have proven to be successful in weakening insurgent and terrorist organizations. The interagency effort by the USAF and CIA to "mow the lawn" has been both militarily and politically effective in containing international terrorist groups and deterring large-scale terrorist attacks on American soil. By contrast, personality strikes target specific individuals such as high-value terrorists and top leaders of nonstate groups, yet these strikes have largely disappointed. Not only have the intelligence requirements for conducting personality strikes been more challenging than those for signature strikes against militant forces, but even in the few instances when leaders have been killed, nonstate groups have proven resilient in quickly replacing them.

---

[50] Externalities include refugee flows and providing safe haven for international terrorist organizations.

In Chapter 3, Tom Hughes evaluates the 1995 NATO intervention in the Bosnian Civil War. After three years of conflict, the combination of NATO air superiority and a Croat-Muslim ground offensive that threatened the Bosnian Serb capitol of Banja Luka convinced President Radovan Karazdic and General Ratko Mladic to grant negotiating power to Serbian President Slobodan Milosevic. NATO air power succeeded militarily by deterring the Bosnian Serb Army from repositioning its forces. Politically, the NATO air campaign succeeded through its indirect support of a Croat-Muslim offensive, which pressured the Bosnian Serbs in the west. Further, NATO air strikes proved politically effective by avoiding collateral damage incidents that might otherwise have undermined NATO's resolve. Economic sanctions against Serbia also played a role in compelling Milosevic to seek a peace deal. It was not sanctions, however, that convinced the Bosnian Serbs to accept the 49/51 split of Bosnia with the Bosnian Federation. It was, rather, the Croat-Muslim offensive that had made such a partition the reality on the ground.

In Chapter 4, Andrew Stigler examines the 1999 Kosovo War in which the United States and NATO conducted three air operations. NATO's air war against Serbian military forces did not deter Serbia from its ethnic cleansing operations against the Kosovar Albanians. They also failed to coerce Milosevic to make any concessions. Further, an incompetent Kosovo Liberation Army never seriously pressured Serbian forces and was unable to coordinate air strikes with NATO aircrew overhead. Meanwhile, a US-only strategic bombing campaign near Belgrade targeted Milosevic's domicile and political headquarters and conducted "crony" attacks on the economic interests of the Serbian elite who supported him. These leadership strikes also did not convince Milosevic to acquiesce. Instead, a limited number of air strikes against Serbian power and transportation infrastructure brought an already stagnant economy to a halt, and the threat of further attacks deterred Serbian producers from reengaging in substantive economic activity altogether. The suffering of the population and its political consequences for the looming election and Milosevic's bid to remain in power finally convinced him to accept a peace deal. Though Russian intervention did contribute to Milosevic's decision, Russian diplomacy alone would not have caused Milosevic to cede Kosovo absent the economic suffering caused by international sanctions and the credibility demonstrated by NATO that it would continue the air war until Serbia capitulated.

In Chapter 5, Nick Blanchette assesses the air operations in Afghanistan in 2001 following the September 11th attacks. Leadership strikes against Al-Qaeda and Taliban leaders failed to decapitate or paralyze either organization. By contrast, the military campaign, which embedded special operators alongside Northern Alliance and anti-Taliban Pashtun fighters to provide US air cover, proved successful in toppling the Taliban both militarily and politically. Though Osama bin Laden escaped to Pakistan and the costly US-led counterinsurgency and counterterrorism operations in Afghanistan continued for nearly two decades, the overthrow of the Taliban did achieve the core political objectives of punishing Al-Qaeda and the regime that harbored them. It further removed a safe haven for the terrorist group to base its global operations.

In Chapter 6, Heather Venable evaluates the 2003 invasion of Iraq by considering the long durée of US involvement in the region in the context of effective air-power employment. Venable argues that the current historiography is flawed because it still relies on studies rushed to print in the wake of the invasion, and these studies advertised the stunning effectiveness of air and ground power in combined arms warfare with advanced military capabilities in the early weeks of the campaign. The reality, though, is that it remains frustratingly difficult to translate a technological advantage into enduring strategic effect, as seen in the coalition operations that shifted into and have continued in a lower grade of violence for almost two decades now. Paradoxically, precisely at the point that Western nations hoped that a technological advantage might nudge the Clausewitzian triangle of passion, reason, and chance into their corner of reason by removing chance, passion has sprung its head. Passion – most closely related to the people – is critical to understanding the decades-long story of air power's employment in Iraq, because war remains a fundamentally interactive process even as one side appears to hold most of the cards. In essence, rather than highlight the sweeping success of the initial first weeks of the 2003 campaign, this chapter turns the tables by providing a more ethnographic treatment of the ongoing use of violence punctuated by brief bouts of conventional force. Ultimately, Operation Iraqi Freedom must be evaluated in a balanced manner that focuses more on the complex interactions between militaries, governments, and people and less on the overwhelming application of US kinetic force in order to appreciate the challenging character of contemporary air wars.

In Chapter 7, Nimrod Hagiladi examines the performance of the Israeli Air Force (IAF) in the 2006 Second Lebanon War. In this one-month-long war, Israel conducted three air operations against Hezbollah's military, leadership, and economy. The IAF succeeded in destroying Hezbollah's medium- to long-range rockets that threatened Tel Aviv and Jerusalem but could not deter the launching of shorter-range

Katyusha rockets that struck Northern Israel throughout the war. The IAF likewise struggled to support the Israeli army once it deployed into southern Lebanon. As with other contemporary wars, the lack of intelligence plagued Israeli efforts to target Hezbollah leaders. The targeting of Lebanese and Hezbollah infrastructure, such as the blockade of its seaports, the bombing of its airports, and the interdiction of its highways, did impose significant economic costs as did the bombing of houses associated with Hezbollah activity in southern Lebanon and the destruction of hundreds of high-rises in a Hezbollah-controlled section of Beirut. These punishment strikes did not compel Hezbollah to stop its rocket attacks while the war was still ongoing. After the UN-mandated ceasefire came into effect, however, the damage already suffered and the expectation that such air strikes would resume should Hezbollah renew its cross-border activities have deterred such actions and the ceasefire has held.

In Chapter 8, Jahara Matisek surveys the 2011 air war over Libya in which NATO targeted the Libyan government and its military. Leadership strikes failed to decapitate President Moammar Qaddafi's regime or prevent him from commanding his forces. By contrast, NATO's enforcement of a no-drive zone in eastern Libya quickly shifted the military balance of power on the ground in favor of the rebels, which, over time, led to the overthrow of Qaddafi's regime. Though the rebels did not directly coordinate with NATO air power, without NATO intervention the rebellion would have been crushed as had previous uprisings. NATO air forces succeeded militarily and politically in achieving the implicit political objective of regime change. The lack of friendly ground forces to keep the peace after the war ended, however, created a security vacuum that contributed to Libya degenerating into a failed state.

In Chapter 9, Ralph Shield assesses the 2015 Saudi-led intervention in the Yemeni Civil War. Saudi Arabia applied multiple air strategies in its effort to restore a friendly regime in Sanaa. An early bombing campaign against Houthi rebel forces was insufficient by itself to reverse the tide of the war. The subsequent introduction of conventional ground forces enabled the Saudis and their allies to recapture Houthi-held territory, but their successes were incomplete and soon gave way to military stalemate. Decapitation strikes, meanwhile, failed to dispatch either Abdul Malik al-Houthi or his principal ally, Yemeni ex-president Ali Abdullah Saleh. Frustrated by campaign stall and collapsed negotiations, the Saudi intervention increasingly relied on the bombing and blockade of Yemeni civilians. That collective punishment strategy did little to resolve the conflict and much to amplify the human suffering associated with this brutal civil war.

In Chapter 10, Ralph Shield evaluates Russia's role in the Syrian Civil War. Here the arrival of Russian air power saved President Bashar al-Assad's regime, tilted the balance of forces on the ground in Assad's favor, and assisted him in regaining control of much of Syria's territory. The Russian Air Force showcased new technologies in its attacks on rebel military forces but also conducted area bombing of rebel-held cities and villages and deployed its improved targeting capabilities against hospitals. The resulting large-scale flight of refugees from rebel-held territory deprived opposition forces of local support and cover. By targeting rebel forces and the population that supported them, and by shrugging off international opprobrium over its direct attacks on noncombatants, Russia successfully secured its limited strategic objectives in Syria.

In Chapter 11, Stephen Renner examines the fall of ISIS in the retaking of Mosul in 2017, the militant group's final stronghold in Iraq. The expansion of ISIS across eastern Syria and northern Iraq in 2014 led the United States to intervene with air strikes to halt their expansion into Iraq but not before Ramadi, Fallujah, Tikrit, and Mosul had all fallen. Although US air power could prevent further ISIS gains, it could not retake these cities absent a credible ground force willing to trade blood for territory. A combined Iraqi security force composed of regular armored and infantry divisions supported by federal police and spearheaded by counterterrorism troops proved equal to the task. In the end, the retaking of Mosul proved to be both a key military and political victory in collapsing the Islamic State in Iraq and Syria.

In Chapter 12, Colin Jackson draws lessons from these ten wars in which air forces played a significant role. Powerful air forces, when working with competent proxy ground forces, have been effective militarily against much weaker state and nonstate actors in almost all cases, but political effectiveness varied by ambition and target. Air power was most likely to be politically effective in denial strategies against weak states; it was least effective when attempting to coerce nonstate actors by punishment. There is a real chance that the scorecard may overstate the political effectiveness of air power; the number of cases is small and the context for each crisis matters. The success of state-on-state coercion in Bosnia and Kosovo hinged on context – it came in cases of vast asymmetries in power, diplomatic isolation of the target, and modest demands. Coercion failed in Lebanon when the demands were greater, the targets more elusive, and adversaries enjoyed the support/sanctuary of patrons. One should not assume that coercion will be equally effective when power asymmetries shrink, demands rise, and the targeted states enjoy powerful patrons. Air power was far more effective in breaking armies and toppling regimes than it was in restoring political order in the aftermath of regime change. The long wars in Iraq and Afghanistan are testaments to the limits of air power as a political instrument of state making; air power, in the context of counternetwork operations, provided a means to degrade and disrupt militant organizations but often fell short of translating the suppression of resistance into the restoration of organized obedience. Some but not all of the strategies of the age of primacy will survive the transition to an age of great power rivalry. The persistence of small wars against nonstate actors will leave a space for the application and refinement of advisory models, close air support, and counternetwork targeting. But missions that were feasible in an era of unchallenged air supremacy – CAS and persistent ISR – may be impossible in an operational environment dominated by enemies possessing resilient IADS and long-range strike capabilities of their own.

# 2    Remote Warfare: A New Architecture of Air Power

*Timothy P. Schultz* *

Major General Qasem Soleimani's flight from Damascus arrived in Baghdad shortly after midnight on Friday, January 3, 2020. Tracked by Western intelligence assets, the "second-most powerful man in Iran" was returning from a meeting with Hezbollah leaders in Lebanon. Two cars whisked Soleimani and his colleagues into the night. Minutes later both vehicles exploded.[1] Although details remain classified, the Congressional Research Service refers to this as "the Soleimani drone strike," suggesting the work of Hellfire missiles launched by remotely piloted aircraft (RPA).[2] Thus ended the life of the commander of Iran's Quds Force, the foreign arm of the Islamic Revolutionary Guards Corps responsible for a network of proxies in the Middle East, including support of Bashar al-Assad's regime in Syria, and listed as a terrorist organization by the United States in 2019.[3]

Soleimani's death fit neatly into a preferred practice of the Bush, Obama, and Trump administrations: targeting specific high-value terrorists in so-called "personality strikes," typically using a combination of manned and unmanned technology. That combination is portrayed here as a kill web, a far-reaching air power architecture increasingly reliant on RPAs controlled from continental distances. This form of remote warfare has thrived since 9/11 in permissive operating environments including Afghanistan, Iraq, Pakistan, Yemen, Syria, Libya, and Somalia. RPAs took on new roles as contemporary air warfare became increasingly

---

* The views expressed by the author do not reflect those of the US government, the Department of Defense, or any of its organizations.
[1] Peter Baker et al., "Seven Days in January: How Trump Pushed US and Iran to the Brink of War," *New York Times*, January 13, 2020.
[2] "US Killing of Qasem Soleimani: Frequently Asked Questions," Congressional Research Service, January 13, 2020, 1,14. https://crsreports.congress.gov/product/pdf/R/R46148
[3] "Statement from the President on the Designation of the Islamic Revolutionary Guard Corps as a Foreign Terrorist Organization," April 8, 2019. https://whitehouse.gov/brief ings-statements/statement-president-designation-islamic-revolutionary-guard-corps-for eign-terrorist-organization

remote, digitized, and precise. In addition to striking known personalities, they could leverage local surrogates and special operations forces to target pernicious threats such as ISIS (Islamic State of Iraq and Syria) or al-Shabaab militants. Although the evolving architecture of air power included policy structures attempting to narrow the use of remote warfare, these competed with its allure as a means to achieve military and political goals. RPAs became vehicles of political expediency. This provoked questions about the efficacy and ethics of remote warfare and air power operations in countries not at war with the United States.

This chapter first highlights the architecture of remote warfare with a brief technical history of RPAs and how they incorporated existing technologies such as laser-guided weapons, sensor data, and global communications and integrated with a complex web of air and ground assets. It then describes the rapacious demand for RPAs and their expansion into various military missions before examining their military and political effectiveness. Although a variety of RPAs have permeated all branches of the US military and many foreign militaries, this analysis focuses on the US Air Force's (USAF) Predator and Reaper aircraft as catalysts of remote warfare. Indeed, Soleimani's erasure in 2020 traces to 2001 when the first armed RPA, a Predator, was employed to find and kill terrorist leaders in Afghanistan.

### The Technology of Remote Warfare

When you visit the Smithsonian Institution's Udvar-Hazy Center, a Predator stares down at you. A veteran of nearly 200 combat missions, Predator #97-3034 is an unmanned aircraft built by General Atomics and operated variously by the Central Intelligence Agency (CIA) and USAF. It is not a "drone" or a "killer robot" – airmen directly control the hunter-killer Predator, even if they don't physically occupy it. Originally Predators were exclusively reconnaissance platforms and identified as RQ-1: "R" means reconnaissance and "Q" means unmanned in USAF lingo. Then in 2001 engineers slung two Hellfire missiles under #97-3034's wings, giving it a reconnaissance-strike role and a new identity as an *M*Q-1, or "*m*ulti-role" unmanned aircraft, illustrated in Figure 2.1. As an RQ it could hunt; as an MQ it could hunt *and* kill. On the opening night of Operation Enduring Freedom, October 7, 2001, MQ-1 #97-3034 became the first Predator to fire a missile in combat, thus earning its elite airspace in the Smithsonian and opening the door to a new era of remote warfare.[4]

---

[4] See https://airandspace.si.edu/collection-objects/uav-general-atomics-mq-1l-predator.

Figure 2.1  MQ-1 Predator (Photo by Lt. Col Leslie Pratt, USAF)

Remote warfare involves much more than RPAs.[5] Bristling with sensors and weapons, RPAs became nodes in a spreading, interconnected architecture transforming the kill chain into a *kill web*. A kill chain traditionally relied on a combination of manned reconnaissance and strike aircraft and ground forces to find, fix, target, track, engage, and assess targets.[6] The more complex kill web is a flexible and persistent network of capabilities spanning global distances and woven together by arrays of streaming data.[7] Although sensors and algorithms gather and order this data, the kill web is human-intensive. At nearly every node reside analysts, operators, and decision makers. Some occupy the combat zone; others are continents away. Humans trap, identify, and dispatch their targets in this web, aided by an increasingly sophisticated mesh of software and manned and unmanned platforms. RPAs often provide the sting but frequently play an indirect role in supporting manned aircraft and ground commanders.

---

[5] This chapter uses the terms "RPA" (Remotely Piloted Aircraft) and "MQ" (Multi-role unmanned aircraft) interchangeably. "RPA" was adopted by the USAF to replace "Unmanned Aircraft System" (UAS) because these aircraft were heavily manned but remotely operated.

[6] For a summary of the kill chain, see David Deptula et al., "Restoring America's Military Competitiveness: Mosaic Warfare," Mitchell Institute for Aerospace Studies, September 2019, 27–31.

[7] Douglas Birkey, David Deptula, and Lawrence Stutzriem, "Manned-Unmanned Aircraft Teaming: Taking Combat Airpower to the Next Level," *Mitchell Institute Policy Papers* 15 (July 2018). The authors apply "adaptive kill web" to a future involving autonomous aircraft interconnected with manned and unmanned nodes. However, "kill web" aptly describes highly automated, but not autonomous, RPAs and connected systems.

Spindly and slow, when the Predator first flew in 1994 it was initially designed as a sensor platform to provide real-time imagery via electro-optical, infrared, and synthetic aperture radar sensors.[8] The Pentagon soon recognized the Predator's potential for long-endurance surveillance and reconnaissance, and in 1995 the Air Combat Command assigned the first two Predators to the 11th Reconnaissance Squadron (RS) at Indian Springs, a complex in the Nevada desert later known as Creech Air Force Base.[9] The Predator's numbers, capabilities, and roles multiplied during its tenure in the 11th RS (and eventually other squadrons in Air Combat Command, AF Special Operations Command, and the Air National Guard) until its retirement in 2018.[10] Several developments essential to this evolution and the modern architecture of remote warfare include equipping Predators with laser designators, arming them with Hellfire missiles, linking them with various players in the battlespace and intelligence community, and controlling them across continental distances.

*Lasers and Hellfires*

Predators gained operational experience detecting enemy vehicles and troop movements during NATO operations in the Balkans from 1995 to 1999 (Chapters 3 and 4). During Operation Allied Force in 1999, Predator's live video feed was enhanced to include geographic coordinates.[11] This coupling of high-resolution imagery with specific location expanded targeting opportunities but required direct interaction between Predator and manned

[8] For histories of Predator and RPAs, see Thomas Ehrhard, *Air Force UAVs: The Secret History* (Arlington: Mitchell Institute Press, 2010); Richard Whittle, *Predator: The Secret Origins of the Drone Revolution* (New York: Henry Holt and Company, 2014); Caitlin Lee, "The Role of Culture in Military Innovation Studies: Lessons Learned from the US Air Force's Adoption of the Predator Drone, 1993–1997," *Journal of Strategic Studies*, September 26, 2019. https://doi.org/10.1080/01402390.2019.1668272; Sean M. Frisbee, "Weaponizing the Predator UAV: Toward a New Theory of Weapon System Innovation," School of Advanced Air and Space Studies, Maxwell AFB, AL, 2004; Joseph L. Campo (Lt Col, USAF), "From a Distance: The Psychology of Killing with Remotely Piloted Aircraft," PhD dissertation, School of Advanced Air and Space Studies, 2015; Timothy Cullen, "The MQ-9 Reaper Remotely Piloted Aircraft: Human and Machines in Action," PhD dissertation, MIT, 2011; Lawrence Spinetta, "Remote Possibilities: Explaining Innovations in Airpower," PhD dissertation, School of Advanced Air and Space Studies, 2012.

[9] "11 Attack Squadron (ACC)," Air Force Historical Research Agency. www.afhra.af.mil /About-Us/Fact-Sheets/Display/Article/432049/11-reconnaissance-squadron-acc

[10] Daryl Knee, "MQ-1B, MQ-9 Flight Hours Hit 4 Million," Air Combat Command Public Affairs, March 11, 2019. www.af.mil/News/Article-Display/Article/1781271/mq-1b-mq-9-flight-hours-hit-4-million

[11] David A. Deptula, "Consolidating the Revolution: Optimizing the Potential of Remotely Piloted Aircraft," Mitchell Institute for Aerospace Studies, Air Force Association, June 2017, 15.

aircraft, adequate training of Predator operators in complex air-to-ground operations, and the integration of Predator capabilities into operational doctrine. A key step was Predator's acquisition of a laser targeting capability, already a combat-tested technology for the targeting pods of manned aircraft. This was integrated in some Predators in 1999, although too late for kinetic operations in Europe.[12] In a cable to senior USAF leaders in May 2000, Air Combat Command (ACC) Commander General John Jumper emphasized the need to transform Predator beyond a reconnaissance role and employ it as "a FAC-like [Forward Air Control] resource" using laser targeting. This would accomplish two goals: first, identify and laser-illuminate, or "buddy-lase," targets for manned aircraft equipped with laser-guided munitions; second, spur "the next logical step" of weaponizing Predators with their own laser-guided weapons.[13]

Buddy-lasing established a fundamental capability for RPAs. Predators could now exploit a real-time, interdependent role in the battlespace because buddy-lasing illuminated targets for a menagerie of fighter, bomber, and gunship aircraft. This formed a key aspect of the kill web architecture, drastically shrinking the amount of time between finding and striking a target. It also created new opportunities for battlespace commanders, FACs, and Joint Terminal Attack Controllers (JTACs) embedded with ground forces.[14]

Nearly concurrent with laser designation was the ability to convert the RQ-1 Predator to the MQ-1 Predator with the addition of a laser-guided Hellfire missile. ACC's General Jumper was not the only senior leader to push for this capability. National Security Council and CIA officials expressed a keen interest as well. In a memo to President Clinton regarding the hunt for Osama Bin Laden in early 2000, National Security Advisor Samuel Berger summarized plans to search for him in Afghanistan with a Predator. This would overcome "our most significant shortfall" of being unable to corroborate reports of the Al-Qaeda leader's location without imagery evidence. Berger also promised a recommendation for presidential action once we "establish a pattern of bin Laden's movements."[15] The

---

[12] Daniel Haulman, "US Unmanned Aerial Vehicles in Combat, 1991–2003," Air Force Historical Research Agency, June 9, 2003, 10.

[13] "RQ-1, Predator, Program Direction," Cable from ACC/HQ to HQ USAF, HQ USAFE, HQ AFMC, HQ PACAF, SAF Washington, DC, May 1, 2000. "Predator: The Secret Origins of the Drone Revolution," National Security Archive Electronic Briefing Book No. 484. https://nsarchive2.gwu.edu/NSAEBB/NSAEBB484

[14] Nadine Barclay, "Guide Me In: MQ-1s, MQ-9s Provide 'Buddy Lase' Capability against ISIL," Creech AFB Public Affairs, June 22, 2016.

[15] Memo from Samuel Berger to Bill Clinton, 2000 (date unclear, but before September 5, 2000). http://tinyurl.galegroup.com/tinyurl/9eiLG7, Gale Document number: GALE \CK2349611780. For additional context, see Richard Whittle, *Predator: The Secret Origins of the Drone Revolution* (New York: Henry Holt and Company, 2014).

success of a CIA-operated Predator in finding bin Laden in September 2000 sparked discussions of whether and how to employ an armed Predator to kill him. Already a fan of Predator video feeds, Richard Clarke, special assistant to the president and NSC Counterterrorism Coordinator, advocated strongly for a Predator strike when he learned the Air Force endeavored to arm it with Hellfire missiles.[16] The Air Force successfully tested a Predator-launched Hellfire missile in February 2001 but employment overseas came too late to dispatch bin Laden.[17]

The first time a live weapon leapt from the rails of an unmanned aircraft in combat operations was on October 7, 2001, the opening night of Operation Enduring Freedom. By the end of 2002 more than forty Hellfires had been launched from Predators against a variety of targets. While Predators sought their marks in Afghanistan, the USAF employed the Predator-Hellfire combination against Iraqi antiaircraft artillery during Operation Southern Watch.[18] A high-profile strike occurred in November 2002 when a Predator-fired missile struck a moving vehicle in Yemen, killing Qaed Salim Sinan al-Harethi and five others. On describing the attack and the new capability afforded by the MQ-1, Deputy Defense Secretary Paul Wolfowitz argued that such strikes not only kill "somebody dangerous," in this case a suspected accomplice in the 2000 bombing of the USS *Cole*, but "impose changes in their tactics, operations, and procedures."[19] Similarly, the MQ-1 helped catalyze changes in US counterterrorism tactics and operations while also influencing strategic and institutional priorities.

Equipping Predators with radios, laser guidance, and Hellfire missiles transformed their role from hunter to killer but also raised questions about institutional control and the legality of assassinating leaders and foreign operatives like bin Laden. CIA Director George Tenet asked, "What is the chain of command? Who takes the shot? Are America's leaders comfortable with the CIA doing this, going outside of normal military command and control?"[20] Such questions highlight important aspects of the kill web's architecture. Effective command and control of RPA assets required clear coordination at the highest levels of government. This was especially highlighted by the fumbling of the MQ-1 Predator's combat debut on the first night of Operation Enduring Freedom.

---

[16] *9/11 Commission Report*, July 22, 2004, 211.
[17] Thomas E. Ricks, "Unmanned US Plane Is Lost over Iraq," *Washington Post*, August 28, 2001.
[18] Dan Haulman, "US Unmanned Aerial Vehicles," 11.
[19] Jane Mayer, "The Predator War," *The New Yorker*, October 19, 2009.
[20] *9/11 Commission Report*, 211.

Air power had a prize opportunity to kill Taliban Supreme Commander Mullah Omar on October 7, 2001. Observers at the Combined Air Operations Center (CAOC), CIA, and Pentagon watched the live video feed of a Hellfire-armed Predator as it observed Mullah Omar and some of his lieutenants dismount from their vehicle and enter a building. A decision was made by someone – to this day it remains unclear whom – for the Predator to strike the vehicle with a Hellfire missile presumably to flush the Taliban leader out of the building for a second, lethal shot from the Predator. This thwarted the CAOC's plan for a nearby F/A-18 to destroy the building with Mullah Omar still in it and have the Predator hold its fire unless Omar squirted out of the building.[21] The Predator's premature strike on the vehicle missed Mullah Omar, who then slipped away into darkness. The literal missed opportunity led to acrimonious debate between the USAF, CIA, and Central Command (CENTCOM). General Tommy Franks, CENTCOM commander, summarized the issue: "In combat there has to be one line of authority. But in this goat rope there had been CENTCOM [including the CAOC], the Pentagon, the White House, the CIA."[22] This incident revealed that a functional kill web was based on much more than technology. It also required command and control expertise to optimize military effectiveness.

### Rover, Chat, and PED

While lines of authority and strategic priorities complicated the architecture of remote warfare, another battlefield technology expanded the effectiveness of manned and unmanned nodes in the kill web. The "Rover" – Remote Operated Video Enhanced Receiver – materialized in late 2001 and transformed battlespace integration. Seeking to acquire MQ-1 imagery for better situational awareness and tactical effectiveness, the Air Force Special Operations Command requested the Air Logistics Center to equip AC-130 gunships with a video receiver from Predator.[23] This would enable a Predator orbiting undetected near a target to extend an air-to-air tendril of streaming video to a Rover-equipped AC-130 many miles away. The AC-130 crew would then know where to train

---

[21] Richard Whittle, *Predator*, 248–54.

[22] Chris Woods, "The Story of America's Very First Drone Strike," *Atlantic* (May 30, 2015): 3.

[23] "High Technology," Warner-Robins Air Logistics Center, May 2005. www.robins.af.mil /history/FY02/CH3.02.htm. See also Frank Grimsley, "The Predator Unmanned System: From Advanced Concept Demonstrator to Transformational Weapon System," 303d Aerospace Wing, Wright Patterson AFB, Air Force Materiel Command briefing (PowerPoint slides), September 2008.

their heavy guns as their aircraft rumbled toward the target, firing before it could be detected by its prey.[24]

While AC-130 crews sought real-time imagery from Predators, so did ground forces. In January 2002, Army Green Beret Chief Warrant Officer Chris Manuel asked for access to Predator video to "see what was over the next hill."[25] Specializing in the swift genesis of operational innovations, the USAF's Big Safari organization scrambled to create a solution, and Special Operations Force (SOF) troops soon had their own portable Rovers. These permitted elite forces to interact directly with RPAs and use that connection to accelerate the kill chain with airborne or land-based weapons. Unsurprisingly, combatants outside of the special operations realm soon noticed SOF forces could arrange for an attack within a minute or two while the process for regular forces took up to forty-five minutes.[26] Why the difference? SOF had Rover; regular forces did not. This sparked a major effort to equip regular units with Rover and also modify Rovers so they could receive streaming data not just from Predators but also manned fighters, bombers, and helicopters.[27]

Such actions enabled Rover to expand beyond a niche capability.[28] Rovers decreased in size and weight to resemble small laptop computers, and this increased their utility for coalition forces. By September 2007 approximately 1,500 were in use in Afghanistan or Iraq with another 2,200 on the way.[29] This multiplied the interconnected nodes in the kill web. According to one report in 2008, 85 percent of Close Air Support (CAS) missions involved a Rover. Moreover, a diverse fleet of air assets and 14 allied nations either provided or received full motion video (FMV) courtesy of Rover.[30] Rover also expanded the roles of manned aircraft. According to one A-10 pilot, Rover turned his aircraft into "a nontraditional intelligence and surveillance platform" since Joint Terminal Attack Controllers (JTACs) miles away could stream video from his A-10 to coordinate attacks from various ground-based or airborne assets.[31]

Not only could JTACs communicate via radio with nearby MQ-1 Predators and various manned aircraft, they could also provide "talk-ons" using Rover imagery highlighted by drawing clear symbols to

[24] Richard Whittle, *Predator*, 300.
[25] Chuck Menza, "ROVER Capabilities Brief," Pentagon, 2008. https://ndiastorage .blob.core.usgovcloudapi.net/ndia/2008/uscg/Wednesday/menzabrief/menza.pdf
[26] Julian E. Barnes, "He Helped Clear the Fog of War," *Los Angeles Times*, September 13, 2007.
[27] Ibid.     [28] Ibid.     [29] Ibid.     [30] Menza, "ROVER Capabilities."
[31] David Kurle, "ROVER Provides Pilot's View to Ground Forces," Air Force Reserve Command, January 18, 2008. www.afrc.af.mil/News/Article-Display/Article/158513/rove r-provides-pilots-view-to-ground-forces

identify the location of combatants and noncombatants.[32] One JTAC
noted, "I can circle an area on my screen, drawing arrows for emphasis,
and what I'm drawing appears on [the pilots'] screens as well."[33] Another
user argued this hands-on graphical interface appealed to the "Xbox
generation."[34] Lasers, Hellfires, Rovers, and RPAs thus created new
opportunities for human creativity in an increasingly relevant and lethal
kill web. Yet other modes of interaction and control were vital to RPAs
and the kill web's evolution.

Another familiar means of modern communication, and one used
extensively in the air combat enterprise, is tactical chat, or multiuser
internet relay chat (mIRC, or mIRC-chat).[35] The kill web is also a giant
online chat room. An RPA crew in a Ground Control Station (GCS)
may use text-based chat as a flexible, low-bandwidth means to communicate globally with manned aircraft, intelligence analysts, operations
centers, commanders at various levels, lawyers, and others during any
given mission.[36] These are succinct and retrievable conversations about
suspected enemy movements, the status of coalition weapon platforms,
weather reports, positive identification of potential targets, etc. Because
a vast array of players in the joint combat environment came to rely on
mIRC-chat, in 2009 the DoD established multi-Service tactics, techniques, and procedures to enhance its usefulness for warfighters.[37] The
modern kill web is thus overlaid with a network of remotely dispersed
intercommunicating experts and operators seeking and scrutinizing
military operations that may have tactical, operational, and strategic
implications. This includes connections to legions of personnel in the
military's broader Processing, Exploitation, and Dissemination (PED)
system.

The PED system anchors the threads of the kill web. It links intelligence and action, rendering information for the swift use of intelligence
organizations and combat forces. Part of the global intelligence, surveillance, and reconnaissance (ISR) architecture, it consists of five
Distributed Ground Systems in the United States (Hawaii, California,
Virginia), Germany, and South Korea. These organizations receive tera-
bytes of raw data collected from key components of the kill web – RPAs,
satellites, and various species of airborne and terrestrial platforms – for

[32] Kurle, "ROVER Provides."     [33] Menza, "ROVER Capabilities."     [34] Ibid.
[35] The "m" in mIRC-chat may stand for multiuser or Microsoft; sometimes it is just
called IRC.
[36] David A. Mindell, *Our Robots, Ourselves* (New York: Viking, 2015), 145–46.
[37] LorRaine T. Duffy and Emily W. Medina, "Military Text Chat Is 'Communication at the
Edge,'" *Air Land Sea Bulletin* (January 2012): 21.

analysts to refine into "decision-quality information" and disseminate to the kill web's nodes for assessment and action.[38]

Despite PED's reliance on cyber-based networks, it is an inherently human, labor-intensive mission. For example, the USAF estimated in 2011 that approximately 4,750 PED personnel would be needed to support RPA operations.[39] According to USAF Chief of Staff General David Goldfein, the priority of populating the architecture of remote warfare caused the Air Force to retire ten squadrons of legacy fighter aircraft in 2010.[40] In addition to PED demands, a vital aspect of managing remote warfare involved another innovation: Remote-Split Operations.

*Remote-Split Operations*

RPAs permit a novel means of control: Remote-Split Operations (RSO), illustrated in Figure 2.2. A team of airmen called the Launch and Recovery Element (LRE) deploys with RPA squadrons to a remote airbase in or near the combat theater. They use line-of-sight radios to control RPAs during critical takeoff and landing phases of flight. Local operators then share – or split – control with a team of airmen at a Ground Control Station (GCS) in the continental United States. Once launched toward the battlespace, the aircraft switches from LRE to GCS control, which uses a combination of satellite and undersea fiber optic transmissions. Although intercontinental distance imposes a nearly two-second communication delay, the officer pilot and enlisted sensor operator in the GCS can still maneuver their aircraft at medium altitude to employ its sensor and weapon capabilities in a near-real-time manner while they also interact with various nodes of the kill web architecture.

RSO debuted on the opening night of Operation Enduring Freedom in the previously discussed CIA-led effort to assassinate Mullah Omar. Predator #97–3034 took off from Uzbekistan under the line-of-sight radio control of airmen in the LRE. For its mission in Afghanistan, control was transferred via a satellite uplink to a relay base in Germany and then to a GCS at CIA

---

[38] "Reachback and Distributed Operations ISR," Annex 2–0 Global Integrated Intelligence, Surveillance, & Reconnaissance Operations, Curtis E. LeMay Center for Doctrine Development and Education, Maxwell Air Force Base, AL, January 29, 2015.

[39] "The Future of Air Force Motion Imagery Exploitation," RAND Technical Report, 2012. www.rand.org/content/dam/rand/pubs/technical_reports/2012/RAND_TR1133 .pdf; RPA Task Force, "RPA Fast Facts," Headquarters USAF, RPA Task Force, January 1, 2011.

[40] Birkey et al., "Manned-Unmanned Aircraft Teaming." This document references General David Goldfein's "Address to the Air Force Sergeants Association Professional Airmen's Conference and International Convention." www.youtube.com/ watch?v=icOQhtEbngo

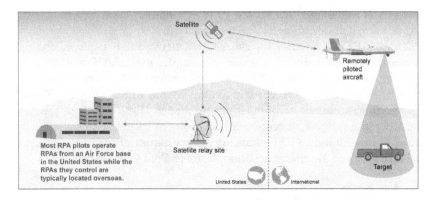

Figure 2.2 Remote-split Operations diagram (US Government Accounting Office Report, GAO-14-316, "Air Force RPA Pilots," April 2014)

Headquarters in Langley, Virginia.[41] An Air Force crew in the GCS flew the Predator; their job was to position it so a CIA officer could push the button that launched the Hellfire. This illustrated a key advantage of RSO, namely the ability to minimize political sensitivities by having "trigger-pullers" located in the United States.[42] Colocating a GCS with an LRE in a country neighboring Iraq or Afghanistan, for example, may pose political and diplomatic difficulties for the host country, especially if it is concerned about fallout over RPA-related combat operations. RSO also provides the pragmatic advantage of deploying far fewer US personnel to the host country, enabling a more covert or politically expedient style of operations.[43]

The DoD continued to refine RSO capabilities in Operations Enduring Freedom and Iraqi Freedom to directly support ground forces. For example, an Air Liaison Officer during Operation Iraqi Freedom recalls the scenario when Marine ground forces needed to neutralize an enemy sniper. A Predator crew operating from Nevada identified the sniper atop a structure and used a laser to mark his location for an F/A-18. The F/A-18 slewed its camera to the location and delivered a GBU-12 laser-guided, 500-lb bomb to eliminate the threat.[44] Similar scenarios

---

[41] M. C. Elish, "Remote Split: A History of US Drone Operations and the Distributed Labor of War," *Science, Technology, & Human Values* 42:6 (2017): 115. For a fuller account of this operation, see Whittle, *Predator*, 223–25.

[42] M. C. Elish, "Remote Split," 115.

[43] "Reachback and Distributed Operations ISR," Richard Whittle, *Predator*, 151.

[44] "How We Fight," US Air Force video featuring Air Liaison Officer Greg Harbin. www.youtube.com/watch?v=3lxJSZQ93gI; see also David Deptula, "Consolidating the Revolution," 38.

involving missions against precision targets and efforts to minimize collateral damage highlight other vital nodes in the RSO architecture that
include a large cast of actors – some in the battlespace, some far from it –
who influence RPA operations. These include pilots, sensor operators,
joint terminal attack controllers, forward air controllers, commanders (up
to four-star and senior-civilian authorities), lawyers, linguists, intelligence
experts, meteorologists, engineers, weaponeers, and others who may play
a real-time role.[45] Woven together by satellites, radios, relay stations,
modems, telephones, chat rooms, and trans-oceanic fiber optic cables,
these people and machines constitute a new architecture of air power.

### Remote Warfare: Pressure and Expansion

Remote Split Operations was just one innovation that made the kill web
inherently adaptable. Equipping Predators with laser guidance capabilities and then arming them with Hellfire missiles elevated RPAs to a new
role. Rover and mIRC-chat multiplied connections in an increasingly
resilient and relevant kill web that exploited ground, air, cyber, and
space domains. These elements enhanced the operational architecture
of manned and unmanned aircraft and spun the kill web into being.
Remote warfare spanned tactical, operational, and strategic seams with
new advances in range, endurance, and sensor and payload capabilities.
These included upgrades to the Predator and the combat debut of the
MQ-9 Reaper in 2007. The efficacy of RPAs in permissive environments
stoked demand and enabled their expansion beyond declared war zones.

*Demand Pressure*

In his speech to Citadel cadets in December 2001, President George
W. Bush extolled the virtues of RPAs while cautioning those who might
resist them. He cited the Predator's ability to loiter over the enemy, feed
information to commanders, and then attack with pinpoint accuracy.
And then came a subtle warning to traditionalists: "Before the war, the
Predator had skeptics, because it did not fit the old ways. Now it is clear
the military does not have enough unmanned vehicles. We're entering
a new era in which unmanned vehicles of all kinds will take on greater
importance – in space, on land, in the air, and at sea."[46] President Bush's
new era of unmanned vehicles was made possible by the lack of a modern

---

[45] Timothy Schultz, "UAS Manpower: Exploiting a New Paradigm," US Air Force
Research Institute, October 2009, 5.
[46] George W. Bush speech at the Citadel, December 12, 2001. www.citadel.edu/root/
presbush01

air threat in the permissive skies over Afghanistan and Iraq, and the White House and Pentagon demand for RPAs escalated in the two decades after 9/11. Theater commanders developed an intense "desire for that unblinking eye" in their quest for *coup d'oeil*.[47] This unrelenting pressure required not only high-tech solutions but an enormous amount of organizational effort and manpower.

The rapacious demand for RPAs manifested in the form of Combat Air Patrols, or CAPs. CAPs were generally defined as the ability to provide 24/7 coverage over a given objective. One CAP required several aircraft rotating into position over twenty-four hours, and it especially needed several sets of GCS aircrew. A single CAP is thus a metric of demand that entails a broad base of resources.[48] "CAP" is also a carefully chosen term regarding RPAs. Why not use "orbit," the term traditionally associated with ISR aircraft? The Air Combat Command favored "CAP" due to its long association with fighter aircraft patrols, and a CAP would therefore sound like something involved with the combat Air Force and not the intelligence community.[49] It was an intentional label to stake out organizational control and highlight the kinetic aspect of multirole MQ aircraft.

New CAPs winked into existence in the remote warfare constellation at a frantic rate. This reflected the intensifying counterinsurgency effort in Iraq and the expanding war on terrorism. General David Petraeus, for example, pressed Secretary of Defense Robert Gates for more CAPS in 2007 to support his surge. Pressure also came from the Special Operations Command commander, who urged Congress in 2008 to facilitate 30 CAPs.[50] Accordingly, the number of CAPs exploded from 5 in 2004 to 65 over the next decade.[51] This required hundreds of more Predators and Reapers and many thousands more personnel because nearly 200 people could be needed to support a single CAP.[52] The demand pull for resources was highlighted in a widely publicized critique of the Air Force by Secretary Gates on April 21, 2008: "I've been wrestling for months to get more [ISR] assets into the theater .... Because people were stuck in old ways of doing business, it's been like pulling teeth. While we've doubled this capacity in recent months, it is still not

---

[47] Senate Armed Services Committee, "Hearing to Receive Testimony on Army Unmanned Aircraft Vehicles and Air Force Remotely Piloted Aircraft," March 16, 2016, 24. www.armed-services.senate.gov/imo/media/doc/16-32_3–16-16.pdf
[48] "The Future," 4.    [49] David Deptula, "Consolidating the Revolution," 42, fn.78.
[50] Caitlin Lee, "The Culture of US Air Force Innovation: A Historical Case Study of the Predator Program," PhD dissertation, King's College, London, 2016, 232–33.
[51] Senate Armed Services Committee, "Hearing," 7.
[52] A RAND report determined "a maximal crew of 192 airmen can be associated with a single CAP, including 30 analysts dedicated to the exploitation of motion imagery alone"; "The Future," 4; M. C. Elish, "Remote Split," 1104.

good enough."[53] Notably, his use of the term "old ways" echoed President Bush's 2001 admonition of the "old ways" of remote warfare skeptics, suggesting the difficulty of overcoming an institution's entrenched cultural and warfighting priorities.[54]

A steep increase in flight hours illustrates the seemingly insatiable demand for RPAs: 250,000 hours from 1995 to 2007, one million by 2011, two million by 2013, three million by 2016, and four million by 2019.[55] These hours were predominantly flown by airmen in GCS complexes at a growing number of locations beyond Creech AFB at active-duty and Air National Guard bases across the United States.[56] RPAs logged these hours over Afghanistan, Iraq, Syria, Libya, Yemen, Somalia, and Pakistan, indicating their penetration of modern conflict.[57]

*Mission Expansion*

During the Bush, Obama, and Trump administrations, RPA missions expanded in terms of military capabilities as well as geographic scope. President George W. Bush, enthusiastic about the era of unmanned vehicles since 2001, oversaw RPA missions in Iraq, Afghanistan, and parts of Pakistan. By the end of his second term, President Obama expanded RPA operations to Yemen, Libya, and Somalia. The Trump administration oversaw RPA activity in all of these countries plus others such as Syria and Niger. This growing list reflects an evolving array of missions and emerging political priorities.

Predator's transformation from an ISR-only to a strike-capable platform became obvious during the Battle for Takur Ghar, later know as Roberts Ridge, in Afghanistan in March 2002. Heavy enemy fire from fortified positions damaged or destroyed several helicopters and claimed numerous US lives. A Predator observed much of this battle, streaming its video to Joint Special Operations Command and tactical operations centers, and then used a Hellfire to destroy an enemy bunker that had pinned down US Special Forces. It also buddy-lased Al-Qaeda positions for destruction by French Mirage 2000D fighter aircraft. A former commander of the 32d Expeditionary Air Intelligence Squadron that flew the

---

[53] Kristin Roberts, "Pentagon Chief Seeks More Drones in Iraq for Intel," *Reuters*, April 21, 2008.

[54] For more on institutional culture, see Caitlin Lee, "The Role of Culture."

[55] Daryl Knee, "MQ-1B, MQ-9 Flight Hours." See also www.creech.af.mil/About-Us/Fact-Sheets/Display/Article/449126/432nd-wing-432nd-air-expeditionary-wing

[56] Caitlin Lee, "The Culture," 264–65.

[57] Jacquelyn Schneider and Julia Macdonald, "US Public Support for Drone Strikes," Center for a New American Security, September 20, 2016. www.cnas.org/publications/reports/u-s-public-support-for-drone-strikes

Takur Ghar Predator later observed, "We were a sideshow up until that point . . . . After that, Predator became what it is today."[58]

The expanding capabilities of RPAs and the kill web occasioned the Operation Iraqi Freedom Coalition Forces Air Component Commander, Lieutenant General Michael Moseley, to admit, "We're at a threshold of something very, very exciting and very, very new with unmanned aerial vehicles . . . ."[59] Key to mission evolution in Iraq was the combination of sensors and weapons incorporated by Predators and Reapers. Their Multi-spectral Targeting System (MTS) included electro-optical video, a laser designator, and an infrared capability permitting a "hunt for heat."[60] While Predator's only armament consisted of two Hellfire missiles, the Reaper could carry more than eight times the payload, including a mix of Hellfires, GBU-12 laser-guided bombs, GBU-38 GPS-guided bombs, and GBU-54 laser-GPS guided bombs capable of striking moving targets[61] (see Figure 2.3). The combination of sensory and kinetic capabilities resulted not from new technologies but new combinations of technologies originally developed for other aircraft.[62]

The evolving capabilities of RPAs enabled them to colonize new roles in the battlespace. The Reaper, for example, began flying combat operations in September 2007, which, a decade later, had expanded to a variety of hunter-killer abilities such as close air support (CAS), including urban CAS; combat search and rescue; precision attack; and overwatch of convoys and strike units.[63] All of this was in addition to classic ISR and warranted RPAs to be characterized as "persistent attack and reconnaissance" aircraft.[64] The Reaper, moreover, cultivated an organic "hard kill" capability because it incorporated the entirety of the kill chain, or the ability to find, fix, target, track, engage, and assess various targets.[65]

[58] Richard Whittle, *Predator,* 298.
[59] Kurt D. Hall, "Near Space: Should Air Force Space Command Take Control of Its Shore?" USAF Air War College, Maxwell Paper No. 38, 4. www.au.af.mil/au/awc/awc gate/maxwell/mp38.pdf
[60] "MQ-9 Reaper Unmanned Aircraft System Selected Acquisition Report," as of FY 2016 President's Budget, Defense Acquisition Management Information Retrieval, 18, March 2015, 6; Lisa Parks, "Drones, Infrared Imagery, and Body Heat," *International Journal of Communication* 8 (2014): 2518–21.
[61] James Thompson, "CSAF Lauds Combat RPA Innovation," 432nd Wing/432nd Air Expeditionary Wing Public Affairs, January 18, 2019. www.af.mil/News/Article-Display /Article/1735173/csaf-lauds-combat-rpa-innovation
[62] Joe Chapa, "The Ethics of Remote Weapons," in *One Nation, Under Drones: Legality, Morality, and Utility of Unmanned Combat Systems,* ed. John Jackson (Annapolis: Naval Institute Press, 2018), 179.
[63] "MQ-9 Reaper Unmanned Aircraft System Selected Acquisition Report," as of FY 2019 President's Budget, December 2017, 8.
[64] Daryl Knee, "MQ-1B, MQ-9 Flight Hours."
[65] Frank Grimsley, "The Predator Unmanned System."

Figure 2.3  MQ-9 Reaper (Photo by Staff Sgt. Brian Ferguson, USAF)

These capabilities continued to develop in the permissive skies of Yemen, Somalia, and Libya as three US presidents balanced the risks and rewards of counterterror air strikes in countries not at war with the United States.

Operations outside of Iraq and Afghanistan highlighted a key distinction in RPA missions: *personality* strikes versus *signature* strikes. Personality strikes target a specific individual or what the White House termed a high-value terrorist (HVT). For example, in Yemen on November 4, 2002, a CIA-operated Predator struck a vehicle carrying Qaed Salim Sinan al-Harethi, one of the planners in the October 2000 attack on the USS *Cole*.[66] The only strike in Yemen during the Bush administration, this was indicative of other personality strikes that occurred in Iraq, Afghanistan, and Pakistan during his administration. In September 2011, President Obama authorized the killing of Anwar al-Awlaki, a prominent Al-Qaeda radical complicit in a number of terror plots. Although an American citizen, the White House viewed him as an HVT and acute threat to US security who likely could not be captured but could be dispatched from the air. Awlaki thus qualified for a personality strike, and Obama reportedly noted "This is an easy one" despite debates over the legality of slaying an American citizen on foreign soil.[67] Signature

---

[66] Eric Patterson and Teresa Casale, "Targeting Terror: The Ethical and Practical Implications of Targeted Killing," *International Journal of Intelligence and Counterintelligence* 18:4, 643–44.

[67] Jo Becker and Scott Shane, "Secret 'Kill List' Proves a Test of Obama's Principles and Will," *New York Times*, May 29, 2012.

strikes, however, were less specific and more tolerant of potential civilian casualties.

A carryover from the Bush administration, signature strikes involved likely but nonspecific participants in terrorist activity; even if their identities were unknown, military-age males participating in things like training camps or transportation possessed the signature of complicity.[68] Guilty by association, they were thus subject to air strikes. Chastened by the accidental killing of several Yemeni civilians in a 2009 air strike, and wary of starting a war in Yemen, Obama forbade signature strikes for nearly two years.[69] Due to Al-Qaeda's metastasis in Yemen, by 2012 the White House reverted to the use of signature strikes only under a different name: Terrorist Attack Disruption Strikes (TADS) against unnamed suspects who showed some evidence of activity threatening the United States.[70] Although the Obama administration still aimed to limit air strikes in Yemen to only time-critical, positively identified targets with no collateral damage, a 2016 New America Foundation report claimed that 131 RPA strikes and 16 manned-aircraft strikes – almost all under President Obama – killed 1,242 people in Yemen.[71]

The United States, in control of the air, sought the high ground of certitude, precision, and just cause to minimize political fallout but still make progress in dismantling extremist organizations that might target Americans. RPAs served that purpose. A 2013 Presidential Policy Guidance permitted precision air strikes outside of the war zones of Iraq and Afghanistan "only when there is near certainty that the individual being targeted is in fact the lawful target" and if "the action can be taken without injuring or killing noncombatants." An HVT's activities, moreover, must "pose a continuing, imminent threat to US persons." Strikes also required direct approval from the president if the target was an American or if the principals (Secretaries of State, Defense, Justice, Homeland Security; Director of CIA; Director of National Intelligence) lacked unanimous consent.[72] Nevertheless, due to the persistence of Al-Qaeda and the rise of Islamic State extremists in Yemen, Somalia, and Libya, the Obama administration strayed from this high standard and reverted to signature strikes with their looser rules of engagement.[73]

[68] Dan De Luce and Paul McLeary, "Obama's Most Dangerous Drone Tactic Is Here to Stay," *Foreign Policy*, April 5, 2016.
[69] "Secret 'Kill List.'"    [70] Ibid.
[71] Dan De Luce and Paul Mcleary, "Obama's Most Dangerous Drone Tactic."
[72] "Procedures for Approving Action against Terrorist Targets Located Outside the United States and Areas of Active Hostilities," Presidential Policy Guidance, May 22, 2013, 1, 14, 17. www.justice.gov/oip/foia-library/procedures_for_approving_direct_action_against_terrorist_targets/download
[73] Dan De Luce and Paul Mcleary, "Obama's Most Dangerous Drone Tactic."

The Obama administration authorized numerous personality and signature strikes under the auspices of US Africa Command (AFRICOM) against al-Shabaab militants in Somalia. For example, a signature strike in March 2016 against a training camp used RPAs and manned aircraft to kill approximately 150 militants.[74] The Trump White House continued in this vein. Acceding to the Pentagon's desire for more latitude, in March 2017 President Trump designated regions of Somalia and Yemen as "areas of active hostilities," thus bypassing the 2013 Presidential Policy Guidance, reducing the degree of interagency coordination, and empowering theater commanders to authorize manned and unmanned air strikes.[75] This helped double the number of strikes in Somalia and triple them in Yemen.[76]

Although the Pentagon divulges few details regarding RPA operations, AFRICOM press releases and broader media coverage cited the Trump administration's sustained campaign to disrupt al-Shabaab forces via air strikes in cooperation with African Union and Somali ground forces.[77] Major General Gregg Olson, AFRICOM Director of Operations, noted in March 2019 how a network of aircraft and ground components enabled striking the enemy network: "whether a single node or a concentration ... we understand the network better than we have in years past."[78] This enabled personality strikes against specific individuals and signature strikes against militant concentrations such as in June 2017 when a Reaper launched by an LRE crew in Djibouti used Hellfire missiles against an al-Shabaab camp to kill eight combatants.[79] These operations are echoed in Pentagon data from 2018, listing 326 suspected combatants killed in 47 strikes, and 225 killed by 24 strikes in the first two months of 2019.[80] This included an air strike killing 52 al-Shabaab militants who attacked Somali army forces.[81]

---

[74] "Statement from Pentagon Press Secretary Peter Cook on Airstrike in Somalia," March 7, 2016. www.defense.gov/News/News-Releases/News-Release-View/Article/687305/statement-from-pentagon-press-secretary-peter-cook-on-airstrike-in-somalia; Gordon Lubold, "US Attack Hits Militant Training Camp in Somalia," *Wall Street Journal*, March 7, 2016.
[75] Charlie Savage and Eric Schmitt, "Trump Administration Is Said to Be Working to Loosen Counterterrorism Rules," *New York Times*, March 12, 2017.
[76] Rebecca Malone, "Trump's First Year: Analyzing the Trump Administration's Use of Drone Strikes as a Counterterrorism Strategy in 2017," *Georgetown Security Studies Review* 6:2 (2018): 9.
[77] Charlie Savage, Helene Cooper, and Eric Schmitt, "US Strikes Shabaab, Likely a First since Trump Relaxed Rules for Somalia," *New York Times*, June 11, 2017.
[78] Charlie Savage and Eric Schmitt, "Trump Administration Steps Up Air War in Somalia," *New York Times*, March 10, 2019.
[79] Charlie Savage, "US Strikes Shabaab."
[80] Charlie Savage, "Trump Administration Steps Up Air War."
[81] "Al-Shabaab Degraded by US, Federal Government of Somalia," AFRICOM press release, January 19, 2019.

Concurrent with operations in Yemen and Somalia, the evolution and expansion of RPA missions under the Obama and Trump administrations also manifested in operations against the Islamic State of Iraq and Syria (ISIS) forces. Notably, Libya showcased the utility of RPAs in countering ISIS expansion via joint air operations and coordination with ground components.

As described in Chapter 8, a Predator identified and helped disable Qaddafi's motorcade in October 2011 as he fled the port city of Sirte, and shortly later he was trapped and executed by a rebel mob. ISIS forces took advantage of the subsequent instability in Libya and occupied Sirte in May 2015. Libya's new Government of National Accord requested US assistance as it fought to reclaim the city in summer 2016, resulting in a return of RPAs and other forces. President Obama designated Sirte as an "area of active hostilities" in order to accelerate the process of military violence, and the resulting five-month AFRICOM campaign, Operation Odyssey Lightning, relied heavily on a combination of Marine jets and helicopters, Libyan government forces, US special operations forces, and Reapers controlled by aircrew in Nevada, Tennessee, and North Dakota.[82]

From one Reaper pilot's perspective, precision combat in Sirte posed new problems and opportunities: "As the battle went on we had to adapt the style to fight the enemy we were engaging ... some of the persistent attack capabilities that hadn't been used widely before were developed because of this operation."[83] This included multi-aircraft coordination between Reapers to optimize target identification, laser designation, and weapon-delivery angles in urban terrain. It also involved hundreds of "danger close" strikes, weapons dropped only thirty yards from friendly forces, the distance from home plate to first base.[84] In some cases Reaper crews eliminated snipers by firing Hellfire missiles into a building's window; one Reaper pilot engaging in similar urban tactics against ISIS in Syria claimed, "I can shoot down an alleyway. If there's a sniper in one of the windows, I can hit that."[85] In assessing nearly 300 Reaper strikes,

[82] Jim Michaels, "How US Drones Helped Win a Battle against ISIS for First Time in Libya," *USA Today*, April 17, 2017; Charlie Savage, "Trump Administration Is Said to Be Working."

[83] Christian Clausen, "Providing Freedom from Terror: RPAs Help Reclaim Sirte," 432nd Wing/432nd Air Expeditionary Wing Public Affairs, August 1, 2017. www.creech.af.mil/News/Article-Display/Article/1225090/providing-freedom-from-terror-rpas-help-reclaim-sirte

[84] Jim Michaels, "How US Drones Helped."

[85] Brian W. Everstine, "The B-2 Body Blow," *Air Force Magazine*, July 2017, 37; W. J. Hennigan, "The US Is Now Routinely Launching 'Danger-Close' Drone Strikes So Risky They Require Syrian Militia Approval," *Los Angeles Times*, August 15, 2017.

60 percent of the total US air strikes in Sirte, the AFRICOM command-ing general affirmed the value of combining RPAs with special operations forces: "I don't think you can do an operation like that without somebody on the ground. You have to have that contact . . . to make sure we can do it with this skill and precision that's required."[86] He also predicted Sirte will "serve as a model for future US operations in the region."[87]

Retaking a city from extremists, however, did not equate to victory. RPAs continued their work against ISIS with signature strikes, including a farewell bombing from the Obama administration. On January 18, 2017, during the final hours of his second term, President Obama authorized a strike by heavy bombers, B-2s laden with 85 bombs and flown nonstop from their base in Missouri. Reapers identified the target: ISIS militants at a training camp 30 miles from Sirte. AFRICOM assessed more than 100 ISIS members were killed.[88] The Trump administration continued efforts to deny safe havens with episodic strikes in Libya. On September 27, 2019, for example, AFRICOM reported killing 17 militants in a signature strike. The report noted: "Currently we assess no civilians were injured or killed as a result of this air strike."[89] This statement indicates the sensitivity and political liabilities concerning noncombatant casualties, a factor that deeply informs the efficacy of remote warfare.

## Remote Warfare and Air Power Efficacy

The evolution of RPA capabilities reflected the effort to deny safe haven to terrorists and disrupt their ability to plot against US interests. RPAs, along with the development of an adaptive and deployable kill web, permitted the White House and Pentagon to project power outside of established war zones. Vehicles of political expediency, RPAs embodied resolve and created at least the appearance of progress against terrorism. Yet the overall effectiveness of RPAs and remote warfare requires a critical assessment.

### Effectiveness

The mission of the first armed Predator was to assassinate top leaders to effect collapse of an extremist organization, a goal with military, strategic,

[86] Brian Everstine, "The B-2 Body Blow," 39.
[87] Jim Michaels, "How US Drones Helped."
[88] "US Conducts Air Strikes on Daesh Camps in Libya," AFRICOM press release, January 19, 2017; Brian Everstine, "The B-2 Body Blow," 40.
[89] "US Africa Command Airstrike Targets ISIS-Libya," AFRICOM media release, September 27, 2019.

and foreign policy implications as witnessed by the turmoil and brinks-manship between the United States and Iran following the January 2020 killing of Quds Force commander Major General Soleimani. This strat-egy reflects aspects of John Warden's Five Rings hypothesis that places senior leaders and their command and control apparatus in the center ring, the highest priority of destruction.[90] Yet eliminating the inner ring of leadership along with as many lower-level insurgents as possible does not necessarily alter the status quo and create peace even though it is a tantalizing use of the kill web. The commander of Multi-National Corps – Iraq noted in November 2006 that even though senior leaders were among the thousands of Al-Qaeda operatives killed in Iraq, "the enemy has shown a sustained capacity for regeneration."[91] One analyst compared an RPA to a lawn mower: "You've got to mow the lawn all the time. The minute you stop mowing, the grass is going to grow back."[92] Something noisy and violent happens but the status quo endures.

This effort at containment via hundreds of personality and signature strikes across numerous countries preserved a manageable state of affairs, a simulacrum of peace in the era of remote warfare. It also reflected President Obama's remarks on "drone strike policy" near the end of his second term: "So part of my job as president is to figure out how I can keep America safe doing the least damage possible in really tough, bad situations. And I don't have the luxury of just not doing anything and then being able to stand back and feel as if my conscience is completely clear."[93] RPAs essentially provided options, even if they were lesser evils.

Remote warfare reduces the military and political costs compared to a troop-intensive strategy by permitting a military effort of smaller mag-nitude and greater duration in a relatively permissive environment. This reflects the Clausewitzian relationship between the political objective and the magnitude of effort and duration necessary to achieve it.[94] Remote warfare minimizes sacrifice, and a "mowing the lawn" strategy may endure over a long period if it does not incur prohibitive political costs. This mandates a discriminating application of force based on persistent

[90] John Warden, "Enemy as a System," *Air Power Journal* 9:1 (Spring 1995): 40–55.
[91] MNC-I Operations Order 06–03," November 5, 2006, by Lt Gen Peter W. Chiarelli, Commander, Multi-National Corps – Iraq; declassified by MG Michael X. Garrett, USCENTCOM Chief of Staff, 201505; document #97. https://ahec.armywarcollege.edu/CENTCOM-IRAQ-papers/0097.%20OPORD%2006–03%2005%201000%20NOV%2006.pdf
[92] Greg Miller, "Plan for Hunting Terrorists Signals US Intends to Keep Adding Names to Kill Lists," *The Washington Post*, October 23, 2012.
[93] Barack Obama comments at University of Chicago Law School, April 7, 2016. http://c-span.org/video/?c4588991/obamas-defense-drone-strike-policy
[94] Carl von Clausewitz, *On War* (Princeton: Princeton University Press, 1989), 92.

ISR and precision destruction, the hallmarks of remote warfare. RPAs may not achieve a violence-free peace, but they may be able to sustain an order stable enough to satisfy political needs. Consider some of the various manifestations of this capability.

The remote warfare architecture creates a panopticon. Adversaries are subject to the unblinking stare of armed observers. Embodied in RPAs, observers may track movements during the day and heat signatures at night. They listen constantly, vacuuming up electronic signals. And they are especially interested in objects of a militant's interest such as guns, vehicles, cell phones, and other people.[95] In this sense the kill web renders adversaries discernible, or at least *potentially* discernible, and likely alters their behavior.[96] A *New York Times* journalist held in custody by the Taliban for seven months recalls his captors' paranoia: They blamed (and executed) local informants for guiding missile strikes, and some "even stopped drinking Lipton tea because they believe the CIA puts homing beacons for the drones in the tea bags."[97] Although remote warfare's panopticon effect and its varying psychological and behavioral influences resist precise measurement, the physical results are more obvious and range from the tactical to the strategic.

The commander of Air Forces Central Command remarked in 2018 that in urban environments RPAs must "consistently stare at and maintain custody of targets ... to strike the enemy when they presented themselves" while not destroying infrastructure.[98] Such efforts blurred the lines between tactical, operational, and strategic perspectives due to the sensitive, high-stakes nature of liberating urban centers from extremist control with minimal collateral damage.[99] RPA operations also provided flexibility to commanders at all levels. For example, in 2007 Multi-National Corps – Iraq utilized RPAs to "maximize collection efficiencies and effectiveness" and support its ISR priorities: counter-IED, target development (kinetic and nonkinetic), sectarian violence,

---

[95] Lisa Parks, "Drones, Infrared Imagery, and Body Heat," *International Journal of Communications* 8 (2014): 2518.

[96] Asfandyar Mir and Dylan Moore, "Drones, Surveillance, and Violence: Theory and Evidence from a US Drone Program," *International Studies Quarterly* 63 (2019): 847.

[97] Andrew Callam, "Drone Wars: Armed Unmanned Aerial Vehicles," *International Affairs Review* XVIII:3 (Winter 2010).

[98] "Next Level of RPA Preparations, USAFCENT Commander Recognizes Airmen," 432nd Wing/432 Air Expeditionary Wing Public Affairs, January 10, 2018. www.creech.af.mil/News/Article-Display/Article/1412436/next-level-of-rpa-operations-usafcent-commander-recognizes-airmen

[99] Joe Chapa, "The Sunset of the Predator."

and border monitoring.[100] The need to "disrupt or neutralize the [IED] network" received special emphasis and became a strategic and political priority. This was a war of networks within the Iraqi battlespace – the Coalition's air-ground network architecture versus the network of insurgents embedded in the population, each wielding new combinations of existing technologies in pursuit of military and political advantage.

Remote warfare also demonstrated combat effectiveness in the campaign against ISIS in Iraq and Syria. During anti-ISIS operations in 2015 and 2016, for example, Predators and Reapers played a role in "pretty much every engagement" according to the senior commander at Creech AFB. Indeed, they participated in more than 81 percent of the 61,723 weapons released by the coalition, while also triggering an increase in Hellfire production due to the amount of RPA strikes.[101]

Overall, the kill web and its RPA components altered factors of time and space in combat operations.[102] Time was exploited by accelerating the kill chain to single-digit minutes. Indeed, the Reaper embodied the entire find, fix, target, track, engage, assess cycle and thus became an engine of increasingly efficient destruction. RPAs also advantaged time in terms of persistence, loitering over targets for extended periods, sometimes weeks, discerning patterns of life for persons of interest. In turn, this slowed the ability of terrorist leaders to communicate, plan, and maneuver.

Space was reframed in terms of expanding the accessible battlespace for US and coalition forces while reducing it for terrorists. RPAs operated in areas too dangerous or politically sensitive for manned aircraft, such as airspace over remote tribal areas in western Pakistan, where the intrusion of manned aircraft would have amplified political complications. The advent of RSO in the early 2000s enabled an RPA aircrew at Creech AFB to dynamically re-task across theaters as their GCS switched control from one aircraft to another, prosecuting a different adversary in another

[100] Multi-National Corps – Iraq, OPORD 08–01, December 14, 2007, PowerPoint brief, 54–55; document #99, https://ahec.armywarcollege.edu/CENTCOM-IRAQ-papers/0099.%20OPORD%2008–01%20Brief%20(FINAL)%2020DEC07.pdf; "MNC-I Operations Order 08–01," December 20, 2007, by Lt Gen Raymond T. Odierno, Commander, Multi-National Corps – Iraq (MNC-I), document #95, https://ahec.armywarcollege.edu/CENTCOM-IRAQ-papers/0095.%20MNC-I%20OPORD%2008–01%2020DEC07.pdf. Both documents declassified by MG Michael X. Garrett, USCENTCOM Chief of Staff, 201505.
[101] Cory T. Anderson et al., "Trust, Troops, and Reapers: Getting 'Drone' Research Done Right," War on the Rocks, April 3, 2018. https://warontherocks.com/2018/04/trust-troops-and-reapers-getting-drone-research-done-right
[102] "Time – Space – Complexity: Strengthening USAF Science and Technology for 2030 and Beyond," April 2019. https://admin.govexec.com/media/u.s._air_force_science_and_technology_strategy_final_master_file_03262019_(1).pdf

region.[103] The commander of an MQ-1 Predator squadron recounts how his airmen shifted on short notice from monitoring shipping lanes in the Arabian Gulf to "assisting with airdrops to rescue civilians trapped on Mount Sinjar in northwest Iraq."[104] The flexibility offered by remote warfare and RSO thus enabled new opportunities for allocating air power across geographic space while minimizing time and cost.

Yet a key problem unsolved by remote warfare is that the wrong lives may be taken. Despite their ability to pursue various military and political goals, plus the advantages of exploiting time and space, RPAs also generated problems that undermined their efficacy.

*Ineffectiveness*

A chief criticism of RPAs is they kill innocents. On the third day of the Obama administration, for instance, poor intelligence in a CIA personality strike against an Al-Qaeda leader resulted in an RPA destroying the home of a pro-government official in South Waziristan and killing his entire family.[105] An analysis of RPA strikes in northwest Pakistan from 2004 to 2010 estimated they killed somewhere between 830 and 1,210 individuals, and nonmilitants allegedly account for nearly a third of that number. The analysts argued this strategy drives large numbers into the Taliban and Al-Qaeda."[106] A Stanford Law School report similarly concluded that RPA strikes inflame anti-American ire in Pakistan and beyond, aiding the recruitment efforts of extremist organizations.[107] If true, this extends the duration and perhaps scale of the conflict, undermining military and political objectives and inviting international criticism.

A 2010 incident that mistook a group of Afghan civilians for Taliban fighters illustrates the connection between killing the wrong people and some inherent weaknesses in the kill web. The *L.A. Times* published the lengthy transcript of radio and mIRC-chat dialogue between ground forces, a Predator crew, intelligence analysts in the PED architecture,

---

[103] Joseph Campo, "From a Distance," 28.
[104] Creech TV, "Air Force Combat RPAs Shape OIR," February 1, 2017. www .dvidshub.net/video/505470/air-force-combat-rpas-shape-oir
[105] Jane Mayer, "The Predator War."
[106] Peter Bergen and Katherine Tiedemann, "The Year of the Drone: An Analysis of US Drone Strikes in Pakistan, 2004–2010," New America Foundation, February 24, 2010, 5.
[107] "Living under Drones: Death, Injury, and Trauma to Civilians from US Drone Practices in Pakistan," International Human Rights and Conflict Resolution Clinic (Stanford Law School) and Global Justice Clinic (NYU School of Law), September 2012, 125. https://law.stanford.edu/wp-content/uploads/sites/default/files/publication/313671/doc/slspublic/Stanford_NYU_LIVING_UNDER_DRONES.pdf

and other aircraft.[108] This evidenced serious flaws in the kill web's ability to distinguish between combatants and noncombatants. Multi-spectral imagery failed to identify women and children, and signals intelligence from a nearby Taliban group was confused with the targeted group. Intelligence analysts and aircrew, moreover, succumbed to confirmation bias as they seized on unclear indications of potential militancy, believing they had seen weapons when none had likely been present, and assuming smaller figures were younger militants rather than women or children. The kill web, despite its sophistication, trapped the wrong prey.

To dispute claims that RPAs inflict reckless violence on noncombatants, President Obama stated in 2016, "And what I can say with great certainty is that the rate of civilian casualties in any drone operation [is] far lower than the rate of civilian casualties that occur in conventional war."[109] That year the Director of National Intelligence (DNI), per the Obama administration's effort to establish a policy structure for conducting and reporting RPA strikes, released summary data of counterterrorist strikes outside of areas of active hostilities, or everywhere except Iraq, Afghanistan, and Syria. Between January 20, 2009, and December 31, 2015, 473 strikes resulted in an estimated 2,372 to 2,581 combatant deaths and 64 to 116 noncombatant deaths.[110] The maximum number of noncombatant deaths is notably less than estimates from civilian organizations that range from "200 to slightly over 900." The DNI claimed, however, that US government estimates were more accurate due to pre- and post-strike data from multiple intelligence sources inaccessible to nongovernment analysts.[111] This may have assuaged some critics, yet the problem remained that perceptions trump an unknowable reality.

Even if the DNI's report was accurate, it may make little difference concerning political attitudes in combat zones. A recent study of Pakistani citizens indicates objective data about even pristinely accurate air strikes fails to positively shape the views of local people.[112] Instead, preexisting political orientation and bias against foreign interlopers cause most people to interpret successful precision attacks as indiscriminate. This creates a dual disadvantage for US interests: Civilian casualties create huge political costs, but strikes that avoid civilian casualties may

---

[108] David S. Cloud, "Anatomy of an Afghan War Tragedy," *Los Angeles Times*, April 10, 2011, A1.
[109] Barak Obama, University of Chicago Law School, April 7, 2016.
[110] "Summary of Information Regarding US Counterterrorism Strikes Outside Areas of Active Hostilities," Director of National Intelligence, January 19, 2017.
[111] "Summary of Information."
[112] Daniel Silverman, "What Shapes Civilian Beliefs about Violent Events? Experimental Evidence from Pakistan," *Journal of Conflict Resolution* 63:6 (2019): 1460–1487.

still impose similar political costs because people tend to dismiss truths not aligned with their worldviews. Military strategists and civilian leaders should realize that remote warfare's persistence and precision may result in military accuracy, but what actually happens may matter less than what people *think* happened.[113] Ironically, it may be easier to strike accurately than be perceived as striking accurately. This indicates the value of partnering with local forces for RPA operations as well as the importance of understanding and, to the degree possible, shaping attitudes in the information environment.[114]

This phenomenon is a form of blowback, a term coined by the CIA to describe the undesirable consequences of operations.[115] Various scholars, national security experts, and human rights organizations contend that RPA strikes generate a net negative effect by stoking anti-Americanism, draining resources, and aiding terrorist recruitment. General John Abizaid, former commander of US Central Command, conjectured in 2015 that RPA strikes became a "potent recruiting tool" and "fueled a 'whack-a-mole' approach" with no end in sight except for greater instability.[116] Three dozen former national security officials signed a letter in March 2017 to Secretary of Defense James Mattis urging adherence to principles such as civilian protection, restrictive rules of engagement, bureaucratic transparency, and careful strategic assessment in order to ensure the efficacy of remote warfare and minimize blowback.[117] Some scholars, however, challenge the notion of blowback, particularly claims that RPA strikes will enrage Muslim populations and inspire support for militants.

In a 2018 *International Security* article, Aqil Shah challenged the blowback thesis with data refuting claims of a causal relationship between RPA strikes and militant recruitment on a local, national, or transnational scale.[118] He based his conclusions on interviews with 167 residents of Pakistan's Federally Administered Tribal Areas, various terrorism experts, and a Pakistani survey of 500 terrorist detainees. Shah determined "most critics of drone warfare assume, rather than demonstrate, the occurrence of blowback," and this is due in part to ill-informed

---

[113] Ibid., 1463.    [114] Ibid., 1481.
[115] John Feffer, "The Coming Drone Blowback," Institute for Policy Studies, May 25, 2016. https://fpif.org/coming-drone-blowback
[116] John P. Abizaid and Rosa Brooks, "Recommendations and Report of the Task Force on US Drone Policy," Stimson Center, April 2015, 9–10.
[117] Rand Beers et al., letter to Secretary of Defense James Mattis, March 10, 2017. www.humanrightsfirst.org/resource/statement-former-us-government-officials-use-force
[118] Aqil Shah, "Do US Drone Strikes Cause Blowback? Evidence from Pakistan and Beyond," *International Security* 42:4 (Spring 2018): 49.

"colonial stereotypes and myths about Pashtuns."[119] Essentially, the decision to join a terrorist group is far more complex than a revenge-based response to RPA strikes. It reflects economic, religious, cultural, and class motivations as well as state repression and strident recruitment efforts.[120] Other researchers similarly question the claim that RPA strikes stoke insurgencies and argue instead that the panopticon-like presence of RPAs dampens insurgent activity and recruitment.[121] Although some scholars dispute Shah's reasoning, such as noting he neglects the downside of RPA strikes and uses an unclear definition of blowback, it nevertheless provides a corrective to the debate and reminds analysts to resist simplistic explanations of human motivations and reactions in modern warfare.[122]

Minimizing the inefficacies of remote warfare and the kill web remains a priority for critics and practitioners alike. In 2017, the Deputy Secretary of Defense called for algorithm-based technology to reduce reliance on human analysts and improve the speed and quality of analysis in the Processing, Exploitation, and Dissemination (PED) system.[123] Replacing various human functions in the kill web with machine intelligence prompted the USAF's Deputy Chief of Staff for ISR to declare in 2018 "PED is dead" because "sensors will do the PE part now."[124] A kill web reliant on sensors mounted on all sorts of platforms and woven together by cloud-based data-sharing and machine-speed analysis thus emerged as the next step in improving remote warfare.[125] In December 2019, for example, the Army, Navy, and Air Force field-tested a computational-intensive version of the kill web that links manned and unmanned nodes across all domains in a real-time construct dubbed Joint All-Domain Command and Control.[126] If this evolution of human-machine teaming enhances discrimination between combatants and

[119] Ibid., 48, 49, 62.    [120] Ibid., 71.
[121] Mir and Moore, "Drones, Surveillance, and Violence," 860.
[122] Ahsan I. Butt, ISSF article review for Aqil Shah, "Do US Drone Strikes Cause Blowback?" February 6, 2019, 7.
[123] Robert Work, "Establishment of an Algorithmic Warfare Cross-Functional Team (Project Maven)," memorandum to senior DoD officials, April 26, 2017.
[124] John A. Tirpak, "'PED Is Dead': ISR Roadmap Reaches Long for New Tech," *Air Force Magazine*, August 2, 2018.
[125] "Action Is Needed to Provide Clarity and Mitigate Risks of the Air Force's Planned Advanced Battle Management System," US Government Accountability Office Report, GAO-20–389, April 16, 2020. www.gao.gov/assets/710/706165.pdf
[126] Cara Bousie and Charles Pope, "Air Force, Navy, Army Conduct First 'Real World' Test of Advanced Battle Management System," December 23, 2019. https://af.mil/News/Article-Display/Article/2046531/air-force-navy-army-conduct-first-real-world-test-of-advanced-battle-management

noncombatants, will it encourage military – particularly air power – solutions to political problems? Remote warfare's evolution so far suggests it will.

## Conclusion

The MQ-9 Reaper likely involved in killing Iranian mastermind Qasem Soleimani in 2020 possessed vastly different capabilities than the MQ-1 Predator assigned to hunt and kill Taliban leader Mullah Omar in 2001. Although these aircraft look roughly similar, their sensors, weapons, communications, and operational procedures represent two decades of rapid evolution in remote warfare that fostered a new architecture of air power. Laser designators, Hellfire missiles, Rover video, mIRC-chat, and Remote-Split Operations helped weave RPAs into an increasingly sophisticated and far-flung kill web that rendered high-value terrorists, suspected enemy concentrations, and military infrastructure even more subject to examination and precision destruction while reducing risk to US forces. This enhanced air power's effectiveness, creating efficiencies at the tactical, operational, and strategic levels as well as providing political opportunities. No wonder the temptations of RPAs seduced three US presidents. Yet drawbacks were evident. Remote warfare became a seemingly perennial commitment in regions rich in turmoil but poor in air defenses, and its usefulness was undermined by high-profile errors concerning the deaths of noncombatants.

Although remote warfare may develop new means of portraying and shaping the battlespace with manned and unmanned elements, its nature and purpose require ongoing examination. The kill web's architecture converts human lives to 0s and 1s, streams of binary data transmuted by network alchemy into pixels on viewscreens. Upon these images decisions are rendered, fates are determined. It is imperfect but not impersonal. RPA aircrews often come to know their adversaries far more than soldiers or pilots of manned aircraft ever will. Remote warfare, ironically, enhances human creativity. Its evolution will remain the result not of machine intelligence but of human purpose, however imperfect that may be.

# 3    Deliberate Force: Ambivalent Success

*Thomas Alexander Hughes* *

On August 28, 1995, elements of the Bosnian Serb Army, a separatist force laying siege to Sarajevo, lobbed five mortar shells into a busy marketplace in the core of the ancient capital. After the explosions cleared, witnesses recalled "hands and feet tossed among odd bits of clothing, torsos strewn amid fresh vegetables, wet scraps of flesh clinging to the stone walls of nearby buildings." A shopkeeper emerged to see the still writhing upper half of a woman along a curbside; 100 feet away her legs still straddled a fallen bicycle.[1] The attack killed forty-three and seriously wounded another seventy-five. Graphic, full-color photos accompanied international reports of the Second Markale Massacre, as the atrocity became known. Each account mournfully reported yet another tragedy in Sarajevo, a city that a decade earlier had hosted the twentieth-century emblem of international comity, an Olympic Game, and now owned another distinction: The Bosnian Serb assault on Sarajevo was already the longest siege of a capital city in modern times, nearly three times the duration of World War II's Battle of Stalingrad and a year longer than the siege of Leningrad.

The First Markale Massacre on February 5, 1994, had actually been worse, claiming 68 deaths and 144 wounded. But the second, coming as it did amid a wave of violence in the complex, nearly four-year Bosnian civil war, at last galvanized the West to a sustained military response to quell widespread carnage. Since 1992 United Nations (UN) and North Atlantic Treaty Organization (NATO) deliberations regarding the region had stumbled for the same reasons all coalitions struggle toward collective action: different capabilities, interests, and viewpoints. Now, however, according to *The Economist*, the West "got tough" following "years of bluffing" and launched Operation Deliberate Force.[2] This compact yet powerful air campaign was designed to end an era of "feckless threats and weak reprisals," added *Newsweek*, restore balance among the warring

---

* The views expressed by the author do not reflect those of the US government, the Department of Defense, or any of its organizations.
[1] Kevin Fedarko, "Louder than Words," *Time* (September 11, 1995): 50.
[2] *The Economist*, September 2–8, 1995, cover, 41.

Figure 3.1  Map of Bosnia (after Dayton Accord)

factions, and compel negotiations to end the violence.[3] Within three days of bombing, each warring party expressed interest in peace talks, and in November a formal accord emerged in the Dayton Agreement, which froze the fighting and established peaceful mechanisms to manage the many disputes plaguing the region (see Figures 3.1 and 3.2).

The armistice was imperfect. But it stopped the fight, an achievement no other effort had yet obtained. It was the product of many influences, preeminent among them Deliberate Force, a campaign that both reflected and confirmed the historic promise of air power to accomplish more with less. In its operational cadence, general scope, and strategic

---

[3] *Newsweek* (September 11, 1995): 37.

Figure 3.2  Map of Serbia (1995)

direction, though, it did so in a manner unfamiliar to airmen, leaving them with deep unease about Deliberate Force and the meaning of air power in a post–Cold War world. In the end, this discomfort left air strategists ambivalent toward their own triumph and wary of pleas for air power to settle political strife later in the decade and beyond, a hesitancy that would have astonished the earliest generations of air theorists who could only have dreamed of such attention from their political masters.

## Lead-Up to Conflict

Both precondition and precipitate begot the Bosnian civil war, which emerged as a flashpoint in a manner at once gradual, sporadic, and, in retrospect, inexorable. A thousand years of periodic ethnic and nationalist conflict in the region found ample echo in 1914 when a Bosnian Serb assassinated the heir to the Austro-Hungarian throne, triggering diplomatic roulette across Europe and sparking World War I, with its 40 million casualties. Following the fight the victorious Allies did not forget the Balkans' leading role in the fiasco. From the region they created Yugoslavia from whole cloth, its unlikely constellation of smaller nations stapled from the "detritus of not merely the most murderous war imaginable, but the final collapse of two great empires, the Ottoman and Hapsburg."[4] Yugoslavia's volatile admixture of Serb Orthodox Catholic, Croatian and Slovenian Roman Catholic, and Bosnian and Kosovar Muslim was a challenge from the start and, unsurprisingly, the years between the world wars were marked first by an unsettled democracy and then, after 1928, by its oft corollary, dictatorship.[5]

During World War II, Axis powers managed to overrun, brutalize, and undergovern Yugoslavia, all at the same time. Amid a crosscurrent of rampage, enemy invaders levied a heavy toll but so did domestic thugs: Fascist strongmen in Croatia set out to kill a third of its Serb population, expel another third, and convert the remainder to Catholicism. Elsewhere, Serbs retaliated in kind. In some southern regions intense clashes with Muslims occasionally united these sworn enemies, and by the end of the war a majority of the million-plus Yugoslavs killed in the fight had died at the hands of fellow countrymen, not Axis outsiders. Of all the world's combatants in World War II, only Germany, Poland, and the Soviet Union had suffered proportionally more death.

Paradoxically, the Cold War bestowed to this seething shamble a degree of stability and a (relative) modicum of tranquility. Reluctance among the major powers to engage in direct confrontation in Europe, as well as the rise of the half-Slovene, half-Croat Josip Broz – better known

---

[4] David Halberstam, *War in a Time of Peace: Bush, Clinton, and the Generals* (New York: Scribner, 2001), 76.
[5] Unless specifically noted, background for this and following paragraphs taken from Laura Silber and Allan Little, *Yugoslavia: Death of a Nation* (New York: Penguin Books, 1997); Steven Burg and Paul Shoup, *The War in Bosnia-Herzegovina: Ethnic Conflict and International Invention* (Philadelphia: Routledge, 2000).

as Tito – as president combined to transform Yugoslavia into something of a favored buffer zone during the Cold War. The unlikely success of Yugoslavia received star billing during the 1984 Winter Olympics in Sarajevo, when commentators nightly reminded a global audience of the region's troubled past and its new status as an affluent destination, a "sophisticated urban venue" where "pluralism seemed to work, and ethnic tensions were largely dormant."[6]

Tito's death in 1980 foretold a return to the past. Energy-related financial crises diminished the Yugoslav standard of living 40 percent from 1982 to 1989, exacerbating old ethic and religious jealousies. Then the end of the Cold War eroded the international value of Yugoslavian stability, leaving the nation to its own devices and designs, which had rarely portended peace and prosperity. At first, it was merely the bustle from the bright promise of freedom in former communist states, but for portions of Yugoslavia, the fall of the Berlin Wall proffered not only freedom from Cold War tensions but also release from Belgrade. Slobodan Milosevic, president of Serbia and leader of the Serbian League of Communists, used separatist tumult to win control of communist parties in Kosovo, Vojvodina, and Montenegro and angled with some success to gain control of portions of the Yugoslavian military, which then became the seed corn for Serb-dominated forces of the like that later shelled the Markale marketplace. Thus threatened, Croatia turned for leadership to its own virulent nationalist, Franjo Tudjman, who extolled the virtues of outright independence from Yugoslavia as preferable to a yoke spun by Serbs.[7]

Croatia and Slovenia declared their respective independence in summer 1991. Now without Croat and Slovene voices to counter Serbian influence in the federated government, Belgrade sent troops into the breakaway regions – with ill-disciplined and impassioned Serb paramilitary units making up the shortfalls from absent Croat and Slovene troops. What followed included the siege of Dubrovnik, the first of numerous episodes of ethnic cleansing throughout the Balkans, and the first serious deliberations elsewhere in Europe over the burgeoning crisis. European authorities were reluctant to nurture these Yugoslav independence movements, yet sympathetic to the impulse of self-determinism from which they sprang. Led by a German diplomatic muscularity not seen since World War II – itself a reminder to other powers of how small Balkan

---

[6] David Halberstam, *War in a Time of Peace*, 121.
[7] Steven Burg, *The War in Bosnia-Herzegovina*, 45–48. For more on Milosevic and his relationship with other leading personalities in the Balkans, see Lenard Cohen, *Serpent in the Bosom: The Rise and Fall of Slobodan Milosevic* (New York: Basic Books, 2000); Adam LeBor, *Milosevic: A Biography* (New Haven: Yale University Press, 2004).

problems had a history of becoming larger if left unattended – the European Community (EC) acknowledged Croatian and Slovenian autonomy in early January 1992 and declared other Yugoslav regions could petition the organization for recognition by the twentieth of that month.

The snap EC invitation "placed considerable pressure" on other republics to move precipitously toward independence.[8] Macedonia, Albanians in Kosovo, and Bosnia Herzegovina (hereafter Bosnia) all applied. The EC granted Macedonia recognition and denied the Albanians in Kosovo the same status, setting aside issues there for yet another Balkan war later in the decade. In an unfathomable decision, the EC then deferred a verdict on Bosnia pending an internal referendum to settle the matter in a forlorn hope that democracy could soothe long-simmering strife.

The opposite happened. In many ways Bosnia was the most naked and vulnerable of all Yugoslav republics. It had long been the most pluralistic of them: Bosniak Muslims comprised 44 percent of its populace; Orthodox Serbs, 31 percent; and Catholic Croats, 17 percent – a combustible mixture lacking only a match to ignite. On February 29, 1992, the independence referendum passed but without support from Bosnian Serbs, who, fearing minority status within an autonomous state, boycotted the election and agitated for their own secessionist republic led by a politician, Radovan Karadzic, and a military tyrant, Ratko Mladic. The vote revealed that Bosnia's harmony had been a patina purchased by inclusion in a larger, pluralistic Yugoslav federation. The prospect of independence exposed it to the conflagration of ethnic, religious, and national jealousies that had by then become a contagion elsewhere.

As if on cue, and with ample assistance from allied groups in neighboring republics, Bosniaks, Serbs, and Croats commenced nothing less than brutal civil war. Bosnian Serbs under Mladic's military command, aided by Milosevic's Serbian Army, secret police, and paramilitary opportunists, quickly overran nearly two-thirds of Bosnia by April 1993. Along the way, they pillaged and massacred untold thousands. In one small city, 2,000 Muslims were executed or disappeared into concentration camps. Across Bosnia in 1993 and 1994 it was nothing for a mortar attack to kill dozens, an artillery barrage to take a hundred, or for rape to be so systemized as to constitute a weapon of war. Along the way Mladic amply earned the moniker "Butcher of Bosnia." Attacks of all kinds

---

[8] Karl Mueller, "The Demise of Yugoslavia and the Destruction of Bosnia: Strategic Causes, Effects, and Responses," in *Deliberate Force: A Case Study in Effective Air Campaigning*, ed. Robert Owen (Maxwell AFB: Air University Press, 1997), 13.

were linked to yesteryear's hatreds, painting an intractable problem with no current solution: One newsman explained the "answer to an artillery attack of yesterday will begin in the year 925, invariably illustrated with maps."[9] Sarajevo itself quickly became a burning hulk, a place where locals mordantly compared it to Auschwitz – a place with no future. By summer 1993, one careful observer described Bosnia as home to the "worst genocidal crimes seen in Europe since World War II,"[10] a judgment with which few would have then disagreed.

All this assaulted Western sensibilities, but whether, when, and how to engage in the Bosnian civil war prompted much angst within and among nations. Diplomatic activity to mediate various Balkan disputes dated back into the 1980s. These earlier talks failed, however, and had produced, in the judgment of one leading diplomat "the greatest collective security failure in the West since the 1930s."[11] This left much harder decisions about military force, a notion itself compounded by a myriad of factors.

For one, the war was bewildering in its complexity, as are many three-way contests – in combat or on the playground. Milosevic and Serbia supported the Bosnian Serbs. Tudjman and the Croats were at first nominal allies of the Bosniaks, but at various times they fought each other and the Bosnian Serbs, sometimes even simultaneously being friend and foe at different locations. There were surely Serbian atrocities aplenty, though Croat forces were not above moral reproach, and the Bosniaks were accused of staging attacks against their own Muslim population to encourage foreign intervention against the Serbs – as many observers suspected had been the case in the gruesome First Markale Massacre.[12]

There were also competing views about the relative culpability of each combatant. As a general proposition, for instance, Germany tended to side with Croatia, Greece with Serbia, and Turkey with the Bosnian Serbs – mostly – but sometimes also with the Bosniaks. Great Britain was usually the least hawkish of the nations; the United States, the most. French views tended to correspond with the British, though not always, and Germans cheered American muscularity, even as their martial exhortations were freighted with their troubled World War II past. The United States viewed Serbian aggression as a root cause of the violence. Britain, France, and other European states tended to see in Bosnia

[9] Ed Vulliamy, *Seasons in Hell* (New York: St. Martins, 1994), 5.
[10] David Halberstam, *War in a Time of Peace*, 123.
[11] Richard Holbrooke, *To End a War* (New York: Random House, 1998), 21.
[12] Steven Burg, *The War in Bosnia-Herzegovina*, 87.

a calamity with no clear innocents anywhere. This smorgasbord of views made any international collective action a difficult proposition.

Finally, two very different international organizations jostled to orchestrate whatever encounter the world order might eventually muster: the United Nations (UN) and the North Atlantic Treaty Organization (NATO). Each claimed different constituencies, charters, and purposes. The UN was a global collective with ambivalent attitudes about military action; NATO, a regional defense pact expressly established to use such force. Both had well-worn cultural and behavioral patterns not well aligned with each other. They were a bit like wary friends, committed to collaborative action in an emergent post–Cold War world but not quite trusting the other. All this meant any response required the explicit approval of both organizations, which became the dreaded "dual key" authorization needed to approve any military strike that later so bedeviled an aggressive international response.[13]

Little wonder, then, that one leading scholar described the lead-up to Deliberate Force as "gradual but inconstant."[14] A less understated assessment would employ words such as "tentative," "tepid," "timid" and always – always – "reluctant." At first no nation focused upon intervention. American Secretary of State James Baker reflected many viewpoints when he recalled his "central focus" diplomatically at the time was "managing the peaceful dissolution" of the Soviet Union.[15] Contrary to popular belief in some quarters, it was the Europeans, not the Americans, who sounded the first real alarms about the Balkans in late 1991 and early 1992 – though no military response was ever to be likely absent US participation. At the time, however, US leaders had no appetite to act without a new consensus, both globally and at home, of its role in a post–Cold War world, a caution heightened by a disastrous excursion into Somalia, where an American force had been ambushed, and underscored in Rwanda, where US might stood unashamedly idle while genocide occurred.

In 1992 bloodshed in Croatia at last prompted the first collective military response. That spring, the United Nations sent a Protection Force (UNPROFOR) to former Yugoslav republics to keep peace or at least maintain safe areas for this or that besieged ethnic group. That summer NATO deployed naval forces to the Adriatic Sea to monitor shipping and curb arms going into the region. That fall, United Nations Security Council Resolution (UNSCR) 781 authorized NATO to patrol

[13] For more on the problems of integrating UN and NATO planning and operations, see Bradley Davis, "The Planning Background," in Owen, *Deliberate Force*, 65–86.
[14] Karl Mueller, "The Demise of Yugoslavia," 17.
[15] James Baker, *The Politics of Diplomacy* (New York: Putnam, 1995), 637.

the Balkan skies to prohibit all flights not approved by UNPROFOR. In March 1993, and following 500 documented violations of this restriction, UNSCR 816 authorized aerial force to ensure compliance with a no-fly zone over Bosnia, and two weeks later NATO commenced Operation Deny Flight to accomplish that goal. In June, UNSCR 836 authorized UNPROFOR to use ground force to ensure safe zones and added close air support to the repertoire of the peacekeepers. That same month, NATO initiated a naval blockade of the Adriatic Sea, dramatically increasing pressure on warring factions to find peace. And early that fall, Deny Flight operations gained authority for attacks not only to defend but also to deter or to punish attacks against UNPROFOR or within any of six designated safe areas, as long as both UN and NATO officials agreed to each strike.

None of this made more than modest progress to stem the fight, in part because the UN was always far more reluctant than NATO to turn its key to actually use rather than to merely authorize military force. On the ground, atrocities continued within safe areas. In the air, all combatants continued to employ helicopters with near impunity, often painted with red crosses to shield their offensive purpose. The First Markale Massacre in February 1994 marked a modest turning point: On the month's last day NATO saw its first combat action ever when two US F-16 jets downed four Yugoslavian – but de facto Serbian – Super Galeb light attack aircraft on a bombing mission against Bosniak forces; on April 10 and 11, NATO flew its first close air support (CAS) mission when UNPROFOR troops came under attack, a strike that prompted Bosnian Serbs to take 150 UN troops hostage; throughout the summer NATO jets periodically struck attacking Serbian units. In November some 30 NATO aircraft from 4 nations struck an airfield and weapon site, a raid described at the time as a "massive attack," although "later contemptuously but accurately labelled pinpricks."[16] In retaliation, Bosnian Serbs grabbed hundreds of UN soldiers, using some as human shields to prevent further NATO air strikes. By early 1995, the Washington Agreement did put an end to fighting between the Bosniaks and Croats, in effect reducing the three-way fight to a duel between them and Bosnian Serbs with their Serbian allies. A shaky cease-fire followed this development as all combatants assessed this new dynamic, but few anywhere believed the region had seen the last of calamity.

Now dealing with a simplified war, the West coalesced around a vague formula to stem the remaining strife. This equation proposed to divide Bosnia, leaving 49 percent of the republic in Serb hands and

[16] Richard Holbrooke, *To End a War*, 61.

51 percent in Bosniak and Croat possession. This tender did not identify the actual areas corresponding to these percentages, and no interested party on the ground rushed to embrace the scheme, which at the time would have required Serbian forces to relinquish areas hard won by arms and that would have demanded the Bosnian government to countenance a continuing hostile presence within its border. Nonetheless, the proposition did give to diplomats a focal point from which to work and to military planners a yardstick from which to orchestrate force.

For a variety of reasons, that force was air power. The hesitancy of Western powers to engage with arms in the Balkans was an overriding factor from the start. Then their UNPROFOR experience reinforced this caution: The challenges keeping the peacekeeping ground force neutral in the eyes of local combatants amid a nasty civil war bedeviled UN leaders, and UNPROFOR vulnerability as a hostage tool precluded further ground commitments. Finally, military aviation was then ascendant in the eyes of many in the West as a military instrument without peer. All this made air power, as a practical matter, the only option available for international intervention.

As many expected, the lull in fighting in early 1995 did not last. In April and June, two Croat offensives reclaimed a bit of territory from Bosnian Serb forces. In May, Bosnian Serb artillery hit Sarajevo safe areas, prompting first two days of NATO retaliatory air strikes and then yet another Bosnian Serbian seizure of UNPROFOR troops as hostages and human shields. In June American pilot Scott O'Grady was shot down patrolling a no-fly zone, greatly focusing the US public on the faraway conflict. In early July, Bosnian Serb units under Mladic's control occupied the safe area of Srebrenica and proceeded to massacre as many as 8,000 Bosniak men and boys and rape and expel an untold number of Bosniak women. Later that month and into early August, Croat and Bosniak forces launched Operation Summer and Operation Storm, wrestling overall momentum of the ground war from the Bosnian Serbs for the first time since 1992: The first captured some 620 square miles of land and the second, the largest land battle in Europe since World War II, placed considerable pressure on Bosnian Serbs heretofore used to battlefield victory. These defeats prompted Karadzic to remove Mladic from field command. Mladic, however, refused to go and, with support from military subordinates, forced Karadzic to retreat, an episode that created yet more murk with which any diplomatic effort would have to contend.[17]

---

[17] Karl Mueller, in Owen, *Deliberate Force*, 23–29; Phil Haun, *Coercion, Survival, and War: Why Weak States Resist the United States* (Stanford: Stanford University Press, 2015), 104.

The summer's spurt of violence heightened Western vigilance in the Balkans. In response to the Srebrenica Massacre, British Prime Minister John Major convened UN, NATO, and EC diplomats to assess the burgeoning crisis. Out of this London Conference came an agreement to threaten Bosnian Serbs with forceful and sustained air strikes if they committed further transgressions and, perhaps more importantly, a decision to remove the UN key required for military action from political representatives and place it in the hands of Lieutenant General Bernard Janvier, a French officer then serving as the senior UN military commander in the region. Seriously contemplating a vigorous military response for the first time, UN and NATO officials also agreed upon four strategic objectives for an air campaign, if it came to that: (1) reduce the threat to Sarajevo and deter further attacks there or in any safe area; (2) force the withdrawal of Serbian heavy weapons from a 20 kilometer exclusion zone circling Sarajevo; (3) ensure complete freedom of movement for UN forces as well as personnel from peaceful international organizations; and (4) ensure unrestricted use of the Sarajevo airport.[18] Neither the London Conference nor these articulated objectives assured commencement of Deliberate Force, but they did guarantee to reveal the West as a paper tiger should the Bosnian Serbs precipitate more violence in or near designated safe areas.[19]

## NATO Air Operations

If they did so, NATO air forces in the area would be ready. Planning for Deliberate Force stretched back many months and was conditioned by NATO's ongoing air operations in the region under the auspices of Deny Flight. These efforts rested with US Lieutenant General Michael Ryan, who later became the younger of the Air Force's only father–son duo as chief of staff. He had served in the early 1990s as an assistant to two successive Joint Chiefs chairmen and as a military advisor to diplomatic groups searching for a Balkan solution. In September 1994 he became commander of both NATO Allied Air Forces, Southern Europe, and of the US 16th Air Force. In this capacity, he would directly oversee the Deliberate Force campaign.

His prior duty and nearly a year in command of NATO air forces in the region made him thoroughly familiar with the political challenges

---

[18] Bradley Davis, "The Planning Background," in Owen, *Deliberate Force*, 44; Christopher Campbell, "The Deliberate Force Air Campaign Plan," in Owen, *Deliberate Force*, 87.
[19] Karl Mueller, in Owen, *Deliberate Force*, 5–26.

attendant to Western military action in the Balkans.[20] Foremost among these was the split chain of command within which he worked.

The UN and NATO each had elaborate command structures, and meshing them at first made for additional challenges. From top to bottom, any UN decisions regarding Bosnia had to travel through four echelons, each with its internal, multinational deliberations, before reaching Janvier as the organization's responsible military officer in the region. A similar line in NATO crossed seven bureaucratic strata before reaching Janvier's counterpart, US Admiral Leighton Smith, who as commander of all NATO forces in Southern Europe was Ryan's immediate boss. Together, Smith and Janvier held the keys required to initiate military action, but the UN and NATO command chains would also integrate at three other echelons at Ryan's level or below for target coordination in the event of actual operations.[21] In both the UN and NATO structures, each organizational layer represented potential for friction, as did each bridge between the two alliances, and of course the whole thing had been a cumbersome arrangement greatly limiting military responses to the Bosnia war thus far.

In such a circumstance Ryan planned with care. From the outset, he believed the level of international and political oversight of the operation demanded he alone designate targets, and later just he and one – and in rare instances two – senior subordinates held authority to authorize actual strikes upon those targets. This tight grip on operations dismayed plenty of other Deliberate Force participants weaned on the air power mantra of "centralized control, decentralized execution," but Ryan believed "if we had committed just one atrocity from the air, NATO would forever be blamed for crimes and the military threat will be lessened," if not removed altogether.[22] Beyond that, given the international community's shaky commitment to the region, Ryan thought casualties – among friendly or enemy forces and particularly among the civilian populace – would so quickly erode support for operations that he deemed force protection and collateral damage as paramount concerns, at times holding them as higher priorities than achievement of broader political objectives.[23] Ryan's close oversight of operations was at odds with decades of command habit among Western air forces and became the focus of discussion then and later about the campaign.

---

[20] Author interview with Michael Ryan, November 13, 2007.
[21] Bradley Davis, in Owen, *Deliberate Force*, 49.
[22] Michael Ryan, cited in Bradley Davis, in Owen, *Deliberate Force*, 57.
[23] Ronald Reed, "Chariots of Fire: Rules of Engagement in Operation Deliberate Force," in Owen, *Deliberate Force*, 415.

The Deliberate Force plan grouped targets into three ascending categories, termed options, available to political leaders willing to employ ever more aggressive force: Option one targets included enemy positions closest to safe areas and posing direct threats to them, such as the artillery units that had so often shelled safe harbors throughout Bosnia; option two targets were those a bit farther afield and posing indirect hazards, such as ammunition depots and supply areas; and option three targets were more distant still, presenting remote risk to safe areas but providing Bosnian Serb forces their staying power, such as infrastructure, arms production factories, and maintenance depots outside of Bosnia proper.[24] Sophisticated Serbian integrated air defenses, much of which was drawn from late Cold War Soviet technology of the kind that had downed O'Grady's F-16, included an estimated seven SA-2, six SA-6, and twelve SA-9 SAM batteries, as well as an unknown number of man-portable missiles.[25] These posed no danger to safe areas by themselves but were the primary threat to NATO aircraft. Air operations to neutralize them were code-named Deadeye and became some of the most important elements of Deliberate Force.

To accomplish Deliberate Force, Ryan could call upon an order of battle that was at once sufficient to the task and modest when compared to its immediate antecedent in the Gulf War. Together, eight NATO nations contributed 300 aircraft of all kinds, flying from 18 land locations throughout southern Europe and as many as 4 aircraft carriers in the Adriatic Sea.[26] By late August 1995, Ryan had distilled 151 specific targets within his option one and two categories (category three targets were always seen as less likely to be struck) into 87 mission-specific objectives for his force. As the campaign occurred, these tallies were further reduced to 56 targets with a total of 338 specific aim points.[27]

Deliberate Force commenced early on August 30, two days after the Second Markale Massacre. On its first day, 122 sorties hammered Deadeye enemy air defenses and option one sites near Sarajevo. The following two days witnessed a magnification of this effort, with 242

---

[24] Mark Bucknam, "Michael E. Ryan: Architect of Air Power Success," in *The Air Commanders*, ed. John Andreas Olsen (Lincoln, NE: Potomac Books, 2012), 352.

[25] Mark Conversino, "Executing Deliberate Force, 30 August – 14 September 1995," in Owen, *Deliberate Force*, 135.

[26] Most of the combat aircraft came from just five nations, and the vast bulk of the sorties were flown from either Aviano Air Base in northern Italy or, to a lesser extent, from aircraft carriers. For the campaign, the United States contributed 120 aircraft; France, 50; the United Kingdom, 33; Italy, 20; the Netherlands, 18; Turkey, 16; Germany, 14; and Spain, 11. Bradley Davis, in Owen, *Deliberate Force*, 53–54.

[27] Christopher Campbell, in Owen, *Deliberate Force*, 107; Mark Bucknam, in Owen, *Deliberate Force*, 358.

sorties flown on August 31 and another 273 on September 1 against a similar range of targets. Collectively, this activity was of an order of magnitude greater than all previous NATO air strikes combined. The campaign's swift start was designed, in part, to destroy as much Bosnian Serb combat capability as possible before either they yielded or the West lost its nerve. To Ryan, this goal to bring balance into the ground equation "was the heart of the bombing operation" and would serve to give Deliberate Force consequence regardless of whatever political effect it might obtain.[28]

As it happened, following the third round of strikes, Richard Holbrooke, the leading American diplomat in the Balkans, and Milosevic interceded to suspend the campaign so that Janvier and Mladic – who had maintained control of most Bosnian Serb forces – could discuss terms to end the bombing. Opinion on this bombing halt varied wildly and divided unsurprisingly among diplomats, who tended to favor it, and military officers, who worried the West could not marshal again the support to resume it if required. On September 3 NATO officials declared the bombing would resume if the Bosnian Serbs did not meet three conditions: one, remove all heavy weapons from the 20-kilometer exclusion zone surrounding Sarajevo; two, cease all attacks in the remaining safe areas; and three, lift the siege of Sarajevo by opening access by road and air to the beleaguered city. By late September 4, it was clear the Bosnian Serbs would not comply. To some surprise within NATO, and to considerable chagrin among Bosnian Serbs, NATO leaders authorized Ryan to resume operations the next day.[29]

For Ryan the bombing pause had been an anticipated concern but also a welcome respite. The tempo of Deliberate Force's opening act had taxed NATO's human and material resources, and Ryan used the short recess as a rest for his air forces. When strikes resumed on September 5, they did so with increased strength and scope. The next week's daily tally of sorties flown ranged from 211 to 294 and aggregated 1,791, a sum exclusive of NATO's first-ever dramatic and highly effective use of precision-guided Tomahawk cruise missiles to destroy particularly hard-to-reach enemy air defenses, an operation that underscored to "Serbs that the Americans in particular were willing to use some of their most advanced weapons."[30] Moreover, missions now included a focus on option two targets, such as ammunition bunkers, command and control facilities, supply areas, and bridges and encompassed as well an expanded range of Deadeye missions to degrade Serb air defenses,

---

[28] Michael Ryan cited in Mark Bucknam, in Owen, *Deliberate Force*, 357; Mark Conversino, in Owen, *Deliberate Force*, 136–48.
[29] Mark McLaughlin, in Owen, *Deliberate Force*, 192–93.
[30] Richard Sargent, "Deliberate Force Combat Air Assessments," in Owen, *Deliberate Force*, 337; Mark Conversino, in Owen, *Deliberate Force*, 153.

not just near Sarajevo but throughout the entire region, which solidified NATO's near total air dominance of the region.[31]

The vigorous week created a potential conundrum. By September 12 Ryan was left with a mere 11 targets with 60 individual aim points from his option one and two lists. Fearing he would exhaust his targets before a political settlement was reached, he reduced sorties from 255 on September 12, to 210 the next day, and just 140 the following day. Still, by September 14 there existed a mere 8 targets, with 43 aim points, a number that a single robust day of air operations could dispatch.[32] Yet, there had been no political resolution, and Ryan worried what might become not only of the air campaign but also of the West's entire strategy in the Balkans if military strategy to win was misaligned with political efforts to end the fighting.

Fortunately for the West, Deliberate Force coincided with two Croat-Bosniak ground offensives. Operation Mistrel 2 stretched from September 8 to 15 and built upon momentum in the ground war established by their summer assaults. Mistrel 2 took an additional 920 square miles of Serb-controlled territory and essentially cut off the majority of Mladic's Serb forces well to the east of newly vulnerable Banja Luka, the de facto Bosnian Serb capital. In the offensive, Croatian and Bosnian forces demonstrated an increasing military capability at the precise moment Deliberate Force strikes at Serb command and control centers inhibited Bosnian Serb ability to coordinate an effective defense. On September 13 these difficulties compounded when Croat-Bosniak forces launched Operation Sana, an eventual month-long campaign that revealed yet more endurance for combat. Taken together, these offensives levied great pressure on Serb and Bosnian Serb leaders to sue for peace before they forfeited any additional real estate.

This is what happened. As Deliberate Force's targets dwindled to near nothing on September 14, Milosevic – whose interest in Bosnia was always secondary to his power base in Serbia – convinced the Bosnian Serb leaders Karadzic and Mladic to acquiescence to the West's ultimatum to end the immediate fighting and seek a fuller agreement at some intermediate, future point. Holbrooke, who had been crisscrossing the region in search of some breakthrough, seized this diplomatic moment, and Smith directed Ryan to suspend military strikes after just twenty sorties on September 15. Following a seventy-two-hour hiatus to confirm a pause in Bosnian Serb aggression, Deliberate Force came to an end.

[31] Mark Bucknam, in Owen, *Deliberate Force*, 363.
[32] Mark Conversino, in Owen, *Deliberate Force*, 154–58.

## Dayton Conference

Most parties then agreed to convene in November at Wright Patterson Air Force Base in Dayton, Ohio, chosen for its combination of sufficient infrastructure, relative seclusion, and distant remove from Balkan killing grounds.[33] A woeful series of peace plans had preceded its commencement. There was, for instance, the Carrington-Cutileiro Plan of February 1992, which might have left a rump government in Bosnia Herzegovina but placed real power in a hodgepodge of local ethnic communities if the resultant Lisbon Agreement had endured longer than its ten-day life in March. There was the Vance-Owen Peace Plan in the spring of 1993, which involved the division of Bosnia into ten semiautonomous regions and reached as far as a national referendum in May before many Bosnians boycotted the vote outright and 96 percent of the rest rejected the initiative. The Owen-Stoltenberg Plan came next in the summer of 1993, a stillborn scheme involving Bosnian partition into three mini-states, giving the Serbs 52 percent of Bosnia-Herzegovina's territory; Muslims, 30 percent; and Croats 18 percent. Along with other initiatives absent even the dignity of a name, this record of futility reduced aspirations to almost nothing, and even the Washington Agreement in March 1994 produced not much more than a shaky, temporary cease-fire of the likes that had periodically marked the Balkan wars.[34]

From this frustration emerged the Contact Group, an association of representatives from America, Britain, France, Germany, Italy, and Russia that was smaller and, the theory went, more cohesive than the UN or NATO writ large to shepherd delicate diplomacy. Informally led by Holbrooke, in the months preceding the Dayton Conference this group had redoubled efforts to cajole a settlement among the warring factions. On the heels of Deliberate Force and apparent Bosnian Serb consent, their labors intensified further, especially within the American and Russian contingents, and begot agreement to convene at Dayton.[35]

The conference took place across the first three weeks of November. Hosted by US Secretary of State Warren Christopher and led by Holbrooke as his chief negotiator, the gathering also included two co-chairmen representing the EC and Russia, Serbian President Slobodan Milosevic – who held the proxy for Bosnian Serb interests – and the Croatian and Bosnia Herzegovina presidents, Franjo Tudjman and Alija Izetbegovic, respectively. The issues were as they always had been

[33] The exception being Karadzic and Mladic, who had by then been indicted by The Hague. Milosevic therefore spoke for the Bosnian Serbs.
[34] Karl Mueller, in Owen, *Deliberate Force*, 17–23.
[35] Richard Holbrooke, *To End a War*, 86–96.

in the Balkans and reflected those contentions common in revolutionary and civil wars: home rule, and who would rule at home. As before, questions about who governed, where, and how all quickly reduced to lines on maps. Diplomacy's goal remained unchanged as well: Mediators aimed not to resolve deep-rooted disputes but rather promote enough peace and enough stability to give tempers a chance to wane. And this they hoped to do with familiar math: a territorial split giving 49 percent to Serbian interests and 51 percent to Croat and Bosniak factions. But which terrain was to be what, and subordinate rifts about territory between the newly allied Croats and Bosniaks, added to tensions that periodically broke into open revolt, threatening the delicate talks.[36]

But agreement came. Bosnia itself was partitioned into ten semiautonomous zones, called cantonments. Through them, Bosnian Serbs accepted control of 49 percent of the nation, the Bosniaks accepted a 30 percent share, and Bosnian Croats agreed to a 21 percent stake – creating, in essence, a wary Croat-Bosniak federation based in Sarajevo and, perilously circling it, a Bosnian Serb republic. The agreement also required a wide range of international organizations to shepherd emergent democratic habits, elections, and civil institutions throughout Bosnia and mandated an ongoing international peacekeeping force to, well, keep the peace. Overall, the Dayton Agreement would have surprised no negotiator from prior efforts and may well have depressed many that years of war had garnered such little tangible result. The accord may well have done more to end the war than promote peace, as Holbrooke lamented afterward, but keep the peace in Bosnia it did – a result no other effort had yet accomplished amid the most virulent European violence since World War II.

A cottage industry of commentary arose to enumerate the precise admixture of influences that begot the cease-fire and the Dayton Agreement.[37] There were, as there often is, a myriad of factors at play. Among them, the UN-sanctioned economic embargo in place since 1992 had at last bitten hard into Milosevic's political base in Serbia and Montenegro by the summer of 1995, creating for the Serbian leader a potent incentive to cooperate with the West and end the war.[38] There were also the powerful Bosniak-Croat ground offensives preceding and then coinciding with Deliberate Force, daily eroding the hard won Serb footprint in Bosnia and promising to erase Serb advantage altogether if

---

[36] This and following paragraph distilled from Richard Holbrooke, *To End a War*, 215–312; Lenard Cohen, *Serpent in the Bosom*, 192–95; and Owen, *Deliberate Force*, 505–14.

[37] The best short distillation of these various factors is found in Phil Haun, *Coercion, Survival, and War*, 108–12.

[38] David Rohde, *Endgame: The Betrayal and Fall of Srebrenica, Europe's Worst Massacre since World War II* (New York: Penguin, 2012), 333.

hostilities continued. Prior to these offensives, Serb interests controlled perhaps 70 percent of Bosnian real estate, but by late September they presided over just 46 percent of the republic, with 28 percent in Bosniak hands and 26 percent under Croat control. This made aspirations at Dayton to essentially split the republic "much easier" to reach, Holbrooke recounted, because the battlefield had already done much of the negotiating.[39] Given the facts on the ground, Milosevic's interests in Serbia were no longer served by ongoing strife in Bosnia, and the Bosnia Serbs were essentially being coerced to accept at the bargaining table what already existed on the map.

Still, Deliberate Force was the preeminent and proximate influence behind the Dayton Agreement. Holbrooke, the American diplomat most familiar with the machinations leading to Dayton – and one not prone to discount neither his own importance nor other nonkinetic factors in the process – flatly declared the air campaign was simply "the most important single factor influencing the Serbs" and "never had air power been so effective in terms of a political result."[40] American Secretary of Defense William Perry, surely informed and bright enough to understand the myriad factors involved, believed "Deliberate Force was the absolute critical step in bringing the warring parties to the negotiating table."[41] Army General Wesley Clark, who later led the coalition war in Kosovo and counted by decade's end as much high-level experience in the Balkans as any person then alive, concurred, in part because it was air power that had most bedeviled Mladic's (by extension Milosevic's) ability to counter Croat and Bosniak ground offensives. There is folly, of course, in relying upon Western assessments alone, but Milosevic shared this view, telling Clark shortly after the Dayton conference: "It was your NATO, your bombs and missiles, your high technology that defeated us."[42] In the end, US Ambassador to the UN Madeline Albright asserted the crisis in Bosnia "showed that the limited use of force – even air power alone – could make a decisive difference."[43]

Few others would have gone quite that far. But when it was said and done, the truth was this: Deliberate Force, given its compact and circumscribed scope, certainly delivered more political gain via less military resources – in

---

[39] Richard Holbrooke cited in Ivo Daadler, *Getting to Dayton, The Making of America's Bosnia Policy* (Washington, DC: Brookings Institution, 1999), 124.

[40] Richard Holbrooke cited in John Tirpak, "Deliberate Force," *Air Force Magazine*, October, 1997, 38; Mark McLaughlin, "Assessing the Effectiveness of Deliberate Force: Harnessing the Political-Military Connection," in Owen, *Deliberate Force*, 194.

[41] William Perry, cited in J. T. Correll, "The New American Way of War," *Air Force Magazine*, October 1996, 22.

[42] Wesley Clark, *Waging Modern War* (New York: Public Affairs, 2001), 68, 430, 432.

[43] Madeleine Albright, *Madam Secretary* (New York: Harper Perennial, 2013), 192.

time, lives, or treasure – than that proffered by any other combat arm of any nation or belligerent. The influence of Croat-Bosniak ground offensives on political calculations at Dayton was immense – maybe dispositive – but their effectiveness owed much to Deliberate Force. The campaign's air dominance over all of Bosnia denied Bosnian Serbs the ability to mass for counterattacks, and particularly "threatened the transport of weapons from eastern to western Bosnia" – a calamitous development for Karadzic and Mladic after Banja Luka fell under Croat danger.[44] Perhaps the strongest evidence of Deliberate Force's impact on ground-fighting emerged after the air campaign ended: By the third week in September, the heretofore successful Croat drive on Banja Luka stalled without NATO air power as an ally and, by early October and now free from aerial stalking, the Bosnian Serbs had stabilized their position and were preparing a counterstrike.[45]

Moreover, the Croat-Bosniak ground assaults consumed massive military resources, accounted for some of the war's atrocities, and exacerbated the most consequential fallout of the whole conflict: ethnic refugees. Operation Summer, for instance, involved 14,000 troops, killed or wounded as many as 1,000, and created 12,000 to 14,000 Bosnian Serb refugees. Storm involved some 170,000 forces, cost well over a thousand lives and at least as many wounded, imprisoned another 4,000 as POWs, and spawned a humanitarian crisis by throwing nearly a quarter of a million people into the countryside as refugees, 80 percent of whom were Serbian, the rest Bosniak or Croat. After the war, investigators concluded that Croat forces chasing Bosnian Serbs during Storm were guilty of some of the most horrible ethnic crimes committed in the Balkan Wars, and by 2012 some 2,380 people had been duly convicted of crimes ranging from looting to arson to rape to murder committed in that battle alone. The two operations concurrent with Deliberate Force were similar: Mistral 2 involved many thousands of troops, more than 600 deaths, and perhaps 20,000 refugees, most of whom fled to areas already inundated by 50,000 made homeless by Operation Storm; Operation Sana necessitated 50,000 troops at its peak, cost nearly 1,200 dead, about 2,000 wounded, and forced another 20,000 refugees on an uncertain and perilous path away from their homes.[46]

Deliberate Force's tally sheet is puny in comparison. Encompassing roughly a fortnight, the campaign employed about 300 aircraft, maybe a thousand aircrew, and another 10,000 supporting forces – many of them

---

[44] Richard Sargent, in Owen, *Deliberate Force*, 318; Phil Haun, *Coercion, Survival, and War*, 106.

[45] Phil Haun, *Coercion, Survival, and War*, 108.

[46] Precise accounting of casualties and refugees in the Bosnian conflict are elusive; here and throughout this essay, numbers represent median approximations and generally hew closely with Central Intelligence Agency, *Balkan Battleground: A Military History of the Yugoslav Conflict, 1990–1995* (Langley, VA: Central Intelligence Agency, 2005).

on densely packed naval vessels in the Adriatic Sea. Deliberate Force's offensive air operations comprised 3,525 sorties and dropped 1,026 bombs, 708 of which were precision munitions – an eight-fold increase as a percentage than in the Gulf War just four years earlier.[47] These bombs killed perhaps 25 enemy combatants and 27 Serb civilians. Deliberate Force created zero refugees on the ground and accounted for zero atrocities. Compared to the heralded air power of Gulf War standards, Deliberate Force achieved its goals more modestly: In two-fifths of the time, Deliberate Force involved only one-fourth the assets, one-twenty-fifth the sorties, and less than one-one hundredth the bomb tonnage.[48] The campaign was not perfect: Deliberate Force cost an America U-2 pilot killed in a flight accident, a Mirage pilot shot down, and another two French pilots taken as POWs; Deadeye strikes did not uniformly eliminate surface-to-air enemy missile threats until the last couple of days; command and control mechanisms between American and coalition forces posed initial problems; less than a handful of actual close air support missions actually fired weapons; and poor weather – the same obstacle that had bedeviled military operations from time immemorial – did the same despite the most advanced technology, on some days thwarting as many as 40 percent of planned NATO air strikes.[49] Still, rarely had air power contributed to a political task with as meager an expenditure, especially in relation to the massive resources consumed by ground offenses.

What irony, then, that the US Air Force, as the world's preeminent air arm, was able to but reluctantly acknowledge Deliberate Force's success. Praise for its manifest tactical prowess was then, and remains now, ubiquitous among airmen, and the closest the Air Force ever got to an official history, *Deliberate Force: A Case Study in Effective Campaigning*, makes apparent in its very title a basic claim of success and repeats it on its final page: The operation "was a decisive element in bringing a new period of peace to Bosnia – quickly, cleanly, and at minimal cost in blood and treasure."[50] But to get to this assessment, the study authors treat Deliberate Force's achievement with equivocation and qualification. Much of their analysis is sound, some of it worthy of admiration, emulation, and – and this essay makes clear – citation. In every instance, however, the authors, nearly to a person, harbored deep unease with Deliberate Force as a model upon which to base future operations.

At base, Deliberate Force was a graduated and incremental air campaign, conducted with significant political oversight and constraint, which worked.

---

[47] There were also 1,091 support sorties. Richard Sargent, in Owen, *Deliberate Force*, 220.
[48] Ibid., 337.     [49] Mark Conversino, in Owen, *Deliberate Force*, 150–55.
[50] Robert Owen, *Deliberate Force*, 515.

This truth, so contrary to received wisdom about air strategy, reduced airmen to a series of befuddled explanations – when they attempted explanation at all. Deliberate Force's political achievement, for instance, was the subject of the volume's most slender chapter, eight pages, and credited ground operations and independent Bosnian and Serbian political calculations as much as it did the air strikes for the Dayton Agreement. Meanwhile the volume's largest chapter, seven times the length at fifty-eight pages, comprised a technical catalogue of the aircraft used in Deliberate Force, long a comfort zone for airmen the world over.[51] To the study authors, Deliberate Force was a "unique operation" replete with strategic ambiguities and political incongruities that "nonetheless seems to have worked."[52] One chapter "endeavored to examine the nature of Deliberate Force's remarkable success, which was largely unpremeditated," and another claimed – or hoped? – "the circumstances in Bosnia are unlikely to be repeated."[53] Deliberate Force as an "effective but not efficient" operation constituted a subplot of the entire study; its success was the product of a "propitious convergence of events," and the campaign had worked "despite the politico-military constraints and sensitivities" pervading the whole affair.[54]

Without a broader frame of reference, American airmen realized neither the operation's resemblance to prior campaigns nor considered that it may have prevailed *because of* and not *despite* strategic constraints, if for no other reason than it was precisely those constraints that made air power in its modern, potent guise the West's only viable option. Instead, for them, the "unusual" mixture of NATO and UN prerogatives "were fertile ground for problems" solved only by temporary "Band-Aid connections." Yet, coalition warfare has nearly always produced air command and control schemes at odds with doctrinal precepts since at least World War II, and in any event once Deliberate Force commenced, the campaign operated via "a de-facto all-American chain of command" wherein Ryan enjoyed "a large amount of autonomy."[55]

Study authors also critiqued Deliberate Force's bombing halt, reminiscent as it was to ill-fated pauses during the Vietnam War, yet nearly to a person diplomats on all sides at Dayton believed the stopping and

---

[51] Mark McLaughlin, in Owen, *Deliberate Force*, 189–97; Richard Sargent, "Aircraft Used in Deliberate Force" and "Weapons Used in Deliberate Force," in Owen, *Deliberate Force*, 199–277.

[52] Bradley Davis, in Owen, *Deliberate Force*, 37.

[53] Christopher Campbell, in Owen, *Deliberate Force*, 126; Ronald Reed, in Owen, *Deliberate Force*, 416.

[54] Ronald Reed, in Owen, *Deliberate Force*, 416; Mark McLaughlin, in Owen, *Deliberate Force*, 193; Richard Sargent, in Owen, *Deliberate Force*, 331.

[55] Bradley Davis, in Owen, *Deliberate Force*, 59; Christopher Campbell, in Owen, *Deliberate Force*, 92; Mark Bucknam, in Owen, *Deliberate Force*, 364.

starting of the air strikes had had "perhaps even more stunning effect on Serbian military leaders than had the initial strikes," belying as it did a heretofore absent Western resolve.[56] Ryan's tight control of the campaign, which "appeared to constitute micromanagement, reminiscent of Vietnam," also came in for special scrutiny; a study author tortuously justified it by dredging up prevailing command habits from the age of Napoleonic warfare.[57] But Ryan's *modus operandi* was both possible, given the compact size of Deliberate Force, and necessary, given the campaign's politically difficult birth and the international community's aversion to casualties; indeed, although the air campaign might not have survived a significant instance of collateral damage, Ryan's close oversight likely gave it its best chance to endure if such an accident had occurred.[58] Perhaps most revealing, an entire chapter of *Deliberate Force* asked whether other approaches more akin to favored means of swift and overwhelming force aimed at strategic centers "would have enjoyed more success than the one actually used in the Balkans," a counterfactual to an otherwise victorious air operation absent in any other official or sponsored history in the annals of the US Air Force.[59]

Deliberate Force was not perfect, just as the Dayton Agreement little resembled a mature political settlement. Both left certain matters to fester, waiting another war over Kosovo lurking just beyond the horizon. There, misperceptions of Deliberate Force's decisive impact in Bosnia – rather than its preeminent contribution – would create an illusionary hope for air power's role amidst yet another power grab by an unreconstructed Serbia and its leader, Milosevic. And in Bosnia, reconciliation among various parties once at each other's throats took decades and wrenching war crime trials – and wounds still sometimes bleed. But throughout the region, and twenty years after the fighting, travel guides trumpeted again the allure of Sarajevo, quaint Bosnian villages, and the Croatian coast, all shimmering in the sun.

[56] Mark McLaughlin, in Owen, *Deliberate Force*, 193.
[57] John Orndorff, "Aspects of Leading and Following: The Human Factors of Deliberate Force," in Owen, *Deliberate Force*, 353.
[58] Author interview with Michael Ryan, 2007.
[59] Robert Pollack, "Roads Not Taken: Theoretical Approaches to Operation Deliberate Force," in Owen, *Deliberate Force*, 432.

# 4    Hoping for Victory: Coercive Air Power and NATO's Strategy in Kosovo

*Andrew L. Stigler**

Operation Allied Force (OAF) began as a determination by the United States and its NATO allies that something needed to be done about Serbian depredations against the Kosovar Albanians. NATO decided, almost reflexively, to execute an operation similar to the one that had worked in 1995. In Bosnia, a brief air campaign contributed to the negotiations that led to the Dayton Accords (see Chapter 3). Partly as a consequence of this successful outcome, NATO elected to engage in a short air campaign designed to convince Serbian President Slobodan Milosevic to cease his harassment of Albanians in Kosovo. When Milosevic responded to the allied air campaign by increasing the pressure on the Kosovar Albanian population, generating almost a million refugees, the alliance found itself inadvertently committed to reversing the situation. Strategic improvisation and graduated escalation became NATO's default strategy.

In the case of Kosovo, however, the desire for a quick and low-cost action led to an unexpected and unwanted strategic commitment. Decision makers overlooked the risk that the situation could deteriorate in Kosovo following allied bombing and that the alliance would feel obligated to at least partially reverse what it, inadvertently, had made worse. As the conflict wore on, some asked if the post–Cold War viability of NATO was on the line. Commitment comes in many forms.

The 1999 conflict over Kosovo points to the importance of identifying when a strategy depends on defeating an enemy's will in order to succeed. Successful coercion in these campaigns involves estimating more than the enemy's current willingness to sacrifice personnel, materiel, and international standing to secure a positive outcome. The coercing party must also assess the likely willingness of the enemy to resist after weeks or months of battle. This is a daunting task, and some of the United States' worst defeats can trace their origin to a failure to successfully estimate an enemy's willingness to sacrifice. The war in Kosovo was not

---

* The views expressed by the author do not reflect those of the US government, the Department of Defense, or any of its organizations.

identical to the conflict in Vietnam, but some of the lessons of the latter were lost on the men and women responsible for planning military strategy in the late 1990s.

Military historian John Keegan later expressed his surprise that the Western alliance had ultimately met with success in the theater, as he had been deeply skeptical that the use of air power alone could achieve such a significant outcome as a change in control over sovereign territory. "Now there is a new turning point to fix on the calendar: June 3, 1999, when the capitulation of President Milosevic proved that a war can be won by air power alone."[1] Keegan simultaneously argued that the war over Kosovo was a singular victory for air power and expressed a measure of puzzlement as to how the victory was achieved. This may be a sage perspective: to note a true and unassisted success for air power while remaining cautious about the lessons for the future. Both of these perspectives will serve as foci of this chapter in an attempt to understand the path to success while offering reservations about OAF's applicability for future conflicts.

Five years before the war over Kosovo, Eliot Cohen published a widely cited article in *Foreign Affairs*, "The Mystique of US Air Power." He argued, "Air power is an unusually seductive form of military strength, in part because, like modern courtship, it appears to offer gratification without commitment."[2] As discussed in the introductory chapter, part of the appeal of air power is the potential for a low-casualty victory while avoiding an occupation and other long-term commitments. Given that US air forces are more powerful than those of any other nation, there was reason to utilize a form of power in which the United States has traditionally held a profound advantage. This theme runs throughout this volume, and this strategic heuristic certainly applies to the war over Kosovo.

This chapter proceeds in six parts. The first reprises major events prior to and during Operation Allied Force. The second critiques NATO's senior general on the alliance's coercive strategy. The third argues that strategies targeting the will of the enemy embrace significant risks. The fourth section shows how NATO's strategy relied on air power and air power alone, while the fifth discusses the evolution of the air campaign. The final section explores why the alliance's effort, one that came to rely on improvisation and was widely critiqued as it unfolded, was ultimately successful.

---

[1] John Keegan, "Please, Mr. Blair, Never Take Such a Risk Again," *The Sunday Telegraph*, June 6, 1999.
[2] Eliot A. Cohen, "The Mystique of US Air Power," *Foreign Affairs* (January–February 1994): 109.

### The Air War over Kosovo

In the conclusion of Richard Holbrooke's memoir, *To End a War*, the American ambassador offers a summation of the 1995 Bosnia crisis that suggests how the decision to bomb was the climactic moment that led to the Dayton Accords.

[I]n only eighteen weeks in 1995 ... the United States put its prestige on the line with a rapid and dramatic series of high-risk actions: an all-out diplomatic effort in August, heavy NATO bombing in September, a cease-fire in October, Dayton in November, and, in December, the deployment of twenty thousand American troops to Bosnia. Suddenly, the war was over – and America's role in post–Cold War Europe redefined.[3]

Holbrooke's summation implies the mindset with which some in the national security community approached the Kosovo crisis: a belief that a relatively brief round of bombing could convince Milosevic to change course.

The Serbian attack on Kosovar Albanians in March 1998 triggered a series of events. The Contact Group of six nations (the United States, France, the United Kingdom, Germany, Italy, and Russia) promptly convened to discuss a unified response. Secretary of State Madeleine Albright set a dramatic tone, warning that "History is watching us."[4] In October 1998, the Contact Group, through Richard Holbrooke, believed it had negotiated a cease-fire and the partial withdrawal of Serb forces.[5] But the agreement proved ill-defined and was soon challenged by the Serbs. Although there were occasional pauses in Serbian depredations, Milosevic largely continued to harass and kill Kosovar Albanians. A bloody massacre at the Kosovar village of Racak on January 15, 1999, proved particularly galvanizing for the alliance, and the forty-five dead garnered wide condemnation. US Ambassador William Walker, a foreign service veteran who had seen his share of atrocities in Central America, called it "an unspeakable atrocity."[6]

A conference convened at Rambouillet, France, on February 6 represented the last effort to resolve the crisis peacefully. The Serbs sent a relatively junior representative, Deputy Prime Minister Ratko Markovic, strongly suggesting Milosevic was not as engaged in the

---

[3] Richard Holbrooke, *To End a War* (New York: Modern Library, 1999), 360.
[4] Walter Isaacson, "Madeleine's War," *Time*, May 17, 1999, 29.
[5] Mike O'Connor, "Kosovo's Albanians Give Truce Pact Poor Reviews," *New York Times*, October 15, 1998.
[6] Ivo H. Daalder and Michael E. O'Hanlon, *Winning Ugly: NATO's War to Save Kosovo* (Washington, DC: Brookings Institution Press, 2000), 64.

diplomatic effort as he had previously been during the negotiations at Dayton. The talks ended in failure on March 18, and NATO launched the air campaign on March 24.

The first day of attacks was limited. Launching under cover of night, a total of 53 targets were struck, almost all related to Yugoslav air defense capabilities.[7] NATO had prepared for a few days of bombing, and when Milosevic showed no change in his negotiating position there was a sudden scramble for additional targets. At the start of the war 219 targets had been selected and approved (most related to air defense or communications, while others related to military facilities such as troop barracks), and NATO had struck half of these by the end of the third day. At one point, American targeteers were producing ten to twelve new targets a day, while Allied planes were striking twice that many.[8] This led to a rush to find more targets; General Clark later set a goal of 2,000 targets, a figure derided by some officers as "T2K." But by the end of the war, even after expanding the target set to include tobacco warehouses and a Yugo automobile factory, the alliance had identified only 1,021 fixed targets.[9]

March 30 marked a significant escalation with the use of the Combined Air Interdiction of Fielded Forces (CAIFF) operational concept. This involved using A-10s during the day and F-16s at night as airborne forward air controllers to locate and identify Serbian fielded forces in Kosovo. The daytime use of the A-10s was partly predicated on the fact that the slower-moving aircraft would have advantages in making positive target identification. Operating above a 17,500-foot "hard deck" proved a challenge, and no attacks were made on the first day of CAIFF sorties due to a lack of opportunity.[10] (This hard deck was later lowered to 15,000 and then 10,000 feet.)

Meanwhile NATO air strikes continued across Serbia. In response, the Serbs had been shifting many of their anti-air assets nightly, not only the missile batteries but radars and support vans as well. On the fourth night of the operation, a Serb surface-to-air missile battery managed to lock onto an F-117 and blow off the left wing. The pilot ejected safely and was

---

[7] Anthony H. Cordesman, *The Lessons and Non-Lessons of the Air and Missile Campaign in Kosovo* (Westport, CT: Praeger, 2001), 25.

[8] The British supplied approximately two dozen targets during the war. The rest were generated by Americans.

[9] Steven Lee Meyers, "The Chinese Embassy Bombing: A Wide Net of Blame," *New York Times*, April 17, 2000, A1.

[10] Christopher E. Haave, "The A-10, Its Missions, and the Hog Units that Flew in Operation Allied Force," in Christopher E. Haave and Phil M. Haun, eds., *A-10s over Kosovo: The Victory of Airpower over a Fielded Army as Told by the Airmen Who Fought Operation Allied Force* (Maxwell AFB, AL: Air University Press, 2003), 26–8, 30.

rescued, but the aura of invincibility surrounding the F-117 had been torn. Serbian street vendors were soon selling souvenir posters in Belgrade with the phrase, "Sorry, we didn't know it was invisible."[11]

The downing of a US stealth fighter was a signal event in the war, though not a turning point. A later investigation noted the weather was imperfect for the mission; it was not a dark night and the F-117 could still find itself silhouetted against stars. The Serbs were clever in how they used their slightly dated air defense technology, employing their radars sparingly to avoid detection. Mobility was also an asset; a Pentagon spokesman offered that the Serbs "are very adept at moving [air defense missiles] around."[12] The head of the USAF investigation into the incident reflected on one lesson: "I think the Air Force needs to learn that we can't afford to let the bad guy get lucky with below-average equipment."[13]

NATO's decision to continue and escalate the air campaign after the first week was seen as a necessary response to Milosevic's escalated attacks on Kosovar Albanians. The UN High Commissioner for Refugees estimated there were fewer than 100,000 international refugees from Kosovo before the start of bombing on March 24, 1999. Less than a month later there were more than 500,000. At the height of the refugee count in early June there were almost 800,000.[14] This ruthless effort, which began two days after the start of bombing, forced the alliance into a corner it had hoped to avoid. Stopping the attack after several days and claiming "Milosevic has been punished" was no longer an option, given that the situation had greatly worsened for the Kosovar Albanians.

Guiding aircraft to targets was a constant challenge. The surveillance technology on a Predator drone allowed the operator to see accurately at a distance, but only through a very narrow field of view akin to a "soda straw." An A-10 pilot has a much wider range of observation. As a result, the Predator operator could often see targets but be unable to guide the pilot to a location from which to make an attack.

On one occasion the head of the NATO air campaign, Lieutenant General Michael Short, observed other officers in the Combined Air Operations Center (CAOC) attempting to guide an American aircraft to a Serbian tank that a Predator operator had located. The aircraft was piloted by his son, Captain Chris Short. The attempt to guide Captain Short's plane to the target continued unsuccessfully. To offer encouragement, the CAOC communicated, "General Short really wants you to find

[11] David Cenciotti, "'Vega 31': The First and Only F-117 Stealth Fighter Jet Shot Down in Combat," *The Aviationist*, March 27, 2014.
[12] Dana Priest, "Yugoslav Air Defenses Mostly Intact," *Washington Post*, April 13, 1999, A1.
[13] Simpson, 273, 275.    [14] Daalder and O'Hanlon, 109.

and kill that tank." Captain Short replied, "Tell Dad I can't find the [expletive deleted] tank!"[15]

And as the target set expanded, the bombing campaign increasingly impacted the Serbian population. By the end of the war, a target set that had been almost solely focused on Serbian air defenses at the outset had been expanded to include civilian infrastructure targets in Belgrade. In mid-May, 85 percent of Serbia's electrical supply was being intermittently interrupted, and these interruptions impacted the civilian water supply.[16] The pressure challenged Milosevic's political support; pro-government protests that had previously drawn tens of thousands now drew just hundreds.

The pressure to find additional targets sometimes came at a cost. Though senior American officers asserted that they were operating under restrictive rules of engagement, there were still a number of highly publicized incidents that involved the deaths of civilians.[17] In one F-16 attack on a suspected military convoy in early April, the Serbs claimed that NATO had actually struck a civilian convoy and that sixty-four Kosovars had been killed.[18] As Benjamin Lambeth argues, "The extraordinary media attention given to these events attested to what can happen when zero noncombatant casualties becomes not only the goal of strategy but also the expectation."[19]

The most politically significant targeting error was the bombing of the Chinese Embassy in Belgrade on May 8, killing three Chinese nationals. Multiple failures led to the mistaken strike. A CIA review of the process claimed there were four primary flaws: (1) the method of identification of the target was inadequately reviewed; (2) the CIA had no procedural guidelines for proposing targets; (3) procedures at EUCOM were designed to check accuracy of geographic data but not to check the designation of the target; and (4) information that the Chinese Embassy was moved in 1996 (a fact well known to American diplomats) was not to be found in any of the targeting databases.[20]

---

[15] Haave and Haun, *A-10s over Kosovo*, 300.
[16] Phil Haun, *Coercion, Survival, and War: Why Weak States Resist the United States* (Stanford: Stanford University Press, 2015), 123.
[17] Joel Havemann, "Convoy Deaths May Undermine Moral Authority," *Los Angeles Times*, April 15, 1999, A1.
[18] David Williams and Michael Seamark, "Who Is to Blame for Death Convoy," *Daily Mail* (London), April 15, 1999.
[19] Benjamin S. Lambeth, *The Transformation of American Air Power* (Ithaca: Cornell University Press, 2000), 205.
[20] Central Intelligence Agency, "DCI Statement on the Belgrade Chinese Embassy Bombing," July 22, 1999.

The Chinese were apoplectic, convinced the strike had been deliberate partly because it struck the Chinese defense attaché's office and the embassy's intelligence cell.[21] Bombing in Belgrade was halted, and the Serbs made the most of this unusual propaganda opportunity. Defense Secretary William Cohen later admitted the erroneous bombing was due neither to mechanical nor to human failure but instead was the result of "an institutional error."[22]

In late May, the Kosovo Liberation Army (KLA) launched Operation Arrow, an effort to seize a highway near the southwestern border with Albania. Involving 4,000 troops, it was a rare example of the KLA mounting a large-scale attack at that point in the conflict. But the Serbs counterattacked, and the KLA was pushed back toward Mt. Pastrik, straddling the border between Albania and Kosovo. Only NATO air support – the first known occasion of NATO offering such support for the Kosovars – saved the KLA from a total defeat. Some US intelligence sources reported after the conflict that the KLA was "near death."[23]

However, the Serbs' success here did not alter the fundamental calculus of the situation Milosevic was facing. The alliance had demonstrated a willingness to persevere. Stephen Hosmer argues it was, by late May, an "obvious fact that NATO could have continued the bombing indefinitely and with virtual impunity."[24] On June 9, after seventy-eight days of bombing, Milosevic – facing the defection of his main ally, Russia, and the threat of continued air attack – capitulated with an agreement to withdraw his forces. The conclusion of the campaign is discussed in more detail later in this chapter. There were efforts by American officials to introduce the distant threat of a NATO ground invasion, though there are strong reasons to believe that these efforts did not contribute to Milosevic's decision to capitulate.

## The Commander's Perspective

The flaws in the alliance's initial strategy should have been apparent. Consider what the commanding general for the operation, Wesley K. Clark, believed to be the three main reasons why the reliance on air power was a satisfactory solution to the Kosovo problem. Clark offered

[21] Meyers, "The Chinese Embassy Bombing: A Wide Net of Blame."
[22] Lambeth, 207.
[23] Dana Priest and Peter Finn, "NATO Gives Air Support to KLA Forces," *Washington Post*, June 2, 1999, A1.
[24] Stephen T. Hosmer, *Why Milosevic Decided to Settle When He Did* (Santa Monica: RAND, 2001), 69.

this assessment after the conflict, but it still allows insight into how the senior commander justified the operation.

Reliance on the air threat was natural for NATO. First, it had worked in 1995, against the Bosnian Serbs, albeit in conjunction with a powerful Croat ground campaign. Second, it promised a low-cost, low-risk statement of political intent. And third, it left open other, more difficult, and costly options. It seemed to be the military means best suited to carry the nations' political dynamic forward.[25]

The weakness of each of the three rationalizations speaks to the quality of the reasoning behind the air campaign. First, as NATO learned to its chagrin, Kosovo was not Bosnia, since Kosovo was seen by Serbs as being more integral and valuable to the Yugoslav state. The 1995 bombing by NATO that led to the Dayton Accords was a particularly tidy outcome (at least compared to other possible outcomes); a very limited and, for the NATO alliance, largely cost-free air campaign contributed to a positive result. On the basis of that single data point, NATO planners apparently felt highly confident they could achieve a similar success. But in 1999, instead of relenting in his depredations against the Kosovar Albanians once the bombing began, Milosevic escalated (as described earlier).

Second, waging a war to make a "statement of political intent" is a questionable rationalization on its face. A limited strike can signal future intent but could also be perceived as a lack of commitment to the cause. Using air power to make a statement can be an uncertain proposal, as the subsequent conduct of the war demonstrates.

Third, justifying a strategy by arguing that, should the air campaign fail, there are "other, more difficult, and costly options" available is a strange way to sell a strategy after the fact. Given that the alliance had decided to get involved in Kosovo in large part because they expected it to be a low-cost conflict, there were many reasons to predict NATO would be allergic to the higher-cost enterprises that Clark had in mind.

A major lesson of OAF is the need to consider the possible spectrum of reactions an enemy may take in response to your initiatives. If you cannot counter those possible responses, you should at least consider your available means to prepare for them or at the bare minimum recognize that they could occur. In an interview after the war, Clark revealed that he was unsure what calculations led Milosevic to give in. When asked shortly after the war why the Serbs retreated, he offered, "You'll have to ask Milosevic, and he'll never tell you."[26]

General Clark viewed the Kosovo campaign as one of "continuous adaptation." This phrase implies both a positive and negative

[25] Wesley K. Clark, *Waging Modern War* (New York: PublicAffairs, 2001), 430.
[26] Michael Ignatieff, "The Virtual Commander," *The New Yorker*, August 2, 1999, 31.

connotation – positive in the sense that the US military and its NATO allies recognized the need for adaptation and collectively agreed on a revised approach. The ability of both military institutions and the individuals operating them to recognize a need to change strategy and to be capable of acting upon that need can be a valuable asset.

The negative face of Clark's embrace of "continuous adaptation" lies in the implication that a regular pace of adaptation was necessary. This is not an intrinsically negative quality in and of itself; fluidity in strategic thinking can be a good thing. But the implication that Operation Allied Force was a tale of constant strategic improvisation cannot be a wholly positive lens through which to view NATO's decision making prior to and during the conflict.

### Targeting the Will

The Kosovo conflict highlights that purely coercive strategies embrace a profound risk that brute force strategies do not. If one employs a strategy that depends on the target changing its mind – and Kosovo is such a conflict – then the attacking state needs to have some confidence that military punishment will lead to that outcome. Contrast this with brute force strategies, which seek to seize what is at issue even if the enemy is willing to fight to the last soldier. If one chooses a strategy that depends on defeating the enemy's will, one's calculations must embrace a host of complexities – human psychology, group dynamics, perceptions of the target, the target's willingness to bear costs, and others. Many defeats have been caused primarily because one state misjudged another state's willingness to bear punishment in order to retain a contested territory.

The United States' long engagement in Vietnam, for example, can largely be explained as a consequence of an American inability to perceive North Vietnam's willingness to bear costs to unify with the South. Americans engaged in a years-long exercise in mirror imaging, expecting that the North Vietnamese would weigh costs and benefits similar to how an American would. This led to profound frustration for American leaders, including three consecutive US presidents. At one point, Secretary of Defense Robert McNamara found it incredible that, even though the North was losing 60,000 troops a year, they continued to fight against the world's richest superpower. In a 1966 report, he conceded "there is no sign of an impending break in enemy morale."[27] McNamara, a man who relied heavily on metrics and statistics, came to recognize he had

---

[27] Robert S. McNamara, *In Retrospect: The Tragedy and Lessons of Vietnam* (New York: Random House, 1995), 262.

incorrectly estimated North Vietnam's dedication and that the vast American effort would fail as a result.

The inherent complexity of gauging an enemy's willingness to resist is a factor that often leads states to choose a brute force strategy. During preparations for the 1991 Gulf War, President George H. W. Bush made it clear he wanted to ready an invasion-capable ground force and delayed the start of the war by weeks to have such a force in place. He dismissed a proposed strategy relying only on coercive air power and sanctions. As General Colin Powell phrased his rejection of air power alone, "You either reverse an invasion [Iraq's invasion of Kuwait], or you don't."[28]

Operation Allied Force offers a rare example of a purely coercive campaign, one that relied entirely on air power and therefore depended for success on overcoming the Serbs' willingness to resist. As the campaign unfolded, some of NATO's civilian and military leaders saw virtue in at least threatening a ground campaign. But NATO focused all of its efforts on the air campaign, partly because a brute force attack entailed a completely different set of political and strategic calculations. At one point, Clark pressed for a land force to be deployed, arguing in part that ground troops would be needed if Milosevic capitulated.[29] US civilian leadership ignored him, even excluding Clark from a key White House meeting on June 3 out of concern that he would press for a ground operation.[30]

The president and other leaders understood the leverage that a threat of a decisive ground strike could generate, as this would have forced Milosevic to contemplate the daunting prospect of NATO forces seizing Kosovo by force. Such a threat also risked the prospect of additional political commitment to a conflict that had already proven to be a volatile one. But ultimately the alliance dedicated its political and military resources to the coercive air campaign, one that embraced all the risks inherent in a strategy that targets the will of the enemy.

### Kosovo: Air Power and Air Power Alone

In Kosovo, given the complete absence of any serious ground threat to Serbian control of the province, air power alone achieved a major political result, namely the decision by Belgrade to relinquish control of Kosovo to an international security force. An evaluation of the only two military factors that could have generated a ground threat – the Kosovo Liberation

---

[28] US News and World Report, *Triumph without Victory: The Unreported History of the Persian Gulf War* (New York: Random House 1992), 51.

[29] Clark, *Waging Modern War*, 282.

[30] Ben Macintyre, "White House Snubs Hawkish General," *Times* (London), June 3, 1999.

Army (KLA) and the NATO alliance – strongly suggests that neither of these potential ground threats played a significant role in Milosevic's final decision to concede. The KLA never posed a serious threat. Some estimate that it may have initially grown to 8,000 or 10,000 soldiers armed only with small arms and grenades procured from neighboring Albania, but with no artillery or other heavy weapons. The training offered to recruits lasted less than two weeks, and there was no meaningful centralized coordination between individual brigades, which numbered a few hundred fighters.[31]

By the end of the war the ranks of the KLA swelled to as many as 17,000, as the civilian Kosovar population became increasingly opposed to the Milosevic regime and more recruits were available.[32] But even so, one observer argues, "[the KLA] was essentially able to hold territory only when there was no opposing force trying to take it away. It was incapable of militarily defending any of these territories against a concerted Yugoslav Army attack . . . ."[33] Daniel L. Byman and Matthew C. Waxman concur: "By the end of Operation Allied Force, [the KLA] still had not defeated the Serbian army in battle and . . . posed no immediate threat to Serbian control over the province." They also note that Milosevic's concessions greatly exceeded anything the KLA could have obtained in the near or medium term.[34] Although there was some limited coordination between NATO forces and the KLA, there is little reason to be swayed from the conclusion that the KLA was not a major military factor.

Similarly, though there were tentative efforts to reconsider a ground operation, the threat of a NATO ground operation did not play a role in Milosevic's decision. The British were perhaps the European ally most in favor of muscular action, even advocating for a ground war at one point.[35] At a meeting of defense ministers on May 27, UK Defense Minister George Robinson pressed this argument, offering 54,000 troops. France and Italy demurred but said they would offer troops if the invasion was approved. Germany and the United States offered no commitment whatsoever.[36] This range of opinions on the possibility of a ground operation did not mar the alliance's commitment to the air campaign, which remained strong.

---

[31] Anthony Schinella, *Bombs without Boots: The Limits of Airpower* (Washington, DC: Brookings Institution Press, 2017), 55–56.
[32] Daalder and O'Hanlon, *Winning Ugly*, 151–52.
[33] Schinella, *Bombs without Boots*, 57.
[34] Daniel L. Byman and Matthew C. Waxman, "Kosovo and the Great Air Power Debate," *International Security* 24:4 (2000): 30.
[35] Daalder and O'Hanlon, 138, 141.    [36] Ibid.,157–58.

But it seems likely the threat of a NATO ground offensive was not a factor in determining the outcome. After the campaign some argued the specter of a NATO invasion, combined with the air campaign and intensive diplomacy by the Russians, convinced Milosevic. President Bill Clinton tried to introduce the threat of a ground campaign on May 18, when he stated that "we have not and will not take any option off the table."[37] Newspaper accounts published after the successful conclusion of the Kosovo campaign suggested there was serious planning for a ground campaign.[38]

The evidence suggests otherwise. High-ranking military and civilian officials in the Clinton administration sent numerous signals that a ground operation was not being seriously considered. On June 3, Chairman of the Joint Chiefs of Staff General Hugh Shelton claimed there was "insufficient domestic and international political support for sending ground troops into Kosovo."[39] Secretary of Defense William Cohen noted afterward that it "was going to be a very tough sell, if not impossible, to persuade the American people that we were going to put up to 150,000 or 200,000 American troops to go in on the ground . . . ."[40] By the time a military technical agreement was signed on June 9 and the war was formally concluded on June 10, NATO had not begun any of the extensive military preparations necessary for a large-scale land operation. If Milosevic caved in partly because he feared a ground operation, the operation he feared was many weeks away. And NATO, which had strong incentive to threaten a ground operation to maximize the pressure on Milosevic, had not come remotely close to doing so in any credible manner. Despite the willingness of some participants – including General Wesley Clark, the NATO commander – to credit a ground threat with the favorable outcome, there is little reason to believe this to be the case.[41]

As a consequence, one is left with the conclusion that OAF is a rare example in the annals of warfare of a particular type of conflict: an air power–only campaign that resulted in the successful coercion of the

---

[37] Kathering Q. Seelye, "Clinton Resists Renewed Calls for Ground Troops in Kosovo," *New York Times*, May 19, 1999. The title of this article suggests the author's perception of the likelihood of a ground campaign.

[38] Dana Priest, "The Commander's War: A Decisive Battle that Never Was," *Washington Post*, September 19, 1999, A1; Steven Erlanger, "NATO Was Closer to Ground War in Kosovo than Is Widely Realized," *New York Times*, November 7, 1999.

[39] Steven Lee Myers, "US Military Chief Firm: No Ground Force for Kosovo," *New York Times*, June 3, 1999.

[40] Interview with US Secretary of Defense William Cohen, *Frontline*, February 22, 2000.

[41] For more on this point, see Andrew L. Stigler, "A Clear Victory for Air Power: NATO's Empty Threat to Invade Kosovo," *International Security* 27:3 (Winter 2002/3): 124–57.

enemy and the change of political and military control over territory at issue. Air power has certainly been used independently to destroy specific targets and to send signals, as with President Ronald Reagan's raid on Libya on April 15, 1986. Powerful coercive air campaigns have been used in combination with significant ground forces to achieve major objectives, as in the Allies' fight against Nazi Germany in Europe. But Kosovo marks the best example of a solely coercive air strategy, and one that gained a significant outcome with control over sovereign territory shifting from Serbia to an international and Western-aligned peacekeeping force.

## The Evolution of the Air Campaign

Numerous indicators suggest that NATO leaders believed Operation Allied Force would not be long. The activation warning, the first stage of the three-stage process for authorizing a NATO military operation, was for a "Limited Air Operation."[42] NATO planes began to run out of targets after three days, a fact that strongly indicated the expectation of a brisk campaign and a quick victory.[43] NATO had only 350 planes in range of Serbia, fewer than the 410 it had in the area as recently as October 1998. No aircraft carriers were within striking range. There were even fears expressed that a longer campaign would be overly encouraging to the KLA.[44]

Serbian air defenses remained a continuous threat, and this concern combined with NATO's aversion to casualties to generate the alliance's cautious approach to bombing. NATO destroyed fewer than six surface-to-air missile sites in the first four weeks of the conflict, partly because of Serbian caution by choosing to conserve SAMs. They frequently turned off their radar systems when enemy jets approached, guaranteeing that Serbia could not shoot down any NATO planes in that encounter but preserving the asset and the threat.[45] Serbian deception operations played a role in luring American planes into striking nonexistent targets, demonstrating ostensibly crude deception efforts can be effective against modern air forces. The Serbs at one point used a telephone pole leaned against a truck axle to mimic an artillery piece. The combination was enough to draw not just one coalition attack, but three.[46]

A group of Apache helicopters, code named Task Force Hawk, deployed to the theater at a cost of $243 million. Yet the Apaches

[42] Clark, *Waging Modern War*, 135.
[43] Interview with Colonel Steve Shinkel, USAF, May 5, 2019. Shinkel flew in support of OAF with the 912th Air Refueling Squadron from the first day of the war.
[44] Daalder and O'Hanlon, *Winning Ugly*, 103, 104.
[45] Haave and Haun, *A-10s over Kosovo*, 227.    [46] Shinkel interview, May 5, 2019.

conducted no combat operations because of concerns that the Serb air defenses had not been sufficiently degraded to allow the helicopters to operate. As Chairman of the Joint Chiefs Hugh Shelton put it after the war, it was decided to keep the Apaches out of harm's way until the effort to counter the Serb air defenses had "reduced the risk to the very minimum."[47] The Task Force Hawk episode is another indication of the Allies' keen desire to avoid any risk of casualties – even to the point of denying themselves a military advantage – suggesting just how closely NATO had embraced a coercive strategy in Kosovo. And despite Clark's claim that the deployment of the Apaches "conveyed a powerful image of a ground threat," it seems equally plausible that the decision not to use them at all similarly communicated a deep reticence on the part of NATO about putting Army helicopters – and, by extension, Army units – in harm's way.[48]

There had been a significant expansion of Clark's authority to select targets. By the start of April, Clark could select from the Phase III target list – everything outside of downtown Belgrade and not an industrial target. NATO's North Atlantic Council required Clark to consult with NATO Secretary General Javier Solana if a strike risked high civilian casualties.[49] One USAF officer suggests that the decision to target bridges and other civilian targets (including the political headquarters of Milosevic's wife) was a particularly significant escalation, since the damage was difficult to repair and also a highly visible escalation for both the civilian population and the Serbian leadership.[50]

Had the increase in strike aircraft continued at the pace the alliance planned, NATO would have been able by the end of June to generate 1,000 strikes a day against Serbian targets, with alliance planes attacking the Serbs from all directions.[51] This would have equaled the highest number of sorties per day during the first week of Operation Desert Storm in 1991 and vastly exceeded the fifty strike sorties launched at the start of OAF.[52] By the end of the war, the alliance would be at 300 strike sorties per day, with planes based in nine countries surrounding Serbia.[53]

In the weeks before the Serbian capitulation, bombing escalated and included more Serbian infrastructure targets. Beginning on May 2, NATO began bombing Serbian electrical transformers with munitions that deployed conductive filaments designed to short out transformers without causing permanent damage. Escalation increased the pressure on Milosevic and the Serbian population, while also warning that worse was

[47] Lambeth, *The Transformation of American Air Power*, 209.
[48] Clark, *Waging Modern War*, 427.    [49] Schinella, *Bombs without Boots*, 71–72.
[50] Shinkel interview, August 6, 2019.    [51] Hosmer, *Why Milosevic Decided to Settle*, 99.
[52] Lambeth, *The Transformation of American Air Power*, 184.    [53] Ibid., 145.

to come if conventional explosives were employed. On May 22, NATO did escalate with conventional attacks on the power grid.[54] Nearly two months into the air campaign, the Serbs were openly admitting that the Serbian economy, already in difficulty from four years of sanctions, was facing severe hardship.[55]

## Why Did Allied Force Carry the Day?

Few would argue that Operation Allied Force should serve as a template for future conflicts in which air power is used independently to achieve a beneficial outcome. The title of Ivo Daalder and Michael O'Hanlon's book on the conflict, *Winning Ugly*, is an apt one. Clark reported that, days after Milosevic conceded and NATO had emerged victorious, a closed-door session of senior alliance military officials was held. One European Defense Minister offered that a fundamental lesson of the war was "we never want to do this again."[56] There was no laughter in response, and the minister in question did not expect any.

It is worth emphasizing the factors that contributed to the successful outcome. The main reason must be the continued and intensifying use of air power, as elaborated in the preceding section. The threat of intensified air strikes had been clearly and successfully communicated to Serb military commanders and military leaders. On May 31, the Serbian military headquarters issued a statement that "[the] NATO air force, intensifying its attacks from day to day, targeted numerous townships . . . . All this is being done systematically and uninterruptedly for 69 days with the clear intent to aggravate the humanitarian catastrophe to an intolerable level."[57]

Russia's decision to side with the West was the most significant diplomatic turning point of the war. For Milosevic, to have a great power and your staunchest defender decide to take the side of the enemy was a serious blow. Had Russian President Boris Yeltsin remained in the Serbs' corner, one could imagine Milosevic would have continued to hold out.

Yeltsin had significant incentives to continue to back Milosevic. Russia, with its fractious neighbors and concerns about NATO enlargement, had

[54] William M. Arkin, "Smart Bombs, Dumb Targeting?" *Bulletin of Atomic Scientists* (May–June 2000).
[55] Robert Block, "In Belgrade, Hardship Grows under Sustained Air Assault," *Wall Street Journal*, May 12, 1999.
[56] Clark, *Waging Modern War*, 417.
[57] Yugoslav Army Information Service, May 31, 1999. Cited in Stephen T. Hosmer, *Why Milosevic Decided to Settle When He Did* (Santa Monica: RAND, 2001), 98.

long been concerned about Western efforts to encroach on the Russian sphere of influence. Strobe Talbott, the Deputy Secretary of State and a long-time Russia expert, relates that there were rumors in Moscow that OAF was a "trial run for a future war when the Alliance would separate Chechnya from Russia."[58]

Tensions between the United States and Russia were high at times. Yeltsin requested a bombing pause from Clinton at one point, arguing that this would send a signal to Milosevic that the West was willing to give diplomacy another chance. Clinton refused, replying that NATO had laid out clear conditions as to what Serb actions would precipitate a pause in the bombing, and he did not think it would be prudent to undercut that Alliance policy. Yeltsin became angry: "Don't push Russia into this war! You know what Russia is! You know what it has at its disposal! Don't push Russia into this!"[59]

A meeting on June 2 between Milosevic, Russian envoy Viktor Chernomyrdin, and Finnish President Maarti Ahtisaari appears to have been critical in convincing Milosevic to make concessions.[60] The terms presented by Ahtisaari called for an end to violence in Kosovo, withdrawal of all Serb forces, and deployment under UN auspices of an effective international security presence. The terms expressly stated that these conditions took into "full account" the matter of Yugoslav sovereignty, offering the suggestion that there was no plan to make Kosovo fully independent.[61] Milosevic asked if there could be revisions and was told no because Chernomyrdin and Ahtisaari were simply present to "emphasize" the document.[62] Ahtisaari then stated that Chernomyrdin, who was sitting at the table, had agreed to these conditions. Milosevic had been presented with a reversal by his only ally on the most critical points of dispute between his government and NATO. The fact that the senior Russian envoy was in the room while Ahtisaari presented Milosevic with this change in Russian policy lent credibility to Ahtisaari's claims.

When a dismayed Milosevic asked, "Is this what I have to do to get the bombing stopped?" and both Ahtisaari and Chernomyrdin replied in the affirmative, the scope of Russia's change of heart was clear.

---

[58] Strobe Talbott, "Bill, Boris, and NATO," in Daniel S. Hamilton and Kristina Sphor, eds., *Open Door: NATO and Euro-Atlantic Security after the Cold War* (Washington, DC: Foreign Policy Institute, 2019), 421.

[59] Talbott, "Bill, Boris, and NATO," 422.

[60] Yeltsin signaled his unhappiness with Russia's lack of success in resolving the matter when he replaced Yevgeny Primakov with Viktor Chernomyrdin as his primary envoy. Haun, *Coercion, Survival, and War*, 124.

[61] Daalder and O'Hanlon, *Winning Ugly*, 173.

[62] Blaine Harden, "The Long Struggle that Led Serb Leader to Back Down," *New York Times*, June 6, 1999.

Chernomyrdin's perspective had changed considerably in just a few days since May 27, when he published an op-ed in the *Washington Post* titled "Impossible to Talk Peace with Bombs Falling."[63] Milosevic had lost his only meaningful ally, and the specter of heightened international isolation with no prospect of improvement on the horizon must have been daunting. Speaking after the war's conclusion, the Serbian Third Army Commander, General Nebojsa Pavkovoc, was candid about his dismay when the Russians turned and supported the Atlantic alliance's demands.

[T]he Russians then came back and said we had to accept the Western plan, that we had to take it or leave it. We were told that if we refused the plan, every city in Serbia would be razed to the ground. The bridges in Belgrade would be destroyed. The crops would all be burned. Everyone would die. Look at the Russians. They have not helped us.[64]

The degree to which Russia was worn down and weary of supporting Milosevic can be seen in the lopsided United Nations Security Council vote adopting UN Resolution 1244, signaling the formal acceptance of the outcome of the war by the international community.[65] The tally was fourteen in favor, none against, with one abstention – China. Russia, which had veto power, also had the option of abstaining in order to send a mild diplomatic signal that Moscow was displeased with the outcome but willing to allow it to go forward. The Russian vote for Resolution 1244 signaled how far President Boris Yeltsin had come in the direction of the West's position and how willing he was to seek even a disadvantageous end to the conflict. Talbott, who was as deeply involved in the negotiations over Kosovo as any American diplomat, credits the "crucial and courageous role of Yeltsin" with the outcome of the war over Kosovo.[66]

Another key reason the operation was successful is that the alliance held together. Although NATO did not emerge covered in glory, it survived its most significant trial by fire. Two years later, in a turn of events never imagined by the authors of the NATO charter, the alliance would come to the United States' defense in the aftermath of 9/11. In 1999, the alliance similarly found itself engaged in a military operation that those who had

---

[63] Viktor Chernomyrdin, "Impossible to Talk Peace with Bombs Falling," *Washington Post*, May 27, 1999.

[64] Chris Hedges, "Angry Serbs Hear a New Explanation: It's All Russia's Fault," *New York Times*, July 16, 1999.

[65] United Nations Press Release SC/6866, "Security Council, Welcoming Yugoslavia's Acceptance of Peace Principles, Authorizes Civil, Security Presence in Kosovo," June 10, 1999.

[66] Talbott, "Bill, Boris, and NATO," 423.

forged the alliance at the outset of the Cold War would not have expected
to be the alliance's first collective military operation.

One alliance member supported the air campaign in the face of great
domestic opposition. In Greece, there was tremendous criticism of the
operation, with most members of the Greek political opposition blaming
the United States and NATO for the conflict. At one point, according to
"one small but representative" poll, 96 percent of the Greek population
opposed the military operation – a remarkable amount of national unity
around a foreign policy.[67] And yet Greece continued to support the action
(though it did not participate), as the government of Prime Minister
Konstantinos Simitis decided it did not care to risk Greece's status in
NATO and so took the unpopular stand of supporting intervention. This
is a potent example of how international institutions can become binding
entities and at times alter states' foreign policies from what they might
have been otherwise. The fact that the alliance was committed to a low-
risk air campaign must have played a role in Athens' calculations.

Daalder and O'Hanlon offer a qualified but strong endorsement of
NATO's ability to remain unified in the face of unexpected difficulties
and internal stress.

Possessing nearly two-thirds of the world's economic strength and military might,
enough international credibility to wage war even without a UN Security Council
mandate, NATO had several fundamental advantages over an atavistic tin-pot
communist dictator .... The world's greatest alliance in history, described by
many as due to recede or dissolve after the demise of the Soviet Union, proved its
capabilities and its continued relevance in Kosovo.[68]

Luck also played a role, as usual in war, as a number of key turning
points could have gone differently and led to alternative outcomes. The
two key players involved in determining whether Serbia would give in to
NATO's demands – Yeltsin and Milosevic himself – could have chosen
alternative views of their interests and their best actions at a number of
important junctures. This is the key risk of coercive enterprises dependent
on the actions of others for success. To illustrate, two alternative and
viable outcomes are considered: the possibility of continued Russian
support for Milosevic and how Milosevic might have tested the alliance's
resolve in June.

Yeltsin's decision to endorse NATO's demands and present Serbia
with an ultimatum was a devastating blow for Milosevic, both psychologically and strategically. But Russia was never a sure bet to side with the

[67] Congressional Research Service, "Kosovo: International Reactions to NATO Air
Strikes," CRS Report for Congress (Library of Congress), RL30114, April 21, 1999, 4.
[68] Daalder and O'Hanlon, *Winning Ugly*, 181.

Western alliance. Yeltsin's personal relationship with Clinton had highs and lows, and Yeltsin was under significant pressure at home to respond more aggressively. Following a NATO summit in late April 1999, Yeltsin and Clinton spoke on the telephone. Yeltsin mentioned there were politicians in the Russian Duma and some military officers pressing for Russia to send naval vessels into the Mediterranean to show support for Serbia. He also claimed to have fired one military commander who had been looking for ways to secretly deploy a Russian battalion.

These could have been bargaining ploys, of course. But considering the angry Russian reaction at the outset of the conflict, it was never a certainty that Russia, even after prolonged NATO operations, would decide to switch sides. Yeltsin could have opted to watch the alliance struggle on and potentially fail, even if the Serbs suffered as a result. Such a decision could have altered the outcome of the conflict.

A second alternative outcome involves NATO's self-imposed and publicized deadline to begin planning for a ground operation. On multiple occasions, senior Western officials signaled that the alliance would have to make a decision on a ground campaign by mid-June in order to be ready to undertake offensive operations before the onset of the Balkan winter.[69] This suggests a missed opportunity for Milosevic: Given that the conflict concluded on June 10, if Milosevic had held out for one more week he could have had considerably greater insight into NATO's future intentions. It is also possible that the alliance would have had difficulty maintaining its consensus if it adopted a ground campaign.

Milosevic had waited out the Western coalition successfully on prior occasions. Part of the reason he precipitated conflict in the Balkans earlier in the decade was his cold observation that the allies had not responded meaningfully to the Serb sieges of Dubrovnik and Vukovar in 1991.[70] To be sure, OAF was a potent signal of NATO's political investment. But the stakes were higher for Milosevic as well, and he could have used the mid-June deadline to explore every opportunity to allow the alliance to fracture.

## Conclusion

NATO emerged victorious, having coerced the Serbian government in Belgrade to accept all five of the demands that the alliance had issued in

---

[69] Katherine Q. Seelye, "Clinton Resists Renewed Calls for Ground Troops in Kosovo," *New York Times*, May 19, 1999. Clark's memoir also suggests that mid-June was a significant decision point.

[70] David Halberstam, *War in a Time of Peace: Bush, Clinton, and the Generals* (New York: Scribner's, 2001), 129.

April while making only minor concessions to utilize UN instead of NATO peacekeepers and not stipulate a referendum on Kosovo's independence. A sustained and expanding campaign of air strikes, combined with tireless and hard-nosed diplomacy, had brought success to what had been NATO's most significant military confrontation to date. Yet despite this success, there was little celebration in Brussels or Washington. Instead, there was consensus that the West had lumbered into a campaign that had spun out of control and had found itself committed to achieving an outcome that it could not guarantee. The strategy of improvisation and escalation had worked, but no one was inclined to use it as a template for future confrontations. Admiral James Ellis, Commander of NATO Southern Forces and Clark's immediate deputy, offered a candid assessment in an unofficial briefing shortly after the war: "We got this one *absolutely* wrong."[71]

The haphazard nature of the conflict and the confessions of senior civilian and military leaders that they could not guarantee a successful outcome with air power alone highlight the risks inherent in employing strategies that depend for success on convincing the enemy to change course. Operation Allied Force, then, is another example of the need to assess the enemy's willingness to resist, and willingness to bear costs, when opting for a coercive strategy. Coercive efforts embrace a host of uncertainties, some of which are unique to coercive endeavors. Milosevic ably demonstrated this in 1999.

Kosovo is a unique case for this volume: A strategy involving air power alone led the target of the strategy to make a major political concession, that of conceding homeland territory. The experience of the 1999 war over Kosovo suggests there are two urgent questions a military planner or civilian official should ask before committing to the employment of air power. First, what opportunities does the enemy have to escalate the conflict? Milosevic promptly began forcing hundreds of thousands of Kosovar Albanians from their homes, and NATO found itself backed into a commitment. Second, and more importantly, does the strategy being considered depend on overcoming the willingness of the enemy to resist? If so, then the operation being considered may depend for success on a wide range of variables that will be difficult or even impossible to estimate. This would be particularly true for conflicts that involve significant political concessions, as opposed to lower-level conflicts that seek policy changes but no change of territorial control. Eliot Cohen describes air power as "the distinctly American form of military

---

[71] James O. Ellis, "A View from the Top," briefing slides, Summer 1999. Emphasis in original. Cited in Daalder and O'Hanlon, *Winning Ugly*, 104.

intimidation."[72] The promise of leveraging the United States' vast investment in air superiority to achieve a quick win will often be appealing in a crisis. But the allure of a low-cost victory must not blind the strategist to the spectrum of uncertainties that a purely coercive strategy will ineluctably embrace.

[72] Cohen, "The Mystique of US Air Power," 53.

# 5    Operation Enduring Freedom
## Evaluating the Effectiveness of Air Power over Afghanistan

*Nicholas Blanchette*

### Introduction

This chapter examines the use of air power during Operation Enduring Freedom (OEF), the US-led military response to the September 11th attacks. It focuses on the initial and major combat phase of military operations in Afghanistan from October 2001 through March 2002, analyzing how the various uses of air power during the campaign contributed to or inhibited the achievement of military and political objectives. After providing historical context for the conflict, its major actors, and the planning process that guided the coalition's air campaign (see Figures 5.1 and 5.2), the chapter critiques the effectiveness of air power in OEF, as well as considers the implications of the campaign for broader debates on contemporary air warfare.

Tasked with eliminating Al-Qaeda in Afghanistan, toppling the Taliban regime that had provided sanctuary for Osama bin Laden's organization, and creating the conditions for a new government in Kabul, air power undertook a major role. For many, the rapid battle-field victory achieved by coalition forces during OEF embodied a new American way of war, a concept adopted to capture the purported revolutionary technical and doctrinal innovations that allowed for the efficient delivery of precision air strikes, comprehensive intelligence, reconnaissance, and surveillance (ISR) support and closely coordinated Special Operations Forces (SOF) actions.[1] In OEF, Afghan forces conducted much of the ground combat, providing a template, an "Afghan model," for leveraging US military power cheaply and efficiently in asymmetric wars, relying on indigenous ground forces and

---

[1] Donald Rumsfeld, "Transforming the Military," *Foreign Affairs* 81:3 (May/June 2002); Max Boot, "The New American Way of War," *Foreign Affairs* 82:4 (July/August 2003); Thomas Ricks, "Bull's-Eye War: Pinpoint Bombing Shifts Role of GI Joe," *Washington Post*, December 2, 2001.

| Date | Key Events |
|------|-----------|
| 1988 | Al-Qaeda founded |
| August 7, 1998 | Al-Qaeda attacks US embassies in Tanzania and Kenya |
| August 20, 1998 | United States launches cruise missile attacks against Al-Qaeda camps in Afghanistan |
| October 12, 2000 | Al-Qaeda attacks USS *Cole* in Yemen |
| September 11, 2001 | Al-Qaeda launches coordinated attacks against the United States using hijacked passenger airliners |
| October 7, 2001 | Operation Enduring Freedom begins as US aircraft commence bombing against Taliban and Al-Qaeda targets in Afghanistan |
| October 19, 2001 | US special operators join local Afghan allies |
| November 9, 2001 | Mazar-i-Sharif falls to the Northern Alliance |
| November 26, 2001 | Northern Alliance fighters capture Kunduz |
| December 7, 2001 | Kandahar falls to Hamid Karzai's fighters in southern Afghanistan |
| December 17, 2001 | Fighting at Tora Bora ends with bin Laden escaping across the border into Pakistan |
| March 2–14, 2002 | Operation Anaconda in the Shah-i-Kot Valley |

Figure 5.1 Operation Enduring Freedom time line

the limited use of embedded special operators to shoulder ground combat responsibilities.[2]

Although the speed of the Taliban's collapse exceeded coalition expectations, air power over Afghanistan and the Afghan model did not produce uniformly effective results. At its most effective, US air power, when directed against Taliban and Al-Qaeda frontline forces with close coordination with embedded tactical air controllers and local Afghan allies, produced major breakthroughs in OEF and accelerated the Taliban's collapse. But when combined with less-skilled allied fighters against determined, dug-in foes, air power failed to achieve key military and political objectives, most critically resulting in the escape of bin Laden and Al-Qaeda members at Tora Bora. Against fixed targets and enemy leadership, air strikes produced similarly underwhelming results, unable to generate anticipated defections among or

[2] Richard Andres et al., "Winning with Allies: The Strategic Value of the Afghan Model," *International Security* 30:3 (Winter 2005/2006); Stephen Biddle, "Allies, Airpower, and Modern Warfare: The Afghan Model in Afghanistan and Iraq," *International Security* 30:3 (Winter 2005/2006).

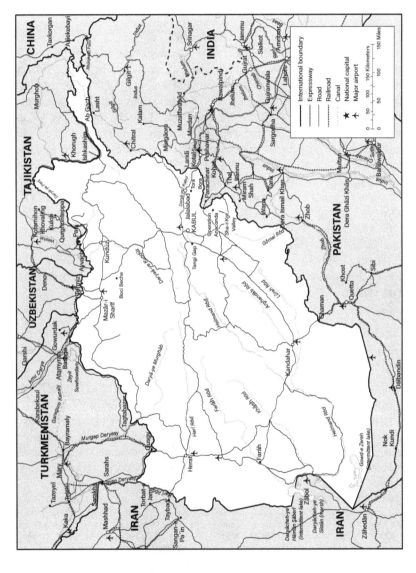

Figure 5.2  Map of Afghanistan

significantly undermine the fighting ability of the Taliban and Al-Qaeda. Further, the failure to achieve the campaign objective to capture or kill bin Laden and significant portions of Al-Qaeda leadership, as well as Taliban leadership, carried important implications for the post-conflict phase of operations in Afghanistan, sowing the seeds for the insurgency in Afghanistan that continue to grip the country.

Twenty years after the opening stage of military operations in Afghanistan, and with US forces having just departed Afghanistan, OEF provides important lessons on the efficacy of air power in contemporary conflicts. Like other air wars of the post–Cold War era, OEF reflected deep asymmetries in power, technology, and interests between the intervening state and its adversaries. Against the Taliban and Al-Qaeda, US air forces quickly achieved air superiority over Afghanistan, leveraging military and technological advantages to project power at great distance and quickly shifting the balance of power on the ground. Whereas US air forces enjoyed an asymmetric advantage in power and technology over the Taliban and Al-Qaeda, inverted asymmetries in interests influenced the course of OEF's air campaign, limiting the use of US ground forces and constraining the application of air power through restrictive rules of engagement. Although the campaign had unusually high levels of support within the United States, the imperative to limit the use of US ground forces nevertheless prevailed during and after the campaign, reflecting widening asymmetries in interest as the war in Afghanistan persisted deeper into the twenty-first century.

## Background

### Objectives and Plans

On September 11, 2001, hijackers crashed two planes into the World Trade Center in New York City and another into the Pentagon in Washington. The terror attacks killed nearly 3,000 people, marking the first major attack on the US homeland since Pearl Harbor.[3] US officials quickly concluded that the Al-Qaeda terrorist organization, which based its operations in Afghanistan, orchestrated the attacks.[4] Within days the George W. Bush

[3] Joseph Collins, "Initial Planning and Execution in Afghanistan and Iraq," in Richard Hooker and Joseph Collins, eds., *Lessons Encountered: Learning from the Long War* (Washington, DC: National Defense University Press, 2015), 21; National Commission on Terrorist Attacks upon the United States, *The 9/11 Commission Report: Final Report of the National Commission on Terrorist Attacks upon the United States* (New York: Norton & Company, 2004).

[4] Seth Jones, *In the Graveyard of Empires: America's War in Afghanistan* (New York: Norton, 2009), 87–88; Collins, "Initial Planning and Execution in Afghanistan and Iraq," 22.

administration planned a rapid and aggressive response against Al-Qaeda and the Taliban, Afghanistan's pro–Al-Qaeda regime that controlled most of Afghanistan, particularly after Taliban leadership refused to hand over bin Laden and close Al-Qaeda's training camps in Afghanistan.[5] The administration's planned military response received wide endorsement from the international community, Congress, and the American public.[6]

Though Al-Qaeda captured American attention during the 1990s following a series of high-profile terror attacks, "there were no plans on the shelf for either the war on terrorism or operations in Afghanistan."[7] Several factors complicated an effective military response. Afghanistan's remote, rugged, and landlocked geography prevented US port access, requiring aircraft and military supplies to either be flown in from a great distance or forward based.[8] The political landscape of Afghanistan, characterized more by ethnic divisions and rival warlords than centralized governance, erected further hurdles for US planners. Although weak Taliban governance and the tendency of Afghan militant groups to switch sides presented opportunities to bolster opposition groups and encourage Taliban defections, it also pressured the United States to foster a broad and diverse anti-Taliban coalition that could balance competing interests and ethnicities.[9] In practice, this requirement led to continuous debate over the relative pace and degree of US support for Northern Alliance forces and Pashtun anti-Taliban fighters in southern Afghanistan.[10]

To overcome the complications of waging war in Afghanistan, the United States required logistical and intelligence support from reluctant regional partners, adding a layer of complexity for US diplomats and military planners.[11] Similarly, backing from Islamic countries in the

---

[5] Ibid.; John Burns, "Taliban Refuse Quick Decision over Bin Laden," *New York Times*, September 18, 2001; "Taliban Again Refuses to Turn Over bin Laden," *New York Times*, October 2, 2001.

[6] US Office of the Press Secretary, "President Signs Authorization for Use of Military Force," *The White House*, September 18, 2001; "Invocation of Article 5 Confirmed," *NATO*, October 3, 2001; Eric Larson and Bogdan Savych, *American Public Support for US Military Operations from Mogadishu to Baghdad* (Santa Monica: RAND Corporation, 2005), 93.

[7] Walter Perry and David Kassing, *Toppling the Taliban: Air-Ground Operations in Afghanistan, October 2001–June 2002* (Santa Monica: RAND, 2015), 12.

[8] Milton Bearden, "Graveyard of Empires," *Foreign Affairs*, November 1, 2001; Donald Wright et al., *A Different Kind of War: The United States Army in Operation Enduring Freedom (OEF) October 2001–September 2005* (Fort Leavenworth: US Army Combined Arms Center, 2010), 4–14.

[9] Peter Baker, "After Taliban, a Power Vacuum?" *Washington Post*, October 7, 2001; Molly Moore and Kamran Khan, "Who Will Rule in Kabul?" *Washington Post*, October 5, 2001.

[10] Ibid.

[11] Eric Schmitt and Michael Gordon, "Top Air Chief Sent," *New York Times*, September 21, 2001.

region was viewed as necessary to reinforce the administration's effort to underline the war as one against terrorism rather than Islam.[12] However, concerns of domestic backlash against US military action in the region led several nations to either limit access to basing for military operations or constrain the types of air operations launched from regional air bases.[13] Both Pakistan and Uzbekistan prohibited the United States from staging combat air operations from their territory, for example, but allowed support missions and critical staging areas for US forces.[14] Saudi Arabia similarly prohibited combat operations but reluctantly allowed the United States to direct its combat air operations from the recently opened Combined Air Operations Center (CAOC) at Prince Sultan Air Base.[15] Though forward basing options improved during the first month of OEF, limited basing options for tactical aircraft led to a reliance on US bombers operating from thousands of miles away, such as bases from within the United States or from Diego Garcia in the Indian Ocean. Carrier-borne Navy strike aircraft also operated off the southern Pakistan coast. The strategy that emerged for OEF was a CIA-initiated military operation that emphasized speed of response and a light footprint rather than a conventional ground invasion. Embedded CIA teams and special operators supported local forces fighting the Taliban, while US air power sought targets of strategic value and, through coordination with embedded US joint tactical air controllers, provided air support for the ground offensive against the Taliban and Al-Qaeda.[16] Central to the operation was an effort to limit the use of US conventional ground forces. A light footprint approach held several advantages. First, it offered the most immediate military response, satisfying the political imperative to retaliate quickly and shift the Taliban and bin Laden onto a backfoot.[17] Second, it alleviated US concerns that a large military presence might spark local resistance as had occurred following the Soviet invasion of Afghanistan. And

---

[12] Henry Crumpton, *The Art of Intelligence: Lessons from a Life in the CIA's Clandestine Service* (New York: Penguin Press, 2012), 172.

[13] Bruce Pirnie et al., *Beyond Close Air Support: Forging a New Air-Ground Partnership* (Santa Monica: RAND, 2005), 50; Michael Gordon, "Gains and Limits in New Low-Risk War," *New York Times*, December 29, 2001.

[14] Rone Tempest, Tyler Marshall, and Robyn Dixon, "US Forces Deploy to Pakistan Bases; Warplanes Pound Kabul for 4th Day," *Los Angeles Times*, October 11, 2001.

[15] Michael Gordon, "Rumsfeld Meets Saudis and Says He's Satisfied with Level of Support," *New York Times*, October 4, 2001.

[16] Keith Shimko, *The Iraq Wars and America's Military Revolution* (New York: Cambridge University Press, 2010), 135; Steve Call, *Danger Close: Tactical Air Controllers in Afghanistan and Iraq* (College Station: Texas A&M University Press, 2007).

[17] Steve Coll, *Directorate S: The CIA and America's Secret Wars in Afghanistan and Pakistan* (New York: Penguin Press, 2018), 39; Crumpton, *The Art of Intelligence*, 178–81.

third, it limited losses of American forces, transferring the core risks of the ground campaign to allied Afghan forces.[18]

In identifying and prioritizing targets for the air campaign, planners focused on eliminating Taliban and Al-Qaeda leadership targets and military facilities, including training camps, command and control networks, and air defense systems. Securing the air domain from enemy aircraft and air defense threats represented the primary military objective for early aerial bombing, allowing coalition aircraft to operate freely over Afghanistan.[19] Early strikes against fixed military targets aimed to degrade the ability of Taliban fighters to easily communicate and resupply, paving the way for a sustained air-ground offensive later in the war.[20] Through targeting leadership, US officials sought to both sever the Taliban and Al-Qaeda's ability to centrally direct operations and to incentivize defections and concessions.[21] By aggressively and visibly striking targets associated with Taliban and Al-Qaeda leadership, US planners hoped that other leaders might be coerced to turn against Mullah Omar, the leader of the Taliban.[22]

Infrastructure targets were avoided for two reasons. First, US planners sought to mitigate collateral damage to facilitate a smoother transition to postwar reconstruction and to counter propaganda against US forces that would result from civilian casualties.[23] The United States desired the intervention be perceived as a fight against Al-Qaeda and their Taliban sponsors, rather than one against the Afghan people. Second, relative to Serbia and Iraq in the 1990s (see Chapters 4 and 6), an impoverished Afghanistan presented few infrastructure targets suitable for a punishment bombing campaign.[24] Reflecting these concerns, the US Air Force (USAF) also carried out humanitarian aid efforts, dropping supplies for Afghan civilians, and operating under strict rules of engagement.[25] Strikes involving sensitive targets or that carried political implications required approval from US Central Command (CENTCOM) officials or Washington.[26]

---

[18] Alexander Salt, "Transformation and the War in Afghanistan," *Strategic Studies Quarterly* 12:1 (Spring 2018): 106.
[19] Wright et al., *A Different Kind of War*, 64.    [20] Ibid.
[21] Tim Weiner and Michael Gordon, "Taliban Leader a Target of US Air Campaign," *New York Times*, October 16, 2001; Alan Sipress and Vernon Loeb, "CIA's Stealth War Centers on Eroding Taliban Loyalty and Aiding Opposition," *Washington Post*, October 10, 2001.
[22] Grenier, *88 Days to Kandahar*, 107.
[23] Pirnie et al., Beyond Close Air Support, 48–49.
[24] Ibid; The Editors, "Rules of Engagement," *Washington Post*, September 23, 2001.
[25] Perry and Kassing, *Toppling the Taliban*, 67.
[26] Benjamin Lambeth, *Air Power against Terror: America's Conduct of Operation Enduring Freedom* (Santa Monica: RAND Corporation, 2005), 311–24.

*Al-Qaeda and the Taliban*

Afghanistan possesses a long history of instability. A Soviet invasion compounded this turmoil in 1979, with the Soviet Union seeking to prop up the Marxist People's Democratic Party against an Islamic Afghan Mujahideen, which was in turn supported by the CIA and Pakistan's Inter-Services Intelligence.[27] Both Al-Qaeda and the Taliban emerged from this decade-long war.[28]

Osama bin Laden, the son of a wealthy Saudi family, founded Al-Qaeda in 1988 with the belief that the organization, a militant brotherhood without borders, could be used to target those oppressing Muslims across the world.[29] The group gained the attention of the US public on August 7, 1998, after Al-Qaeda detonated truck bombs simultaneously at US embassies in Tanzania and Kenya, killing 224.[30] Two weeks later, the Clinton administration retaliated with cruise missile strikes against Al-Qaeda training camps in Afghanistan and a pharmaceutical factory in Sudan.[31] The attacks did little to dent Al-Qaeda's ambitions, with the group attacking the USS *Cole* and killing seventeen sailors on October 12, 2000, while the ship anchored at Aden, Yemen.[32] At the time of the September 11 attacks, Al-Qaeda, supported by the Taliban regime and expanding its ranks with foreign fighters, operated numerous terrorist training camps in Afghanistan.[33]

In contrast to Al-Qaeda, the Taliban movement emerged from deep divisions among the Afghan Mujahideen in the aftermath of the Soviet-Afghan War.[34] A group of Islamist clerics and students predominantly of Pashtun origin, the Taliban adopted a strict interpretation of Islam and conservative social customs consistent with Pashtun tribal traditions.[35] After four years of civil war between rival Mujahideen groups, the Taliban eventually controlled Kabul by late 1996 but could not achieve stability or legitimacy across the country. Severe diplomatic isolation and economic sanctions from the international community due to its harboring Al-

[27] Bearden, "Graveyard of Empires."    [28] Ibid.
[29] US Library of Congress, Congressional Research Service, *Al Qaeda: Profile and Threat Assessment*, by Kenneth Katzman, RL33038 (2005), 1–3.
[30] Bearden, "Graveyard of Empires."
[31] "US Missiles Pound Targets in Afghanistan, Sudan," *CNN*, August 21, 1998.
[32] Anthony Cordesman, "The Ongoing Lessons of Afghanistan," *Center for Strategic and International Studies*, May 6, 2004, 11–12.
[33] Ahmed Rashid, *Descent into Chaos: The US and the Disaster in Pakistan, Afghanistan, and Central Asia* (New York: Penguin Books, 2008), 17.
[34] Bearden, "Graveyard of Empires."
[35] US Library of Congress, Congressional Research Service, *Afghanistan: Post-Taliban Governance, Security, and US Policy*, by Kenneth Katzman and Clayton Thomas, RL30588 (2017), 4.

Qaeda, an inability to consolidate power internally amid resistance from opposition groups, and draconian governance left the Taliban with weak control over Afghanistan.[36] Even so, by the fall of 2001, the Taliban controlled roughly 80–90 percent of Afghanistan and had between 40,000 and 50,000 fighters.[37]

The Taliban concentrated power in the Pashtun-majority region of southern Afghanistan. As a fighting force, Taliban members varied in terms of combat ability and levels of motivation. Some Afghan Taliban and aligned foreign fighters had combat experience and/or had received conventional training and understood the basics of ground operations. Others were unskilled seasonal fighters, fighting when agricultural calendars or family obligations allowed.[38] In addition, elite Al-Qaeda fighters, including 500 to 1,000 largely foreign fighters, comprised a motivated and more capable force supporting the Taliban forces.[39]

The Taliban's military arsenal consisted of rudimentary equipment, including modest numbers of Soviet T-55 and T-62 tanks, armored personnel carriers, and field artillery pieces left over from the Soviet-Afghan War.[40] The Taliban operated military aircraft and air defense systems, but these were far more limited in quality and quantity than the Iraqi and Serbian air defenses encountered by US air forces in previous air campaigns.[41] The Taliban's air force included a handful of MiG-21 fighters and Su-22 fighter bombers, as well as a limited inventory of transport aircraft and helicopters.[42] Though not a serious threat to US forces, the Taliban demonstrated a limited capacity to conduct air attacks against Afghan rivals. Taliban surface-to-air defenses were similarly weak. Beyond a handful of radar-guided SA-2 and SA-3 surface-to-air missile batteries defending major cities and hundreds of antiaircraft guns, the Taliban also operated man-portable air defense systems (MANPADS), including Stinger missile systems supplied to the Mujahideen by the United States in its fight against the Soviets.[43] The US-made Stinger, difficult to detect with its thermal guidance system, posed a danger to coalition helicopters and slower aircraft operating

---

[36] Wright, *A Different Kind of War*, 21–24; Zachary Laub, "The Taliban in Afghanistan," *Council on Foreign Relations*, July 4, 2014.

[37] Wright, ibid., 73.     [38] Biddle, "Allies, Airpower, and Modern Warfare," 167.

[39] Rory McCarthy, "The Elite Force Who Are Ready to Die," *The Guardian*, October 27, 2001.

[40] Anthony Schinella, *Bombs without Boots: The Limits of Airpower* (Brookings, 2019), 105; Molly Moore, "In the Taliban's Hands, an Old, Varied Arsenal," *Washington Post*, September 23, 2001; "Analysts Say Limited Weaponry, Forces Hamper Taliban," *CNN News*, October 3, 2001.

[41] Cordesman, "The Ongoing Lessons of Afghanistan," 16.

[42] Moore, "In the Taliban's Hands, an Old, Varied Arsenal."

[43] Michael Gordon, "Routine Start in Novel War," *New York Times*, October 8, 2001.

below 10,000 feet, a lethal capability that had been demonstrated by the Mujahideen against Soviet forces during the Soviet-Afghan War.[44]

### The US-Led Coalition

The anti-Taliban opposition in Afghanistan fell broadly into a northern and southern coalition. The United States had a ready, if loose, partnership with the Northern Alliance, comprised largely of Uzbek, Tajik, and Hazara ethnic minority groups long opposed to Taliban rule.[45] In 2001, the Northern Alliance fielded 12,000 to 15,000 fighters, supplemented by less formal militias throughout northern and central Afghanistan. Combat experienced, Northern Alliance commanders and veteran soldiers had fought during the Soviet-Afghan War and against Taliban forces in the years preceding OEF. Armed with only rudimentary light weapons, however, the Northern Alliance fighters lacked access to the heavier weapons and equipment employed by the Taliban.[46] On September 11 the Northern Alliance possessed only a limited amount of territory in the rugged region of northeastern Afghanistan, which its experienced fighters had been able to hold after several years of conflict against the Taliban.

Conversely, southern Afghanistan, the power base of the Taliban movement, had virtually no organized resistance.[47] This presented a challenge for US military leaders who, sensitive to Afghan ethnic and regional politics, sought a balanced coalition of Afghans to include Pashtun fighters from southern and western Afghanistan.[48] Forces led by Hamid Karzai and Gul Agha Shirzai, both Pashtun anti-Taliban leaders from the Kandahar region, formed the basis of a Southern Alliance. The fighters available to Karzai and Shirzai, less numerous, organized, or combat experienced compared to their Northern Alliance counterparts, further lacked operational expertise and depended heavily upon US support.[49] Balancing and sequencing the level of support for the northern and southern anti-Taliban resistance groups proved to be a challenge for the United States since too much support for the more capable Northern Alliance, primarily comprised of ethnic minority

---

[44] Joseph Fitchett, "What about the Taliban's Stingers?" *New York Times*, September 26, 2001.
[45] Wright, *A Different Kind of War*, 72–73.    [46] Schinella, *Bombs without Boots*, 108–09.
[47] Pirnie et al., *Beyond Close Air Support*, 52–53.
[48] Wright, *A Different Kind of War*, 93–95; Molly Moore and Kamran Khan, "Who Will Rule in Kabul?" *Washington Post*, October 5, 2001.
[49] Schinella, *Bombs without Boots*, 113.

groups, risked encouraging the Pashtun population to coalesce around the Taliban.[50]

US allies, with the exception of the United Kingdom, played a minor role during the first months of OEF. US concern that a larger coalition might complicate campaign planning and operations as it had in Kosovo, as well as the broader imperative for US forces to respond quickly, limited the willingness of the United States to directly involve its allies, particularly those from the North Atlantic Treaty Organization.[51] US allies gradually introduced air and ground forces to Afghanistan in late 2001 and 2002, as the United States sought to internationalize its coalition following criticism of the campaign, while other nations provided logistical and humanitarian support. After OEF the United States further shifted responsibilities to allies in Afghanistan as the United States prepared to invade Iraq.

### The Air Campaign: The Fall of the Taliban and the Search for Bin Laden

Operation Enduring Freedom's air campaign began on the evening of October 7 when US air forces bombed Taliban and Al-Qaeda positions across Afghanistan.[52] The first strikes were carried out by US Navy carrier strike aircraft, USAF bombers, and cruise missiles.[53] The objective of the initial strikes was to establish air superiority over Afghanistan by destroying the Taliban's limited air force and air defense capability. Even though pilots reported limited antiaircraft fire, US strike aircraft flew above the threat by enemy ground fire to ensure against combat losses.[54] Air superiority was achieved at the outset of the first night of the campaign, with air force leaders so confident in their ability to operate freely within Afghan airspace that USAF C-17s flying from Germany dropped food and medical supplies within an hour of the first bomb release.[55]

[50] Grenier, *88 Days to Kandahar*, 107.   [51] Perry and Kassing, *Toppling the Taliban*, 14.
[52] "Afghanistan Wakes after Night of Intense Bombings," *CNN*, October 7, 2001; Department of Defense, "DoD News Briefing – Secretary Rumsfeld and Gen. Myers," October 8, 2001.
[53] Five B-1B and ten B-52 bombers launched from Diego Garcia in the Indian Ocean, while twenty-five F-14 and F-18 aircraft operated from the aircraft carriers USS *Carl Vinson* and USS *Enterprise* in the North Arabian Sea. In addition, two B-2 bombers flew directly from Whiteman AFB, Missouri, while fifty Tomahawk Land Attack Missiles were fired by US and British ships and submarines. Dan Balz, "US, Britain Launch Airstrikes against Targets in Afghanistan," *Washington Post*, October 8, 2001.
[54] Department of Defense, "DoD News Briefing – Secretary Rumsfeld and Gen. Myers," October 9, 2001; Steve Vogel, "They Said No. This Is Our Answer; Carrier Pilots, Crew Describe Challenges of Afghan Mission," *Washington Post*, October 8, 2001.
[55] Patrick Tyler, "A Nation Challenged: The Attack; US and Britain Strike Afghanistan, Aiming at Bases and Terrorist Camps; Bush Warns 'Taliban Will Pay a Price,'" *New York Times*, October 8, 2001; Lt. Gen. David Deptula, interview by author, June 23, 2020.

Other targets during the initial strikes included the Taliban's leadership, communication networks, military facilities, and Scud launchers.[56] In the first night, 31 targets were struck with initial battle damage assessments reporting 85 percent damaged or destroyed.[57] Air strikes continued throughout the first week of OEF at varied intensity, reflecting a paucity of fixed targets with any strategic value. During the second day of bombing, fewer aircraft were committed with only thirteen targets serviced.[58] However, the third day produced heavier bombing, with targets struck in Kabul, Kandahar, and Herat, with the USAF utilizing bunker-busting munitions for the first time against suspected leadership targets.[59] Air strikes during the first week also targeted mountain cave complexes believed to be harboring Al-Qaeda leadership.

Despite destroyed targets and the quick achievement of air superiority over Afghanistan, these early efforts produced limited effects against the Taliban and Al-Qaeda. The impact of initial strikes against fixed targets was largely blunted by the Taliban and Al-Qaeda's abandonment of its facilities and the dispersal of its forces and supplies.[60] Air strikes directed against Taliban and Al-Qaeda leadership proved similarly fruitless as many leaders went into hiding well before the first bombs fell.[61] The United States also missed an opportunity to kill Mullah Omar, the leader of the Taliban, on the opening night of the air campaign after an armed Predator identified him in his compound in Kandahar but instead struck a nearby vehicle (see Chapter 2).[62] Few fixed targets of strategic value, targeting indecision, and countermeasures pursued by the Taliban and Al-Qaeda largely limited the anticipated effectiveness of independent air strikes and defections among Taliban ranks in the opening stage of OEF.[63] Further, in southern Afghanistan, little progress was made

[56] Molly Moore, "In the Taliban's Hands, an Old, Varied Arsenal," *Washington Post*, September 23, 2001; Michael Hirsh and John Barry, "Behind America's Attack on Afghanistan," *Newsweek*, October 7, 2001.
[57] Lambeth, *Air Power against Terror*, 88.
[58] Clyde Haberman, "A Scaling Back, Anger in the Streets and American Determination," *New York Times*, October 9, 2001; Lambeth, ibid.
[59] Department of Defense, "DoD News Briefing – ASD PA Clarke and Maj. Gen. Osman," October 11, 2001.
[60] Judith Miller, "The Damage: Pentagon Says Bombs Destroy Terror Camps," *New York Times*, October 10, 2001; Peter Baker, "Rulers' Key Defenses Crippled, Say Rebels, Whose Gains Are Few," *Washington Post*, October 9, 2001.
[61] Vernon Loeb and Thomas Ricks, "Bin Laden's Location Sketchy; US Gets Conflicting Intelligence Reports," *Washington Post*, September 30, 2001.
[62] Richard Whittle, "How We Missed Mullah Omar," *Politico*, September 16, 2014.
[63] Robert Pape, "The Wrong Battle Plan," *Washington Post*, October 19, 2001; John Mearsheimer, "Guns Won't Win the Afghan War," *New York Times*, November 4, 2001; Peter Baker, "Growing Impatient with US, Rebels Plan Attack on Kabul," *Washington Post*, October 14, 2001.

toward building a Pashtun anti-Taliban opposition, leading some to question the viability of the US strategy along with the reticence to support directly Northern Alliance fighters against Taliban frontlines.[64]

The air campaign shifted from fixed to emerging targets of opportunity at the end of the second week of OEF.[65] Pilots began to pursue Taliban and Al-Qaeda targets identified within designated engagement zones, a concept reminiscent of the kill boxes employed in Desert Storm and used thereafter in Iraq and Kosovo. Aircrew exercised discretion to attack emerging targets within an engagement zone, though they still required target approval before conducting air strikes.[66] More significantly, a shift toward targeting of frontline Taliban forces was coupled with the deployment of US special operators and joint terminal attack controllers (JTACs) within Afghan ally armies on October 19.[67] This critical campaign development allowed coalition forces to target enemy positions from the ground and coordinate the safe movement of partner ground forces during the combined air-ground offensive.[68] Although progress remained slow against the Taliban in the south, the introduction of special operators to fight alongside the Northern Alliance accelerated air strikes against frontline Taliban units in northern Afghanistan.[69]

Even with the insertion of special operators and the air campaign's transition to targeting fielded forces, progress against Taliban and Al-Qaeda frontlines remained fleeting throughout October. On the ground, Afghan allies failed to secure lasting victories against dogged Taliban resistance, while air strikes had not produced breakthroughs or defections among Taliban fighters.[70] In the south, Karzai continued to struggle to gain a foothold against Taliban forces, requiring frequent US intervention to avert military disaster and eventually orchestrate an evacuation in early November after successive defeats.[71] For some US commentators, the sclerotic pace of the bombing campaign could be blamed on the low

---

[64] Michael Gordon, "Fast Track, Slow Track," *New York Times*, October 15, 2001.

[65] James Fallows, "Behavior Modification," *The Atlantic*, April 2002.

[66] Lambeth, *Air Power against Terror*, 93; Department of Defense, "DoD News Briefing – ASD PA Clarke and Rear Adm. Stufflebeem," October 17, 2001.

[67] Department of Defense, "DoD News Briefing – Gen. Myers," October 20, 2001.

[68] "US Sends in Special Forces," *The Telegraph*, October 19, 2001; Vernon Loeb and Thomas Ricks, "Special Forces Open Ground Campaign; Small Numbers Are Said to Be Operating to Aid CIA Effort in Southern Afghanistan," *Washington Post*, October 19, 2001.

[69] Alan Sipress and Bradley Graham, "Rebels to Advance on Kabul Soon; Allies Reportedly Bombing Near Taliban Front Lines," *New York Times*, October 22, 2001.

[70] R. W. Apple, "Military Quagmire Remembered: Afghanistan as Vietnam," *New York Times*, October 31, 2001; Molly Moore and Kamran Khan, "Strategy Fails to Splinter Taliban; US, Pakistani Efforts Not Yielding Significant Defections," *Washington Post*, October 26, 2001.

[71] Schinella, *Bombs without Boots*, 142; Grenier, *88 Days to Kandahar*, 202–03.

number of valuable targets for aerial bombing, a tool best employed against industrialized and target-rich societies. In Afghanistan the unskilled Afghan allies allowed Taliban and Al-Qaeda fighters to dig-in against air strikes and repel poorly coordinated ground attacks.[72] Others argued against a restrained US military strategy, calling for the introduction of US ground forces and lifting restrictions on air strikes in support of the Northern Alliance.[73] Domestic and international criticism also increased as reports of civilian casualties mounted. US officials confirmed several collateral damage incidents, and the Taliban readily exploited and exaggerated these reports in an attempt to undermine the war effort.[74] On the ground, Northern Alliance commanders, underwhelmed by American air power, criticized the air strikes as ineffective pinpricks.[75] Other Northern Alliance fighters argued air strikes actually helped the Taliban, improving morale by demonstrating their ability to withstand air attacks.[76]

But despite these criticisms and slow initial progress, air-ground operations between the Northern Alliance and US air forces improved as special operators established stronger relationships with Afghan commanders and began operating at the frontlines.[77] With growing trust between Afghan allies and special operators, JTACs more effectively controlled air strikes while mitigating the risk of friendly fire.[78] As a result, the number of US strike sorties and percentage of missions dedicated to directly supporting the Northern Alliance saw an uptick at the end of October.[79] These factors proved critical during the Northern Alliance's subsequent campaign to take Mazar-i-Sharif.

[72] Mearsheimer, "Guns Won't Win the Afghan War"; Patricia Cohen, "Getting It Right: Strategy Angst," *New York Times*, October 27, 2001.

[73] Charles Krauthammer, "Wars of Choice, Wars of Necessity," *Time*, October 28, 2001; Apple, "Military Quagmire Remembered"; Robert Kagan and William Kristol, "The Gathering Storm," *The Weekly Standard*, October 29, 2001; William Branigin, "US Planes Bomb Taliban Front Lines; Strategy Aims to Help Rebels Advance, but Strikes Remain Limited," *Washington Post*, October 23, 2001.

[74] Ewan MacAskill, Michael White, and Luke Harding, "Bombs Go Astray, the Casualties Mount ... and the Doubts Set In," *The Guardian*, October 29, 2001; Edward Cody, "Taliban Claims Large Civilian Casualties; Afghan Rulers Increase Efforts to Win Support from Islamic World," *Washington Post*, October 12, 2001.

[75] Alan Philps and Michael Smith, "B-52 Carpet Bombing 'Can Oust Taliban,'" *Telegraph*, November 1, 2001; William Branigin and Sharon Lafraniere, "Anti-Taliban Forces Get US Assistance; Opposition in Key City Describes Limited Aid," *Washington Post*, October 20, 2001.

[76] David Rohde, "Anti-Taliban Forces Say Light US Strikes Lift Foes' Morale," *New York Times*, October 26, 2001; Gary Schroen, *First In: An Insider's Account of How the CIA Spearheaded the War on Terror in Afghanistan* (New York: Presidio Press, 2006), 160–62.

[77] David Rohde, "Sight of a B-52 Makes Northern Alliance Troops Shout with Joy," *New York Times*, November 1, 2001.

[78] Call, *Danger Close*, 16.    [79] Schinella, *Bombs without Boots*, 132.

During the first week of November, after intense bombing around the city of Mazar-i-Sharif, Northern Alliance fighters began dislodging Taliban forces in a series of engagements that opened a path to the city.[80] On November 5, Northern Alliance General Abdul Rashid Dostum's forces overran Taliban and Al-Qaeda forces at Bai Beche in a key engagement. Dug-in Taliban and Al-Qaeda fighters in the village utilized Soviet-era defensive positions that tested both Dostum's fighters and US air power. When Dostum's horseback cavalry withdrew after a failed charge against the enemy's defensive lines, US special operators called for further air strikes. Misinterpreting a warning regarding the forthcoming air strikes, Dostum again ordered a charge of the Taliban and Al-Qaeda positions just as bombs fell on Bai Beche. Though special operators feared a major friendly fire incident, Dostum and his fighters charged through enemy lines just after the bombs exploded, emerging through the smoke to encircle and rout the shocked defenders.[81]

This fortuitous outcome demonstrated the benefits and pitfalls of the Afghan model. At the model's best, well-timed and coordinated air and ground attacks between US air forces and local Afghan allies could force breakthroughs against entrenched Taliban defenders. While dug-in and pinned down by US air power, the Taliban were left vulnerable to ground attack from mobile Northern Alliance forces. At the model's worst, difficulty coordinating air operations with the movement of Afghan allies risked major friendly fire incidents and threatened to undermine the air-ground effort.

Tajik and Hazara forces won similar victories around Mazar-i-Sharif, joining up with Dostum on November 8 at the outskirts of the city. The next day B-52 strikes created a breakthrough at the Tangi gap, a natural gateway into the city where Taliban fighters massed to repel the Northern Alliance offensive.[82] With the path to Mazar-i-Sharif open, Northern Alliance forces swept through the city, meeting little resistance. The capture of Mazar-i-Sharif marked the first major victory for the coalition forces and a critical turning point in the war. The defeat significantly undermined the Taliban's position in Northern Afghanistan and set the stage for successive losses at Kabul and Kunduz.[83] In the Mazar-i-Sharif campaign, 15,000 Northern Alliance fighters, supported by US air power

[80] "B-52 Jets Attack Taliban Positions," *The Guardian*, November 1, 2001; Schroen, *First In*, 311–12.
[81] Biddle, *Afghanistan and the Future of Warfare: Implications for Army and Defense Policy* (Carlisle: Strategic Studies Institute, 2002), 38–39.
[82] Wright et al., *A Different Kind of War*, 78–79.
[83] Perry and Kassing, *Toppling the Taliban*, 48; Steven Morris and Ewan MacAskill, "Collapse of the Taliban," *The Guardian*, November 17, 2001.

controlled by SOF JTACS, defeated a numerically superior Taliban force. The timing of the operation and location of the city proved significant. With winter approaching, the defeat at Mazar-i-Sharif forced the Taliban into the mountains, further cut off from supply lines. The city itself carried important benefits as it offered a "land bridge ... to Uzbekistan, [providing] a humanitarian pathway to move supplies ... into Afghanistan."[84] Most importantly, the battle triggered a wave of defections and desertions, depleting the Taliban of much-needed troops as the coalition advanced.[85]

Within days of the fall of Mazar-i-Sharif, Northern Alliance forces captured Herat and Kabul, the Afghan capital. Indeed, the pace of the Northern Alliance's advance led US officials to delay preparations to attack Kabul to allow time for greater involvement from anti-Taliban Pashtun fighters. The United States feared that Pashtuns might coalesce around the Taliban should the Northern Alliance take the Afghan capital.[86] The heavy bombing of massed Taliban and Al-Qaeda front-line units again opened the approach to Kabul for allied Afghan fighters, while defections within the Taliban ranks along with a hasty retreat by the Taliban and Al-Qaeda toward strongholds at Kandahar and Tora Bora, respectively, led to an easy victory for Afghan allied forces. Though the Taliban continued to fight hard at Kunduz and Kandahar, the Northern Alliance soon captured Kunduz on November 26, and Karzai's forces, after several weeks of close calls and significant US air support, captured Kandahar on December 7, marking the formal end of Taliban rule.[87]

As Kandahar fell, US and Afghan forces engaged Al-Qaeda fighters in the mountainous terrain of Tora Bora, which contained a series of cave complexes that offered Al-Qaeda militants the option to dig in or escape into bordering Pakistan.[88] Al-Qaeda leadership, thought to be in the mountains at the time, fled from Jalalabad toward the border, presenting the United States a crucial window of opportunity to capture or kill bin Laden before he escaped.[89]

---

[84] "Why Mazar-e Sharif Matters," *CNN*, November 10, 2001.
[85] Lambeth, *Air Power against Terror*, 132; Department of Defense, "DoD News Briefing – Secretary Rumsfeld and Gen. Myers," November 13, 2001.
[86] Schinella, *Bombs without Boots*, 137.
[87] "Konduz Falls to Northern Alliance," *CNN*, November 26, 2001; Department of Defense, "DoD News Briefing – Deputy Secretary Wolfowitz and Rear Adm. Stufflebeem," December 10, 2001.
[88] Benjamin Runkle, "Tora Bora Reconsidered: Lessons from 125 Years of Strategic Manhunts," *Joint Force Quarterly* 70 (July 2013): 41.
[89] Ibid.

At Tora Bora, only a few US special forces fought alongside 2,500 local Afghan fighters hastily recruited for the operation. Unlike other Afghans who had fought with US forces in earlier battles, the allied fighters at Tora Bora, comprised of soldiers aligned with three different warlords, were unmotivated to fight against Al-Qaeda and less capable than those in the Northern Alliance.[90] With this patched-together army, US aircraft bombed the cave complexes of Tora Bora throughout the battle, conducting up to 100 close air support missions a day and delivering 1,000 precision munitions and a 15,000lb BLU-82 bomb.[91] Despite the sustained bombing, motivated and well-trained Al-Qaeda forces at Tora Bora took advantage of the rough terrain and prepared defenses, maintaining their positions against local Afghan fighters for several weeks. Fighting ended on December 17 after defenders in the last cave complex had been overrun. Despite the battlefield victory, bin Laden and many of his associates had escaped across the border into Pakistan. Neither the local Afghan nor Pakistani militias tasked with blocking bin Laden's escape succeeded. In fact, bribed militias at the border assisted bin Laden's escape.[92]

With the collapse of the Taliban regime and Al-Qaeda's withdrawal to the mountains bordering Afghanistan and Pakistan, coalition objectives shifted to the more difficult and ambitious undertaking of supporting the new Afghan government in its effort to consolidate control throughout Afghanistan. Following the Battle of Tora Bora, nine weeks of continuous combat operations ended, with the coalition transitioning to a concurrent counterterrorism and reconstruction strategy that marked a new phase in the war.[93]

**Operation Anaconda**

In early March 2002, the coalition identified an opportunity to eliminate resurgent Taliban and Al-Qaeda forces after US intelligence indicated enemy fighters regrouping in the Shah-i-Kot Valley in Eastern Afghanistan.[94] The resulting effort, Operation Anaconda, marked the first large-scale involvement of US conventional ground forces.

---

[90] Peter Krause, "The Last Good Chance: A Reassessment of US Operations at Tora Bora," *Security Studies* 17 (2008): 649.

[91] The massive BLU-82 was designed to clear terrain and maximize enemy casualties with its large overpressure effects. US Senate Committee on Foreign Relations, *Tora Bora Revisited: How We Failed to Get Bin Laden and Why It Matters Today* (Washington, DC: Government Printing Office, 2009), 2–7; Krause, "The Last Good Chance," 650.

[92] Krause, "The Last Good Chance," 652.

[93] "Operation Anaconda: An Air Power Perspective," *Headquarters United States Air Force*, February 7, 2005, 17–18.

[94] Ibid., 19–23.

The operation began on March 2 with the insertion of combat teams comprising US ground forces and local Afghan allies in blocking positions to prevent the escape of enemy forces.[95] As it turned out, intelligence reports underestimated the strength and preparedness of Taliban and Al-Qaeda fighters in the Shah-i-Kot Valley. Post-battle assessments indicated that, instead of the 150–200 enemy fighters expected in the area, there were as many as 1,000 militants.[96] Inserted coalition troops quickly became pinned down by enemy small arms and mortar fire.[97] Unreliable local allies again undermined coalition efforts, with Afghan proxies abandoning the battlefield early in the fight and leaving US ground forces vulnerable to attack.[98] Compounding the unraveling situation facing US ground forces, Apache helicopters attempting to provide close air support received heavy fire and were forced to withdraw.[99] Lacking rotary-wing fire support against a stronger-than-expected foe, US ground forces turned to US air forces to relieve pressure on ground units and then dislodge Taliban and Al-Qaeda forces from the valley.

The sudden demand for air support from air controllers and the hastily organized air operation led to problems managing the high volume of fixed-wing strike sorties within an extremely restricted airspace, with several close calls occurring in the sky above the Shah-i-Kot Valley.[100] During the first 3 days of the battle, US aircraft dropped 751 bombs day and night, with 674 of the munitions dropped with troops in contact.[101] The confusion facing the air component with its last-minute addition into the operation along with congestion over the battlefield combined to create challenging circumstances for fielding multiple CAS requests. US air forces nevertheless managed to fly an average of 60 sorties per day, delivering some 3,500 munitions during the 12 days of battle.[102] As the heavy and persistent air support improved in efficiency and effectiveness, coalition forces eventually turned the tide against Taliban and Al-Qaeda forces, with air strikes accounting for the majority of enemy casualties during Operation Anaconda.[103]

---

[95] Perry and Kassing, *Toppling the Taliban*, 99–100.

[96] "Operation Anaconda: An Air Power Perspective," 28, 66; Sean Naylor, "The Lessons of Anaconda," *New York Times*, March 2, 2003; Paul Hastert, "Operation Anaconda: Perception Meets Reality in the Hills of Afghanistan," *Studies in Conflict & Terrorism* 28:1 (January–February 2005).

[97] Biddle, "Afghanistan and the Future of Warfare," 14; Vernon Loeb, "General Defends Tactics in Afghan Battle; Commander Denies Al Qaeda Fighters Escaped into Pakistan, Says Hundreds Killed," *Washington Post*, March 12, 2003.

[98] Lambeth, *Air Power against Terror*, 179–80.

[99] Perry and Kassing, *Toppling the Taliban*, 101–02.

[100] "Operation Anaconda: An Air Power Perspective," 80.    [101] Ibid.    [102] Ibid., 101.

[103] Lambeth, *Air Power against Terror*, 199.

Coalition forces ultimately met Operation Anaconda's core objective to attrit Taliban and Al-Qaeda fighters in the Shah-i-Kot Valley, killing up to 800 enemy fighters.[104] However, poor planning and coordination of joint operations in the valley undermined coalition efforts, risking a major debacle and triggering interservice debate over whether the air or land component should shoulder the blame for Operation Anaconda's shortcomings.[105] In a late-2002 interview with *Field Artillery* assessing Operation Anaconda, Army Major General Franklin Hagenbeck, the operation's joint force commander, criticized the Air Force and the limits of its precision bombing and ISR assets.[106] For Hagenbeck, fixed-wing aircraft provided limited support to US ground forces during the battle, with the Air Force particularly encumbered by the slow delivery of weapons and processing of close air support requests.[107] He further suggested that Air Force assets were overly timid in their provision of close air support in comparison to Navy and Marine aircraft and limited in their effectiveness largely to attacks on fixed targets, favorably highlighting instead the fire support of Army rotary aircraft and mortars.[108]

Air Force officials, for their part, challenged both Hagenbeck's account of air support during Operation Anaconda and the manner in which its broader planning process was conducted.[109] In particular, Air Force officials high-lighted that planning for Operation Anaconda, nominally a joint operation, was carried out solely by Army officials with insufficient coordination with the air component.[110] Indeed, Combined Joint Task Force (CJTF) Mountain only included Army officers in its organizational structure and did little in the run-up to Operation Anaconda to integrate the air component into the planning for the operation.[111] Air Force planners were left out of the loop of the planning process, with the air component caught by "total surprise" when they learned of the impending operation just days before it was set to

---

[104] Eric Schmitt and Thom Shanker, "Body Count; Taliban and Qaeda Death Toll in Mountain Battle Is a Mystery," *New York Times*, March 14, 2002; Lester Grau and Dodge Billingsley, *Operation Anaconda: America's First Major Battle in Afghanistan* (Lawrence: Kansas University Press, 2011), 344.

[105] Robert McElroy, "Afghanistan: Fire Support for Operation Anaconda," *Field Artillery* (September–October 2002); Richard Andres and Jeffrey Hukill, "Anaconda: A Flawed Joint Planning Process," *Joint Force Quarterly* 47 (January 2007).

[106] Vernon Loeb, "General Defends Tactics in Afghan Battle," *Washington Post*, March 12, 2003; Elaine Grossman, "Army General Cites Lapses in Afghanistan Air Support: Left in Dark for Most of Anaconda Planning, Air Force Opens New Probe," *Inside Defense*, October 7, 2002. McElroy, "Afghanistan: Fire Support for Operation Anaconda."

[107] McElroy, "Afghanistan: Fire Support for Operation Anaconda."       [108] Ibid.

[109] Elaine Grossman, "Left in the Dark for Most Anaconda Planning, Air Force Opens New Probe," *Inside the Pentagon*, October 3, 2002.

[110] Perry and Kassing, *Toppling the Taliban*, 99.

[111] Lambeth, *Air Power against Terror*, 168–69; Lt. Gen. David Deptula, interview by author, June 23, 2020.

commence.[112] The flawed joint planning of Operation Anaconda would contribute to several of the battle's core challenges, including poor use and coordination of ISR to prepare the battlefield beforehand, limited tactical coordination between the land and air component for the effective application of close air support, and difficulties in managing and deconflicting an influx of requests for air support.[113] Although Hagenbeck would later retract his critiques, the episode nevertheless highlighted interservice differences in the understanding and application of contemporary air power.[114] More critically, Operation Anaconda further underlined the need for conducting closely integrated joint planning in contemporary security environments.

## Air Power over Afghanistan: A Retrospective

Air power played a central role throughout OEF, shifting the balance of power on the ground in Afghanistan. During the course of the war, the US-led coalition killed an estimated 8,000 to 12,000 Taliban and Al-Qaeda militants, representing roughly 20 percent of their fighting strength.[115] In total, pilots flew 6,500 strike sorties and delivered 22,000 munitions.[116] The air campaign represented further refinement in American use and reliance upon precision weapons, which represented 60 percent of expended munitions.[117] Civilian casualties remain difficult to verify, but it is generally estimated that 1,000 civilian Afghans lost their lives in US air strikes, a figure higher than air campaigns in Bosnia and Kosovo.[118]

Overall, OEF proved an incomplete success. Although the coalition's combined air-ground campaign accomplished a central political objective by removing the Taliban regime from power faster than anticipated, it was only partially effective against Al-Qaeda militants, with bin Laden and Al-Qaeda remnants escaping into Pakistan, sowing the seeds for future instability in the region.[119] In many respects, air power proved a vital tool during OEF, allowing the United States to mount a rapid,

---

[112] Ibid., 171; Andres and Hukill, "Anaconda: A Flawed Joint Planning Process."

[113] Andres and Hukill, "Anaconda: A Flawed Joint Planning Process," 137–39.

[114] Grau and Billingsley, *Operation Anaconda*, 343–59; Elaine Grossman, "Anaconda: Object Lesson in Ill Planning or Triumph of Improvisation?" *Inside the Pentagon* 20:34 (2004): 18–28.

[115] O'Hanlon, "A Flawed Masterpiece."

[116] Perry and Kassing, *Toppling the Taliban*, 46–47.

[117] Lambeth, *Air Power against Terror*, 252.

[118] O'Hanlon, "A Flawed Masterpiece"; Carl Conetta, "Operation Enduring Freedom: Why a Higher Rate of Civilian Bombing Casualties," *Project on Defense Alternatives*, January 24, 2002.

[119] Krause, "The Last Good Chance"; US Senate Committee on Foreign Relations, *Tora Bora Revisited*.

technologically sophisticated military response at great distance, with little prior planning or commitment of ground forces. Air power further bridged tremendous logistical gaps for US forces operating in Afghanistan. Yet, importantly, the US air campaign over Afghanistan also encountered stumbling blocks: Air strikes against fixed Taliban and Al-Qaeda targets often produced disappointing results; and in support of the air-ground offensive, the effectiveness of air strikes depended upon the ability of ground forces to capitalize upon the advantages it conferred against Taliban and Al-Qaeda forces.

### Collateral Damage and Rules of Engagement

Beyond questions over the efficacy of competing approaches to the application of air power, OEF's air campaign informs ongoing debates concerning rules of engagement, precision warfare, and efforts to limit civilian casualties. Throughout the planning and execution of OEF's air campaign, the mitigation of collateral damage played an important political and military role for US officials in an effort to limit the degree to which Afghan civilians united around the Taliban regime and ensure continued support from Islamic partner nations in the longer-term fight against terrorism. Indeed, General Tommy Franks and CENTCOM maintained tight control over the use of air power and its targeting process throughout the eleven-week air campaign.[120] Though this target approval process loosened somewhat during the course of the air campaign, particularly as aircraft focused on frontline targets and struck targets within designated engagement zones and in coordination with JTACs, air strikes that risked civilian casualties still required stringent and centralized approval from CENTCOM.[121]

This command and control dynamic between CENTCOM and the CAOC proved a source of frustration for those operating in the air component for several reasons. First, the target-vetting process that accompanied the air campaign's strict rules of engagement was viewed by air planners as prohibitively inefficient, creating "target approval bottlenecks" that allowed time-sensitive targets to disappear while individual strikes were transmitted for approval and vetted thousands of miles away through a time-intensive chain of sign-offs.[122] Such delays in receiving target approval occurred in several high-profile cases, including a Taliban convoy of nearly 1,500 fighters during the battle of Mazar-i-

[120] Lt. Gen. David Deptula, interview by author, June 23, 2020.
[121] Perry and Kassing, *Toppling the Taliban*, 45–46.
[122] Lambeth, *Air Power against Terror*, 312–13; Lt. Gen. David Deptula, interview by author, June 23, 2020.

Sharif and an opportunity to kill Mullah Omar on the opening night of the air campaign.[123] Second, CENTCOM not only controlled target selection but also held authority over desired mean point of impact and weapon selection in certain cases.[124] As Lieutenant General David Deptula, the first CAOC director during OEF, suggested, CENTCOM officials (with more limited air campaigning experience) "micro-managing" decisions over weapon selection and allocation often led to air strikes that were less than optimal in meeting campaign objectives.[125] Although the adverse impacts of tightly centralized rules of engagement and approval processes, with the exception of several important incidents of targeting delay and indecision, were ultimately minimal in the broader picture of the campaign, tension between CENTCOM and the CAOC during OEF provided an important lesson of the need for better interservice integration and joint planning that would be incorporated into Operation Iraqi Freedom in 2003.[126]

Compounding concerns surrounding rules of engagement and the application of air power, Taliban and Al-Qaeda forces exploited the degree to which US airmen adhered to rules of engagement, utilizing similar tactics to those used against US air power during the Kosovo and Iraq wars.[127] This effort began in the weeks preceding the air campaign, with Taliban spokesmen stressing the misery already suffered by the Afghan people and the dearth of targets "worth the price of a single missile fired at us," as well as the broader mistrust that military action would cause "between the people in the region and the United States."[128] Following the initial air strikes, Taliban and Al-Qaeda fighters began operating from residential areas, using their proximity to schools, mosques, and hospitals to provide cover from air strikes, exacerbating the risk of civilian casualties as a means to turn the propaganda tide against the US-led coalition.[129] Regardless of US claims that "no nation in human history has done more to avoid civilian casualties," targeting errors inevitably occurred.[130] Collateral damage in Afghanistan, most likely worsened by tactics utilized by the Taliban and Al-Qaeda, created political and military challenges for coalition

---

[123] Ibid., 314; Coll, *Directorate S*, 71–76.
[124] Lt. Gen. David Deptula, interview by author, June 23, 2020.    [125] Ibid.    [126] Ibid.
[127] Ibid.
[128] Barry Bearak, "Taliban Plead for Mercy to the Miserable in a Land of Nothing," *New York Times*, September 13, 2001.
[129] William Branigin, "Taliban's Human Shields," *Washington Post*, October 24, 2001.
[130] Department of Defense, "DoD News Briefing – Secretary Rumsfeld and Gen. Myers," October 29, 2001; "UN Confirms Destruction of Afghan Hospital," *Guardian*, October 23, 2001; John Pomfret, "Afghans Now Question US Strikes; Refugees Say Civilian Deaths Are Softening Opposition to Taliban," *Washington Post*, October 18, 2001.

forces and US policy makers from domestic, international, and Afghan sources.[131] The consequences of collateral damage and civilian casualties were less acute during the opening stages of OEF than air campaigns in humanitarian interventions like Kosovo or Libya. This reflected higher levels of domestic and international support for US military operations in Afghanistan in 2001. Conflicting pressures to prioritize military accomplishment by loosening the rules of engagement or restricting targeting to reduce collateral damage highlight an important dilemma for contemporary air power.[132]

## Conclusion

OEF presents an important case for ongoing debates over the proper application of air power in limited, asymmetrical conflicts. Analysis of the war reveals the qualified success of air power over Afghanistan but also raises questions over the replicability of the Afghan air campaign. This line of query is necessary considering the long shadow of OEF and the apparent applicability of the campaign for today's conflicts in the Middle East. Air power's role during OEF provides a useful historical template for the effective execution of air-ground operations with local allies, and it illustrates the critical importance of highly capable air controllers and operators, as well as allied ground forces capable of and motivated to capitalize on the advantages of a coordinated offensive against a vulnerable enemy. This set of conditions proved essential in turning the balance of power in Afghanistan against the Taliban, driving their collapse in late 2001.

Additionally, OEF's air campaign offers further evidence of the challenges of executing strategic interdiction air operations against a target-poor adversary and successfully eliminating enemy leadership targets as part of a decapitation strategy. With few targets of strategic value to hit and Taliban and Al-Qaeda leadership difficult to track and eliminate, air power in strategic interdiction and leadership decapitation roles proved ineffective. The near-miss of Mullah Omar at the beginning of the campaign and the escape of bin Laden at Tora Bora, in particular, contributed to the ensuing instability and insurgency in Afghanistan. Last, though concerns regarding rules of engagement and collateral damage played a relatively minor role during the 2001 air campaign over Afghanistan, owing to the high levels of support for

---

[131] William Arkin, "Fear of Civilian Deaths May Have Undermined Effort," *Los Angeles Times*, January 16, 2002.
[132] David Petraeus and Michael O'Hanlon, "Take the Gloves Off against the Taliban," *Wall Street Journal*, May 20, 2016.

the conflict and the political imperative to strike quickly following the September 11 attacks, the case nevertheless highlights important challenges in the contemporary execution of air operations. This underlies the difficulties of limiting collateral damage while achieving military and political objectives.

# 6     The Result Is Never Final: Operation Iraqi Freedom

## The Greater Thirty Years War, 1990–

*Heather Venable** [*]

> The real winner is the side that has established the framework for the next war
>
> (a decidedly realist strategic position) or the conditions for a lasting peace (an idealist outlook).[1]

Although it is common to refer to operations in Afghanistan as the "longest war," the United States and its coalition partners have been applying air power in Iraq for more than three decades, ranging widely across the spectrum of nonkinetic roles, including mobility and reconnaissance, to kinetic missions from strategic attack to close air support. In this vein, Operation Iraqi Freedom (OIF), the US invasion of Iraq in 2003, is better told not as the story of a relatively quick and overwhelmingly successful joint air-ground campaign but as one chapter of a thirty years' war. Placed in this context, OIF reveals how technological superiority may enable short-term goals yet distract attention from the long-term complexities of war.

From this perspective, Operation Desert Storm, the US-led coalition's liberation of Kuwait in 1991, and the initial weeks of OIF are outbreaks of conventional conflict amidst a longer trend of low-level air power employment. This framework highlights decades of low-grade violence punctuated by bouts of more traditional conflict, without long-term decisive effect. Neither Desert Storm nor OIF ended in a clear-cut manner because nation states, nonstate actors, and individuals never stopped using violence to achieve their political objectives.[2]

---

[*] The views expressed by the author do not reflect those of the US government, the Department of Defense, or any of its organizations.

[1] Everett Dolman, quoted in Rich Ganske, "Counter Terrorism, Continuing Advantage, and a Broader Theory of Victory," *Strategy Bridge*, March 23, 2014. https://thestrategy bridge.org/the-bridge/2016/1/10/counter-terrorism-continuing-advantage-and-a-broade r-theory-of-victory

[2] See, for example, Richard McCutcheon, "Rethinking the War against Iraq," *Anthropologica* 48:1 (2006): 11–28; also see Dilip Hiro, *Iraq: In the Eye of the Storm* (New York: Thunder's Mouth Press, 2002).

The American way of war, though, seeks the exact opposite. It assumes that a clear advantage in military capabilities translates neatly, and in a linear fashion, to enduring strategic advantage. Precision capabilities, for example, are admirable in their desire to spare lives; meanwhile, though, opponents skillfully manipulate media and emotion.[3] This distanced view of war can lead at times to an unbalanced Clausewitzian trinity in which reason is assumed to trump emotion and chance, as can be seen in an influential but misguided work published shortly after Operation Desert Storm: Ullman and Wade's *Shock and Awe*. Published by the National Defense University in 1996, the authors claimed to offer a new way to affect an enemy's "will, understanding, and perception" rather than by decisively defeating the enemy's military capabilities.[4] But the underpinning of this desired psychological effect rested, uniquely in their opinion, on "the confluence of strategy, technology, and the genuine quest for innovation." Technology – and the innovative process through which one creates it – would be the cornerstone of psychologically convincing the enemy to cease fighting.[5] In essence, Clausewitz's "reason" leg of his famous trinity of reason, chance, and emotion would trump the enemy's "emotion."

This approach is highly problematic. Clausewitz experts Christopher Bassford and Edward J. Villacres explain that an "approach to theory that denies or minimizes the role of any of these forces or the interaction among them is, therefore, by definition wrong."[6] It is ironic that Clausewitz's most famous concept of the trinity rests not on the art of warfare, for which he is renowned, but on a scientific principle: As a pendulum swings between three magnets, it uncontrollably and unpredictably shifts and pivots between the magnets until it comes to rest on one of them. As such, it is unpredictable when reason – most closely connected with the military – will become most important, despite tremendous increases in US military capability. Passion and chance continue to have just as much possible influence. Indeed, what one scholar has described as the "West's decades long effort to bottle up passion in war, its well-meant denial of the purchase that hatred and enmity has on the collective psyche of a population that believes itself at war, has

---

[3] David Betz, *Carnage and Connectivity: Landmarks in the Decline of Conventional Military Power* (New York: Oxford University Press, 2015), 6–10, 83.

[4] Harlan Ullman and James Wade Jr., *Shock and Awe: Achieving Rapid Dominance* (Washington, DC: National Defense University, 1996), 18.

[5] Ullman and Wade, *Shock and Awe*, 4–6, 14–15, 22.

[6] Christopher Bassford and Edward J. Villacres, "Reclaiming the Clausewitzian Trinity." www.clausewitz.com/readings/Bassford/Trinity/TRININTR.htm, originally published in *Parameters*, August 1995.

produced a surfeit of it – seething to be unleashed."[7] Or, as Robert Mihara similarly points out, the "agency of individuals limits the potential of intervention by subverting the influence of rationality (i.e., policy) on the direction and outcome of conflicts."[8]

Viewed in this light, OIF no longer appears as an outlier in a work focused on contemporary air campaigns. One may design and employ precision weapons, but no amount of engineering can prevent them at times having sweeping and often unintended consequences. In other words, technology does not always translate neatly into desired political outcomes. Thirty years of warfare in Iraq reveal how overwhelming technological advantage cannot overtake the essential battleground for and in the human domain, especially for anything but the most straightforward of political objectives. Yet, for the most part, national defense strategy as recent as 2018 suggests that, in response to the changing character of war, the Department of Defense stress "lethality" above all else.[9]

But, importantly, as Colin Gray reminds us, "strategic effect is decided by the target, not by the attacking air power."[10] And the target, according to Clausewitz, consists of the complex interplay of governments, militaries, and people.[11] Western historiography on US interventions in Iraq, however, largely omits the Iraqi people from these accounts. It similarly breaks up decades of violence into two conventional phases of Desert Storm and OIF, separated by an extended interval of sanctions, and with minimal "collateral damage." This focus stresses overwhelming US capabilities and decisions in regard to employing force, thus removing the interactive nature of war from contemporary campaigns while ignoring less conventional periods of conflict.[12] In essence, lessons learned from these conflicts overemphasize the military "leg" of the Clausewitzian triangle while neglecting the leg of the "people" that plays such an important role in contemporary air conflicts in light of Iraq and other similar postcolonial nations' complex population dynamics. The point of this chapter is not to overturn all aspects of previous

---

[7] David Betz, "The Strategic Bystander: On Mayhem in Century 21," *Infinity Journal* 5:2 (Spring 2016): 32.

[8] Robert Mihara, "The Inutility of Force," *Infinity Journal* 5:3 (Fall 2016). https://militarystrategymagazine.com/article/the-inutility-of-force

[9] Olivia A. Garard and B. A. Friedman, "Clausewitzian Alchemy and the Modern Character of War," *Orbis* 63:3 (2019): 363.

[10] Colin S. Gray, "Airpower Theory," in *Airpower Reborn: The Strategic Concepts of John Warden and John Boyd*, ed. John Andreas Olsen (Annapolis: Naval Institute Press, 2015), 168.

[11] This interpretation is contentious, but Clausewitz generally believed that these categories corresponded to rationality, passion, and chance. For a useful article considering these two competing triangles, see Bassford and Villacres, "Reclaiming the Clausewitzian Trinity."

[12] McCutcheon, "Rethinking," 13.

accounts of OIF or to critique air power per se but rather to highlight often underemphasized aspects of ethnic diversity given how important it has been in many recent contemporary conflicts.

Thus, this chapter seeks to add nuance to accounts like Benjamin Lambeth's *Unseen War* – the only full-length work on air power in OIF. *Unseen War*, despite being published in 2013, ignores the subsequent challenges of applying air power after the initial campaign. Such works portray air power in OIF as a model of planning and application for future conventional operations. Air Force General Michael T. Moseley, for example, describes air power's role in OIF as exemplifying "air power's final maturation" for "high-intensity warfare."[13] Lambeth echoes this refrain, praising a "concurrent and synergistic" campaign.[14] Celebratory accounts emphasizing the revolutionary characteristics of US capabilities are problematic, though, because they prevent the US military from taking a more introspective look at war's enduring nature – to include Clausewitz's magnetic pole of the people – despite the vast increase in lethality, as seen in the ability to project enormous amounts of force where desired.[15]

Gravitating toward the short-term decisiveness of the conventional air and ground campaigns in Desert Storm and Iraqi Freedom makes it easy to miss the enduring nature of these conflicts as ones of "durable disorder."[16] Sean McFate uses this terminology to stress how the US military has become imprisoned to "'conventional war' strategy" by focusing on individual nation states rather than more "systemic" and enduring threats.[17] Even as air power historiography reflects that "conventional" approach, there is an increasing need to understand longer trends in air power application and the context in which the United States sought to achieve its strategic goals.

## Operation Desert Storm: An Early Lesson in Planning for a Better Peace

American airmen have long sought to employ air power precisely to strike more directly at an opponent to paralyze it with as little destruction as

---

[13] General Michael T. Mosely, foreword to *Unseen War: Allied Air Power and the Takedown of Saddam Hussein*, Benjamin Lambeth (Annapolis: Naval Institute Press, 2013).

[14] Lambeth, *Unseen War*, 2–4.

[15] Bassford and Villacres, "Reclaiming" www.clausewitz.com/readings/Bassford/Trinity/TRININTR.htm; for the Army shaping narratives see Michael R. Gordon and Gen. Bernard E. Trainor, *The Generals' War* (Boston: Little, Brown and Company, 1995), 184.

[16] Sean McFate, *The New Rules of War: Victory in the Age of Durable Disorder* (New York: William Morrow, 2019), Kindle location, 173.

[17] McFate, *New Rules of War*, Kindle location, 125, 159.

possible. And, for many, the employment of air power during Operation Desert Storm seemingly validated that concept in the winter of 1991. Precision weapons appeared to allow the fulfillment of an almost blood-less application of air power against key infrastructure and leadership targets and enabled a short thirty-eight-day campaign, restoring Kuwaiti sovereignty that had been violated when Iraq invaded the previous August (see Figure 6.1).[18]

The narrative has shifted over time, however, to stress other air power roles, particularly the critical importance of decimating the Iraqi Army in the Kuwaiti theater of operations, which ultimately received about 75 percent of coalition air efforts.[19] More specifically, battlefield interdiction far more so than close air support (CAS) contributed to the destruction of the Iraqi army, particularly in the Kuwaiti theater.[20]

The relative contributions of strategic attack as opposed to CAS and interdiction can be argued. It is less debatable whether or not the coalition succeeded in achieving its desired ends, including the most important objective: the removal of Iraqi troops from Kuwait and the restoration of the Kuwaiti government. The military achieved many of its other responsibilities as well, including defending Saudi Arabia and other neighboring states and making the Republican Guard combat ineffective.

One objective, however, stood out for being far more intangible: encouraging regional stability in the Persian Gulf.[21] Likewise, the White House also sought even more vaguely to "weaken Iraqi popular support" for its government.[22] In this vein, it wanted to avoid "damage to non-military economic infrastructure" and "energy-related facilities."[23]

Yet targeting electricity, long seen by some airmen as the best way to disarm an opponent, served a variety of purposes even as it resulted in unintended consequences despite the employment of precision weapons. The traditional strategic target of electricity had multiple objectives ranging from degrading Iraqi air defense networks to depriving the population of electricity in hopes that civilian anger might undermine the Iraqi

---

[18] Richard T. Reynolds, *Heart of the Storm: The Genesis of the Air Campaign against Iraq* (Maxwell AFB: Air University Press, 1995); Olsen, "Operation Desert Storm," 177; John Warden, "Success in Modern War: A Response to Robert Pape's *Bombing to Win*," *Security Studies* 7:2 (Winter 1997/97): 183.

[19] See Thomas A. Keaney and Eliot A. Cohen, *Gulf War Air Power Survey Summary Report* (Washington, DC: Government Printing Office, 1993), 91, 235.

[20] Olsen, "Operation Desert Storm," 195; Keaney and Cohen, *Gulf War Air Power Survey*, 91.

[21] The White House, National Security Directive (NSD) 54, January 15, 1991, 2. https://nsarchive2.gwu.edu/NSAEBB/NSAEBB39/document4.pdf

[22] NSD 54, 2.   [23] NSD 54, 3; GAO; *Desert Storm*, 153.

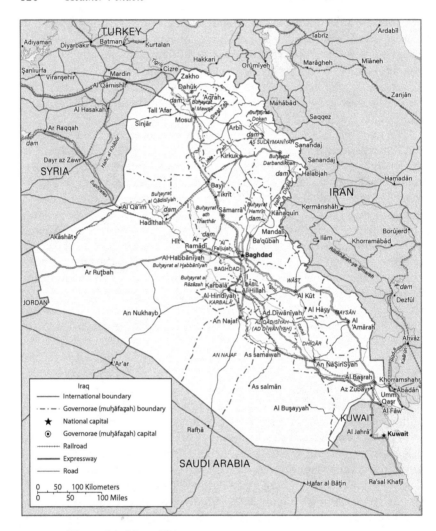

Figure 6.1  Map of Iraq

regime.[24] Even some air planners hoped that shutting off electricity might turn Iraqi civilians away from supporting their government.[25]

[24] Olsen, "Operation Desert Storm," 189.
[25] GAO, 153; Michael W. Lewis, "The Law of Aerial Bombardment in the 1991 Gulf War," *The American Journal of International Law* 97:3 (July 2003): 488. For debates about electricity, also see Daniel T. Kuehl, "Airpower vs. Electricity: Electric Power as

While planners adhered to a philosophy of effects-based operations (EBO) – or the idea that one need not destroy a target to achieve one's desired effect – operators often did not, thus resulting in unnecessary damage to the nation's electric system.[26] Not only did planners and operators envision the destruction of electricity somewhat differently, but planners in particular had competing objectives for what effects they sought to achieve.

This trend continued in OIF. The Air Force hoped EBO would allow it to understand how the enemy responded to its efforts.[27] But as Clausewitz explains, emotion is difficult to "pin down, being as it is an intangible, largely ephemeral force."[28] Reports conducted after OIF found that physical damage, more than enemy's intent, continued to be the only practical way of assessing a sortie's success.[29] The effects of wartime destruction and postwar sanctions also merged in the conflict's immediate aftermath, challenging the neat distinction between war and peace. The *Gulf War Air Power Survey* does not deal with sanctions' effects on civilians, despite being published in 1993; however, one researcher has pointed out that the destruction of the electric grid had "unintended consequences" on water supply and sanitation. Furthermore, he concludes that these effects are difficult to separate out in terms of what the bombing caused and what sanctions caused.[30] Others paint an equally grim picture of the years following Desert Storm in terms of harm caused to ordinary Iraqi citizens resulting from lack of access to food, medicine, and other necessities.[31] The point is not to quantify whether air power or sanctions caused more damage to Iraqi society but rather to challenge traditional air power historiography that tends to discount such developments because it focuses excessively on the US employment of force.[32]

---

a Target for Strategic Air Operations," *Journal of Strategic Studies* 18:1 (January 2008): 237–66.

[26] *Gulf War Air Power Survey*, 71–72; "Law of Aerial Bombardment," 486. Dave Deptula took a different view. See "Law," 486, 505–06.

[27] Col. Gary Crowder, "Effects-Based Operations," March 19, 2003, HQ Air Combat Command. https://premium-globalsecurity-org.aufric.idm.oclc.org/military/library/news/2003/03/mil-030319-dod01.htm

[28] Thomas Waldman, *War, Clausewitz and the Trinity* (New York: Routledge, 2016).

[29] Vince Crawley, "Missing the Target: Major Parts of War-Fighting Code Were Not Effective," *Air Force Times*, April 19, 2004, 22.

[30] Kuehl, "Airpower vs. Electricity," 254.

[31] Beth Osborne Daponte and Richard Garfield, "The Effect of Economic Sanctions on the Mortality of Iraqi Children Prior to the 1991 Persian Gulf War," *American Journal of Public Health* 90:4 (April 2000), 546–52. More recent work available in "Economic Sanctions: A Blunt Instrument?" *Journal of Peace Research* 50:1 (2013): 121–35.

[32] Nimrod Hagiladi argues with regard to the Second Lebanon War in Chapter 7 that destruction in a conventional conflict can have an impact in the postwar environment, deterring further violence.

These narrow perspectives appear in the *Gulf War Air Power Survey*, which largely dismisses any claims that air power injured civilians during the war, deriding "peace activists who visited Iraq immediately after the war looking for evidence" of damage.[33] Such commentary seeks to exonerate the United States more than it does to understand the long-term consequences of military force. Moreover, if air power destroys infrastructure that leads to long-term civilian suffering, then air power is responsible for that suffering even if civilians are not killed in the initial bombing.

But these kinds of concerns remained secondary for the military, which felt it had eradicated the ghost of Vietnam. This seeming overwhelming victory led many in the United States to believe that "something truly profound had occurred in the desert," making it difficult for any power to challenge it.[34] Certainly, the context of the desert environment played to air power's strengths.[35] The Air Force in particular believed it had contributed extensively – if not the majority – to a decisive military victory. Still, air power advocates overstated these effects. Subsequent assessments conducted by the GAO also challenged many statements made by various individuals and organizations in the Air Force.[36] Air power, for example, had only destroyed 24 percent of the Republican Guard, thus allowing it to put down civilian uprisings that occurred after the war, which resulted in a drastically changed society after Hussein retaliated.[37]

Air power did do amazing things in the desert, hobbling the Iraqi Army at the cost of remarkably few coalition casualties. Although the media tended to amplify strategic attacks that may have ultimately provided little effect, air power did achieve air superiority quickly and decisively, making ground operations substantially easier. But airmen and air power history have overstressed that point for the last thirty years in a way that overemphasizes the military leg of the Clausewitzian triangle while marginalizing that of people. What happened in the

---

[33] *Gulf War Air Power Survey*, 249.

[34] Bacevich, "Terminating," 280. For the contrarian view that this was an overreaction given the ease of the desert compared to Vietnam according to Assistant Secretary of Defense James Webb, see Betz, *Carnage and Connectivity*, 48.

[35] Olsen, "Operation Desert Storm," 196; Keaney and Cohen, *Gulf War Air Power Survey*, 235.

[36] General Accounting Office, "Operation Desert Storm: Evaluation of the Air Campaign," GAO/NSIA-97-134, June 1997, 110–38. For an optimistic Air Force assessment, see Office of History, HQ 37th Fighter Wing, Twelfth Air Force, Tactical Air Command, *Nighthawks over Iraq: A Chronology of the F-117A Stealth Fighter in Operations Desert Shield and Desert Storm*, January 1992. https://nsarchive2.gwu.edu/NSAEBB/NSAEBB39/document9.pdf

[37] For a critical view of air power, see Daryl G. Press, "The Myth of Air Power in the Persian Gulf War and the Future of Warfare," *International Security* 26:2 (Fall 2001): 5–44.

months after a seeming clear-cut battlefield victory set into play forces just as powerful as the seemingly overwhelming and unstoppable military weapons the United States had rained on portions of Iraq and Kuwait, inviting new forms of domestic instability. Even as the United States sought to contain Hussein after the war, the forces that Desert Storm unleashed subsequently boiled over as Hussein took drastic steps to alter Iraq's political landscape.

American commentators, though, offered influential interpretations of the war that ignored these very forces, including the authors of *Shock and Awe.* Given such "overwhelming capabilities," victory was "largely a matter of drafting a cogent and coordinated operation plan based on using the entire system of capabilities and then executing that plan to produce a decisive victory."[38] In their telling, the complex and foggy nature of war Clausewitz depicted could be reduced to the calculated employment of weapons.

### Operations Southern and Northern Watch

Desert Storm's end certainly marked a significant downturn but by no means an end to violence. In the eleven years between the end of Desert Storm and the beginning of Iraqi Freedom, the United States maintained economic sanctions and enforced no-fly zones. The former had the consequence of reshaping the dynamics of Iraqi society while the latter increasingly demonstrated a pattern of the systematic and intensifying application of force.[39] The no-fly zones gradually transformed from an effort to protect Iraqi civilians into sustained attacks on Iraqi military infrastructure, bringing these actions ever closer to outright war. Yet these no-fly zones have been characterized as something different than war.[40] Richard Swain, for example, calls them "neither war nor not war."[41] But if war is the use of violence to achieve political objectives, then the no-fly zones certainly should be considered a war, even if imposed for humanitarian reasons to uphold UN Security Council Resolution 688, which sought to safeguard the Shiites after the Safwan

---

[38] Ullman and Wade, *Shock and Awe*, 28.

[39] For the British perspective of effects on Iraqi society, see Select Committee on Defense, Thirteenth Report, "Relations with Iraq," August 2, 2000. https://publications .parliament.uk/pa/cm199900/cmselect/cmdfence/453/45305.htm

[40] Kevin Shi and Paul Scharre, "Phases of War and the Iraq Experience," November 22, 2016; *War on the Rocks*, http://warontherocks.com/2016/11/phases-of-war-and-the-iraq-experience

[41] Richard Swain, quoted in Col. Joel D. Rayburn and Col. Frank K. Sobchak, eds., *The US Army in the Iraq War: Invasion, Insurgency, Civil War*, volume 1 (Carlisle, PA: Strategic Studies Institute and US Army War College Press, 2019), 15.

130     *Heather Venable*

cease-fire agreement failed to prohibit the regime's use of helicopters. Notably, however, some argue that the UN resolution did not specifically authorize a no-fly zone in northern or southern Iraq, which is important given the waning international support for the US-led measure.[42]

Hussein responded to the no-fly zone in a variety of ways. At times he ignored them. In 1994, for example, he sent elements of the Republican Guard toward Kuwait in a worrisome move, which the United States followed up with Operation Vigilant Warrior, deploying more than 13,000 service members while putting more than 150,000 on alert.[43] Iraq also attacked coalition aircraft on more than 700 occasions using both antiaircraft fire and surface-to-air missiles and launched aircraft into the no-fly zone more than 150 times.[44] The United States replied with a range of what it considered to be a scalable menu of five-tiered "response options."[45] In the 1996 Operation Desert Strike, for example, it sent cruise missiles against Iraqi air defense sites.[46]

In response, Hussein developed a strategy aimed at creating tension between the United States, which advocated more kinetic solutions to dealing with Iraq, and its partners. Over time, nations in the region tired of the US presence, while European nations proved more hesitant to use force. Meanwhile, Hussein recognized that he could endure short bursts of kinetic force if required, but he generally tried to remain just below the level of provoking such force.[47] Thus he "exploit[ed] the gray area where the US fe[lt] provoked to act" while not making enough threatening actions that might invoke fear in the Gulf Cooperation Council's member nations.[48] This kind of "low-end of the spectrum of conflict with no termination point" activity far better characterizes the general trend of air power employment in the thirty years' war.[49]

Over time, these operations changed significantly, becoming far more offensive in nature, especially after Operation Desert Fox in December 1998, a short 4-day operation targeting the regime's weapons of mass destruction after Iraq refused visits from weapons inspectors.

[42] Von Sponeck, *Different Kind of War*, 209; United Nations Security Council Resolutions, Resolution 688: Iraq (April 5, 1991). http://unscr.com/en/resolutions/688
[43] Lt. Col. Merrick Krause, "Modern Air Occupation Strategy Case Study: Operation Southern Watch," thesis, National Defense University, 2001. www.apps.dtic.mil/dtic/tr/fulltext/u2/a437040.pdf; Eric Herr, "Operational Vigilant Warrior: Conventional Deterrence Theory, Doctrine, and Practice," thesis, School of Advanced Airpower Studies, 1996, 31–32.
[44] Krause, 3.
[45] Bob Woodward, *Plan of Attack* (New York: Simon & Schuster, 2004), 10.
[46] Rayburn and Sobchak, *US Army in the Iraq War*, 17.     [47] Krause, 17–19.
[48] Ibid., 19.     [49] Ibid., 23.

This operation consisted of firing 415 cruise missiles and dropping 600 plus precision-guided bombs.[50]

Desert Fox marked the most kinetic phase of the period between Desert Storm and Iraqi Freedom, although some argued it had little lasting effect other than to further punish a small number of unfortunate Iraqi civilians.[51] It also marked a change in US strategy from one of containment to one seeking regime change.[52] This shift is important because, as Donald Stoker argues, it pushed a limited conflict into the realm of the unlimited in terms of the political objective sought, although this ebbed and flowed depending on individual US presidents.[53] The point is not to critique the operational use of air power or engage in debates about the tendency of presidents to use air power as a ready tool, however problematically, but rather to stress the *longue durée* of US force employment against Iraq and its changes over time.

In that vein, it is important to place this claim within the context of the increased attacks on the Iraqi military after Desert Fox's conclusion. Indeed, the United States continued to target more than just military targets but leadership ones as well in hopes of undermining Hussein's regime.[54] In effect, the United States militarized the no-fly zones and loosened rules of engagement, shifting the primary reason for the NFZ's purpose from humanitarian concerns to regime change.[55] Nine days after Operation Desert Fox, for example, the United States struck an Iraqi base near Mosul.

This trend continued after Desert Fox, when attacks on the Iraqi air defense system from mid-December 1998 to February 1999, averaging one strike every three days, caused more damage than those launched in Desert Fox.[56,57] This kind of continuity in the application of kinetic effect, however, tends to be lost in standard depictions of this time frame, which paint a starker contrast between the seeming relative calm of Southern Watch and the violence of Desert Fox.

[50] Gordon and Trainor, *Cobra II*, Kindle location, 327.
[51] H. C. Von Sponeck, *A Different Kind of War: The UN Sanctions Regime in Iraq* (New York: Berghahn Books, 2006), 200. The British government took a more positive view. See Select Committee on Defense, "Relations with Iraq."
[52] Rayburn and Sobchak, *US Army in the Iraq War*, 17. Republicans drove some of this change during the Clinton administration by getting the Iraq Liberation Act passed in 1998, which authorized spending up to $97 million in support of an army to overthrow the Hussein regime. Gordon and Trainor, *Cobra II*, Kindle location, 316.
[53] Donald Stoker, *Why America Loses Wars: Limited War and US Strategy from the Korean War to the Present* (New York: Cambridge University Press, 2019), 63.
[54] Conversino, "Operation Desert Fox," 7 (n.p.).    [55] Krause, 2; Von Sponeck, 204–05.
[56] "Daily Airstrikes More Damaging than Four-Day Campaign," *The Herald* (Jasper, Indiana), February 4, 1999, 17.
[57] Von Sponeck, *A Different Kind of War*, 210.

Meanwhile, Iraqi civilians experienced violence in a period seen from a more US-centric perspective as far more akin to a time of peace.[58] In 1999, for example, the United States used more than 1,800 bombs to strike 450 targets, many of which were dumb bombs.[59] Meanwhile, its British ally tried to limit itself to reconnaissance missions.[60] This ongoing low-grade violence in concert with the effects on civilians of sanctions is often lost in conventional treatments of the air-ground campaign that began Operation Iraqi Freedom.

Efforts against military targets subsequently intensified as President George W. Bush took office, given his far greater commitment to removing Hussein.[61] The Bush administration increasingly used operations in the no-fly zones to undermine the regime, in part by using Iraqi provocations to justify "disproportionate response(s)," such as by seeking out antiaircraft fire in order to retaliate, including dropping laser-guided cement bombs on antiaircraft batteries located near mosques and other "sensitive sites."[62]

It could be argued that the destruction of conventional Iraqi military capabilities was counterproductive as Hussein already had decided to invest little in those same capabilities. It did not matter how decisive the United States believed its victory in Operation Desert Storm to be; what mattered was the effect on the enemy, and the "formative military crisis" of Hussein's experience was not Desert Storm but the Shiite revolt after Desert Storm.[63] Hussein, worried about a military coup, shifted resources into paramilitaries rather than the conventional military.[64] But the US intelligence apparatus did not glean any of these developments; thus, it did not prepare adequately for the more unconventional fight that characterized Iraq's military response during the initial campaign.[65]

[58] McCutcheon, "Rethinking," 17.    [59] Ibid.

[60] Thomas E. Ricks, "Containing Iraq: A Forgotten War," *Washington Post*, October 25, 2000. www.washingtonpost.com/archive/politics/2000/10/25/containing-iraq-a-forgotten-war/6f4525ad-8928-4040-891e-8be2486354e6

[61] Gordon and Trainor, *Cobra II*, Kindle location, 338–49.

[62] Ricks, "Containing Iraq," *Washington Post*; Gordon and Trainor, *Cobra II*, Kindle location, 369.

[63] Gordon and Trainor, *Cobra II*, Kindle location, 1130; Kevin M. Woods et al., *Iraqi Perspectives Project: A View of Operation Iraqi Freedom from Saddam's Senior Leadership* (US Joint Forces Command, 2006), 48. https://hsdl.org/?view&did=461392. Perspectives of Hussein's top leaders slant toward overstressing conventional conflict. See, for example, Woods, *Perspectives*, 45.

[64] Rayburn and Sobchak, *US Army in the Iraq War*, 13, 45; Gordon and Trainor, *Cobra II*, Kindle location, 1245.

[65] Rayburn and Sobchak, *US Army in the Iraq War*, 18; Gordon and Trainor, *Cobra II*, Kindle location, 1266. The main source of human intelligence for the United States

Hussein also infused more radical Muslim ideas into Iraqi society, helping to establish the groundwork for inflaming sectarian differences. Understanding how the Ba'athist party's secularism had been "replaced by a strange fusion of Ba'athists and Islamists, mirrored outside the regime by a seething Shi'a Islamist mass movement" with ties to Iran and militia groups could have provided invaluable insights. Many in the US foreign policy establishment, however, geared their assumptions to personal preferences for the large-scale conventional fight.[66] Similarly, other leaders viewed OIF through the lens of iconic historic operations, including the Normandy invasion, believing that Iraq need only be "liberate[d]" rather than occupied.[67] Ignorance of Iraqi society may have been the most significant failure in prewar planning or so the authors of the *US Army in Iraq* contend.[68] But those dizzied by the vast technological capabilities resulting from the Revolution in Military Affairs had determined that a strategy based on "shock and awe" could quickly overwhelm Iraq.[69]

Meanwhile, on the ground in Iraq, sanctions had their effects on the population at large, transforming Iraqi society from a relatively affluent Middle Eastern country to an impoverished one, which ultimately allowed for the "disintegration of the fabric of Iraqi society."[70] Many Iraqis and critics of US policy also blamed the United States for the misery resulting from the sanctions, which had implications for future military operations.[71] Further reshaping of Iraqi society resulted after the Shiite and Kurdish uprisings, with more than one in ten Iraqis being forced to find new homes. The drainage of the southern marshes, for example, resulted in Shiite tribesmen flocking into Baghdad's slums.[72]

### Operation Southern Focus

The USAF and its joint and coalition partners increased kinetic operations almost a year prior to OIF. In summer 2002, the United States had ramped

during this period appears to be the Polish embassy in Baghdad. Gordon and Trainor, *Cobra II*, Kindle location, 570.

[66] Rayburn and Sobchak, *US Army in the Iraq War*, 22, 58. Some of these tensions can also be seen in pilots enforcing the no-fly zones. See Ricks, "Containing Iraq," *Washington Post*.

[67] Rayburn and Sobchak, *US Army in the Iraq War*, 35, 66; Gordon and Trainor, *Cobra II*, Kindle location, 1556.

[68] Rayburn and Sobchak, *US Army in the Iraq War*, 43. Some wary planners predicted a "sectarian bloodbath," but their voices went against conventional wisdom.

[69] Gordon and Trainor, *Cobra II*, Kindle location, 909.

[70] Celso N. Amorim, foreword to *A Different Kind of War: The UN Sanctions Regime in Iraq*, H. C. Von Sponeck (New York: Berghahn Books, 2006), xiii–xiv, 16–17; McCutcheon, "Rethinking," 19; Rayburn and Sobchak, *US Army in the Iraq War*, 18.

[71] Rayburn and Sobchak, *US Army in the Iraq War*, 45.     [72] Ibid., 12.

up its military activities against Iraq, with Operation Southern Watch morphing into Operation Southern Focus, which began targeting Iraq's air defenses. Most of the targets gave the United States air superiority when OIF commenced.[73] Altogether, the United States hit 391 targets with more than 606 bombs during this period, many of them striking the "cable repeater stations" required for Iraqi Command and Control (C2).[74] Some targeting also went beyond the integrated air defense system (IADS) itself to include communications and headquarters.[75] US Central Command's (CENTCOM's) highest-ranking Air Force general, Michael Mosely, praised the precision required to hit targets the "size of a manhole cover," but hitting a target is no guarantee of having a precise effect or, indeed, any effect at all if redundancy is built into the system.[76] Thus, although coalition air efforts successfully gained air superiority in OIF, one should not over-stress the efficacy of precision weapons in conventional air wars.

As it had done since the end of Desert Storm, the United States continued expanding the scope of military force in ways that they likely would have condemned any other nation for doing. As the United States hit a greater variety of targets, Iraqis worked harder to shoot down allied aircraft, which the United States then used to justify further escalation. As a result, some attempted a delicate balancing game to keep their actions from garnering public attention.[77] General Mosely explained that US actions were justified because its pilots only "became a little more aggressive based on them shooting more at us, which allowed us to respond more."[78] Mosely later "admitted" that the war really had begun in mid-2002.[79] One might reply that it never really ended after Operation Desert Storm. This is not a critique of air power but rather an important aspect of many contemporary campaigns.

## Operation Iraqi Freedom

In shifting toward more formal campaign operations, planners worked from relatively clear objectives in support of a preemptive war. The

[73] Crowder, "Effects-Based Operations."
[74] Gordon and Trainor, *Cobra II*, Kindle location, 1412.
[75] Bruce R. Pirnie, John Gordon IV, Richard R. Brennan Jr., Forrest E. Morgan, Alexander C. Hou, and Chad Yost, "Air Operations" in *Operation Iraqi Freedom: Decisive War, Elusive Peace*, ed. Walter L. Perry (Santa Monica: RAND, 2015), 149.
[76] Haag, "OIF Veterans Discuss Lessons."
[77] Gordon and Trainor, *Cobra II*, Kindle location, 1421.
[78] Gordon and Trainor, *Cobra II*, Kindle location, 1412; Staff Sgt. Jason L. Haag, "OIF Veterans Discuss Lessons," July 31, 2003. https://af.mil/News/Article-Display/Article/138783/oif-veterans-discuss-lessons
[79] Julian Borger, "Iraq War 'Began Last Year,'" *The Guardian*, July 20, 2003.

regime should be removed, the nation should be made unwelcome for terrorists, and weapons of mass destruction should be destroyed. Additionally, the desired long-term strategic objective was the creation of a "stable" nation.[80]

By January 2003, CENTCOM planned to meet these objectives by integrating a short air operation with a land operation led by US Army V Corps and the I Marine Expeditionary Force launched out of Kuwait while the 4th Infantry Division created a northern front after crossing from Turkey into Iraq.[81] Yet State Department officials warned in February 2003 that CENTCOM had not devoted enough attention to "short-term civilian public security issues."[82]

Meanwhile, planners at CENTCOM focused on the initial phases of the war, including how long the air war should last. Air power advocates wanted a campaign of about two weeks focusing primarily on air superiority and decapitation targets consistent with a traditional strategic attack seeking paralysis of one's opponent.[83] By contrast, the Army desired a shorter air campaign, which may have resulted in a compromise to start the ground and air campaigns simultaneously.[84] Civilian officials also shaped the planning, with Secretary of Defense Donald Rumsfeld seeking to avoid the "massive build-up" of forces that characterized Desert Storm with more of a "running start."[85]

Iraqi military planning, by contrast, was far more limited and was controlled tightly by Saddam Hussein, which prevented the development of a more viable strategy. The Iraqi regime did not expect a repeat of Operation Desert Storm but something more like Operation Desert Fox, believing that the United States would not commit ground troops.[86] As a result, the strategy it adopted centered on surviving until the tide of world opinion turned against the Coalition's air war, as Hussein worried more about internal security or even a conflict with Iran than a US-initiated attack.[87]

---

[80] Catherine Dale, CRS Report for Congress, *Operation Iraqi Freedom: Strategies, Approaches, Results, and Issues for Congress*, March 28, 2008. https://fas.org/sgp/crs/mideast/RL34387.pdf. Stated British objectives focused more on WMD. Ministry of Defence, "*Operations in Iraq: First Reflections*" (London: Director General Corporate Communication, 2003), 10, 39–40. Also see John Lewis Gaddis, "A Grand Strategy of Transformation," *Foreign Policy* (2002), 57, for the argument that President George W. Bush did not just have in mind a simple strategy for underpinning Iraq but a cohesive and sweeping grand strategy.

[81] Dale, *Iraqi Freedom*, 13.

[82] State Department Information Memorandum for Paula J. Dobriansky, Under Secretary of State for Democracy and Global Affairs, Iraq Contingency Planning, February 7, 2003. https://nsarchive2.gwu.edu/NSAEBB/NSAEBB163/iraq-state-03.pdf

[83] Murray, "Operation Iraqi Freedom," 282.    [84] Ibid.    [85] Ibid.    [86] Ibid., 283.

[87] Murray, "Operation Iraqi Freedom," 284; Gordon and Trainor, *Cobra II*, Kindle location, 1123.

For all the prewar debates over whether the air or the ground should lead and for how many days, the Iraqis had by no means lost all agency. Despite months of prewar planning, the United States also shifted its strategy in response to fears that Iraq had begun to light its oil wells on fire, beginning its offensive ahead of schedule.[88] Now the land attack would begin a day before on March 20, with the air campaign beginning as planned on March 21.[89] After this point, however, the war dissolved into a "dynamic of its own," which all of the prewar planning in the world could not dictate.[90] Again, this reality is often lost in air-centric accounts of the campaign that focus on stressing air power's apportionment to a variety of roles.

The war technically began earlier than planned on March 19, 2003, with an attempt to decapitate the regime after erroneous intelligence indicated that Hussein and his two sons might be located at Dora Farms. In many ways, the "strategic" air war in Iraqi Freedom differed dramatically from Desert Storm. First, the strategy relied less on whole-sale paralysis to affect the regime. Second, in part because of techno-logical advances in precision and in part because of a desire to not have to rebuild Iraq, the coalition largely sought to avoid damaging the nation's infrastructure. Still, the key limitation of air power in regard to leadership decapitation strategies continues to be the limits of intelligence, despite advances in technical sophistication.

The coalition employed air power primarily in support of friendly ground operations, especially targeting mobile ground forces and assets as opposed to fixed targets, striking a total of 15,592 targets. "Strategic" targets came in second at the far lesser number of 1,799 targets, to be followed by 1,441 targets falling into the air superiority category, to include attacks against air defenses and airfields.[91] These figures, how-ever, represent the typical recounting of the war from a fundamentally air-centric perspective, as if air power strategy is created in a vacuum in which the enemy does not get a vote. They constitute measures of performance, not measures of effectiveness.

Air power historiography suffers for this and other reasons. Lambeth's *Unseen War,* sponsored by the USAF, provides a detailed account of an air power campaign that the author characterizes as "all but flawless."[92] Lambeth also relies heavily on works that authors rushed into publication in 2003. In one case he highlights "effective air power performance" by stating that the United States destroyed thirty tanks, citing Williamson

---

[88] Gordon and Trainor, *Cobra II,* Kindle location, 3263, 3285.    [89] Ibid., 3295.
[90] Ibid.    [91] Perry et al., *Operation Iraqi Freedom,* 156.    [92] Lambeth, *Unseen War,* xv.

Murray and Robert H. Scales, Jr.'s *The Iraq War*.[93] This work, however, lacks a single substantiating reference for that purported fact.[94] This is not to say that air power *was* ineffective; rather, the intent is to highlight that the current OIF air power historiography builds on flimsy evidence. Thus initial, tentative views about OIF continue to receive questionable amplification, resulting in the recirculation of the same narratives hurriedly provided to make sense of the war's first year. But Anthony Cordesman modestly pointed out in 2003 how challenging it is to "trace the interaction between land and air forces, the extent to which land action forced Iraqi forces into exposed maneuvers, and the extent to which air strikes exhausted the Iraqi land forces before they could engage coalition efforts."[95] Others point to the overwhelming "confusion" even in the face of a "new information grid."[96] A reporter embedded with Marines wryly explained, "Even with the best optics and surveillance assets in the world, no one knows what happened to nearly ten thousand pounds of bombs and missiles dropped a few kilometers outside the encampment. They may as well have been dropping them in the Bermuda Triangle."[97] This reality has bedeviled the accurate assessment of air power for decades.[98]

Air power planners themselves became overwhelmed with information in the conflict's early weeks. Thus, although there is evidence about what aircraft and weapons the United States used, there is far less about the resulting effects or even the kind of numbers they faced.[99] Regarding the examination of battle damage, one planner admits, " ... we just did not prepare for that amount of information. When each morning General Franks asked Moseley, 'How we doing?' he was forced to say, 'I don't know.' In the end, we had to send an officer out to the bomb dumps to count how many bombs were missing."[100] In this case, air planners had little sense of the progress they were making, and these realities should be acknowledged more in scholarship and official histories on OIF.

By looking at challenges more so than successes, one can mine more insights into contemporary air campaigns. Southern Iraq cities had been "front-loaded" with militias supported by small numbers of Republican

---

[93] Ibid., 100.
[94] Williamson Murray and Robert H. Scales, Jr., *The Iraq War* (Cambridge: The Belknap Press of Harvard University Press, 2003), 172.
[95] Cordesman, *Iraq War*, 9.
[96] Bing West, quoted in David Betz, *Carnage & Connectivity*, 78.
[97] Evan Wright, quoted in David Betz, *Carnage & Connectivity*, 78.
[98] Ian Gooderson, *Air Power at the Battlefront: Allied Close Air Support in Europe, 1943–45*, vol. 6 (Psychology Press, 1998).
[99] Cordesman, *Iraq War*, 9.
[100] Quoted in Knights, *Cradle of Conflict*, 316. Also see Cordesman, *Iraq War*, 32.

Guard troops drawing upon "asymmetric methods, fighting in civilian clothes, using human shields extensively" to undermine the coalition's conventional capabilities.[101] Air Marshal Brian Burridge, who commanded British forces during the invasion, explained that even before the operation began he believed the "regular army would not fight," leading him to characterize the conflict as consisting of "very long lines of communication with ... irregular forces able to apply irritation."[102] As Thomas Ricks described, US forces found themselves in the last week of March 2003 in a challenging situation in which they could either

maximize the advantages of their overwhelming firepower and bomb a wily adversary hiding heavy weapons in built-up areas, which would inflict civilian casualties and set back the US campaign for public opinion. Or they can try to attack precisely with low-flying helicopters and ground forces, which could mean losing more US troops.[103]

Coalition forces had expected to fight the Republican Guard, *not* the Fedayeen.[104] CENTCOM struggled on how to respond to this challenge, with some wondering how to proceed while others like General Franks struggled to appreciate the nature of the conflict as he gazed at computer screens showing the location of US and Iraqi forces.[105]

This kind of urban warfare, which could have been even more confounding had Hussein more deliberately pursued such a strategy, challenges Williamson Murray's depiction of an air-ground campaign as a "throwback to the earliest days of air power" because he fundamentally depicts a conventional campaign.[106] The extent to which the initial portion of the conflict is viewed predominantly as conventional reflects the biases of the US military more than it does the reality on the ground. The same problematic conventional assumptions that shaped US planning for OIF continued in many ways in the initial waging of the campaign.

[101] House of Commons Defense Committee, *Lessons of Iraq: Third Report of Session 2003–04*, vol. II (London: The Stationery Office Limited), 2004, Ev 48, 60; David Blair, "Why the Fedayeen Fight for Their Lives," *The Telegraph*, March 25, 2003. https://telegraph.co.uk/news/worldnews/middleeast/iraq/1425607/Why-the-Fedayeen-fight-for-their-lives.html; Gordon and Trainor, *Cobra II*, On Point, 102.
[102] House of Commons Defense Committee, *Lessons of Iraq*, Ev 49.
[103] Thomas E. Ricks, "Unfolding Battle Will Determine Length of War," *The Washington Post*, March 25, 2003, A1.
[104] Gordon and Trainor, *Cobra II*, Kindle location, 5991, 6015, 6035; Col. Gregory Fontenot et al., *On Point: The United States Army in Operation Iraqi Freedom* (Fort Leavenworth: Combat Studies Institute Press, 2004), 245.
[105] Gordon and Trainor, *Cobra II*, Kindle location, 6026, 6096.
[106] Murray, "Operation Iraqi Freedom," 279.

A press briefing given the day the war began on Effects-Based Operations (EBO) – which has been critiqued for being too scientific in approach – may provide some insights into how this mentality shaped Air Force planning.[107] Even as EBO helpfully stresses the importance of effects rather than capabilities as the starting point for planning military operations, Air Force doctrine in 2003 insisted that EBO could "produce distinct, desired effects while avoiding unintended or undesired effects."[108] But this pronouncement was profoundly linear in nature, assuming that US actions led neatly to outcomes. Similarly, Air Combat Command's Colonel Gray Crowder insisted repeatedly that planning for war was not entirely quantitative, yet even as he allowed for enemy interaction he narrowed his concept of war to explain the "thing about war is it's against two humans ... and the adversary is thinking." And this requires "evaluat[ing] the enemy as target systems, or as a system of systems."[109] The colonel anticipated OIF being a clash primarily between CENTCOM and Hussein, a conflict that could be won by carefully analyzing targets and precisely destroying or neutralizing them.

Some airmen subsequently realized, however, that they did not have enough information to assess the implementation of EBO. They also acknowledged some of the challenges of employing precision weapons, explaining the importance of thinking about "precise effect, not just weapon precision per se."[110] The vast array of US air- and space-based intelligence assets upon which the US way of warfare relied, moreover, could not make up for the gaping lack of human intelligence that made it difficult for US commanders to understand their opponents and to identify where strategic leadership targets might be.[111]

Only three weeks after conventional action began, the regime effectively ceased to exist. And the conflict seemed to be over, in part because of the typically one-sided and short-sighted way that the United States expects to achieve victory on its own time frame. As Ambassador Charles Freeman explains, "Wars end not because the victor declares success, but when the vanquished accept defeat."[112] As seen, the previous decade altered the fabric of Iraqi society significantly and that helps to

[107] James N. Mattis, "USJFCOM Commander's Guidance for Effects-Based Operations, *Parameters* (August 2009): 19. https://apps.dtic.mil/dtic/tr/fulltext/u2/a490619.pdf
[108] US Air Force, Air Force Doctrine Document 1, November 17, 2003, 18.
[109] Crowder, "Effects-Based Operations."
[110] Ministry of Defence, *Operations in Iraq: Lessons for the Future* (London: Directorate General Corporate Communication, 2003), 13–14.
[111] Gordon and Trainor, *Cobra II*, Kindle location, 3493, 3621.
[112] Quoted in Document 943, "Phase IV: Reconstruction," January 14, 2003. https://ahec.armywarcollege.edu/CENTCOM-IRAQ-papers/index.cfm

illuminate why the US attempt to cycle through its six phases of operations – shape, deter, seize initiative, dominate, stabilize, and enable civil
authority – ground to a halt after the dominate phase. And it is certainly
likely that better Phase IV planning could have prevented an insurgency,
but this counterfactual cannot be proven.[113] Although some might argue
this point is overdrawn given the importance of General Order #1 in de-
Baathifying the Iraqi armed forces, it is important to consider the issue of
indigenous agency in these types of postcolonial conflicts. Moreover, as
Clausewitz points out, war's very interactive nature means that when two
wrestlers engage, it is more complicated than a cause-and-effect relationship. Rather, "bodily positions and contortions that emerge in wrestling
are often impossible to achieve without the counterforce and counterweight of an opponent."[114]

In effect, a counterfactual about what could have prevented sectarian
violence from erupting in Iraq has been accepted as a truism in a way that
overstresses US agency in determining an outcome for Iraq. Sectarian
conflict in Iraq may or may not have broken out due to any number of
reasons. War is always a gamble, yet the argument over putting the ideal
Phase IV planning into operation assumes, again with the "right" strategy, the United States can craft a seamless transition while ignoring the
complexities of Iraq itself and the interactive process of each phase of war.

Many of these perspectives also fail to account for the element of time.
The United States sought to shift, understandably, as quickly as possible
from Phase III to Phase IV operations. But just because military operations ceased did not mean the conflict had come to a definitive end.
Gordon and Trainer, for example, insist that the outbreak of insurgency
was not "inevitable." Again, this kind of perspective suffers from being
US-centric, as it makes Americans the central actors. By contrast,
a different view suggests the possibility that non-US actors other than
Hussein willingly bided their time. Shiite and pro-Iranian forces may have
"largely held [their] fire" early on because they wanted to wait until the
Americans had built up the Iraqi Security Forces in order to infiltrate
them rather than engage them more symmetrically and thus
disadvantageously.[115] This possible approach is epitomized by the

[113] See, for example, Joe Buccino, "Turning Battlefield Victory into Strategic Success:
Reviewing War and the Art of Governance," *Strategy Bridge*, January 31, 2020. https://
thestrategybridge.org/the-bridge/2020/1/31/turning-battlefield-victory-into-strategic-s
uccess-reviewing-war-and-the-art-of-governance
[114] Alan Beyerchen, "Clausewitz, Nonlinearity, and the Unpredictability of War,"
*International Security* 17:3 (Winter 1992/93): 67.
[115] Nader Uskowi, *Temperature Rising: Iran's Revolutionary Guards and Wars in the Middle
East* (London: Rowman & Littlefield), 57. For Al Quds' participation in OIF, see
Gordon and Trainor, *Cobra II*, Kindle location, 5881.

purported quip of insurgents for decades that, "Americans have the watches; we have the time."[116] Even more importantly, Abu Musab al-Zarqawi had begun establishing "underground cells, creating auxiliary networks, and laying down weapons caches" as early as the middle of 2002.[117] The seeds of insurgency had been sown even prior to the occupation's beginning.

Policy makers will continue to use and abuse military power, especially air power, because it is a flexible tool. Some air power scholars like John Andreas Olsen argue that "[m]odern" air power can offer "more and better options."[118] The danger, of course, is that improved technology in air power capabilities continues to beguile civilian policy makers, leading to an excessive focus on air power's capabilities at the expense of an appreciation for the complexities of applying force against not only an opposing nation state's ruler but its people, even if indirectly.

The seeming success of the air campaign in OIF resulted in continuing misleading insights into the revolutionary nature of air power. As one commentator described it,

the stunningly rapid advance of US ground forces toward Baghdad – and even yesterday's incursions into the capital itself – is continuing testimony to the soundness of the concept that modern air power, applied to the battlefield with devastating speed, accuracy and lethality, is indeed a revolutionary force that has fundamentally changed the way wars are fought and won on the ground.[119]

Steve Call's *Danger Close,* for example, highlights the many user-led innovations that increased air-ground coordination to include introducing kill boxes to overcome fire support coordination line disputes. But, in the tradition of almost all OIF historiography, he relies solely on interviews, and his work lacks a single endnote. Though this is not to suggest that the participants deliberately exaggerated or obfuscated their experiences, it is to state that it can be very difficult to assess one's performance, especially amidst the fog and friction of war.

In a related vein, some air power commentators tend to label anything and everything air power does worthy of the moniker "revolutionary."[120] They similarly stress each new conflict as a further harbinger of a new way

---

[116] Lucia Martinez Ordonez, *Military Operational Planning and Strategic Moves* (Cham, Switzerland: Springer, 2007), 82.

[117] David Kilcullen, *The Dragons and the Snakes: How the Rest Learned to Fight the West* (New York: Oxford University Press, 2020), 93; Mary Anne Weaver, "The Short, Violent Life of Abu Musab al-Zarqawi," *Atlantic,* July–August 2006.

[118] John Andreas Olsen, *Airpower Reborn: The Strategic Concepts of John Warden and John Boyd* (Annapolis: Naval Institute Press, 2015), xi.

[119] Budiansky, *Washington Post.*      [120] Lambeth, *Unseen War.*

of war, often in the way that air power should now coexist with ground power in different ways.

### From "Fast Air" to "Helicopter Governance": The Unconventional Air War, 2003–

Primary evidence for the use of air power after the conventional phase has ceased is also thin. As such, it is instructive to turn to the work best approximating a theory of air power in small wars to understand air power's historical effectiveness. Wray R. Johnson and James S. Corum argue that air power makes the greatest contributions in counterinsurgency with nonkinetic effects, such as airlift and intelligence, surveillance, and reconnaissance (ISR). In essence, then, they place air power in a supporting role except at occasional times where one's opponent is waging war more conventionally, in which case kinetic air power will be most useful.

More specific literature on this portion of OIF, however, is almost nonexistent.[121] In part this is due to the limited number of sources released by the Air Force in contrast to the Army's declassification of hundreds of sources from CENTCOM.[122] As a result, this attempt to illuminate how air power contributed to OIF will be somewhat Army-centric by virtue of the sources. Air power is virtually invisible in CENTCOM documents, dominated as they are by ground operations ranging from kinetic attacks to the need to provide social services to Iraqi civilians.

One airman asserts that air power could not be integrated fully into planning because much of it took place at the brigade and battalion levels, where air planners were not present, leading to an "operational-tactical disconnect."[123] While the Army plans in a more decentralized manner, the Air Force prefers to view matters from the theater level and thus takes

---

[121] James Corum and Wray Johnson, *Airpower in Small Wars: Fighting Insurgents and Terrorists* (Lawrence: University Press of Kansas, 2013), 8. By contrast, note the kinetic-centric approach of Williamson Murray, who cites exact numbers of aircraft only for fighters and bombers but refers only vaguely to a "whole host of support aircraft." See Murray, 285. For complete numbers of all aircraft, see Anthony H. Cordesman, *The Iraq War: Strategy, Tactics, and Military Lessons* (Washington, DC: Center for Strategic and International Studies, 2003), 24.

[122] Anthony Cordesman notes that this dearth of information contrasts with a more generous sharing of information in the wake of Operation Desert Storm. See *Iraq War*, 7.

[123] Clint Hinote, *Centralized Control and Decentralized Execution: A Catchphrase in Crisis* (Maxwell Air Force Base, AL: Air University Press, 2009), 35–36. Although Hinote makes an interesting point, he does not elaborate on how air power might be used more effectively in support of "ground maneuver plans," being only capable of advising regarding how to provide close air support. Hinote, *Centralized Control*, 36.

a more centralized approach to planning. As Clinton Hinote – Chief of the Strategy Division at the Combined Air Operations Center for OIF from 2006 to 2007 – argues, air power could have been used to achieve greater operational effects, although he gives few specific suggestions as to how air power could be integrated more effectively with the ground component.[124] The author also chides Army restrictions that only allowed the use of ordnance when approved at the division level, although Corum and Johnson argue that in most cases the kinetic application of air power is generally the least effective in such conflicts.[125] As such, it is interesting to note that aircraft with kinetic capabilities were used first and foremost as nontraditional ISR, even if they infrequently produced useful information.[126] Hinote frets at the idea that "air power was the equivalent of an insurance policy for the unexpected events that could happen in Iraq," insisting that it could have had more effect at the operational level although never explaining how.[127] Essentially, he wants to carve out a larger role for air power than it historically has had in counterinsurgency as a supporting element for ground forces although, in keeping with much of the current historiography, there is little evidence provided.[128] Certainly assets like Predator and Reaper provided increasing amounts of coverage through combat air patrols as well as kinetic effect, but the question remains how one translates these tactical effects into operational ones.

This is problematic given the nature of the counterinsurgency fight in Iraq, as he himself points out.

Hinote, in comparing air power's effectiveness in Iraq to that of Afghanistan, explains that air power simply had fewer opportunities to be effective in Iraq because of the environment and other contextual factors. With less mountainous terrain, better road networks, and far smaller groupings of enemy combatants, air power was not as necessary in Iraq as it was in Afghanistan, where it functioned as a greater force multiplier.[129]

One notable exception is the idea of "helicopter governance." This nonkinetic use of air power used helicopters to transfer government officials quickly and efficiently around their provinces in order to

---

[124] Ibid., 35–45.    [125] Ibid., 38, 40.    [126] Ibid., 40–42.    [127] Ibid., 44.
[128] Hinote's wording is typically vague in accord with other air power writing. In one paragraph, for example, he writes: "it was what the ground commanders did with the resources entrusted to them, including air power that was most impressive. Operations in the Baghdad belts kicked off during the summer of 2007, and by all accounts, they were successful. Through the heroic actions of coalition forces integrated with air power, the tide turned in Iraq." Other than referring to air power being integrated with the ground, there is no sense of what air power did. Hinote, *Centralized Control*, 49.
[129] Ibid., 26–28.

demonstrate engagement with a wide range of communities.[130] At other times, the presence of air power worked to undermine civilians' "confidence" in their surroundings, such as when F-16s "continued roaring overhead" in a meeting with local leaders.[131]

Reference to air power assets in Army documents is also interesting in that it highlights air power's transient qualities. The distant supporting role played by air power is apparent not only in its rare appearances in CENTCOM documents but also in regard to how the Army characterized USAF close air support assets as "fast air." For example, a typical report mentions the use of strike assets as consisting of "UAV/PRED, AH 64, fast air and AS 90/M109 EXCALIBUR."[132] Thus, by its very nature, air power's speed, at least in terms of some platforms, responded as required to emergencies as needed but often was unseen.

Still, with the rise of ISIS, one can see air power's ability to provide a kind of scarecrow effect. Marine Corps Brigadier General Thomas Weidley, chief of staff of the Combined Joint Task Force for Operation Inherent Resolve in 2014, explained how ISIS had begun shifting from the offensive to the defensive since the deployment of coalition troops. Air power in particular pushed them to "transition to the defensive when coalition air started to enter the battlespace."[133] This included donning similar uniforms to Iraqi soldiers and driving similar vehicles so pilots frequently thought they had identified ISIS targets only to learn that they had found Iraqi units.[134] Despite increased air and space surveillance capabilities to provide continued ISR, the opportunity for deception still exists in contemporary air wars, with the potential for the enemy to gain an outsized strategic advantage.

Although air power has key limitations in unconventional conflict, it is still important to recognize many of its contributions. One of the most important may be that it does much to prevent the massing of individual

[130] Document 14, "Enclosure 7-MNF-W Assessment," 3, undated; Document 19, "Interview of Brig. General John R. Allen, Deputy Commanding General Multinational Force West," June 27, 2007, 12, 20–23, 26. https://ahec.armywarcollege.edu/CENTCOM-IRAQ-papers/index.cfm
[131] Document 672, Official memorandum to LTG Ricardo Sanchez, April 11, 2004, 1. https://ahec.armywarcollege.edu/CENTCOM-IRAQ-papers/index.cfm
[132] Document 13, "Enclosure 9-MND (SE) Assessment," undated; Document 44, S-MND (SE) MNF-1 Conference Slides-AMA, October 10, 2007, 2. https://ahec.armywarcollege.edu/CENTCOM-IRAQ-papers/index.cfm.
[133] Quoted in Marcus Weisberger, "General Says ISIS Is on the Defensive amid Contrary Reports," *Defense One*, May 15, 2015. https://defenseone.com/threats/2015/05/general-says-isis-defensive-amid-contrary-reports/112969
[134] Andrew Tilghman, "Commander Defends ISIS Air War's Effectiveness," *Military Times*, June 5, 2015.

opponents.[135] In other words, as difficult as it is to measure what air power does, part of air power's greatest strategic effect is what it prevents one's opponent from doing, which is even more difficult to measure.

## Conclusion

For more than thirty years, a conventional mindset of applying force has clashed with the passions of the people, complicating decisive outcomes despite US-led coalitions possessing overwhelming technological superiority. Air power dominated and shaped the use of force for many years, starting with Operation Desert Storm and lasting through Operation Northern and Southern Watch. In Desert Storm, air power shifted from a campaign of strategic attack into one of interdiction and ground attack that decimated Iraqi ground troops, enabling coalition ground forces to achieve their objectives of liberating Kuwait relatively quickly. Subsequent operations focused on protecting Shiite and Kurdish populations but, over time, these operations morphed from humanitarian operations to more offensive operations that increasingly targeted weapons of mass destruction as well as Iraqi air defenses. Simultaneously during this period, sanctions along with President Hussein's actions rewove the very fabric of Iraqi society, weakening and fissuring it, which had ramifications for the waging of and the aftermath of Operation Iraqi Freedom.

Operation Iraqi Freedom began very differently than Desert Storm. Because the air superiority campaign had commenced almost a year prior, the coalition could shift briefly to a strategic campaign before focusing its efforts on supporting the ground war. Also, Desert Storm was far more traditional in terms of conventional troops facing off against conventional troops. By contrast, Iraqi Freedom – as much as Hussein sought to employ military force – unleashed militia forces in urban areas in southern Iraq before US troops encountered conventional forces dispersed among highly populated areas of the Euphrates River Valley before entering Baghdad.

Air power continued in a supporting role as insurgency festered in the ensuing years. If Benjamin Lambeth's *Unseen War* wants to highlight the underappreciated contributions of air power in the most conventional phase of OIF, then it is ironic how truly unseen it was in the unconventional air campaign.[136] This provides a paradox for airmen: OIF and OEF were key experiences to a decade of airmen, but traditional combat air power was somewhat of a sideshow. Instead, many airmen played subtler

---

[135] Hinote, "Drawdown," 51.     [136] Lambeth, *Unseen War,* 6.

roles, such as enabling the Army to go in lighter and faster, while precision strikes and ISR increased from uncrewed platforms. But, until the Air Force begins declassifying its records, it is difficult to justify claims of air power efficacy.

For some of those in CENTCOM, including those engaged in stabilizing and pacification efforts, air power tended to stay at 30,000 feet in their thinking, when and if it ever figured in their minds even as it played important roles in armed overwatch of convoys, IED detection, and other roles. Air support to the task force in its mounting attacks on AQI and later the Shia groups, for example, was crucial. Special forces may have led the targeting cycle, for example, but they could not have done it without some mix of ISR, air mobility, and air strikes.

In Operation Desert Storm, the US-led coalition benefited from employing air power in a way that played not only to its capabilities but also to its nature. Since then, though, it has been applied in more challenging contexts. For example, the US Air Force prefers to employ air power in overwhelming ways in parallel operations. But it often finds itself more constrained, such as when it employed a strategy of gradualism in Operation Allied Force in 1999 (see Chapter 4), one which those leaders who had experienced Vietnam vowed never to repeat. In that campaign to protect ethnic Kosovars against Slobodan Milosevic's ethnic cleansing, the United States had to adhere to its NATO allies' considerations. Likewise, though the Air Force might also prefer to claim success in a high-tech air war as it did regarding the first few weeks of OIF, it should expect that those kinds of conventional campaigns will be the outlier rather than the norm. Indeed, the US military spent eighteen months planning for a war it did not get: another version of Operation Desert Storm.[137] Moreover, the short-term success of the conventional spring 2003 campaign only makes traditional air campaigns that play to US advantages more unlikely.[138] In other words, these kinds of successes have a strategic effect on shaping future warfare far beyond the conflict itself, because those contemplating war against the United States tend to work harder to develop asymmetric means of challenging the United States. OIF may even be the last large-scale campaign where the United States and its coalition partners had the luxury of launching a massive conventional attack from safe nearby bases, all the while its own territory remained safe from attack.[139] The

[137] Gordon and Trainor, *Cobra II*, Kindle loc 9676, 9784, 9693.
[138] Gen. David G. Perkins, "Multi-Domain Battle: Joint Combined Arms Concept for the 21st Century," November 14, 2016, *Association of the United States Army* (AUSA), December 13, 2016.
[139] Adam Taylor, "Amid Tension with Iran, US Air Force Shifts Middle East Command Center from Qatar to South Carolina," *Washington Post*, September 29, 2019.

proliferation of technology – especially the ability of weaker nation states as well as nonstate actors to access capabilities such as cyber, drones, and even cruise missiles – further challenge conventional advantages in air power. Air power made enormous contributions against the military "leg" of the Clausewitzian triangle over the course of thirty years with precision and stealth capabilities. But it is important to reevaluate OIF as an air power campaign in a balanced manner that focuses more on the complex interactions between militaries, governments, and people and less on the overwhelming application of US kinetic force. As John Guilmartin put it, "whatever the technology, war remains as Carl von Clausewitz characterized it, a test of will and faith."[140]

---

[140] John F. Guilmartin, Jr., "Technology and Strategy: What Are the Limits," *Technology, Violence, and War: Essays in Honor of Dr. John F. Guilmartin, Jr.*, eds. Robert S. Ehlers, Jr., Sarah K. Douglas, and Daniel P.M. Curzon (Boston: Brill, 2009), 36.

# 7    Israeli Air Force Effectiveness during the Second Lebanon War (2006)

*Nimrod Hagiladi**

On the morning of July 12, 2006, Hezbollah fighters attacked an Israeli Defense Force (IDF) patrol along the northern border of Israel, killing three, wounding two, and abducting two others. An Israeli tank crossed into Lebanon to foil the kidnapping and drove over a large IED, killing four more. An infantry soldier in the rescue force was also killed. In total, eight IDF soldiers were killed outright with two wounded. The two kidnapped soldiers also died of their wounds soon after. This bloody engagement occurred shortly after an incident near the Gaza Strip, in which Hamas kidnapped an Israeli soldier. At 2230 that night, following a two-hour meeting, the Israeli government unanimously decided to initiate what became known as the Second Lebanon War (see Figure 7.1).

In 34 days of war, 165 Israelis died – 121 soldiers and 44 civilians – and 2,000 more were wounded. In addition, 4,000 rockets fell on northern Israel, resulting in heavy economic damage. The extent of the losses and damage to Hezbollah was also severe. Some 1,200 Lebanese were killed, just over 600 Hezbollah fighters and a few dozen combatants in other military organizations, and approximately 500 civilians. Many more were seriously injured. Hezbollah economic and military capabilities were damaged by Israeli air strikes which flattened over a hundred high rise apartments in the Dahiya neighborhood of Beirut where Hezbollah's leadership resided.[1]

As soon as the war ended, sharp public criticism of the IDF and the government led to an official inquiry. The Winograd Committee subsequently made numerous allegations, including:

The government did not want war, did not intend to start a war, and did not know that it was going to war. However, this was the significance of the decision of July 12 .... A prolonged war initiated by Israel ended without Israel winning militarily .... The rocket fire on the home front continued throughout the war until the very last moment and was stopped only because of the cease-fire ....

---

* The views expressed by the author do not reflect those of the government of Israel, the Israeli Defense Force, or any of its organizations.
[1] Ken Ellington, "Israeli Premier Testifies about Hezbollah War," *Los Angeles Times,* February 2, 2007.

148

Figure 7.1  Map of Israel and Lebanon

A quasi-military organization of thousands of fighters managed to stand for many weeks in front of the most powerful army in the Middle East and its absolute air superiority and great advantages in size and technology.[2]

---

[2] The commission of inquiry into the events of military engagement in Lebanon 2006 (Winograd Committee), Final Report, vol. 1, January 2008, 33–34 (Hebrew) [emphases by author]. Only on March 25, 2007, did the government decide to call the military campaign of the summer of 2006 a "war."

Several studies since 2006 assessing the functioning of the Israeli Air Force (IAF) in the Second Lebanon War argue "the primary tool that Israel chose to use – standoff precision fires – simply could not achieve its overarching goals."[3] Others claim that the belief that air power could decide the outcome of the war by itself was the root of failure, especially in such an asymmetric war.[4] Although both sides suffered militarily and by some measures the war could be declared a draw, "there is little question that Hezbollah won a political victory, at least in the short term."[5] One scholar called it a "divine victory" for Hezbollah from which it emerged more powerful than ever.[6] These critiques, however, ignore that from 2000 to 2006 Hezbollah conducted more than 200 attacks on Israel, but very few occurred since the Second Lebanon War ended, with only four from Lebanon. This chapter argues that, although the IAF struggled during the war, in the long term the damage imposed on Hezbollah deterred further cross-border attacks, and Israel achieved its primary goal of restoring peace.

Considering the controversial opinions regarding the outcome of the Second Lebanon War and the central role played by Israeli air power, this chapter examines the effectiveness of the IAF. Measuring effectiveness requires a military operation to have a clear, achievable objective that considers both the capabilities and limitations of an air force. Overly ambitious goals or unclear objectives that create confusion can lead an air force toward continuous, unremitting operations and a war of attrition that gradually loses momentum until reaching the point of physical and/or mental exhaustion. To be effective, a culminating point must be identified, and political and military leadership must endeavor to end the war prior to reaching it.

In the Second Lebanon War the effectiveness of Israeli air operations at the operational level was minimal, with success limited to a subset of targets for which there was good intelligence and proved to be easy to find from the air, such as Hezbollah's medium-range rocket launchers. However, Hezbollah's rocket campaign against Israel, the IAF's partial response to this challenge, and Israel's unwillingness to end this military struggle without defeating Hezbollah developed into an attrition air campaign. In the short term it appears both Israel and Hezbollah achieved

---

[3] Anthony M. Schinella, *Bombs without Boots: The Limits of Airpower* (Washington, DC: Brookings Institution Press, 2019), 221–22.

[4] Avi Kober, "The Israel Defense Forces and the Second Lebanon War: Why the Poor Performance?" *Journal of Strategic Studies* 31: 1 (February 2008): 3–40.

[5] Daniel Byman, *A High Price: The Triumphs and Failures of Israeli Counterterrorism* (Oxford: Oxford University Press, 2011), 260.

[6] William M. Arkin, *Divining Victory: Airpower in the 2006 Israel-Hezbollah War* (Maxwell Air Force Base: Air University Press, 2007), 145.

some of their political goals in the war – a mixed outcome in a war of limited political aims. Yet the cumulative damage to Hezbollah from Israeli air strikes ultimately generated significant, long-lasting effects. In this asymmetric conflict air power proved ineffective in stopping the war, but it was effective in the long run by imposing costs that deterred further conflict.

### Historical Background

Established as an independent state in 1943, Lebanon has a diverse population. Although all Lebanese are Arabs, the major population groups are Christians, Druze, Shiite Muslims, Sunni Muslims, and, after 1948, Palestinian refugees. In the 1970s, Palestinian terrorist organizations based in Lebanon embarked on a series of attacks across the southern border into Israel. In the summer of 1982, during the First Lebanon War, following years of cross-border terrorist attacks and after Katyusha short-range rockets bombarded Northern Israel, IDF forces invaded southern Lebanon, occupied the capital of Beirut, and evicted the Palestinian Liberation Organization (PLO) from Lebanon. In June 1985, Israel evacuated its forces from Lebanon only to have the IDF return in 1986 to prevent collapse of the Israeli-backed South Lebanon Army (SLA) and to establish a "security zone" to serve as a buffer from terrorist attacks along the border. Although various groups fought the IDF until its departure in 2000, by the early 1990s Hezbollah emerged as the IDF's main enemy in Lebanon.

Hezbollah, the "Party of God," was established in 1982 as a union of religious Shiite movements supported by the Iranian Islamic Revolutionary Guard Corps (IRGC).[7] In its early stages, from 1983 to 1986, the organization operated through various terrorist methods to include thirty-five suicide bombings, placing explosive charges, conducting ambushes, and abducting foreign soldiers and diplomats. In 1990, with the assistance of the IRGC, Hezbollah reorganized as a professional regular military force. Hezbollah divided its several hundred soldiers according to professional expertise: intelligence, offensive operations, and rocket launching. These forces were backed by local militias serving as reservists. Hezbollah became the main military organization in southern Lebanon, gradually evolving to more advanced guerrilla, commando-style, and even regular warfare capabilities. Synchronized with its military action, Hezbollah conducted an extensive social and political campaign

---

[7] Eitan Azani, *Hezbollah: The Story of the Party of God* (New York: Palgrave Macmillan, 2009).

with the objective of occupying southern Lebanon. Foundational to its strategy was a ceaseless low-intensity conflict aimed at exhausting Israel and destroying the SLA.

By contrast, Israel's political goal was withdrawal from Lebanon in exchange for an arrangement that would ensure that the northern border remain free from further attacks. The IDF adopted a defensive strategy, where IDF and SLA forces attempted to thwart Hezbollah's military activities while absorbing as few casualties and with as little effort as possible. On two occasions, in an effort to deter Hezbollah from firing rockets into Israel, the IDF embarked on limited offensive operations, utilizing air strikes and artillery fire while minimizing the deployment of ground forces.

Operation Accountability, from July 25 to 31, 1993, included 1,000 bombing sorties, artillery barrages, and raids by Special Forces.[8] As a result, 300,000 internally displaced Lebanese moved temporarily from southern Lebanon to Beirut. In the attacks, 50 Hezbollah fighters and 65 Lebanese civilians were killed, while 2 Israeli civilians and 3 Israeli soldiers died. Lebanese infrastructure was severely damaged in the bombings. At the end of the military operation both sides signed a cease-fire agreement, agreeing to refrain from firing at civilian populations.

Three years later, following an increase of rockets attacks, the IDF launched Operation Grapes of Wrath from April 11 to 27, 1996, with the objective of renewing its deterrence against Hezbollah. The strategy was to damage national and economic infrastructure to coerce the Lebanese and Syrian governments to pressure Hezbollah to renew the "Accountability" agreement. The operation consisted of air strikes, artillery fire, and Special Forces raids against pinpoint targets. The IDF imposed a naval blockade on Lebanon, and on the night of April 14–15 attacked electricity stations near Beirut (Jumhur and Salam). Grapes of Wrath claimed 3 IDF soldiers, 19 Hezbollah soldiers, and 180 Lebanese civilians while displacing 350,000 Lebanese civilians.

The IAF's assessment of Operation Grapes of Wrath highlighted frustration regarding the inability to directly suppress Hezbollah's rockets. IAF commanders noted, "Against guerrilla warfare, according to what we learned in the operation, we cannot win with the air force . . . . What an air force knows how to do is to strike in a painful place . . . . That is infrastructure in Lebanon, and the supply routes from Syria to Lebanon."[9] Many agreed, including then-IAF Chief of Staff Dan Halutz, who would

---

[8] Raphael Rudnik and Ephraim Segoli, "The Israeli Air Force and Asymmetric Conflicts, 1982–2014," in *Airpower Applied*, ed. John Andreas Olsen (Annapolis: Naval Institute Press, 2017), 285–341.

[9] *Operation Grapes of Wrath* (Hebrew), "The History of the Israeli Air Force," 1999, 304.

be the IDF Chief of Staff a decade later in the Second Lebanon War: "I think we should reduce the treatment of [rockets] ... be willing to absorb some of them, do everything possible, but do not make it our main task .... We need to expand the targets for a painful attack, the so-called disruption of life in Lebanon."[10] It was clear to IAF leaders there would be another military operation in Lebanon, and the preferred mode of operation for Israel would be to rely on air strikes and not to reintroduce ground forces to occupy Lebanon.[11]

The limited air operations against Hezbollah during the 1990s expressed a change in the IDF's operational approach with a shift from ground maneuver supported by air power toward firepower warfare where air power dominated. Though the "maneuver" approach was considered effective against regular forces, it seemed less applicable in irregular warfare. Other problems included sensitivity to casualties and a crisis of legitimacy for the IDF, along with domestic and international concerns regarding ground engagements and occupation of territory. On the other hand new capabilities emerged, such as aerial precision munitions, which further shifted the politicians' preference for firepower over maneuver.[12] Additionally, the political goal for these firepower operations was a return to the security status quo without a change in the political reality on the ground, a goal inconsistent with deployed ground forces. Despite the advantages of the firepower approach, limitations inherent in applying air power against irregular forces prevented a short, decisive outcome and instead led to longer-duration wars, extensive damage to the home front, and ethical problems associated with bombing residential areas.

The prolonged and continuous fighting in the security zone provoked public debate in Israel about the IDF's purpose in staying in southern Lebanon. As a result, in the spring of 2000 Prime Minister Ehud Barak ordered the IDF to withdraw unilaterally from Lebanon. Without a political agreement to back Israel's withdrawal the SLA ceased to exist. The IDF redeployment was touted by Hezbollah leader Hassan Nasrallah as a victory. "I tell you: this 'Israel' that owns nuclear weapons and the strongest air force in this region is more fragile than a spiderweb."[13]

Israel's withdrawal did not stop the evolution of Hezbollah or its attacks against Israel. Hezbollah increased its regular and reserve forces, trained to conduct defensive battles, and acquired a wide variety of weapons and

---

[10] Ibid., 310.    [11] Ibid., 306, 314.
[12] Rudnik and Segoli, "The Israeli Air Force and Asymmetric Conflicts," 288–98.
[13] Hassan Nasrallah's victory speech in Bint Jbeil, Lebanon, May 26, 2000; Jeffrey Goldberg, "In the Party of God," *The New Yorker*, October 14, 2002.

ancillary equipment.[14] It further provided socioeconomic aid and supported educational and religious programs among Lebanese Shiites to attract support. Also, for the first time since its inception, Hezbollah participated in elections and won seats in the Lebanese parliament.[15]

By 2006 Hezbollah had the capabilities of a regular army, including command and control facilities, advanced communications systems, regional units of well-trained combat soldiers, and advanced weapons to include 2,000 antitank missiles, C-802 antiship missiles, and unmanned aerial vehicles. Its rocket arsenal doubled from 7,000 missiles in 2000 to 14,000 in 2006.[16] Hezbollah expanded its military infrastructure across southern Lebanon and in Beirut, including constructing headquarters, rocket-launching sites, and combat positions, some underground.

Hezbollah's ultimate goal had never been restricted to southern Lebanon. Adjusting to the new situation in which there were no Israeli troops in Lebanon, Hezbollah began attacking Israel mostly with short-range rockets and mortars but also by conducting cross-border commando raids aimed at ambushing, killing, and kidnapping Israeli soldiers.[17] For six years, from the autumn of 2000 until the summer of 2006, the IDF was fully occupied fighting the Palestinian Terror Offensive within the Israeli border with almost 1,150 Israelis killed, most of them civilians, and with thousands more wounded. Compared to the approximately 26,000 Palestinian terror attacks within Israel, the 176 Hezbollah attacks along the border, which killed 21 and wounded 102, paled in importance. As a result, the Israeli government and the IDF were not willing to open a second front in response to Hezbollah attacks, instead responding weakly to each incident – if at all.

Following the withering international criticism of its assassination of Lebanese Prime Minister Sa'ad Hariri, Syrian forces withdrew from Lebanon in April 2005. Israeli war plans to strike Syrian forces in Lebanon to coerce Syria to in turn pressure Hezbollah thus became irrelevant. In August 2005, Israel further withdrew from the Gaza Strip, and Nasrallah assessed Israel vulnerable to military pressure. On June 25, 2006, Hamas attacked an IDF tank near the Gaza Strip fence, killing two soldiers and taking another hostage. The IDF commenced an operation

---

[14] Arkin, *Divining Victory*, 22–28.

[15] Daniel Sobelman, "Hizbollah – from Terror to Resistance: Towards a National Defence Strategy," in *Israel and Hizbollah: An Asymmetric Conflict in Historical and Comparative Perspective*, eds. Clive Jones and Sergio Catignani (London: Routledge, 2010), 49–66.

[16] Yitzhak Ben-Israel, *The First Missile War: Israel and Hezbollah Summer 2006* (Tel Aviv: Tel Aviv University, 2007), 7–9.

[17] Thus, in October 2000, three Israeli soldiers were killed, and their bodies abducted to Lebanon. Hava Mudrik Evroni, "Abductions on the Northern Border" (Hebrew) IDF, 2016, 11–13.

in the Gaza Strip with air strikes, targeted killings, and ground raids in an effort to coerce Hamas to return the soldier.[18] Two weeks later, with fighting unabated in Gaza, Hezbollah opened a second front by attacking an IDF patrol along the Lebanese border.

### Second Lebanon War: Political Objectives and Military Goals

Immediately following the attack on IDF soldiers on the morning of July 12, 2006, IAF aircraft bombed Hezbollah border posts and bridges on routes from southern Lebanon to the north. Following an IDF meeting, Chief of Staff Lieutenant General Dan Halutz recommended a change in the defensive policy toward Hezbollah: in order to restore deterrence, attack and thereby impose costs on Hezbollah and Lebanese national infrastructure.[19]

Defense Minister Amir Peretz then held a meeting focused on whom to attack: Hezbollah, Lebanon, or the Syrian government. The meeting also discussed the two primary target sets: Lebanese national infrastructure and Hezbollah's rocket arsenal. Gadi Eizenkot, Chief of Operations, recommended to "not confront Hezbollah but the Lebanese State . . . . The understanding is that if we confront Hezbollah, they will react, and if we hit Lebanese infrastructures, it will create a dilemma."[20] Halutz agreed. However, the head of the Mossad, Meir Dagan, claimed that in the past these operations did not provide any benefits, and if the IDF's proposal was accepted, "we are going to descend into a long-term confrontation, with a high potential for attacks against Israel's home front."[21] Dagan recommended attacking terrorist targets in Syria, but Defense Minister Peretz declared Hezbollah the enemy, and it was therefore necessary to act against them. Halutz recommended attacking power stations, which supply up to 50 percent of the electricity in Lebanon, but Peretz rejected the proposal. Another dispute arose over the attack on Hezbollah's medium-range Fajr rockets, with Halutz and the commander of the IAF, Eliezer Shkedi, recommending they should not be attacked immediately but only in the next stage of the campaign. This assessment was in part due to the potential for collateral damage per operational analysis; this could kill between 100 and 400 civilians living near their storage sites.[22] The Defense Minister objected to targeting infrastructure,

---

[18] The soldier was returned five years later in a prisoner exchange.
[19] Winograd Committee, Interim Report, 68–70.    [20] Ibid., 70.    [21] Ibid., 71.
[22] Amos Harel and Avi Issacharoff, *Spider Webs: The Story of the Second Lebanon War* (Tel Aviv: Ma'ariv, 2008), 163.

declaring instead "the issue of medium-range rockets is a strategic matter and a top priority."[23]

Later in a conference with Prime Minister Ehud Olmert, Peretz again objected to the bombing of national infrastructure that would "primarily harm the Lebanese population, which mainly does not support Hezbollah" and again proposed strikes on deployed medium-range rocket sites. The Prime Minister accepted Peretz's reasoning, adding that damage to Lebanon's infrastructure would incite the international community against Israel.[24] In the cabinet meeting that followed, consensus grew that the operation should be air-only, and soldiers should not be endangered. The military leaders again proposed attacking Lebanese infrastructure as well. Since the Defense Minister and the Prime Minister rejected this proposal, the government security forum approved striking only the medium-range rocket launchers.[25]

Because Israel planned only a large-scale air operation and not an all-out war, IDF plans did not include a transition to a wartime footing, which would have mobilized reserve forces, made preparations for a Hezbollah attack, or made plans for the occupation of southern Lebanon. The Israeli government stated it viewed the Lebanese government responsible for Hezbollah's actions and demanded Lebanon exercise sovereign control over all its land. At the same time, Israel also judged Hezbollah directly responsible for the attack and responded against the terrorist organization "in a manner required by its actions."[26]

From these political statements, IDF leaders defined the military objectives of the operation as enhancing deterrence, coercing the Lebanese government to secure control of southern Lebanon, and exerting pressure on Hezbollah to return the captives.[27] These political objectives would be achieved by a military strategy that imposed a naval and air blockade on Lebanon and severely damaging Hezbollah. Meanwhile, the IDF continued military operations in Gaza in response to a Palestinian attack two weeks earlier as it prepared for a prolonged campaign on the home front.

---

[23] Winograd Committee, Interim Report, 71, 74.
[24] Ibid., 76; Harel and Issacharoff, *Spider Webs*, 165–66.
[25] Government Decision, July 12, 2006, Winograd Report, 82. The ministers in the security forum were Prime Minister Olmert, Defense Minister Peretz, Foreign Minister Tzipi Livni, Shimon Peres, Shaul Mofaz (former Chief of Staff), Eli Yishai, and Avi Dichter (former Shin Bet Chief).
[26] The Government's Decision, July 12, 2006, Winograd Report, 82.
[27] IDF Operations Division, July 12–13, Operation "Appropriate Pay" – Order no. 1, 02:00, 13.7.2006

*Operation Density*

Intelligence played a crucial role in the air operations. In the summer of 2000, intelligence material had been collected on Hezbollah's rocket arsenal in Lebanon, which included details of the location of medium-range rockets and the storage sites of launchers. Hezbollah operated a clandestine system of storing the rocket array inside ordinary "innocent-looking" homes in villages in southern Lebanon. The Lebanese families who agreed to hold rockets in their homes received payment from the organization and allocated rooms to store the launchers. Each launcher was aimed in advance at a specific target in Israel so that when necessary a wall could be quickly torn down and the rocket launched. Obtaining the locations of these storehouses was a major effort by Israeli intelligence, which included more than forty special operations. In some cases, even the specific room was located.[28]

A joint team comprised of the Military Intelligence Directorate and IAF Intelligence accurately identified the targets, and a special planning team was established in the Operations Department to incorporate detailed planning into an operation order. In October 2000, an operational plan formed concerning the best methods to attack the launchers. In 2001, an order called "Density" was issued, which included intelligence findings about the mid-range rockets. The operational order was distributed by the end of 2001, and the IAF began the training to implement it. When the IAF received GPS-guided JDAMs (joint direct attack munitions), precise coordinates were calculated for all targets. In addition, JDAMs made possible extensive operation at night and in bad weather, which could shorten the duration of attacks. The operational idea was "to destroy a significant part of the medium-range rocket launchers, while creating an effect of 'intelligence exposure' and a sense of being hunted within Hezbollah. This was to be done by a simultaneous surprise attack of dozens of targets."[29] With the decision to strike, the discussion turned to the issue of collateral damage. Attorney General Menachem Mazuz ruled that from the point of view of international law, houses belonging to civilians who store weapons can be legally attacked, or as Peretz phrased it, "He who sleeps with a rocket in his house must know that he might get hurt."[30]

---

[28] Ofer Shelah and Yo'av Limor, *Captives of Lebanon* (Hebrew) (Tel Aviv: Miskal-Yedi'oth Ahronopth Books, 2007), 77–81; Ilan Kfir, *The Earth Shivered: 33 Days, Lebanon* (Hebrew) (Tel Aviv: Ma'ariv, 2006), 132–35; Amir Rappaport, *Fire on Our Forces* (Tel Aviv: Ma'ariv, 2007), 87–91.
[29] Ibid.   [30] Shelah and Limor, *Captives of Lebanon*, 50.

Operation Density commenced at 0400 on July 13, 2006. Within 45 minutes, IAF air strikes, primarily with JDAMs, destroyed 44 launchers along with hundreds of rockets. The ferocity of the strikes surprised Hezbollah, which, based on previous incidents, had not anticipated such a powerful response and believed the rocket locations to be secret. Hezbollah's ability to conduct mid-range strikes was severely degraded. In addition to the effectiveness of the strikes, civilian casualties were fewer than expected, with 20 Lebanese killed.[31] The success of the operation was the culmination of a 6-year intelligence and operational effort, and the efficient and precise manner of execution minimized the threat to Israeli pilots.

As the Israeli intelligence services had anticipated and warned, Hezbollah responded by firing its short-range Katyusha rockets at the Galilee. Throughout the day Hezbollah launched 125 rockets, killing 2 civilians and wounding another 69. The next day rockets killed another 6 Israelis. Hezbollah continued its salvos of rockets, and the struggle to suppress them became a distinctive characteristic of the Second Lebanon War. Moreover, Israeli military operations deteriorated into a series of actions and reactions without the Israeli government deliberately deciding to go to war. Initiating Operation Density, which ended the Israeli "containment" policy, meant the beginning of a war of attrition, in which the IAF played a central role.

### Bombing Infrastructure in Lebanon

From the beginning of the war, Chief of Staff Lieutenant General Halutz viewed the bombing of Lebanese national infrastructure as the key to achieving Israel's objectives of stopping the rocket attacks and coercing Hezbollah to return the kidnapped soldiers. Considering the lessons learned from previous operations and the inability to directly attack and destroy all Hezbollah rocket launchers, Halutz and other senior commanders supported an indirect approach, which meant exerting pressure on the Lebanese government to convince Hezbollah to accept the dictates of Israel.

Though the Prime Minister initially disapproved the IDF's initial request to attack electricity facilities, Halutz expected that the retaliatory rocket fire from Hezbollah would change the politician's mind. However, Prime Minister Olmert continued to refuse to damage the power stations because he assumed Israel would lose American and international

---

[31] Benjamin Lambeth, *Air Operations in Israel's War against Hezbollah* (Santa Monica: RAND, 2011), 95–105.

support.[32] Repeatedly rejected through the end of the war, Halutz continued to request to bomb power stations and Lebanese infrastructure targets on a larger scale to motivate the Lebanese government to "take a stand."

The Israeli government nevertheless authorized destruction of numerous infrastructure elements. The IAF attacked bridges between southern Lebanon and central Lebanon to prevent the transportation of the abductees to the north. Beirut International Airport was bombed and partially paralyzed on the second day of the war to prevent air traffic to and from Lebanon. The following day the IAF also bombed airfields at Riak and Kliat. To stop armed convoys from Syria to Lebanon, the IAF bombed bridges and cratered chokepoints along the Beirut-Damascus highway. Additional bridges, including those along the coastal road between Beirut and Tripoli, were disabled to further isolate southern Lebanon. In total, 92 bridges were targeted, and 430 chokepoints were cratered.[33] Besides the attacks on transport infrastructure, two fuel tank facilities near Beirut and 46 petrol stations in southern Lebanon and near Beirut were disabled. The IDF's desire to stop Hezbollah's movement paralyzed Lebanon and inflicted cumulative damage that gained significance over time.

### Bombing the Dahiya Neighborhood in Beirut

Hezbollah located its central headquarters underneath the Dahiya neighborhood in Beirut. In lieu of targeting Lebanese government infrastructure, General Halutz proposed to attack this senior command facility in the hope this would convince Hezbollah to cease the rocket campaign. Both the Israeli Prime Minister and the Minister of Defense approved the recommendation, and that night several bridges and road intersections were struck in Dahiya.[34]

The following day, on June 14, the Israeli cabinet reconvened to discuss how to further damage Hezbollah. Halutz proposed and the cabinet approved targeting Hezbollah's security zone in Dahiya. The IAF dropped leaflets on the neighborhood warning residents to leave.[35] The bombing commenced that evening, demolishing high-rise buildings under which housed Nasrallah's bunker, Hezbollah headquarters, and its television station Al-Manar. The IDF also disrupted Al-Manar's broadcasts and broadcast on the channel anti-Hezbollah propaganda.[36]

---

[32] Harel and Issacharoff, *Spider Webs*, 187.     [33] Lambeth, *Air Operations*, 21, 27.
[34] Winograd, Interim Report, 91.
[35] During the entire war the IAF dropped 17,300,000 leaflets warning residents of targeted areas to move away before it or other IDF units attacked those areas.
[36] Arkin, *Divining Victory*, 111–15.

In response, Nasrallah announced that Hezbollah rockets would now target Haifa.[37] Meanwhile, the IAF continued strikes in the Dahiya area on Saturday and Sunday against the Supreme Council of Hezbollah's "Shura" headquarters, the organization's secretariat headquarters, and many other buildings. Israeli air strikes in the Dahiya neighborhood continued until the end of the war, destroying more than one hundred high-rise buildings and another hundred severely damaged. The IAF employed mainly JDAM GPS-guided bombs, and there were few civilian casualties in part because the civilian population heeded IDF warnings.[38]

In addition to making rubble of Hezbollah's political infrastructure, Israel tried to pressure Hezbollah by targeting its leaders, including bombing the homes of Nasrallah and Fadlallah, the spiritual leaders of Hezbollah. The IAF had extensive experience in targeted killings of terrorist organizations' leaders, including the assassination of Nasrallah's predecessor, Abbas Musawi, in 1992. The key to successful targeted killings is accurate intelligence. On the first day of the war Israel intelligence knew the location of several Hezbollah leaders, but the government disapproved strikes to avoid escalating the crisis. Later the government approved leadership strikes, but accurate and timely intelligence no longer existed. Therefore, though the IAF bombed 450 suspected command sites, Hezbollah senior officers suffered minimal casualties.[39] IDF Special Forces also raided the suspected locations of Hezbollah commanders at Ba'al-Beq, in northeastern Lebanon, on August 2 and two days later in Tyre. However, despite their boldness, both operations failed due to inaccurate intelligence.[40] Moreover, attempts to degrade Hezbollah leadership's command and control systems by bombing its communications lines did not paralyze the organization as Hezbollah maintained multiple methods for communication, which functioned throughout the war.[41]

### IAF Fighting Hezbollah Rockets

The main challenge for the IAF was targeting Hezbollah's short-range rockets. On the eve of the war, Hezbollah had 14,000 rockets that varied in range and size of warheads. Twelve thousand were 107 mm and 122 mm rockets with a range of 20 kilometers, and of these most were located near Israel, between the Lebanese southern border and the Litani River. Another thousand 122 mm rockets had an extended range of 40

[37] On July 16 a rocket hit a train garage in Haifa, killing eight Israelis.
[38] Lambeth, *Air Operations*, 27, 35.
[39] Lambeth, *Air Operations*, 154–57; IAF, "The War against Hezbollah," Air Force Activity and Key Lessons, 2006, 13.
[40] Harel and Issacharoff, *Spider Webs*, 327–31.    [41] Arkin, *Divining Victory*, 107–15.

kilometers and could reach Haifa. The most threatening were 1,000 Iranian-produced 240 mm "Fajr" and 610 mm "Zelzal" rockets with ranges of 70 to 150 kilometers and with large warheads with hundreds of kilograms of explosives. These rockets, located north of the Litani River, could reach Tel Aviv and Jerusalem.[42]

Even before the war, planners recognized "the effectiveness of aerial hunting of rockets and Katyusha and attacking them by air-strikes only is expected to be low."[43] Therefore, planners estimated the IAF could destroy 20 to 50 percent of the rocket launchers, which would reduce launches by 10 to 30 percent. This estimate ignored the possibility that Hezbollah would attack Israel daily with 100 to 200 rockets. Even if the IAF destroyed half of the launchers, this still left sufficient rockets and launchers to maintain an extended-duration attrition campaign.

Operation Density destroyed most of the medium-range Fajr and Zelzal launchers; however, the IAF had little effect on the thousands of 20- to 40-kilometer range rockets. From the second day of the war, Hezbollah commenced mortar and rocket attacks on Israeli civilian and military targets along the border and deeper into northern Israel. As Israeli air strikes on leadership had not prevented but instead precipitated Hezbollah's attacks, and with the Israeli government having no intention of sending ground forces to occupy southern Lebanon, the IAF was forced to act directly to reduce the rocket threat. The IAF responded by attacking rocket launchers and ammunition depots, hunting rockets to disrupt rocket fire, isolating Lebanon from Syria, and cutting off southern Lebanon from the north to prevent the transfer of more rockets into the launching areas.

Throughout the war, the IAF continued to attack rocket deployments with priority placed on the remaining medium-range rockets, but success depended on intelligence. Five days into the war, on July 18, a Zelzal rocket site was located, attacked, and all its launchers destroyed.[44] On the other hand, when intelligence was not accurate, other air strikes failed. Although obtaining the requisite intelligence grew more difficult as the war progressed, no medium-range rockets ever reached central Israel.

*Disrupting Rocket Launches*

The concept of "disrupting rocket launches" had been developed in the 1990s. The idea was to identify the areas in southern Lebanon from which

---

[42] Ibid., 31–38.
[43] Harel and Issacharoff, *Spider Webs*, 282. Katyusha was the Israeli nickname for the 122 mm rockets – based on the designation of a World War II Soviet rocket.
[44] Itai Brun, "The Second Lebanon War, 2006," in *A History of Air Warfare*, ed. John Andreas Olsen (Dulles: Potomac Books, 2010), 310.

rockets were likely to be fired and then preemptively bomb these areas to deter the rocket operators from firing. The results would then be analyzed to determine the effectiveness of the bombing. The areas bombed were in uninhabited brush areas, nicknamed "nature reserves," where Hezbollah rocket launch and fighting complexes had been built under the foliage, with some even subterranean. Even if no specific targets, such as vehicles or launchers, could be identified in an area, bombing the zone was intended to disrupt the rocket operations and reduce the overall number of launches. During Operations Accountability and Grapes of Wrath, the IAF determined this method of deterring rocket launches was inefficient.[45] However, absent a viable alternative, and as rockets continued to land on Israel, the IAF was forced to continue such daily area bombings across southern Lebanon.

In the first two weeks, deterrent attacks used general-purpose bombs, usually one bomb per "disruption-point." To avoid antiaircraft fire, fighter pilots remained above 12,000 feet.[46] An attack from this altitude using a free-fall bomb was not precise, but hitting within 50 meters of the desired aim point was deemed good enough for a disruption mission. Nevertheless, with the rocket launches continuing and the disruption attacks ineffective, within two weeks the IAF transitioned to cluster bomb unit (CBU) munitions. CBUs could cover a wider area to include the routes used by the Hezbollah operators. Also, efforts were made, but failed, to burn the brush foliage that hid the launch sites.[47]

Of the 7,000 targets attacked during the war, 34 percent were part of the disruption effort.[48] Analysts determined the IAF was ineffective at significantly reducing rocket launches from the designated areas. For example, many short-range 122 mm "Grad" rockets fired from camouflaged multiple barrel fixed launchers had been fired either by remote control or with preprogrammed timers.[49] Against such tactics, disruption bombing had little effect. Despite the great effort put into these sorties by the IAF, the pace of Hezbollah launches remained unchanged.[50]

---

[45] *Operation Grapes of Wrath*, 246, 258, 262.
[46] Lambeth, *Air Operations*, 86. The actual average altitude above ground was 10,000 feet.
[47] Harel and Issacharoff, *Spider Webs*, 289–90. During the war more than 1,000 CBU bombs were dropped, and many more cluster bombs were fired by MLRS. See Arkin, *Divining Victory*, 63–67. Human Rights Watch, *Flooding South Lebanon: Israel's Use of Cluster Munitions in Lebanon in July and August 2006*, 2008, 29–48.
[48] Ben-Israel, *The First Missile War*, 41.
[49] Uzi Rubin, "The Rocket Campaign against Israel during the 2006 Lebanon War," Besa Center for Strategic Studies, 2007, 8–9.
[50] Brun, "The Second Lebanon War, 2006," 318–19.

*Rocket Hunt*

Another effort by the IAF was attacking rocket launchers immediately after they were discovered, before or after launching, a method called "rocket hunting." An interagency team led by the IAF developed the processes and systems for swiftly detecting and geolocating launch sites. A special task force assigned to the IAF headquarters planned the "hunt" mission and trained IAF personnel. Due to limited intelligence, the IAF concentrated on attacking mobile launchers, usually found mounted in the bed of a pickup truck, rather than searching for the stationary launchers, which were more difficult to find.

Israeli intelligence, surveillance, and reconnaissance (ISR) platforms, usually remotely piloted aircraft (RPAs), flew continuously over the combat zone day and night, monitoring for suspicious activity. The RPA operators occasionally discovered launchers prior to launch but more often just after the firing of the first rocket. Once located, the launcher position was automatically transferred to the IAF 's control system, which, in turn, assigned an aircraft to attack the target coordinates with guided munitions. The time from launch detection to a bomb on target usually took several minutes.[51]

Detection and attack techniques improved over the course of the war with most medium-range launchers destroyed immediately after launch, a total of thirty-six out of forty-one and another seven destroyed prior to launch.[52] Though an impressive operational achievement, Hezbollah's launchers were disposable as they had a sufficient supply to continue firing through the last day of the war.[53]

*Short-Range Rockets*

The vast majority of Hezbollah rockets were short-range with 95 percent of launches originating between the Israeli-Lebanese border and the Litani River, 10 to 15 kilometers to the north.[54] Northern Command had responsibility for reducing short-range rocket fire, but the operational order did not assign this task until August 3.[55]

Gradually, the IAF attacked the short-range launchers with the same tactics as the medium-range rocket "hunt." Eighty-seven short-range

---

[51] Ben-Israel, *The First Missile War*, 44–46.
[52] This is in addition to the forty-four medium-range launchers destroyed on the opening night.
[53] Rubin, "The Rocket Campaign," 21, 24–28.
[54] Ben-Israel, *The First Missile War*, 18–19; Lambeth, *Air Operations*, 145.
[55] Shelah and Limor, *Captives of Lebanon*, 240–41; Harel and Issacharoff, *Spider Webs*, 288–91.

launchers were destroyed near the border, with dozens of suspected launchers also targeted. However, this was only a small fraction of Hezbollah's arsenal, and the air strikes had no effect on overall short-range rocket launch rates. The IAF improvised the "hunt" because prior to the war it had not been deemed an effective mission for air power. Intelligence was therefore sparse, and it was not until the last week of the war that a concerted effort was made to locate the launchers based on intelligence and not just a visual search. Rocket munition storage sites were located as well as the houses of the Hezbollah personnel who conducted the launches. Yet these strikes came too little and too late to affect the outcome of the war.

An organizational problem that hampered efficient operations was the division of responsibilities between Northern Command and IAF headquarters. In general, Northern Command oversaw the fighting zone up to the Litani River, and IAF headquarters controlled the territory beyond. On the eve of the war Northern Command had the authority to approve attacks only up to 7 kilometers north of the border, and above this line IAF headquarters maintained air strike control. This created an area in which Northern Command had responsibility but not authority to operate aircraft, whereas IAF headquarters had the authority to operate planes, but prioritized other missions over hunting short-range rockets. In practice, this area, from which Hezbollah launched 69 percent of its short-range rockets, was barely attacked.[56]

A by-product of the short-range rocket hunt was unintended civilian casualties. The most significant incident occurred in the village of Qana on July 30, when aircraft attacked a Hezbollah launch site, but an adjacent building collapsed, killing twenty-eight civilians. Following this incident Israel halted air strikes for forty-eight hours. Hezbollah also reduced its launches during this time, with only fifteen rockets fired on Israel on August 1 and 2.

### Preventing the Transfer of Rockets

Another way to reduce rocket launches was to prevent the transfer of rockets from Syria to Lebanon. The IAF attacked 200 targets on the Syrian-Lebanese border and along its major motor routes in northern Lebanon, the Tripoli area, the Bekaa Valley, and along the mountain passes south of the Beirut-Damascus road. In total the IAF struck 50 trucks and other vehicles carrying weapons. These attacks were based on intelligence gained on the vehicles' movements and, though some

---

[56] Ben-Israel, *The First Missile War*, 50.

vehicles still made it through, the IAF's interdiction campaign reduced arms transfers from Syria to Lebanon.[57]

Similarly, the IAF attacked 69 crossings and bridges along the Litani and Zaharani rivers to cut off South Lebanon from the north. Additionally, 230 chokepoints were cratered to block the roads, and 300 vehicles driving south were attacked. However, Hezbollah had prepared rocket storage sites in southern Lebanon to reduce dependence on supply lines. Further, the coastal road was not attacked to allow access for humanitarian vehicles and evacuation of the population. As a result, the Israeli interdiction effort had minimal effect on short-range rocket launches.

To sum, IAFs efforts to reduce short-range rocket launches failed. During the war Hezbollah fired 3,990 rockets and mortars into Israel. The pace of attacks even increased over time. In total, 901 rockets hit Israeli towns, killing 12 soldiers, 44 civilians, and injuring 1,445 (see Figure 7.2).[58]

### IAF Assistance to Ground Forces

Hezbollah rocket attacks continued despite the IAF's efforts and, without a cease-fire in sight, Israel finally felt compelled to deploy troops in Lebanon. The Israeli military presence in Lebanon expanded gradually along with the missions imposed upon them.

On July 19, a week after the war began, the IDF conducted an infantry battalion raid on the Hezbollah compound in Maroun al-Ras, followed by similar raids elsewhere along the border. On July 23, two brigades advanced slightly deeper into Lebanon to capture the town of Bint Jbeil, followed by similarly sized operations against other villages and towns identified with Hezbollah facilities. At the beginning of August, the Israeli Army initiated the recruitment and training of its reserve divisions, with four divisions ordered to advance into and capture all the Lebanese territory from the border up to the Litani River. This operation, however, failed to meet senior command expectations due to planning and training constraints that led to poor execution. Hezbollah, rather than being put on the defensive, employed effective guerrilla tactics. This final act of the ground war halted mid-stride with the cease-fire on August 14.

Even before the ground forces entered Lebanon, IAF aircraft were allocated to Northern Command. Initially, air strikes by Northern

---

[57] Lambeth, *Air Operations*, 40.
[58] Rubin, "The Rocket Campaign," 14. Arkin, *Divining Victory*, 60.

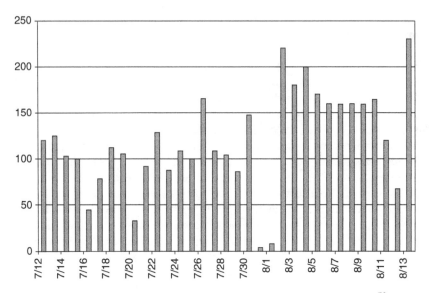

Figure 7.2  Rocket impacts per Day (July 12–August 13, 2006)[59]

Command were directed against Hezbollah infrastructure and rocket launchers. The IAF allocated even more aircraft to Northern Command once Israeli ground forces entered Lebanon. Because the IAF's sortie rate was much higher than the targets it was finding, there was an abundance of available aircraft to assist the ground forces.

During the war the IAF provided 2,500 fighter close air support (CAS) sorties, provided aerial resupply, and conducted medical evacuations.[60] The slowness of air operations and the relatively small number of troops engaged in ground combat at any given time allowed for tactics that ran counter either to doctrine or previous experience. Nine hundred air strikes were conducted within 1,000 meters of IDF ground forces, and some close situations required strikes within 200 meters. What made this so different was that the air strikes were carried out by indirect coordination, without direct communications between aircraft and ground units. It should be noted that despite the danger involved in these attacks, no IDF soldier was killed.[61]

[59] Jewish Virtual Library, November 2006. www.jewishvirtuallibrary.org/hezbollah-rocket-attacks-during-second-lebanon-war
[60] Ben-Israel, *The First Missile War*, 43–44. Lambeth, *Air Operations*, 78–83.
[61] Ben-Israel, *The First Missile War*, 43.

In addition to its fighters, the IAF operated attack helicopters in close cooperation with ground forces, engaging the enemy at very close range. One example was the engagement between Battalion 51 of the Golani Brigade and a Hezbollah force in the town of Bint Jbeil. After a few hours of stubborn infantry fighting, the battle was decided by the helicopters firing missiles at Hezbollah fighters only a few dozen meters from the Golani troops.[62]

Though Israeli ground forces operated only a few kilometers from the border, the combination of a lack of good roads, along with the threat from Hezbollah's long-range anti-tank missiles and improvised explosive devices (IEDs) that threatened existing roads, hindered supplying Israeli troops. From July 27 on, IAF helicopters resupplied these ground forces nightly. As additional forces deployed, supply requirements mounted such that by August 6 the IAF employed its C-130 cargo planes to air drop supplies into Lebanon. Given the proximity of the rival forces, each air drop required a high degree of coordination to ensure C-130s accurately hit the drop site while avoiding Hezbollah ground fire. This aerial resupply capability matured during the war, despite the difficulties and risk, with 360 tons of much needed supplies delivered.[63]

Finally, despite the proximity of most of the fighting to the border, aerial medical evacuation received a high priority because of the lack of suitable roads. Many wounded soldiers were evacuated by helicopter from the line of contact, sometimes under fire, and not from rear-gathering stations as defined in combat doctrine. In total, 93 percent of the sixty-two critically injured were evacuated by helicopters as well as several hundred less seriously wounded.[64]

### Summary of the Aerial Warfare – Data and Lessons

The Second Lebanon War began when Israel responded to a successful Hezbollah cross-border ground attack. As the war progressed, the IDF failed to achieve a decisive victory as Israeli air power failed to prevent Hezbollah rockets from being continually launched into Israel. Though not defeated in battle, Hezbollah did suffer many casualties. Although 121 Israeli soldiers and 44 civilians were killed during the war, Lebanese deaths were much higher, with approximately 1,190 people killed in Lebanon, 650 of whom were Hezbollah members.[65] Hezbollah had not planned for a war but instead had intended to use the kidnapping of Israeli

---

[62] Shelah and Limor, *Captives of Lebanon*, 188.    [63] Lambeth, *Air Operations*, 76.
[64] Ben-Israel, *The First Missile War*, 43–44; Lambeth, *Air Operations*, 78–83.
[65] Arkin, *Divining Victory*, 60, 98.

soldiers to pressure the release of Hezbollah operatives from prison. As a result of the casualties suffered along with the high level of damage to its infrastructure, Hezbollah was ready for a cease-fire while it could declare it had stood toe-to-toe against Israel without surrendering.

A cease-fire agreement, signed in accordance with UN Security Council Resolution 1701, went into effect on August 14. In comparison to the hundreds of attacks that occurred in the six years leading to the war, Hezbollah has subsequently conducted only a handful of attacks against Israel since 2006. The threat of another war with Israel has deterred a return to the provocation attacks, which used to characterize Hezbollah's tactics. Conversely, over this same postwar period Israel has conducted hundreds of strikes against Hezbollah personnel, equipment, and infrastructure. Thus, in the new balance following the Second Lebanon War Hezbollah seems more cautious than Israel in exercising force.

The IAF expended significant resources in the Second Lebanon War. Nearly 12,000 combat sorties by fighters and attack helicopters were flown, more than in the 1973 Yom Kippur War. The physical results of air strikes were numerous, as seen in Table 7.1, including thousands of buildings destroyed that were utilized as command posts, storage facilities, or rocket launcher sites. Also destroyed were a number of Hezbollah headquarters, hundreds of mobile launchers, and thousands of rockets.

The damage caused by Israeli air strikes may not have won the war, but they did prove significant after the war in realizing Israel's primary political objective – to compel Hezbollah to cease its attacks against Israel. Since 2006 there has been no further war in Lebanon, and Hezbollah's terrorist activities along the Lebanese border have ceased. The Lebanese

Table 7.1 *Hezbollah targets attacked by Israeli Air Force*[66]

| Number of targets attacked | Type of object attacked |
| --- | --- |
| 3,000 | Buildings/bunkers/tunnels |
| 2,400 | Disruption of activity on launching sites |
| 500 | Attacking bridges and blocking roads |
| 700 | Rocket launchers and suspicious vehicles |
| 200 | Armed Hezbollah fighters |
| 100 | Communication and radar objectives |
| **6,900** | Total |

[66] Ben-Israel, *The First Missile War*, 41; Lambeth, *Air Operations*, 79.

government's responsibility for the south Lebanon region has grown, though it remains limited due to structural problems in Lebanon and Hezbollah's strength in the Shiite area. Hezbollah has conducted a handful of attacks on Israeli citizens overseas and, for a brief period, attempted to "open a new front" on Israel's border with Syria, but aggressive Israeli responses halted these activities without the escalation in violence as in 2006.

In the decade after the war the IAF added new capabilities. It established a multilayered interception system against missiles and rockets: The Arrow became operational in 2000, before the war, but it was designed against long-range ballistic missiles such as the Scud and was not activated in the war. The Arrow has since been joined by the Iron Dome, which intercepts short-range rockets. After 2006 the Iron Dome became the major defensive weapon in Gaza campaigns, and David's Sling also added capability against medium-range missiles. Thus, the IAF can now intercept missiles of different size and range to provide an active defense of its population, which in turn creates greater breathing space for political leadership to handle crises as they arise.

During the war the IAF's operational headquarters became a bottleneck in the management of information. Therefore, in the years that followed it increased in size, reorganized, and restructured the targeting process to be able to quickly convert actionable intelligence into operational missions. The effectiveness of the Air Force was further examined with regard to the rate at which targets could be attacked. More targets serviced per day required greater aircraft availability, so the IAF invested in its logistics and operational administration to increase daily sortie rates.

The Second Lebanon War shaped development of new air combat operations. Following the war, the IDF initiated the "Campaign between the Wars," a concept to conduct routine operations to hinder enemy force buildup for the next conflict. As part of this campaign, the IAF has attacked hundreds of targets to delay the escalation to war or face a less-capable enemy should war occur.[67] If escalation occurs, Israel stated it intends to act aggressively in what is known as the "Dahiya doctrine," a military strategy designed to conduct massive strikes on Hezbollah's political and military headquarters located in the Shiite quarter of Beirut. The Dahiya doctrine thus makes clear the high costs Hezbollah and its supporters will suffer.[68]

---

[67] Amos Yadlin and Assaf Orion, "The Campaign between Wars: Faster, Higher, Fiercer?" *INSS Insight*, 1209 (August 30, 2019): 1–6.
[68] Amos Harel, "IDF Plans to Use Disproportionate Force in Next War," *Haaretz*, October 5, 2008; Daniel Byman, *A High Price*, 263.

The IAF also plans to conduct "High-Intensity Strikes." This reflects changes in the IAF's command structure, administration, intelligence, and logistics to multiply daily sortie rates four times its capacity in 2006. This creates the potential to strike thousands of targets per day, compared to a total of 7,000 targets in 34 days.[69] In 2006, the limiting factor was the availability of actionable intelligence. Since Israel adopted the Dahiya doctrine and High-Intensity Strikes, both the IDF Chief of Staff and the IAF commander have publicly stated the deterrent value of these measures to create a credible threat against Hezbollah assets and thus prevent or delay the next war.

## Air Force Effectiveness in War: Strategy, Operational Design, and Tactics

When the Winograd Committee assessed IAF operations, it noted:

The IAF had very impressive achievements in the Second Lebanon War. It carried out most of its planned missions, and many unplanned missions, successfully and with dedication and high risk .... The IAF presented exceptional capabilities in the war, there is no doubt about its nature and quality, and it is an important component of Israel's deterrent capability.

Despite the IAF being judged as tactically and operationally proficient, the committee members acknowledged the war "ended without Israel winning militarily."[70] This highlights the complex relationship between the tactical, operational, and strategic levels of war in modern air campaigns. Tactical and operational virtuosity may not translate into strategic success, nor may a prudent strategy be achievable in the absence or denial of military ability.[71] War is an act of politics, so strategic decisions should be overseen by the government to ensure military operations are commensurate with political goals.

### *Implications of Air Power on the Strategic Level*

In the Second Lebanon War, the overall political goal was to compel Hezbollah to discontinue its periodic attacks on Israel. As the fighting escalated and rockets fell on Israeli residential areas, the government added the reduction of the rocket threat as an immediate military

---

[69] Major-General Amir Eshel, "Israel's Air Force Capabilities to Increase 400%," *Israel Defense*, May 29, 2014.
[70] Winograd Committee, Final Report, 326, 330.
[71] Clifford J. Rogers "Strategy, Operational Design and Tactics," *International Encyclopedia of Military History*, ed. James C. Bradford (New York: Routledge, 2006).

objective. These two objectives provide indices for evaluating the IAF's effectiveness.

Since the 1990s Israel has chosen to conduct its major military operations with stand-off fire and a minimum of ground maneuver. The reasons for this military strategy have been the desire to minimize risk to soldiers, to lessen the collateral damage to the Israeli population, and to avoid an occupation of Lebanon invoking international hostility. These reasons remained valid in 2006, and the government accepted the Chief of Staff's recommendation to refrain from using ground forces for the first two weeks of the war. However, an air force is not a tool suitable for every mission, and as IAF commanders noted in the Grapes of Wrath inquiry from 1996:

> We took on a task that we could not carry out . . .it is like Michael Jordan playing baseball instead of playing basketball . . . . It was the Air Force vs. Katyusha rockets and eventually we were unable to win.[72]

Achieving military victory against an enemy ground force by stand-off fire alone, without employing ground forces, is a very challenging if not impossible task. In this case air power failed. The enemy response to air strikes with rocket fire led to a campaign of gradual attrition. The Israeli population, particularly those in the north, suffered from the Hezbollah rockets, and Israeli political leaders became more and more sensitive to civilian pressure. Eventually the government felt it had no choice but to add ground forces to place direct pressure on Hezbollah to end the war.

The IDF commander, Lieutenant General Halutz, the former Chief of Staff of the IAF, knew the limits of air power against a guerrilla organization and therefore recommended attacking Hezbollah and Lebanon's infrastructure, particularly the electric power stations. Halutz hoped such targeted strikes and the potential for escalating strikes further would coerce Lebanese leadership, who would in turn pressure Hezbollah to change its behavior. Yet in the 1990s such air strikes against the Lebanese government had not, in turn, influenced Hezbollah. Furthermore, the politicians' concerns over international blowback further placed limits on IDF action, so that the damage inflicted to Lebanon's infrastructure was only partial. In the end, the escalation and continuation of the war was due to the IAF lacking the ability to destroy Hezbollah's entire rocket array. The damage caused by Israeli air strikes was not sufficient to compel Hezbollah to desist its operations. Rather the cease-fire resulted from the accumulation of losses of its fighters, Hezbollah's realization it would not be able to achieve more politically,

---

[72] *Operation Grapes of Wrath* (Hebrew), 233.

and the risk to the organization's very survival as casualties mounted with 2,000 dead or wounded out of a total force of 10,000.

The damage imposed on both Lebanon and Hezbollah has had long-term implications. In Lebanon, thousands of houses were destroyed, including 178 multistory buildings, with another 540 damaged. According to the Lebanese government, the cost of the damage reached two billion dollars.[73] This harm had a cumulative effect felt long after the war, when hundreds of thousands of southern Lebanese who fled north during the war returned to find their homes destroyed. The reconstruction process has taken years, and the extent of the damage and the true cost of war has long been felt and arguably been a restraining factor on Hezbollah actions since.

### Implications of Air Power on Operational Design

The effectiveness of air power depends on proper operational design at the campaign level. In the 2006 air campaign the IAF, instead of focusing on the opponent's vulnerabilities and centers of gravity, such as with Operation Density, instead struck everything it could find without priorities, with the planning criteria being to maximize efficiency, which meant management of aircraft traffic for short stays over the target and a large number of attacks each day. In such a war of attrition, the aggregate level of destruction was significant to the postwar establishment of deterrence. Moreover, coordinated attacks on quality targets, such as in Operation Density and the Dahiya doctrine, have operational advantages such as surprise and simultaneity that can prevent the opponent from defending itself and thus lower the morale of the opponent.

The IAF fought Hezbollah by hitting infrastructure, targeting leadership, rocket hunting, bombing rocket logistic sites, blocking Lebanon's borders, and isolating southern Lebanon. None of these operations defeated Hezbollah. Throughout the war there was not one central strategy but many, each with a different set of actions and logic for victory. The asymmetric nature of the war allowed the IAF to employ almost anywhere without threat to their aircraft. In this "age of waste," large quantities of sophisticated munitions were expended without achieving the goal of bringing the war to an end. Moreover, after a few days, the IAF abandoned critical analysis altogether and instead focused on servicing targets and then fitting them with a rationale. The targets, instead of the means, became the ends without necessarily fitting the broader strategic aims.

[73] Arkin, *Divining Victory*, 75–103.

The IDF received serious criticism for abandoning a traditional doctrine of ground maneuver for one focused on achieving victory by air
power alone, based on older concepts of strategic bombing now expressed
in the convoluted language of effects-based operations (EBO).[74] This
priority accorded to air power did not reflect a belief that war could be
decided from the air alone, but rather an outcome of a long process of
increasing social and political restraints placed on military operations.[75]
The new approach shifted the role of air power from a supporting element
to the main factor of the war. But the lack of conventional military targets
for attack, as Hezbollah had no tanks or fighter jets, and its opponent's
emphasis on dispersion and concealment prompted the IAF to use an
indirect approach, known as "levers," in an effort to pressure Hezbollah
to accept a cease-fire.

Clausewitz introduced the concept of the "culminating point of the
offensive" to indicate the point where the intensity of an attack and its
effectiveness begin to diminish. In the 2006 air campaign the culmination
point stemmed from the principle of diminishing marginal productivity.
In the first days of the war the IAF destroyed the long- and medium-range
rockets, collapsed Hezbollah's headquarters in Dahiya, and damaged
Lebanese infrastructure. After two weeks Lieutenant General Halutz
claimed "most of the strategic objectives of the operation were achieved
during the first ten days of the operation and now a continued effort must
be made to prevent a failure of tactical events."[76] He thus identified the
culmination point at ten days into the war, but the problem remained how
to translate these military achievements into the desired political achievements, to compel the opponent to agree to a cease-fire on Israeli terms.

Even though the IAF recognized it had reached the culminating point,
the war continued for another 3 weeks, during which time Israel suffered
losses without much gain. Of Israeli casualties, 27 were killed in the first
week of the war, while in the final 2 weeks 109 died, two-thirds of all
Israelis killed.[77]

Was Halutz's assessment correct? Hezbollah did not yet feel the need to
capitulate as the pain inflicted by the air strikes alone was insufficient.
One possible solution would have been to find many more targets to
dramatically cause more damage. Another possible option would have

[74] James N. Mattis, "USJFCOM Commander's Guidance for Effects-Based Operations
(EBO)," *Joint Force Quarterly* 51 (4th Quarter, 2008); Avi Kober, "The Israel Defense
Forces."
[75] Brun, "The Second Lebanon War," 306–08.
[76] Dan Halutz, "Summary of Situational Awareness," July 26, 2006. Brigadier General Ido
Nehushtan claimed, "I think we achieved our strategic achievements a week ago."
General Staff meeting, Winograd Committee Final Report, 113.
[77] Winograd Committee Interim Report, April 2007, 154–63.

been to increase the intensity of aerial attacks to "shock and awe." Alternatively, essential Hezbollah and Lebanese infrastructure could have been held hostage, with a hierarchy of targets established with low-level attacks gradually escalating to credibly threaten and compel a cease-fire. The IAF failed to win the war with any of these air-only strategies. Only when the ground forces entered Lebanon and the pressure on Hezbollah increased did Israel succeed in achieving a cease-fire that held.

The entry of ground forces necessitated a more complex management of operations to synchronize the air and ground efforts. In practice, the IDF conducted two separate and largely unrelated campaigns: the air war and the ground war. Although the IAF had an extension of its headquarters within Northern Command, operations were not sufficiently coordinated. This lack of harmonization could be seen with Hezbollah's short-range rockets that fell between the lines of responsibility of the IAF and Northern Command, rockets that continued to fall on Israel throughout the war.

Israeli military commanders feared that the unintentional harming of Lebanese civilians could undermine the achievement of their campaign objectives. One of Israel's challenges, therefore, was the complex human terrain in which Hezbollah operated. In two incidents in the village of Qana, one in 1996 during Operation Grapes of Wrath involving artillery strikes and again during the Second Lebanon War's air strikes, many civilians perished.[78] In both cases world public opinion, which until then supported Israel, changed, and international pressure to end the war was not necessarily in accordance with Israel's goals.[79]

The operational design of the campaign was also influenced by the media's real-time reports, which shaped public opinion. In this arena the government and IDF had a number of goals. First, communicate, via Israeli media, to the Israeli public to win their trust, which is especially important for a long-term campaign in which the population is at risk. Second, communicate, via global media, to the international community to explain Israel's goals and reasons for its actions and to make the case against Hezbollah and its terrorist activities, which violate international law. Finally, communicate with the Lebanese public to warn them to leave the battle areas and to blame Hezbollah for their suffering. Thus, during the war, IAF planes blocked Hezbollah's media channels and dropped 17,300,000 leaflets in Lebanon, warning residents of southern Lebanon to leave their homes.

[78] Byman, 237–38, 257.    [79] Lambeth, *Air Operations*, 56–57.

## Implications of Air Power on the Tactical Level

Due to the nature of aerial warfare, actionable intelligence is essential for effective operations as aircrew are generally unable to obtain this information independently. There is a strong correlation between successful attacks and reliable intelligence, and in its absence air strikes are woefully inefficient, hence, the vital requirement for in-depth and current intelligence research on any potential opponent. The issue of accurate targeting data becomes even more acute with precise data required by GPS-guided weapons as it does when fighting an irregular group whose disappearance into the population is one of its distinguishing features.

An example of the ineptness of Israeli air strikes absent reliable intelligence were the raids to disrupt Hezbollah short-range rocket launches. Despite the considerable effort invested by the IAF, rocket fire did not stop. Inaccurate area bombing required an enormous quantity of munitions and even then proved not to be significant. During World War II, in Operations Goodwood and Cobra, the Allies dropped thousands of tons of bombs in an extremely dense pattern within a short time over a limited number of kilometers and achieved only marginal success. Similarly, the disruption attacks in 2006 were diluted over time and space and therefore proved ineffective. At a time where area bombing of civilians is not relevant, given reasons of international legitimacy and limited resources, the disruption strikes are an example of the incorrect tactical use of air power.

Conversely, the IAF demonstrated impressive capabilities in developing quick solutions to unforeseen problems and adapting to the battlefield. A culture of flexible thinking and a willingness to internalize rapid changes led to many tactical successes. For example, the prewar rocket hunt concept, the capability to quickly locate and attack rocket launchers immediately after launch, improved during the war as new sensors were added to detect the launches. IAF doctrine was subsequently updated as a result of combat experience.[80] Because the enemy will always create unexpected challenges on the battlefield, it is of great tactical importance to maintain a mindset able to quickly adapt and to retain flexibility in doctrine.

### Summary

The IAF in recent decades has been the main instrument used by the IDF to deal with Israel's primary security concerns. However, a nonstate

---

[80] Ben-Israel, *The First Missile War*, 44–46; Lambeth, *Air Operations*, 106–07.

military actor such as Hezbollah, with relatively small forces that disappear into urban areas, but that also have advanced weapons such as rockets that pose a serious threat to the Israeli home front, presents a complex challenge to the IAF. During the Second Lebanon War many expectations were pinned on the promise of air power. Although some were realized, Hezbollah managed to impose a long war on Israel in which both sides experienced success and failure. In the end, Hezbollah was brought to a peace deal by exhaustion and has been deterred from further attacks by the threat of heavy costs such as those imposed on it and the Lebanese government infrastructure.

The war revealed the limitations of air power, especially regarding the removal of the rocket threat to the home front and the ability to create conditions that impose surrender. Since 2006, Hezbollah's capabilities have strengthened both quantitatively and qualitatively, and its rocket and missile arsenal has increased more than tenfold.[81] To overcome these challenges, the air force must coordinate with the ground force's effort, guided by clear political goals and achievable military objectives, and joint actions must be adapted and synchronized at the tactical, operational, and strategic levels.

---

[81] Assaf Orion, "Yellow Hands on the Blue Line: Hezbollah's Military Deployment along the Border Area Increases the Risks of Escalation," *INSS Insight*, 1321, May 21, 2020.

# 8    Libya 2011: Hollow Victory in Low-Cost Air War

*Jahara Matisek**

## Introduction

The United States and an international coalition, backed by a UN Security Council Resolution (UNSCR), began a military campaign in March 2011 to establish a "No Fly Zone" (NFZ) to protect civilians caught in the middle of the Libyan Civil War.[1] Led by dictator Colonel Muammar Qaddafi, Libya's regime was no stranger to international ire. Yet Qaddafi's heavy-handed coercive internal security measures in the wake of Arab Spring uprisings sparked international outcry. The African Union, Arab League, and the Secretary General of the Organization of the Islamic Conference condemned Qaddafi for violating human rights and international humanitarian law.[2] This precipitated the UN's condemnation of the regime and authorization to establish the NFZ and protect civilians.[3] The result was a 227-day coalition-based air campaign that prosecuted regime targets and resulted in the summary execution of Qaddafi as he fled rebel forces and coalition aircraft. The air campaign and this seemingly propitious end ultimately formed a hollow victory.

---

[*] The views expressed by the author do not reflect those of the US government, the Department of Defense, or any of its organizations.
[1] The analysis presented in this chapter draws from deployed experience and interviews with Ralph Jodice (Lieutenant General, US Air Force, retired), who was the Commander of NATO's Allied Air Command at Izmir, Turkey, in 2011; Thomas Torkelson (Colonel, US Air Force, retired), who was the Wing Commander at Royal Air Force Mildenhall in 2011; and dozens of US and NATO personnel, to include a former German diplomat. The author was deployed from January to May 2011 to the Combined Air and Space Operations Center (CAOC) at Al Udeid Air Base, Qatar, enabling detailed perspective and insights on the Libyan conflict. Some of these insights were initially published: Jahara Matisek, "Dealing with the Arab Spring from the Combined Air Operations Center," *Small Wars Journal*, April 17, 2017. Finally, this chapter builds upon Karl P. Mueller, ed., *Precision and Purpose: Airpower in the Libyan Civil War* (Santa Monica: RAND, 2015).
[2] UNSCR 1970, February 26, 2011. www.nato.int/nato_static_fl2014/assets/pdf/pd f_2011_02/20110927_110226-UNSCR-1970.pdf
[3] UNSCR 1973, March 17, 2011. www.nato.int/nato_static_fl2014/assets/pdf/pd f_2011_03/20110927_110311-UNSCR-1973.pdf

The collective resolve to avoid a humanitarian tragedy in Libya gave proponents of the 2005 internationally established Responsibility to Protect (R2P) norm, to stop "mass atrocity crimes of genocide, war crimes, ethnic cleansing and crimes against humanity," an opportunity to give some "teeth" to ideas of humanitarian interventionism.[4] Libya served as a prime candidate even though it was not a vital national interest to any country in the coalition (see Figure 8.1). As the coalition enforced R2P via UN mandate, it became apparent that the militarized humanitarian intervention of imposing costs on the regime was materially aiding anti-regime groups. This, according to the commanding general of US Africa Command (AFRICOM), resulted in a "very problematic situation" as the air campaign eventually included an extensive degree of cooperation with rebels seeking the overthrow of Qaddafi as it sought to achieve its mission of protecting civilians.[5] Despite the coalition's technological prowess in the air campaign, the final result served to undermine air power's efficacy for pursuing humanitarian goals in the future.

The NFZ over Libya, a multilateral air campaign established by the United States and labeled Operation Odyssey Dawn (OOD), first required the creation of a safe operating environment for US and allied aircraft.[6] However, this was not the typical sort of NFZ seen in previous air power–centric interventions. A key aspect of the NFZ was how quickly it transformed into an air campaign against Qaddafi's pro-regime forces, a sort of "no-drive zone" as described by then US Secretary of State Hillary Rodham Clinton.[7] The reality was that this NFZ created a de facto policy of regime change, which enabled critics to undermine proponents of future R2P humanitarian interventions. At the end of March, the United States drastically reduced the number of strike missions in the NFZ coalition, as control of the air war shifted to NATO, ending OOD. This began the new phase of the air campaign, Operation Unified Protector (OUP), maintaining the Libyan NFZ and undermining regime control via NATO strike missions with the United States in a supporting rather than dominant role.

---

[4] UN General Assembly, Resolution adopted by the General Assembly, September 16, 2005. 60/1. 2005 Summit Outcome. A/RES/60/1. New York: United Nations, 2005. www.globalr2p.org/what-is-r2p

[5] Spencer Ackerman, "US General: We Won't Help Libya's Rebels (Unless We Do)," *Wired*, March 21, 2011.

[6] OOD included strike forces from Belgium, Canada, Denmark, France, Netherlands, Norway, United Kingdom, and the United States plus support missions from Greece, Italy, Spain, Turkey, Qatar, and the United Arab Emirates. Karl P. Mueller, ed., *Precision and Purpose: Airpower in the Libyan Civil War* (Santa Monica: RAND, 2015).

[7] Hillary Rodham Clinton, *Hard Choices: A Memoir* (New York: Simon and Schuster, 2014), 375.

Figure 8.1  Map of Libya

The air campaign to enforce the UN No Fly Zone was made remark-able by virtue of its coalition members, consisting of fourteen NATO countries plus Sweden, Jordan, Qatar, and UAE, not suffering casualties while conducting naval and air force activities against Libya.[8] Without sending in ground troops – albeit some coalition members unilaterally deployed intelligence and special operations personnel – the NFZ coalition exercised considerable restraint in bombing targets to avoid being perceived as pursuing regime change and to minimize collateral damage, which could have undermined diplomatic and political support for the operation.[9] Concerns for regime change were a product of the previous decade's crises with Libya over weapons of mass destruction as well as lingering instability in Afghanistan and Iraq.

At the same time, advanced technologies lowered the political threshold and risk for employing military might, thus enabling the Western-led coalition to intervene by leveraging its precision capabilities to target pro-Qaddafi forces. The combined air campaigns of OOD and OUP were a limited yet intense affair that ended a week after rebels captured and killed Qaddafi. Throughout the campaign, the eighteen-member coalition adapted to an evolving and austere operating environment to achieve the end state of protecting civilians by weakening, if not removing, the regime. Air power eroded the fighting capability of pro-Qaddafi forces, spurring many to desert or defect, and thus boosted anti-Qaddafi rebels.[10] Yet such actions were fraught with long-term political risk given the absence of any post-conflict strategy. Indeed, the aftermath of Qaddafi's removal demonstrated the difficulties of stabilizing and rebuilding a fractured polity. By that measure, the air war in Libya was a hollow success: Civilians were protected and Qaddafi was removed, but tribalism trumped a stable democratic transition and Libya descended into chaos. President Barack Obama would later lament the intervention as his biggest foreign policy mistake, describing the Libyan situation as a "shit show," and it heavily influenced his views on the merits of R2P as evidenced by his decision to not impose a NFZ against the Assad regime during the Syrian Civil War, which occurred on the heels of the Libyan intervention.[11]

---

[8] Thirteen countries also provided naval blockade support in OUP. Mueller, *Precision and Purpose*.

[9] Jeffrey H. Michaels, "Able but Not Willing: A Critical Assessment of NATO's Libya Intervention," in *The NATO Intervention in Libya*, eds. Kjell Engelbrekt, Marcus Mohlin, and Charlotte Wagnsson (New York: Routledge, 2013), 37–60.

[10] "NATO Strikes Gadhafi Compound in Tripoli," *VOA News*, May 11, 2011. www .voanews.com/africa/nato-strikes-gadhafi-compound-tripoli; Nick Carey, "NATO Says Hit Military Targets in Libya's Brega," *Reuters*, June 25, 2011. www.reuters.com/article/ us-libya/nato-says-hit-military-targets-in-libyas-brega-idUSTRE7270JP20110625

[11] Dominic Tierney, "The Legacy of Obama's 'Worst Mistake,'" *The Atlantic*, April 15, 2016. www.theatlantic.com/international/archive/2016/04/obamas-worst-mistake-libya /478461

## The Libyan Context: Actors and Objectives

In December 2010, Mohammed Bouazizi immolated himself after Tunisian police seized his local market fruit stand for lacking permits.[12] His act of defiance ignited mass protests and demonstrations, leading to the Tunisian government being overthrown less than a month later. The initial success in Tunisia fueled Arab unity and inspired protests in Egypt, Morocco, Oman, Syria, Yemen, and smaller movements in other Middle Eastern countries. In February, within days of the Egyptian president resigning, anti-Qaddafi protests erupted in Benghazi. Qaddafi, who had been ruling the country with an iron fist since coming to power in 1969 through a military coup d'état, made grandiose pledges about the rebels being "hunted down street by street, house by house and wardrobe by wardrobe."[13] Qaddafi quickly followed through, using his army, air force, militias, and mercenaries (e.g., Tuareg from Mali) to attack anti-Qaddafi protests.[14] The violent crackdown led to international outcry, leading many of Libya's top diplomats and officials to defect en masse.[15]

Informed by a growing consensus to stop Qaddafi's violence under R2P principles, UNSCR 1973 was passed on March 17, 2011. It authorized UN member states "to take all necessary measures ... to protect civilians and civilian populated areas under threat of attack in the Libyan Arab Jamahiriya, including Benghazi, while excluding a foreign occupation force of any form on any part of Libyan territory."[16] This permitted the use of air power against Libya and was built upon the Council of the League of Arab States decision on March 12, 2011, to support an NFZ against Libya to protect civilians.[17] Arab support for an international military intervention was important for many international actors considering an intervention – even China and Russia – due to the symbolic nature of being approved to attack a fellow Arab nation.[18] It stemmed

---

[12] Robert F. Worth, "How a Single Match Can Ignite a Revolution," *New York Times*, January 21, 2011.

[13] Daniel Kawczynski, *Seeking Gaddafi: Libya, the West and the Arab Spring* (London: Biteback, 2011), 242.

[14] Kareem Fahim and David D. Kirkpatrick, "Qaddafi's Grip on the Capital Tightens as Revolt Grows," *New York Times*, February 22, 2011.

[15] "Libyan Diplomats Defect en Masse," *Al Jazeera*, February 22, 2011.

[16] UNSCR 1973, March 17, 2011, 3. Many up until this point speculated that China and/or Russia would veto any military operation against Qaddafi's regime. However, China and Russia abstained, as did Brazil, Germany, and India, permitting UNSCR 1973 passage, giving credibility and legitimacy to military operations against Libya.

[17] The outcome of the Council of the League of Arab States meeting at the ministerial level in its extraordinary session on the implications of the current events in Libya and the Arab position, Resolution 7360, March 12, 2011, Cairo, Egypt.

[18] Ivo H. Daalder and James G. Stavridis, "NATO's Victory in Libya: The Right Way to Run an Intervention," *Foreign Affairs* 91:2 (2012): 2–7.

from the initial unanimous support for UNSCR 1970, passed on February 26, 2011, which demonstrated international consensus against Qaddafi by imposing an arms embargo, banning regime travel, freezing regime assets, and considering Qaddafi's actions worthy of referral to the International Criminal Court (ICC).[19]

Within days of UNSCR 1970 passing, several nations moved naval assets into the region to enforce the arms embargo against the Libyan regime, although many governments had already been using military aircraft to evacuate their citizens and embassy staffs.[20] These UN-sanctioned efforts built upon the foundations of R2P, enabling a legal framework to support a naval blockade while authorizing air power to keep civilians safe for human rights purposes.[21]

Given American reluctance to pursue military actions against Libya, British and French leaders were the most vocal advocates of intervention, leading to the initial attacks on March 19.[22] Worried about lacking American military and political support, the British and French generated a narrative about the pitfalls of American isolation, which convinced the Obama administration to support the Libyan intervention.[23] Such a diplomatic push for standoff strikes was part of a troubling historic shift in diplomatic strategies that increasingly rely on "risk-free coercion."[24] With UNSCR 1973 passage on March 17, France, the United Kingdom, and the United States (and others) already had naval assets in the vicinity, and coalition aircraft had already been conducting ISR (intelligence, surveillance, and reconnaissance) flights since March 8 near Libyan airspace.[25] It would take two or three days of planning to deploy the bulk of allied aircraft needed to enforce the Libyan NFZ and conduct ISR missions to determine the most critical regime targets. Without seeking consent from allies, twenty French aircraft conducted

[19] UNSCR 1970, February 26, 2011.
[20] "UN Arms Embargo on Libya," *SIPRI*, June 13, 2019. www.sipri.org/databases/embar goes/un_arms_embargoes/libya/libya_2011
[21] Sam Fitzpatrick, "United Nations Security Council Resolution 1973 and the Future of the Responsibility to Protect Doctrine," *The Michigan Journal of International Law*, March 6, 2015. www.mjilonline.org/united-nations-security-council-resolution-1973-and-the-future-of-the-responsibility-to-protect-doctrine/#_edn2
[22] Rebecca Adler-Nissen and Vincent Pouliot, "Power in Practice: Negotiating the International Intervention in Libya," *European Journal of International Relations* 20:4 (2014): 889–911.
[23] Laura Roselle, "Strategic Narratives and Alliances: The Cases of Intervention in Libya (2011) and Economic Sanctions against Russia (2014)," *Politics and Governance* 5:3 (2017): 99–110.
[24] Douglas Peifer, "Risk-Free Coercion? Technological Disparity and Coercive Diplomacy," *European Security* 18:1 (2009): 7–31.
[25] CNN Wire Staff, "NATO Starts 24/7 Surveillance of Libya," *CNN*, March 8, 2011. www.cnn.com/2011/WORLD/africa/03/07/libya.military.response/index.html

the first strikes against pro-Qaddafi forces around Benghazi on March 19.[26]

Air strikes and more than 100 Tomahawk Land-Attack Missile (TLAM) launches followed the next day from the United States and United Kingdom to cripple Qaddafi's coastal defenses, air defenses, and command and control (C2) abilities, so that critical centers of gravity could be more easily attacked.[27] These were not the typical centers of gravity seen in previous conflicts (e.g., economic, infrastructure, army), as these strikes were meant to disrupt and destroy Qaddafi's informal networks and hierarchies of control, undermining the way he exercised authority and power. Moreover, such coercion was meant to convince Qaddafi not to use his loyalists to attack civilians. As the United States relied on AFRICOM coordinating UNSCR 1973 enforcement and activities with coalition aircraft, it became readily apparent that AFRICOM lacked capabilities (e.g., staff, resources, aircraft) to conduct a long-term air war in Libya.[28] In fact, the Air Force Targeting Center at Langley Air Force Base in Virginia ended up taking a lead role in supporting the NFZ, as it was responsible for more than 75 percent of targets in Libya.[29]

Because of the Obama administration's desire to make the operation fall under NATO control, intense politicking by the United States with various NATO partners aided the conclusion that NATO would lead, not the United States. This meant a slow transition from dependence on American fighter/attack aircraft toward supporting other NATO members to carry the burden of air strikes. On March 31, NATO formally took command of all air operations from AFRICOM. Indeed, the US Joint Task Force had already given command of the arms embargo and NFZ mission to NATO on March 24. US aircraft would continue to conduct air strikes to protect civilians until March 30.[30] Notably, US tankers would remain a key factor in supporting NATO missions throughout

[26] David Cenciotti, "Operation Odyssey Dawn Explained (Day 1)," *Aviationist*, March 20, 2011. https://theaviationist.com/2011/03/20/operation-odyssey-dawn-explained

[27] "DOD News Briefing by Vice Adm. Gortney on Operation Odyssey Dawn," *Navy News Service*, March 22, 2011. www.navy.mil/submit/display.asp?story_id=59240

[28] Other geographic combatant commanders had to lend aircraft and staff, US European Command (EUCOM) especially, to help AFRICOM take charge of the air war and associated duties (e.g., planning, targeting, air-tasking orders). The author, while deployed to the CAOC in Qatar, repeatedly engaged with AFRICOM staff concerning the complexity of moving aircraft in their area of responsibility (AOR).

[29] Aaron W. Clark, "In Absentia: Airpower and Proxy Ground Forces in the Balkan and Libyan Conflicts," *School of Advanced Air and Space Studies* (PhD Dissertation, May 15, 2018), 299.

[30] Todd R. Phinney, "Reflections on Operation Unified Protector," *Joint Force Quarterly* 73 (2nd Quarter, 2014): 86–92.

the entire Libyan NFZ, as the United States provided 80 percent of NATO air-refueling missions.[31]

While the new OUP phase created a patchwork of participating members and rules of engagement (ROEs) in the Libyan NFZ coalition, it improved upon the efficiency of past NATO practices, such as Operation Allied Force where some nations refrained from striking certain targets they deemed sensitive.[32] At the same time, it forced NATO to innovate and adapt due to the United States only committing its F-16 CJ aircraft for the suppression of enemy air defense (SEAD) missions, though the definition of what was included as part of the Libyan integrated air defense system (IADS) was loosely interpreted. This allowed the targeting of more of Qaddafi's hardware and bases as long as intelligence could justify how such targets were related to air defenses.

As the OUP phase commenced in early April, poor weather and a lack of intelligence, surveillance, and reconnaissance (ISR) assets hampered the ability of NATO to target and attack pro-Qaddafi positions. Moreover, loyalist troops adapted to the new threat environment of NATO air superiority by attempting to move forces more covertly and by trying to blend in with civilians.[33] NATO was further hamstrung by its combined air operations center (CAOC) in Poggio Renatico, Italy, which did not have the resources, facilities, or staff to support ambitious NATO efforts of planning 300 sorties a day. OUP only launched about 150 sorties daily throughout the air campaign. The sheer scale of Libya, similar in size to Alaska, only made it more problematic in terms of identifying targets and attempting to provide an air umbrella for rebels. Delay with the NATO transition to OUP led to many rebel offensives stalling from April through early August.[34] Moreover, many NATO members struggled against the implications of imposing the Libyan NFZ. The protection to civilians also entailed attacking pro-Qaddafi forces near rebel positions, which in turn shifted the military balance of power on the ground and thus slowly contributed toward regime change.[35] This only added more to the problems of a poorly constructed end-state that was facilitated by risk-averse political leaders

---

[31] Ben Barry, "Libya's lessons," *Survival* 53:5 (2011): 5–14.

[32] During Operation Allied Force, NATO members would decline targeting assignments. In the case of OUP, willingness to engage in kinetic operations was dependent upon what each member wanted to do. Interview with AFRICOM intelligence officer who supported OUP, July 22, 2019; Paul E. Gallis, "Kosovo: Lessons Learned from Operation Allied Force," *Congressional Research Service*, November 19, 1999.

[33] Christian F. Anrig, "Allied Air Power over Libya," in *Air Power in UN Operations: Wings for Peace*, ed. A. Walter Dorn (Farnham, UK: Ashgate Publishing, 2014), 255–82.

[34] Mueller, *Precision and Purpose*, 28.

[35] "NATO Allies Question Their Role in Libya," *NPR*, April 16, 2011.

who refrained from deploying ground forces both during and after the war.

### Colonel Qaddafi's Loyalist Forces

Before the outbreak of anti-Qaddafi protests on January 13, 2011, the Armed Forces of the Libyan Arab Jamahiriya had on the books 76,000 personnel in its army, navy, and air force. Despite also having 2,000 tanks, several thousand armored personnel carriers and mobile rocket launchers, 216 surface to air missile systems (SAMs), and 394 combat aircraft, the Libyan pro-government force was a paper army.[36] Qaddafi had coup-proofed his regime by limiting their training and access to munitions. As with most dictators he promoted loyalty over competency.[37] He developed a cult of personality and maintained power through the imposition of various control mechanisms, a divide-and-rule approach, with a core group of loyalists – handpicked militias and elite military units – while the rest of Libya's security architecture remained fragmented, with these components competing with one another, rather than uniting against their master.[38] Over decades of rule, Qaddafi's military exhibited very low military effectiveness.[39] Although US/NATO planners assumed his air force and IADS capable and functional, OOD/OUP aviators never encountered any credible counter-air resistance.[40]

Core elements of Qaddafi's military nevertheless could be lethal against civilian protestors. When anti-Qaddafi demonstrators staged "Day of Rage" protests across numerous cities on February 17, 2011, the Libyan Civil War slowly emerged as Qaddafi ordered security forces and loyal gangs to attack dissidents.[41] The regime's heavy-handed approach caused numerous Libyan officials, diplomats, and military leaders to defect, with 8,000 soldiers in eastern Libya mutinying to join

---

[36] "Chapter Seven: Middle East and North Africa," *The Military Balance* 111:1 (2011): 293–342.

[37] Kenneth M. Pollack, *Armies of Sand: The Past, Present, and Future of Arab Military Effectiveness* (New York: Oxford University Press, 2018), 299–305.

[38] Ariel I. Ahram, "Why States Choose Paramilitarism," *Georgetown Journal of International Affairs* 7:1 (Winter/Spring 2006): 65–70.

[39] During Qaddafi's rule, his army consistently underperformed in wars despite having better military equipment and more troops, such as the Uganda-Tanzania War (1978–79) and the Great Toyota War (1986–87). Kenneth M. Pollack, *Arabs at War: Military Effectiveness, 1948–1991* (Lincoln: University of Nebraska Press, 2004), 358–424.

[40] Personal communication with US/NATO planners and pilots who flew missions in Libya during OOD/OUP, November 2011–June 2015.

[41] Al Jazeera and Agencies, "Deadly 'Day of Rage' in Libya," *Al Jazeera*, February 18, 2011. www.aljazeera.com/news/africa/2011/02/201121716917273192.html

anti-Qaddafi resistance movements.[42] Due to decades of coup-proofing, military units around Tripoli were less likely to defect or desert, as those without kinship/ethnic/clan ties to Qaddafi and others stationed in Benghazi quickly joined rebel forces. Qaddafi's forces began brutally retaking numerous rebel-controlled cities with artillery and air strikes, giving the international community the impetus to implement an NFZ to halt Qaddafi's advance.[43]

By June, NATO air strikes, tribal fissures, defections, desertions, and rebel seizure of territory had left Qaddafi with only about 15,000 personnel. Qaddafi's objectives initially transitioned from the repression of protestors to the annihilation of rebels. But over time as his troops were halted and fell back on the defense, he finally reverted to just survival mode, so weak that he increasingly relied on the loyalty purchased from mercenaries from other African nations. Primarily drawing upon Tuareg mercenaries to fight the rebels and put down protests, Qaddafi paid upwards of $1,000 a day, as coup-proofing had left him with few loyal units.[44] After Tripoli fell, Qaddafi fled to his birthplace, Sirte, where his few remaining Jamahiriya fighters made their final stand until rebels seized the city. As Qaddafi fled the rebel assault on October 20, his convoy was identified by a US Predator aircraft (see Chapter 2), and he was then "caught like [a] 'rat' in a drain, humiliated and shot" by rebel forces (see Figure 8.2 for a time line of events).[45]

### The Anti-Qaddafi Rebels: Benghazi-Based National Transitional Council (NTC)

Formed on February 27, 2011, the NTC was a loose coalition of anti-Qaddafi rebel groups seeking to consolidate actions against Qaddafi's loyalist forces.[46] Because of Qaddafi's iron-fist rule, the NTC could leverage elite grievances – despite tribal differences – to grow the anti-Qaddafi forces.[47] Although difficult to confirm, in early March the NTC

[42] Florence Gaub, "The Libyan Armed Forces between Coup-Proofing and Repression," *Journal of Strategic Studies* 36:2 (2013): 221–44.
[43] Anthony M. Schinella, *Bombs without Boots: The Limits of Airpower* (Washington, DC: Brookings Institution Press, 2019), 230–33.
[44] Peter Gwin, "Former Qaddafi Mercenaries Describe Fighting in Libyan War," *Atlantic*, August 31, 2011. www.theatlantic.com/international/archive/2011/08/former-qaddafi-mercenaries-describe-fighting-in-libyan-war/244356
[45] Tim Gaynor and Taha Zargoun, "Gaddafi Caught Like 'Rat' in a Drain, Humiliated and Shot," *Reuters*, October 21, 2011. www.reuters.com/article/us-libya-gaddafi-finalhours-idUSTRE79K43S20111021
[46] Maya Bhardwa, "Development of Conflict in Arab Spring Libya and Syria: From Revolution to Civil War," *The Washington University International Review* (Spring 2012): 76–97.
[47] Christian Caryl, "Mogadishu on the Mediterranean?" *Foreign Policy*, October 20, 2011. https://foreignpolicy.com/2011/10/20/mogadishu-on-the-mediterranean

| 2011 Time Line | Important Events |
| --- | --- |
| January 13 | Arab Spring protests start against Qaddafi |
| February 15–17 | Massive "Day of Rage" protests: Qaddafi uses loyalist forces to attack civilian demonstrators |
| February 20 | Anti-Qaddafi rebels seize Benghazi |
| February 26 | UNSCR 1970 passed: Sanctions imposed on Libya |
| February 27 | National Transitional Council (NTC) is formed in Benghazi with numerous rebel groups |
| March 10 | Qaddafi's air force bombs Brega and his loyalist forces crush the NTC rebels at Zawiyah and Bin Jawad, giving the international community the impetus to intervene |
| March 10 | France recognizes the NTC as the legitimate government of Libya |
| March 17 | UNSCR 1973 passed: Authorizes UN members to take all necessary measures to protect civilians in Libya |
| March 19 | Operation Odyssey Dawn begins with French air strikes: Qaddafi's forces halt offensive operations against NTC rebels |
| March 23 | Operation Unified Protector begins: United States drastically reduces strike missions and shifts control to NATO |
| March 31 | Operation Odyssey Dawn ends: NATO takes formal command over all air operations from AFRICOM |
| April 25–May 15 | Misrata counteroffensive: NTC rebels repel pro-Qaddafi forces |
| July 28–August 18 | Nafusa Mountains offensive: NTC rebels seize control of critical roads that supply Qaddafi in Tripoli |
| August 20–28 | Operation Mermaid Dawn ("Battle of Tripoli"): Libyan capital seized by NTC rebels and Qaddafi flees to Sirte |
| September 15–October 20 | Battle of Sirte: Four rebel offensives to encircle loyalist positions |
| October 20 | Qaddafi killed |
| October 23 | NTC declares Libya liberated |
| October 25 | NATO only operating ISR missions to monitor situations |
| October 31 | Operation Unified Protectors ends: All NATO-led air operations cease |

Figure 8.2 Time line of important events and battles in Libya, 2011*

military council claimed it had approximately 6,000 civilian fighters and was attempting to integrate 6,000 Jamahiriya personnel who had defected.[48] With so many fighters available, one defector, a Libyan

---

* For more details on the anti-Qaddafi rebel forces and important battles, see Andrei Netto, *Bringing Down Gaddafi: On the Ground with the Libyan Rebels* (New York: St. Martin's Press, 2014).

[48] James Kirkup and Adrian Blomfield, "Libya: Britain to Step Up Support for Rebel Forces Fighting Gaddafi," *The Telegraph*, March 4, 2011. www.telegraph.co.uk/news/w orldnews/africaandindianocean/libya/8362636/Libya-Britain-to-step-up-support-for-rebel-forces-fighting-Gaddafi.html

colonel, stated "We can accept supplies … We don't need soldiers."[49] Regardless, the nascent opposition force was motivated and willing to fight but initially was helpless against Qaddafi's firepower; moreover, it lacked "experienced military leadership at the strategic, operational, or tactical level."[50]

Going counter to the provisions in UNSCR 1970, which imposed a general arms embargo on Libya, several countries decided to support the rebels with supplies and advisors. The NTC formed the Libya Contact Group as a liaison cell with foreign militaries seeking to assist rebel ground forces. Shortly after air strikes began, France and Britain began supplying the NTC with war matériel, and advisors came from British Special Forces, American CIA, France, and Italy.[51] Qatar followed suit by sending military aircraft into Benina airport near Benghazi with medical supplies, war matériel, and hundreds of Qatari Special Forces to mentor NTC rebels.[52]

Within two months of the NTC forming, dozens of Qaddafi's generals stationed primarily in eastern Libya defected by "opening their armories to the rebels."[53] As the size of the anti-Qaddafi rebel force grew through territorial expansion, the NTC was equally concerned about recognition as the legitimate government of Libya. France was the first country to recognize the NTC as the legitimate regime on March 10, 2011, followed by Qatar on March 28 and then two dozen more countries by July 15, to include the United States, allowing the fledging government to access more than $30 billion worth of frozen assets.[54] It was not until September 16 – after many more countries recognized the NTC – that the United Nations finally recognized the NTC government, easing sanctions.[55]

---

[49] Martin Chulov, "Libya's Anti-Gaddafi Rebels Gather Sparse Forces for Battles Ahead," *The Guardian*, February 28, 2011. www.theguardian.com/world/2011/feb/28/libya-anti-gaddafi-rebels-gather

[50] Schinella, *Bombs without Boots*, 234.

[51] Olivier Corten and Vaios Koutroulis, "The Illegality of Military Support to Rebels in the Libyan War: Aspects of Jus contra Bellum and Jus in Bello," *Journal of Conflict and Security Law* 18:1 (2013): 59–93; Sebastian Moffett, John W. Miller, and Stacy Meichtry, "France and Italy to Send Military Officers to Libya," *The Wall Street Journal*, April 20, 2011. www.wsj.com/articles/SB10001424052748704658704576274571364104798

[52] Tim Ripley, "Power Brokers – Qatar and the UAE Take Centre Stage," *Jane's Intelligence Review* 24:2 (February 2012): 22–25.

[53] Few Jamahiriya stationed in western Libya defected. Nicolas Pelham, "The Battle for Libya," *New York Review of Books*, April 7, 2011. www.nybooks.com/articles/2011/04/07/battle-libya

[54] Sebnem Arsu and Steven Erlanger, "Libya Rebels Get Formal Backing, and $30 Billion," *New York Times*, July 15, 2011. www.nytimes.com/2011/07/16/world/africa/16libya.html

[55] "Battle for Libya: Key moments," *Al Jazeera*, April 30, 2017. www.aljazeera.com/indepth/spotlight/libya/2011/10/20111020104244706760.html

## Operation Odyssey Dawn (OOD) and Operation Unified Protector (OUP)

As the Arab Spring took root in Libya, Qaddafi gave a defiant televised speech. He promised to "die a martyr at the end" and encouraged his supporters to go out and attack the "cockroaches" that were protesting against his rule, leading Secretary of State Hillary Clinton to urge President Obama to support the anti-Qaddafi rebels and a no-fly zone to prevent a "massacre" by Qaddafi.[56] Days later, a loose coalition of anti-Qaddafi rebel groups formed into the NTC on February 27, receiving military assistance from numerous countries, helping them maintain control of Benghazi and eastern Libya.[57] Qaddafi's status as pariah in the international system was best highlighted by China and Russia surprising the international community by abstaining during the UNSCR 1973 vote, which removed the barrier to an R2P-justified militarized intervention.[58]

In the late afternoon of March 19, 2011, French aircraft commenced Operation Odyssey Dawn, destroying four Libyan tanks. Hours later, American and British ships fired TLAMs at critical IADS and C2 infrastructure to enable follow-on air strikes against mobile pro-Qaddafi military units.[59] These initial actions caught the international community off-guard as members had expected strikes only against Libyan airbases, aircraft, and anything else that could challenge Franco-American-British air power. By virtue of UNSCR 1973 permitting "all necessary means," notions of a traditional NFZ gave way to a broader interpretation of protecting Libyan civilians from all of Qaddafi's pro-regime forces.[60] A key point of this new thinking was that sizable coalition technological advantages permitted and/or encouraged this broader view of the UN's authorization to attack anything "threatening" civilians, all justified via R2P. It also led many political leaders to believe that they could punish Qaddafi enough through air strikes that he would relent attacks against civilian centers.

[56] "Libya Protests: Defiant Gaddafi Refuses to Quit," *BBC News*, February 22, 2011. www .bbc.com/news/world-middle-east-12544624; "Clinton: Trump 'Temperamentally Unfit' for White House," *Anderson Cooper 360 Degrees: CNN Transcripts*, June 2, 2016. www.cnn.com/TRANSCRIPTS/1606/02/acd.01.html
[57] "Death of a Dictator: Bloody Vengeance in Sirte," *Human Rights Watch*, October 16, 2012. www.hrw.org/report/2012/10/16/death-dictator/bloody-vengeance-sirte
[58] During the Libyan NFZ, Cuba, Nicaragua, and Venezuela remained supportive of Qaddafi's regime.
[59] "Libya: French Plane Fires on Military Vehicle," *BBC News*, March 19, 2011. www .bbc.com/news/world-africa-12795971; Alex Crawford, "Evidence of Massacre by Gaddafi Forces," *Sky News*, March 23, 2011. https://web.archive.org/web/2013062113 3935/http://news.sky.com/story/843866/evidence-of-massacre-by-gaddafi-forces
[60] UNSCR 1973, 3.

On the second day of OOD, B-2 bombers eliminated the ability of loyalists to launch aircraft from various civilian and military airfields. Other US military aircraft continued the SEAD mission while psychological operations (psyops) aircraft broadcasted warnings about operating a regime military ship, aircraft, or vehicle. By day three, the threat was eliminated, leaving only the minimal threat of mobile surface-to-air missiles (SAMs) and shoulder-launched man-portable air defense systems (MANPADS). This enabled the day four transition: destroying important fixed and mobile ground targets that threatened cities under rebel control. These air-to-ground operations enabled numerous allied aircraft to join the NFZ operation on the sixth day because Libyan ground-to-air systems had become a "negligible threat."[61]

On March 25 command and control was passed to NATO due to the Obama administration's desire to avoid congressional criticism of America's role in Libya, thus formally making OOD an internationalized military operation. Tactical air strikes against Qaddafi's fielded forces had essentially rescued rebel forces, especially in Benghazi. Under duress from coalition air strikes, loyalist forces retreated from Ajdabiya, Brega, Ras Lanuf, and Bin Jawad, giving the rebels the psychological advantage in shifting from defensive positions to conducting offensive operations in those areas.[62] Moreover, air strikes had essentially ended Qaddafi's ability to resupply loyalist forces, exhausting them enough to give the rebels a tactical and operational advantage. By the eighth day of OOD, AC-130s and A-10s began conducting interdiction sorties against pro-Qaddafi forces and naval assets. This further shaped the battlespace as loyalist forces were fractured and dispersed, giving rebels an opportunity to counterattack.

By day thirteen of OOD, AFRICOM handed over all control of the Libyan NFZ to NATO. Besides the symbolism of transferring operational coordination of the air war to NATO, the United States dramatically reduced its commitment, only allocating F-16 CJs for SEAD missions and other aircraft for supporting roles such as C2, ISR, and aerial refueling. American support aircraft continued to serve as critical enablers to OUP coalition strike aircraft, which by the end of April had attrited nearly 40 percent of Qaddafi's forces.[63] NATO escalation of air strikes against

[61] Pentagon Press Briefing, "Transcript: DOD News Briefing with Rear Admiral Hueber via Telephone from USS *Mount Whitney*," *AFRICOM*, March 23, 2011. www.africom.mil/media-room/article/8114/transcript-dod-news-briefing-with-rear-admiral-hue

[62] Schinella, *Bombs without Boots*, 250–51.

[63] Phil Stewart, "Libyan Ground Forces Degraded by up to 40 Percent: U.S.," *Reuters*, April 22, 2011. www.reuters.com/article/us-libya-usa-military/libyan-ground-forces-degraded-by-up-to-40-percent-u-s-idUSTRE73L13Q20110422

pro-regime forces, especially by mid-April, was focused on attempting to compel Qaddafi not to target civilians.[64] This trapped the coalition into the logic of trying to increase coercion against Qaddafi, while also inadvertently protecting rebel forces, tying the success of coalition air strikes to the survival of the rebels.

Several notable battles shaped the conflict in 2011. The battle of Misrata was important for the NTC rebels, as dozens of NATO air strikes against pro-Qaddafi forces enabled the rebels to re-take the city by May 15.[65] NATO commenced attacks on April 8 in the Nafusa Mountains Campaign with escalating strikes on loyalist forces, destroying hundreds of pro-Qaddafi military targets. This involved the CAOC saturating the area with ISR, especially unmanned aircraft, to effect destruction of command and control capabilities and a sizable number of loyalist forces.[66] France's unilateral decision in June to airdrop weapons and ammunition to rebels near Nalut in the Nafusa Mountains complemented this effort by undermining the ability of Qaddafi's forces to resist NTC operations.[67] This enabled the rebel forces to encircle Tripoli by August 18.[68] The Battle of Tripoli began on August 20. The regime capital fell in eight days under the combination of NTC assaults and NATO air strikes that destroyed twenty-one loyalist military positions.[69] After sixty-four NATO air strikes against his headquarters, Qaddafi and his core of loyalists fled Tripoli as a "tactical move."[70] His destination: the coastal town of Sirte.

The Sirte redoubt was Qaddafi's birthplace and his final stand. Deep familial ties with the Qadhadhfa tribe and loyal Berber friends in Sirte made it a natural fallback position. A rebel offensive would not occur in Sirte until September 15. It would take four assaults – with the help of NATO air strikes against forty-nine pro-Qaddafi positions – for the rebels to finally encircle loyalists by October 19.[71] The following day,

[64] Clark, "In Absentia," 340–41.
[65] Refer to NATO press releases from April 1 to May 16, 2011. www.nato.int/cps/en/nato hq/news_71994.htm?selectedLocale=en
[66] Clark, "In Absentia," 327–38.
[67] Michael Birnbaum, "France Sent Arms to Libya Rebels," *The Washington Post*, June 30, 2011. www.washingtonpost.com/world/france-sent-arms-to-libyan-rebels/2011/06/29/AGcBxkqH_story.html
[68] Ibid.    [69] Ibid.
[70] Peter Graff and Ulf Laessing, "Gaddafi Flees Tripoli HQ Ransacked by Rebels," *Reuters*, August 23, 2011. www.reuters.com/article/ozatp-libya-20110824-idAFJOE77N00F201 10824
[71] "NATO and Libya: Operational Media Update for 15 September," *NATO* (press release), September 16, 2011. www.nato.int/nato_static/assets/pdf/pdf_2011_09/20110 916_110916-oup-update.pdf. Refer to the *NATO* (press release) archived site to view daily air strike updates from September 15 to October 20, 2011.

approximately seventy-five vehicles, many of them "technicals," attempted to flee the city at high speed toward Wadi Jarif, twenty-five miles away.[72] Suspecting that Qaddafi was hiding in Sirte, an American MQ-1 Predator, along with other coalition ISR assets, had been surveilling the area for more than a month. Observing this suspicious convoy, the MQ-1 fired two Hellfire missiles, destroying one of the vehicles.[73] Then, a NATO AWACS off the coast coordinated with two French Rafaele fighter jets to attack ten more vehicles with two 500lb GBU-12 laser-guided bombs.[74]

Unbeknownst to NATO, this convoy was attempting to sneak Qaddafi out of Sirte in a black SUV. However, due to the air strikes that damaged the fleeing vehicles, a wounded Qaddafi sought sanctuary (and his final hiding spot) in a nearby storm drain. British SAS soldiers and Qatari Special Forces in Sirte advising NTC coordinated the rebel response with the Watan revolutionary brigade, the first rebel group on the scene. A mob of civilian fighters had also arrived who had lost relatives to Qaddafi's brutality. They tortured and taunted him and then came a simple ending: a gunshot to the temple.[75]

Qaddafi's ignominious death on October 20 resulted in remaining loyalists surrendering en masse. NATO interpreted this as achievement of the UNSCR 1973 goal "to protect civilians and civilian populated areas under attack or threat of attack." By October 25, NATO decided ISR missions would only be conducted "to monitor the situation."[76] A US Air Force general's remarks captured the mood at the CAOC in Italy when the date of October 31 was set to cease all NATO air operations in Libya: "Many NATO personnel didn't know what to

---

[72] A "technical" is a makeshift weapon system used in undeveloped countries. It involves the bolting down of a large-heavy gun into the bed of a pickup truck. "NATO and Libya: Operational Media Update for 20 October," *NATO* (press release), October 21, 2011. www.nato.int/nato_static/assets/pdf/pdf_2011_10/20111021_111021-oup-update.pdf

[73] Eric Stover, Victor Peskin, and Alexa Koenig, *Hiding in Plain Sight: The Pursuit of War Criminals from Nuremberg to the War on Terror* (Berkeley: University of California Press, 2016), 2.

[74] Thomas Harding, "Col Gaddafi Killed: Convoy Bombed by Drone Flown by Pilot in Las Vegas," *The Telegraph*, October 20, 2011. www.telegraph.co.uk/news/worldnews/afri caandindianocean/libya/8839964/Col-Gaddafi-killed-convoy-bombed-by-drone-flown-by-pilot-in-Las-Vegas.html

[75] Ben Farmer, "Gaddafi's Final Hours: NATO and the SAS Helped Rebels Drive Hunted Leader into Endgame in a Desert Drain," *The Telegraph*, October 22, 2011. www .telegraph.co.uk/news/worldnews/africaandindianocean/libya/8843684/Gaddafis-final-hours-Nato-and-the-SAS-helped-rebels-drive-hunted-leader-into-endgame-in-a-des ert-drain.html

[76] "NATO and Libya: Operational Media Update," *NATO* (press release), October 25, 2011. www.nato.int/nato_static/assets/pdf/pdf_2011_10/20111025_111025-oup-update.pdf

think. 'NATO had never ended a military operation without a plan' was a common remark from most working at the CAOC. So we were left thinking 'What now?'"[77]

## Air Power's Effectiveness in Libya: A Hollow Victory

OOD and OUP involved more than 26,500 sorties with more than 9,700 strike sorties.[78] The air campaign was a historic first: 100 percent of air strikes used precision-guided munitions.[79] Even *Human Rights Watch* praised NATO for having "taken extensive measures to minimize civilian harm, and those measures seem to have had a positive effect" with no more than 72 verified civilian deaths.[80] Precision weapons in conjunction with coalition risk-aversion were successful in keeping collateral damage at a historic low, making the air campaign appear effective. Yet it was a hollow victory.

Libya's sprawling territory and minimal infrastructure, combined with political sensitivities inherent to OOD and OUP objectives, limited the air strike opportunities available to air planners. Geographical constraints and proximity to air-refueling aircraft orbiting in the Mediterranean Sea limited the reach of the coalition, meaning that more than 95 percent of air strikes occurred within 50 miles of the coastline.[81] For example, despite Sabha being home to substantial numbers of easily identifiable pro-Qaddafi forces, the coalition struck fewer than 50 targets there the whole campaign because it was 400 miles inland. Other targeting issues involved a dynamic battlespace where encounters with pro-Qaddafi

---

[77] Interview, retired US Air Force general, June 13, 2019.

[78] Approximately 40 percent of all sorties were strike sorties flown by manned or unmanned aircraft, although not every strike sortie released munitions. For example, of the 1,825 US strike sorties in OUP, only 397 conducted actual strikes. Mueller, *Precision and Purpose*, 4; Amy McCullough, "The Libya Mission," *Air Force Magazine* (August 2010): 28–32; "Operation UNIFIED PROTECTOR: Final Mission Stats," *NATO Fact Sheet*, November 2, 2011; Jorge Benitez, "National Composition of NATO Strike Sorties in Libya," *Atlantic Council*, August 22, 2011; Pencer Ackerman, "Libya: The Real US Drone War," *Wired*, October 20, 2011; "NATO and Libya (Archived)," *NATO*, November 9, 2015; "Operational Media Update: NATO and Libya," *NATO*, October 25, 2011. www.nato.int/cps/en/natohq/news_71994.htm?selectedLocale=en; "Report of the International Commission of Inquiry on Libya," United Nations, advanced unedited edition, A/HRC/19/68, March 2, 2012, 161.

NATO data, in International Commission of Inquiry on Libya, Report of the International Commission of Inquiry on Libya – advance unedited version, New York: United Nations Human Rights Council, A/HRC/19/68, March 2, 2012, 206.

[79] Mueller, *Precision and Purpose*, 4.

[80] "Unacknowledged Deaths: Civilian Casualties in NATO's Air Campaign in Libya," *Human Rights Watch*, May 13, 2012. www.hrw.org/report/2012/05/13/unacknowledged-deaths/civilian-casualties-natos-air-campaign-libya

[81] Clark, "In Absentia," 311, 315, 322, 325, 335.

forces occurred on multiple fronts with different anti-Qaddafi rebel groups, and coordination with rebels was confounded by technical obstacles and political sensitivities. Loyalist forces multiplied this difficulty by dispersing and reorganizing into smaller fighting units to complicate targeting for coalition aircraft.[82] This required ad hoc planning and innovation by coalition forces beset by the challenges of complex coordination with minimal staffing.[83] Because R2P doctrine included the necessity of minimizing collateral damage, international scrutiny permeated the coalition's evolving efforts to maintain the NFZ and conduct operations that hastened the demise of regime forces.

Throughout most of OOD, coalition members found it increasingly difficult to find suitable targets that met the intent of UNSCR 1973. For instance, B-1 crews that launched from the United States on March 27 to strike targets in Libya dropped forty-eight Joint Direct Attack Munitions (JDAMs) on munition storage facilities and bunkers. The two B-1s continued to Al Udeid Air Base, Qatar, where they were reloaded with forty-eight JDAMs, and on their return flight to the United States ended up attacking the same targets due to a lack of new targets.[84] Air planners, moreover, had to be wary of targeting bunkers and weapon storage sites that might contain yellow cake uranium. Any intelligence that indicated a bunker might be storing such material removed it from the target list to avert a humanitarian disaster that could also play into regime interests. Thus, numerous pro-Qaddafi bases throughout Libya had their bunkers and weapon storage sites bombed multiple times, but a few remained untouched out of concern of radioactive fallout.[85] This notable deterrent of a "yellow cake" shield suggests similar restrictions in future conflicts.

Targeting issues were also influenced by the Obama administration's desire to prevent a flow of arms out of Libya, fearing the civil war would spill into neighboring countries. Thus, according to one USAF

---

[82] Schinella, *Bombs without Boots*, 251–53.

[83] John Barry, "Lessons of Libya for Future Western Military Forays," *European Institute*, August 2011. www.europeaninstitute.org/index.php/130-european-affairs/ea-august-20 11/1417-lessons-of-libya-for-future-western-military-forays; Andrew Tilghman, "US Official: NATO Military Capability Ebbing," *RP Defense*, December 2, 2011. http://rp defense.over-blog.com/article-u-s-official-nato-military-capability-ebbing-91021934. html

[84] Author's personal knowledge from involvement in the operation. Nick Penzenstadler, "Air Force Releases Details of 24-Hour Libya Mission from Ellsworth," *Rapid City Journal*, August 4, 2011. https://rapidcityjournal.com/news/local/communities/ells worth/air-force-releases-details-of-hour-libya-mission-from/article_830a4cec-bf15-11e 0-8f60-001cc4c002e0.html

[85] Sumita Katira, "Gaddafi's Yellowcake Stockpile Found in Libyan Desert," *Arabian Gazette*, September 27, 2011. https://arabiangazette.com/gaddafis-yellowcake-stockpile-libyan-desert; interview, Michael Fowler, PhD, Department of Military and Strategic Studies, US Air Force Academy, July 19, 2019.

intelligence officer who supported the targeting process for F-16 CJs during OUP, the normally restrictive ROEs for the targeting of IADS were interpreted in a "loose" manner. In many cases, USAF F-16 CJs attacked sites that could be interpreted as being a part of the IADS network, as either a command and control node or a weapons storage bunker that might store missiles to replenish a SAM site.[86] Weakening the regime aligned with the UN-sanctioned effort to prevent human rights violations and ensure Libyan authorities complied with international law, and this translated into other developments concerning the escalating conflict between regime loyalists and NTC rebels. As the campaign progressed, coalition operations blurred the lines between protecting civilians from regime forces and aiding rebels in seizing pro-Qaddafi territory.

NATO's strikes against "concentrations of troops, lines of communication, ammunition depots, maintenance depots, and command and control nodes" weakened loyalist forces while minimizing risks to noncombatants and anti-Qaddafi rebels.[87] For a time, this forestalled the bombing of loyalist forces in populated areas or in proximity to rebel forces. However, as the Libyan civil war dragged on into the summer months, "the credibility of NATO was at stake," compelling NATO leadership to provide air strikes in support of rebel operations, especially in the Nafusa Mountains and near Tripoli.[88] This complicated resource allocation because it required an increasing degree of ad hoc planning and execution concerning ISR assets, strike platforms, and coordination – or at least deconfliction – with friendly ground components.

As described by many US and NATO personnel involved in the Libyan NFZ, there was a desire to avoid being perceived as openly supporting the rebels on the ground. Accordingly, the coalition did not want to provide close air support to rebels engaged in open combat with pro-Qaddafi forces.[89] That, however, did not mean the OUP coalition could not leverage innovative means to aid rebel goals. Lacking the ability to deploy Joint Terminal Attack Controllers (JTACs) with NTC forces, NATO forces turned to open-source cues for targeting Qaddafi's army in the vicinity of anti-Qaddafi rebels. For instance, Twitter became the open-source

---

[86] Ibid.
[87] Lieutenant General Charles Bouchard (transcript by Jason Harmala), "Coalition Building and the Future of NATO Operations: 2/14/2012 – Transcript," *Atlantic Council*, February 14, 2012. www.atlanticcouncil.org/commentary/transcript/coalition-building-and-the-future-of-nato-operations-2–14–2012-transcript
[88] Ibid.
[89] Personal communication with US/NATO planners and pilots who had flown missions in Libya during OOD/OUP, November 2011–June 2015.

mainstay for NTC rebels to communicate "in-the-open" the positions of loyalist forces. This bridged the ISR gap for the NATO CAOC in Italy, especially after a friendly fire incident on April 8 that made the NTC rebels more proactive in communicating via Twitter and other open-source channels.[90] Moreover, despite UNSCR 1973 restrictions, some coalition members stationed military personnel at the NTC headquarters in Benghazi to facilitate intelligence sharing and improve efficacy in targeting pro-Qaddafi forces.[91] Such innovations fostered close air support operations without a formal ground presence, thus permitting the coalition to reduce the political costs of supporting NTC forces. As best described by an MQ-1 Predator pilot, "The challenges of limited ISR and restrictive ROEs meant that we [United States and coalition] were operationally conducting air interdiction strikes, but were in reality, providing close air support."[92] The ability of NTC rebels to refine their tactics and capabilities also improved NATO's efficacy, as demonstrated during the well-coordinated Operation Mermaid Dawn assault and capture of Tripoli.[93]

In many cases, NATO air strikes had more of a psychological effect. During the siege of Misrata, NTC leaders pled with NATO planners to drop bombs every night, to give hope to civilians and rebels trapped in the city.[94] In the case of the Nafusa Mountains Campaign and the battle of Tripoli, NATO air strikes disrupted pro-Qaddafi forces, making many desert and/or defect to the rebels. NATO also airdropped more than 9 million leaflets in an attempt to shape the battlespace against loyalists through psychological operations.[95] Many NTC rebel commanders believed that coalition operations in their vicinity led to more anti-Qaddafi rebel recruits while making their NTC fighters more confident in their assaults.[96] These outcomes indicate the potential psychological power of air power in the Information Age and the necessity to manage perceptions in the battlespace.

The reluctance to be perceived as proactively supporting regime change led the coalition to employ air power in a risk-averse fashion and send mixed messages in the way forces were used.[97] Such unwillingness

---

[90] Gregory, *Clean Bombs and Dirty Wars*, 185–203.

[91] Netto, *Bringing Down Gaddafi*, 60.

[92] Interview with an MQ-1 pilot who flew Libya NFZ sorties. April 11, 2020.

[93] Gregory, *Clean Bombs and Dirty Wars*, 184–85; David Perry, *Leading from Behind Is Still Leading: Canada and the International Intervention in Libya* (Ottawa: Conference of Defence Associations Institute, 2012), 9.

[94] Mueller, *Precision and Purpose*, 43–68.

[95] Bouchard, "Coalition Building and the Future of NATO Operations."

[96] Mueller, *Precision and Purpose*, 50–66.

[97] Stephen R. Weissman, "The Law: Presidential Deception in Foreign Policy Making: Military Intervention in Libya 2011," *Presidential Studies Quarterly* 46:3 (2016): 669–90.

to commit – alongside risk-aversion – translated into very little desire to develop a post-conflict NATO plan once OUP concluded. Importantly, the Libyan NTC did not ask NATO for any support or assistance as OUP concluded. Coalition and NTC members failed to understand the implications of a fragmented security environment after OUP, making it difficult for Libya to achieve any modicum of short- or long-term peace and security. Such short-sighted optimism came from perceptions of positive consensus from various anti-Qaddafi factions in holding elections and transitioning to a liberal democracy.[98] Unfortunately, the new Libyan government was unable to create a monopoly over the legitimate use of violence. To the present, the fragmentation of militias has been the greatest driver of political instability in Libya.[99]

As indicated by many interviewees who had been US/NATO planners, there was confusion and surprise when it became obvious that there would be little to no Western involvement after Qaddafi died. His death ended the rationale for the Libyan NFZ with the NTC claiming to represent Libya. Unfortunately, the way in which air power was used to undermine Qaddafi's internal control of Libya did not undermine the logic of politics that Libyans had institutionally come to know from his decades of rule. Myopic optimism by the international community and Libyans alike ignored the implications of Qaddafi's legacy of autocratic governance.

### Post-Qaddafi Era

From 2011 to 2014, Libya experienced continued unrest as factional violence broke out between various armed groups in each region, vying for power in the new Libyan government. This created a new breeding ground for terrorism as the Islamic State (IS) established an affiliate in 2014 at Derna in eastern Libya.[100] The Libyan National Army, one of the strongest factions in the east and headed by General Khalifa Haftar, initiated military operations against IS groups in western Libya. Haftar's actions produced the Second Libyan Civil War (2014–present) and in the process earned him military support from Egypt and UAE. The Egyptian and UAE air forces have supported Haftar's operations, as their warplanes have been striking IS

---

[98] Dirk Vandewalle, "After Qaddafi: The Surprising Success of the New Libya," *Foreign Affairs* 91:6 (2012): 8–15; Christopher S. Chivvis and Jeffrey Martini, *Libya after Qaddafi: Lessons and Implications for the Future* (Santa Monica: RAND, 2014).

[99] Ricardo René Larémont, "After the Fall of Qaddafi: Political, Economic, and Security Consequences for Libya, Mali, Niger, and Algeria," *Stability: International Journal of Security and Development* 2:2 (2013): 29.

[100] Raphaël Lefèvre, "Is the Islamic State on the Rise in North Africa?" *The Journal of North African Studies* 19:5 (2014): 852–56.

targets and other rebel groups in Libya to support Haftar's aim of seizing Tripoli for the Libyan House of Representatives.[101]

The Second Libyan Civil War suggests the sort of long-term blowback one might see in future R2P air power interventions. Numerous scholars and policy makers argue that another R2P-styled military intervention is highly unlikely due to how NATO expanded its interpretation of the USNCR 1973 mandate.[102] A second civil war was largely due to NATO ignoring another aspect of R2P, namely the "Responsibility to Rebuild."[103] Indeed, as noted in a British government report by the House of Commons: Foreign Affairs Committee, "By the summer of 2011, the limited intervention to protect civilians had drifted into an opportunist policy of regime change. That policy was not underpinned by a strategy to support and shape" a Libya after Qaddafi.[104] Hence, air power on the cheap provided only a fleeting victory: Air strikes may kill, destroy, and demoralize an adversarial force but cannot transform how local politics play out on the ground. Though the "ultimate determinant ... in war is the man on the scene with a gun," air power can only shape the battlespace and strategic approaches to asserting control, but it cannot alone resolve the reality on the ground.[105]

Finally, based on the numerous lessons learned from the Libyan intervention, it seems unlikely for the foreseeable future that the international community would agree to another R2P intervention, air power centric or not. A future R2P intervention would likely require an upfront commitment to long-term stabilization. Moreover, this would require a strategy to deal with the externalities that would result from an intervention, especially if it inadvertently caused regime change. This suggests the paradox of "peacekeeping" in the modern era. Risk-averse Western capitals may be enchanted by precision air power's ability to destroy belligerent state and nonstate actors to protect civilians, but this does not assure an end to the logic of violence and politics in weak and collapsed states.

[101] Ulf Laessing and Hani Amara, "Explosions in Libya Capital after Late Night Air Strike," *Reuters*, April 20, 2019. www.reuters.com/article/us-libya-security/explosions-in-libya-capital-after-late-night-air-strike-idUSKCN1RW0E2

[102] Shahram Akbarzadeh and Arif Saba, "UN Paralysis over Syria: The Responsibility to Protect or Regime Change?" *International Politics* 56:4 (2019): 536–50.

[103] Paul Tang Abomo and Carter Ham, *R2P and the US Intervention in Libya* (New York: Palgrave Macmillan, 2018), 243.

[104] "Libya: Examination of Intervention and Collapse and the UK's Future Policy Options," *House of Commons: Foreign Affairs Committee*, Third Report of Session 2016–17, September 14, 2016, 3.

[105] J. C. Wylie, *Military Strategy: A General Theory of Power Control* (New Brunswick: Rutgers University Press, 1967), 85.

## Conclusion

Almost a year after establishing the Libyan NFZ, NATO chief Anders Fogh Rasmussen stated the air war highlighted "significant shortfalls in a range of European capabilities – from smart munitions, to air-to-air refueling, and intelligence surveillance and reconnaissance."[106] French General Marcel Druart made similar comments: "European allies provided most of the assets but only the United States could offer these capabilities. The EU needs to ensure that similar capabilities are available."[107] Despite these lessons, it was still a remarkable air campaign, as *The New York Times* described the Libyan NFZ as "nearly flawless – a model air war that used high technology, meticulous planning and restraint to protect civilians from Colonel Qaddafi's troops, which was the alliance's mandate."[108]

Regardless, the R2P-inspired intervention in Libya epitomized the problem of ambiguity and mission creep. Anti-Qaddafi rebels likely would not have survived against the onslaught of regime firepower had there not been an international coalition providing air cover. Coalition air power disrupted the ability of pro-Qaddafi forces to mass, resupply, wage conventional assaults, and besiege cities under rebel control. However, the definition of protecting civilians as mandated in UNSCR 1973 introduced the contradictory messaging of destroying regime forces that threatened cities under rebel control, giving rebels the ability to counterattack and seize new territory. The use of air power to coerce and compel an authoritarian leader who has nothing to gain from compliance also demonstrated the futility of such an approach. Resolving future R2P crises will likely require the international community to commit more resources and willpower than a low-cost air war.

Despite Qaddafi's removal, this was not the end of foreign air strikes. Since the end of OUP, there have been at least 550 drone strikes by the United States and at least another 4,056 air strikes by various countries – to include France, Turkey, and Israel.[109] This is suggestive of a "mowing

---

[106] Anders Fogh Rasmussen, "Rasmussen: 'Not Much Progress Has Been Made' on NATO-EU Cooperation," *Atlantic Council*, March 21, 2012. www.atlanticcouncil.or g/blogs/natosource/rasmussen-not-much-progress-has-been-made-on-natoeu-cooperation

[107] Nikolaj Nielsen, "NATO Commander: EU Could Not Do Libya without US," *EU Observer*, March 20, 2011. https://euobserver.com/news/115650

[108] C. J. Chivers and Eric Schmitt, "In Strikes on Libya by NATO, an Unspoken Civilian Toll," *New York Times*, December 17, 2011. www.nytimes.com/2011/12/18/world/afri ca/scores-of-unintended-casualties-in-nato-war-in-libya.html

[109] "Airstrikes and Civilian Casualties: Libya," *New America*, March 31, 2020. www.new america.org/in-depth/americas-counterterrorism-wars/airstrikes-and-civilian-casual ties-libya

the lawn" strategy (see Chapter 2), whereby the international community works to suppress insurgency and terrorism in weak or failed states. Participating nations, however, are constrained by their domestic political systems and therefore prefer the risk-adverse strategy of precision air strikes to "do something" but not enough to actually change the dynamics of local-level politics.

Overall, there are many implications of the Libyan air campaign, namely in the areas of tactical and operational adaptation, the military and political implications of advances in precision strike technology, the determinative influence of domestic and international politics, international humanitarian laws and norms, alliance dynamics, and the challenges of aligning air power's capabilities with indigenous ground forces. Even with these advances this conflict highlights the perennial questions that remain concerning what air campaigns can achieve, particularly under conditions of ambiguous guidance, open-ended political objectives, and coalition members unwilling to risk long-term commitments.

# 9 Coercing a Chaos State: The Saudi-Led Air War in Yemen

*Ralph Shield**

### Introduction

In March 2015 Saudi Arabia launched an air-led military campaign to restore a friendly regime in the neighboring Republic of Yemen. The Royal Saudi Air Force (RSAF) and its Gulf partners unleashed an arsenal of the latest Western weapons against a materially outclassed adversary. Seeking to tip the scales of a still inchoate conflict, Riyadh anticipated a quick and low-cost victory. More than six years later, however, the mission once branded *Decisive Storm* has delivered no decision. The war in Yemen grinds on, racking up civilian suffering and international opprobrium but with little measurable progress toward anything that might be sold as strategic success. Why?

Saudi Arabia's struggle to reverse the coup in Yemen provides an opportunity to assess how an authoritarian state approaches the employment of contemporary air power. The Yemen intervention also represents an additional data point to inform long-running debates about the overall utility of air power, both as a coercive tool of first resort and as a critical enabler to achieving victory on the cheap through support to local-proxy ground forces. On the first count, the Saudi coalition's travails cast doubt on the potency of independent air strikes as a coercive instrument in an internal conflict.

On the second, Yemen echoes the oft-made counterargument that air attack is most effectively employed in support of ground forces. A review of what few and qualified successes the Saudis have achieved, though, counsels prudence in calibrating realistic expectations about the types of end-states a light-footprint approach can attain in an internationalized civil war (see Figure 9.1).

---

* The views expressed by the author do not reflect those of the US government, the Department of Defense, or any of its organizations. This chapter draws some insights from the author's earlier article "The Saudi Air War in Yemen: A Case for Coercive Success through Battlefield Denial," *Journal of Strategic Studies* 41:3 (2018): 461–89, by Taylor and Francis. www.tandfonline.com

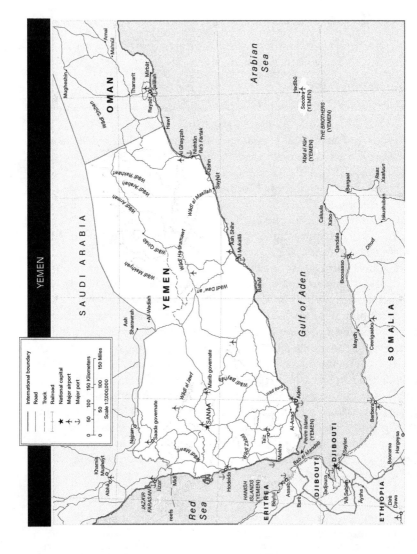

Figure 9.1 Map of Yemen

This chapter examines the Saudi-led air and combined arms campaign from its start through the beginning of 2020. Though no primary accounts have yet emerged that unpack Saudi deliberations and decision making, sufficient data and analyses now exist to deconstruct and characterize the campaign. The ensuing discussion maps coalition air actions to the mechanisms through which they should, if functioning properly, affect enemy behavior. It then evaluates how these mechanisms have actually performed over the duration of the conflict and draws some first-cut conclusions about the determinants of air power efficacy in a civil war context.

## Actors and Objectives

### The Saudi-Led Coalition

Operation Decisive Storm commenced on March 26, 2015, as the Saudi-led response to a desperate appeal for help from the government of Yemeni President Abd Rabbu Mansour Hadi. Undertaken by an ad hoc coalition of Gulf allies, the operation sought to save Hadi's displaced regime from a complete rout. Air strikes and a naval blockade were initiated to blunt the advance of the ascendant Houthi-led rebels toward the port city of Aden, the seat of Hadi's government-in-exile in the south.[1] The prospect that the Houthis might consolidate their takeover of Yemen raised considerable alarm in Riyadh. The Saudi monarchy had supported Sanaa, the Yemeni capital, in a clumsy and inconclusive campaign to quell an earlier Houthi insurrection in 2009 and so had good reason to anticipate a hostile relationship.[2] Perhaps more importantly, Riyadh's perception of the rise of the Shiite Houthi movement was colored by the Kingdom's sectarian rivalry with Iran and the monarchy's heightened sense of regime insecurity following the tumult of the 2011 Arab Spring.[3]

Saudi Arabia headed a collective of Gulf and Arab contributor states that variously included the UAE, Bahrain, Kuwait, Qatar, Egypt, Jordan, Morocco, and Sudan. This coalition itself backed a collection of indigenous anti-Houthi groups in Yemen, some of whom, it would eventually become clear, were only nominally aligned with President Hadi.

---

[1] Statement by Saudi Ambassador Al-Jubeir, *Market Watch*, March 25, 2015. https://marketwatch.com/press-release/statement-by-saudi-ambassador-al-jubeir-on-military-operations-in-yemen-2015-03-25.

[2] Lucas Winter, "Riyadh Enters the Yemen-Huthi Fray," *Middle East Quarterly* 19:1 (Winter 2012). www.meforum.org/articles/2012/riyadh-enters-the-yemen-huthi-fray

[3] Marc Lynch, *The New Arab Wars: Uprisings and Anarchy in the Middle East* (New York: Public Affairs Press, 2016), 2, 15, 61–62.

Supported Yemeni elements included formal military units still loyal to the president and an unsteady and shifting alliance of mainstream Islamists, Salafist militants, tribal irregulars, and southern separatist militias. As the war progressed, the Saudis and Emiratis worked to augment this amalgam of extant proxies with cadres of new Yemeni recruits trained and equipped abroad.[4]

Saudi Arabia's objectives in Yemen were threefold. First, the Saudis sought to preemptively eliminate the threat posed to the Kingdom by Yemen's air force and ballistic missiles, which had fallen into Houthi hands. Second, with respect to control of Yemen, Riyadh demanded that the Houthis relinquish all occupied territories, unilaterally disarm, vacate Sanaa, and allow the Hadi government to return to power. These ambitious demands were codified nearly verbatim in UN Security Council Resolution 2216 on April 14, 2015.[5] Finally, but less tangibly, Saudi Arabia meant to block the Houthis' suspected state-sponsor Iran from expanding its strategic influence on the Arabian Peninsula.[6] As the operation name implied, Saudi officials believed they could accomplish all these ends in rapid and dramatic fashion.[7]

### The Houthi-Saleh Alliance

The Houthi militants that the Saudis endeavored to evict from Sanaa were northern tribesman of the Zaydi sect of Shia Islam. Their rebellion had its genesis in a movement that began in 2001 advocating for Zaydi minority rights and against the central government's complicity in the US-led war on terror, which the group's founder and namesake, Hussein Badreddin al-Houthi, portrayed as a crusade against Islam.[8] Though Houthi-inspired dissent was initially confined to their restive homeland in the northwest highlands, the group's appeal and ambitions surged after the Hadi regime failed to deliver on promised reforms. In September 2014, the Houthis swept into Sanaa, taking control of the capital city in just four days as much of the army, sympathetic to their cause, either stood down or joined them. In the weeks that followed, the

---

[4] Emile Hokayem and David B. Roberts, "The War in Yemen," *Survival* 58:6 (December 2016–January 2017): 166, 170–74.

[5] UN Security Council Resolution 2216, April 14, 2015. www.securitycouncilreport.org/atf/cf/%7B65BFCF9B-6D27-4E9C-8CD3-CF6E4FF96FF9%7D/s_res_2216.pdf

[6] Mark Mazzetti and Eric Schmitt, "Quiet Support for Saudis Entangles US in Yemen," *New York Times*, March 13, 2016. www.nytimes.com/2016/03/14/world/middleeast/yemen-saudi-us.html?_r=0

[7] Ibid.

[8] Barak A. Salmoni, Bryce Loidolt, and Madeleine Wells, *Regime and Periphery in Northern Yemen: The Huthi Phenomenon* (Santa Monica: RAND, 2010).

Houthis and their allies solidified their grip on Sanaa and advanced into the south and east in a bid to capture the remainder of the country.[9]

The Houthis' principal ally in 2014 was Ali Abdullah Saleh, the former president of Yemen. Having held that office for thirty-three years, Saleh was forced to step down and hand power to his vice president, Hadi, as part of an internationally brokered deal to preserve order after protests rocked the capital in 2011. When in power, Saleh's government fought a series of indecisive wars to suppress six separate Houthi uprisings in their home governorate of Sa'dah, the last of which the Saudis directly assisted. Out of power and threatened by a security force restructuring that would dismantle his patronage networks and further marginalize him, Saleh joined with his erstwhile enemies to topple his successor. He brought with him sections of the Yemeni security services that remained loyal to him, including most of the country's elite Republican Guard.[10]

### The War

Saudi Arabia shouldered the lion's share of the air war burden with more than 100 RSAF aircraft participating. These included high-performance, front-line F-15S, Tornado, and Typhoon strike fighters, many outfitted with advanced targeting pods. The next largest force contributor, the UAE, deployed approximately 30 aircraft, including F-16E/F and Mirage 2000s.[11] Most remaining coalition partners operated fewer numbers of similar-make fighter-bombers, predominantly F-16 variants. The only nonwestern types were three Sudanese Su-24 M Fencer-Ds.[12] In addition to strike assets, coalition numbers also included a variety of support aircraft. Among them, Saudi C-130s, and later Emirati C-17s, conducted combat airdrops, delivered humanitarian supplies, and provided intratheater airlift.[13]

The United States and Great Britain, meanwhile, supplied political top-cover, low-profile intelligence and air-refueling support, and multiple

---

[9] International Crisis Group (ICG), "Yemen: Is Peace Possible?" February 9, 2016. www.crisisgroup.org/middle-east-north-africa/gulf-and-arabian-peninsula/yemen/yemen-pea ce-possible; Peter Salisbury, "Yemen: Stemming the Rise of a Chaos State," Chatham House Research Paper, May 2016, 18–25. www.chathamhouse.org/publication/yemen-stemming-rise-chaos-state

[10] Ibid.     [11] Jon Lake, "Conflict in Yemen," *Air Forces Monthly* 327 (June 2015): 36–40.

[12] Ibid.

[13] Alexandre Mello and Michael Knights, "The Saudi-UAE War Effort in Yemen (Part 1): Operation Golden Arrow in Aden," Washington Institute, August 10, 2015. www.washingtoninstitute.org/policy-analysis/view/the-saudi-uae-war-effort-in-yemen-part-1 -operation-golden-arrow-in-aden; Rasha Abubakar, "Arab Coalition Announce Success of First Food and Water Drop Trial in Northern Tuhaita, Yemen," *Emirates News Agency*, July 15, 2018. http://wam.ae/en/details/1395302698912

transfusions of precision guided munitions. The extent of Anglo-American intelligence assistance remains undisclosed but appeared to be robust, driven by a desperation to reduce civilian casualties. It included sharing of satellite imagery as well as motion video and probably signals intelligence from various platforms.[14] The scope of refueling assistance is similarly uncertain as US authorities backed away from their own statistics; the last published tally before USCENTCOM officially disavowed its metrics suggested that US tankers had serviced 9,000 coalition sorties by 2017. By November 2018, when American tanker support was terminated, about one-fifth of the coalition's sorties were being refueled by USAF aircraft.[15]

The most visible and controversial enabling support provided to the coalition has been the sale of laser- and GPS-guided precision munitions. By all accounts these make up the overwhelming majority of the coalition air weapons used in Yemen. Immediate deliveries included the initial British transfer of 2,400 Paveway guided bombs to Saudi Arabia in spring 2015.[16] This was followed by urgent Saudi and Emirati appeals that summer and fall to the United States for an additional 15,000 Paveways, JDAMs, and Hellfires at an estimated total value of $1.7 billion.[17] With brief interruptions, sales from the United States

[14] Maggie Michael and Jon Gambrell, "Saudi Coalition Used US Bombs in Obliterating Yemen Market," *Military Times*, April 7, 2016. https://militarytimes.com/news/your-military/2016/04/07/saudi-coalition-used-u-s-bombs-in-obliterating-yemen-market; Joseph Trevithick, "Houthi Rebels Shoot Down US Air Force MQ-9 Reaper over Yemen," *The Drive*, October 2, 2017. https://thedrive.com/the-war-zone/14806/hou thi-rebels-shoot-down-u-s-air-force-mq-9-reaper-over-yemen; Arron Merat, "'The Saudis Couldn't Do It without Us': The UK's True Role in Yemen's Deadly War," *The Guardian*, June 18, 2019. https://theguardian.com/world/2019/jun/18/the-saudi s-couldnt-do-it-without-us-the-uks-true-role-in-yemens-deadly-war

[15] Samuel Oakford, "US Doubled Fuel Support for Saudi Bombing Campaign in Yemen after Deadly Strike on Funeral," *The Intercept*, July 13, 2017. https://theintercept.com/2017/07/13/u-s-doubled-fuel-support-for-saudi-bombing-campaign-in-yemen-after-de adly-strike-on-funeral; Samuel Oakford, "The US Military Can't Keep Track of Which Missions It's Fueling in Yemen War," *The Intercept*, September 18, 2017. https://thein tercept.com/2017/09/18/the-u-s-military-cant-keep-track-of-which-missions-its-fuel ing-in-yemen-war; Phil Stewart, "US Halting Refueling of Saudi-Led Coalition Aircraft in Yemen's War," *Reuters*, November 9, 2018. https://reuters.com/article/us-usa-yemen-refueling/u-s-halting-refueling-of-saudi-led-coalition-aircraft-in-yemens-war-idUSKCN1NE2LJ

[16] Stockholm International Peace Research Institute's (SIPRI) arms transfer database, accessed September 25, 2019. https://sipri.org/databases/armstransfers

[17] DSCA News Release Transmittal No. UAE 15–14, May 29, 2015. https://dsca.mil/m ajor-arms-sales/united-arab-emirates-uae-guided-bomb-units-gbu-31s-and-gbu-12s; DSCA News Release Transmittal No. UAE 15–51, November 5, 2015. http://dsca.mil/major-arms-sales/united-arab-emirates-uae-joint-direct-attack-munitions-jdam-sus tainment-and-support; Aaron Mehta, "US Clears Sale of Air-to-Ground Weapons to Saudi Arabia," *Defense News*, November 16, 2015. https://defensenews.com/air/2015/11/16/us-clears-sale-of-air-to-ground-weapons-to-saudi-arabia

and United Kingdom continued and vastly increased in volume over the course of the conflict despite legislative scrutiny and pushback in both capitals.[18] In 2019 the Trump administration approved the sale to Saudi Arabia of 120,000 air-delivered precision munitions over bipartisan congressional opposition.[19]

When the campaign began in late March 2015, the coalition attained air superiority quickly against light opposition. As many as forty surface-to-air missiles may have been launched during the disorganized response to initial raids but none found their mark, Yemen's air defenses having been disrupted by a Saudi-led suppression effort.[20] Those anti-air systems not destroyed in the first few days ceased to present a serious threat soon after.[21] Taken by surprise and bereft of many of its pilots – the bulk of whom remained loyal to Hadi – Yemeni Air Force warplanes never left the ground. Most of Yemen's aircraft and air defense equipment, and many of its missile holdings, were quickly destroyed or disabled.

Air raids also struck Houthi and Saleh leadership headquarters and residences and a variety of traditional interdiction targets. These included garrisons, supply dumps, roads, bridges, ports, and airfields. Sustained attention on air and seaports would continue throughout the war, part of a blockade intended to cut Houthi access to material support from abroad. Following these pre-planned attacks, strike emphasis recentered on the defense of Aden. Coalition airlift assets air-dropped weapons and ammunition to pro-Hadi military units and militias there and across the country in an effort to shore up local resistance.[22]

---

[18] Patrick Wintour, "Shelve UK Arms Sales to Saudis over Yemen, Say Two MPs' Committees," *Guardian*, September 15, 2016. https://theguardian.com/world/2016/se p/15/crispin-blunt-report-foreign-affairs-committee-says-arms-sales-to-saudis-yemen-judged-high-court; Helene Cooper, "Senate Narrowly Backs Trump Weapons Sale to Saudi Arabia," *New York Times*, June 13, 2017. https://nytimes.com/2017/06/13/world/middleeast/trump-weapons-saudi-arabia.html?module=inline

[19] Michael LaForgia and Walt Bogdanich, "Trump Allows High-Tech US Bomb Parts to Be Built in Saudi Arabia," *New York Times*, June 7, 2019. https://nytimes.com/2019/06/07/us/saudi-arabia-arms-sales-raytheon.html

[20] Tom Cooper, "The Houthis' Do-It-Yourself Air Defenses (Part Two)," *War Is Boring*," January 16, 2018. https://warisboring.com/the-houthis-do-it-yourself-air-defenses-2

[21] Jeremy Binnie and Sean O'Connor, "Initial Saudi Air Strikes Lacked Intensity," *Jane's Defence Weekly*, April 13, 2015; Jeremy Binnie and Sean O'Connor, "Indecisive Storm: Assessing the Saudi-Led Air Campaign in Yemen," *Jane's Defence Weekly*, July 1, 2015.

[22] Michael Knights and Alexandre Mello, "The Saudi-UAE Effort in Yemen (Part 2): The Air Campaign," Washington Institute, August 11, 2015. www.washingtoninstitute.org/p olicy-analysis/view/the-saudi-uae-war-effort-in-yemen-part-2-the-air-campaign; Michael Knights, "Gulf Coalition Operations in Yemen (Part 2): The Air War," Washington Institute, March 25, 2016. www.washingtoninstitute.org/policy-analysis/view/gulf-coalition-operations-in-yemen-part-2-the-air-war

On April 22, three weeks into the war, Saudi authorities announced the transition from Operation Decisive Storm to Operation Restoring Hope.[23] Though marketed as a shift from kinetic operations to humanitarian assistance, in reality this rebranding signaled no change in targets or tempo. The coalition continued to hammer Houthi positions, generating roughly ninety strike sorties per day, but with little headway toward the positive end-state objective of pacifying the rebellion and recovering Sanaa.[24] The Houthis and their Saleh-loyalist allies retaliated in kind, ambushing Saudi frontier outposts and patrols, and lobbing rocket, mortar, and SCUD missile fire against civilian population centers across the border.[25]

By three months later, in July, the coalition had recognized that heavy application of air power alone was not working and so switched gears. Under the new moniker Operation Golden Arrow, the Emiratis led a daring amphibious reinforcement of Aden, landing a conventional battlegroup at the encircled port. Composed of an Emirati mechanized brigade, Saudi special operations troops, and a cadre of transplanted Yemeni resistance fighters, this mixed force consolidated a foothold in Aden and then launched a counteroffensive north to recapture the nearby airbase and former US counterterrorism hub at al-Anad in August.[26]

The Aden breakout shifted the war into a new and more dynamic phase. The coalition followed up with a second ground offensive in September, driving southwest from Saudi Arabia's al-Wadiah border crossing into central Yemen. This column set up a forward operating base and airfield at the Safir oil refinery in Ma'rib governorate and then pushed west in the direction of Sanaa. Further south, meanwhile, the Aden battlegroup advanced toward Taizz, Yemen's third-largest city. Though unable to break the siege of Taizz – a city that would suffer as a fiercely disputed prize for much of the war – a portion of the Aden force did reach the west

---

[23] "Saudi Ambassador Holds Press Conference on Operation Renewal of Hope," published April 22, 2015. www.youtube.com/watch?v=ZCOqTyRzvtA; the operation name is more commonly translated as *Restoring Hope*.
[24] Meda Al Rowas, "Saudi Arabia to Enforce Embargo in Yemen and Conduct Airstrikes as Needed, Sustaining Maritime and Aviation Risks," *Jane's Intelligence Weekly*, April 22, 2015; Knights, "Air War."
[25] Jeremy Binnie, "Yemen's Ansar Allah Unveils Its Rocket Power," *Jane's Defence Weekly*, May 29, 2015; Binnie and O'Connor, "Indecisive Storm"; Michael Knights and Alexandre Mello, "The Escalating Northern Front in Yemen," Washington Institute, September 24, 2015. www.washingtoninstitute.org/policy-analysis/view/the-escalating-northern-front-in-yemen; Alexandre Mello and Michael Knights, "Gulf Coalition Operations in Yemen (Part 1): The Ground War," Washington Institute, March 25, 2016. www.washingtoninstitute.org/policy-analysis/view/gulf-coalition-operations-in-yemen-part-1-the-ground-war
[26] Mello and Knights, "Golden Arrow."

coast, liberating the port of Mocha and threatening a coastal advance on Sanaa from the south.[27] The coalition opened a third cross-border offensive in the winter of 2016, this time in the extreme northwest of the country. Pushing north-to-south along the Red Sea coast, this thrust captured the Yemeni port of Midi, thus denying the Houthi another gateway for maritime resupply, but bogged down soon thereafter.[28]

Coalition ground force operations had reclaimed significant territory in the six months since Golden Arrow, but progress on all axes stalled by February 2016. In the interim, the Houthis progressively escalated the border war. Raids and rocket fire into the Kingdom incurred mounting Saudi casualties and equipment costs.[29] Adding to these steady rear-front losses were several high-toll Tochka mobile missile strikes against the coalition's forward operating bases in Yemen, a butcher's bill for Riyadh's failure to completely eliminate these weapons in garrison early on.[30] In a predictable replay of the US Air Force's SCUD-hunting hardships in Iraq in 1991, the Saudi air component struggled to find and destroy road-mobile missile launchers once dispersed.[31]

By spring 2016 the war appeared to have reached a stalemate. Official Saudi and Emirati statements signalled a waning appetite for further commitment.[32] Both sides consented to a tentative ceasefire in April and ended up participating in serious peace negotiations brokered by the United Nations in Kuwait that summer.[33] Sadly, a combination of

[27] Mello and Knights, "Ground War."
[28] Jigmey Bhutia, "Yemen: Scores of Houthi Rebels and Government Troops Killed in Fresh Fighting Near Saudi Border," *International Business Times*, December 20, 2015. www.ibtimes.co.uk/yemen-scores-houthi-rebels-government-troops-killed-fresh-fighting-near-saudi-border-1534191; "Pro-Government Troops Recapture Strategic Yemeni Port Town," *Middle East Eye*, January 7, 2016. www.middleeasteye.net/news/pro-government-troops-yemen-recapture-strategic-port-town-143743280
[29] Knights and Mello, "Northern Front"; Lori Plotkin Borghardt and Michael Knights, "Border Fight Could Shift Saudi Arabia's Yemen War Calculus," Washington Institute, December 6, 2016. www.washingtoninstitute.org/policy-analysis/view/border-fight-could-shift-saudi-arabias-yemen-war-calculus; Knights, "Air War."
[30] Binnie and O'Connor, "Initial Saudi Air Strikes"; Jeremy Binnie, "Arab Coalition Reportedly Hit by Second Tochka Missile Attack in Yemen," *Jane's Defence Weekly*, December 16, 2015.
[31] Lucas Winter, "Yemen's Houthi Missiles Keep Saudi Arabia Mired in Conflict," *Terrorism Monitor* 15:13 (June 30, 2017). https://jamestown.org/program/yemens-houthi-missiles-keep-saudi-arabia-mired-conflict
[32] "Saudi Arabia to Scale Back Operations in Yemen after Deadly Strike," *Middle East Eye*, March 27, 2016. www.middleeasteye.net/news/saudi-arabia-plans-draw-down-operations-yemen-after-deadly-air-strike-1437795930; Noah Browning, "UAE Says Its War in Yemen 'Practically over,'" *Reuters*, June 16, 2016. www.reuters.com/article/us-yemen-security-emirates-idUSKCN0Z20HU
[33] Peter Salisbury, "Yemen: National Chaos, Local Order," Chatham House Research Paper (December 2017): 35–36. www.chathamhouse.org/publication/yemen-national-chaos-local-order

factors conspired to foil the Kuwait talks. Despite being a primary party to conflict, Saudi Arabia was not directly represented, and Hadi appears to have played the role of a spoiler, revealing himself to be a less pliable client than Riyadh perhaps originally envisioned. The Houthis, for their part, may have lacked the political experience and savvy to define and extract an acceptable compromise.[34]

In the ensuing two years Yemen sank into entrenched and stagnant conflict. The contours of territorial control changed little, with intense fighting delimited to several distinct and geographically disparate contact fronts. Factionalized terrain and loose allegiance patterns on either side, meanwhile, gave rise to local arrangements that perpetuated the conflict with minimal actual ground combat across the remainder of the country, portions of which suffered nevertheless under incessant coalition bombing.[35] Although air raid tempo was lower now than during the initial nine months of the war, slackening to between twenty to seventy sorties per day, attacks continued to hit targets such as residential blocks and markets with little obvious military value.[36] The Houthis home governorate of Sa'dah, moreover, remained the focus of a high share of punishment, absorbing almost a quarter of all recorded strikes since the beginning of the intervention.[37] Notably, air strike activity surged following breakdowns in negotiations or successful Houthi missile and drone attacks against strategic targets on Saudi territory as bombing intensity appeared to function as an expression of Riyadh's frustration with the war.[38]

Despite Saudi-led efforts to disable Yemen's coastal defenses and retake its seaports, the fighting also spilled into the maritime domain. The Houthis sporadically attacked Saudi, Emirati, and even US warships operating offshore, the last eliciting a spate of American naval counterstrikes.[39] These and other attacks were conducted with new weapons not previously in Yemen's inventory, like suicide boats, sea

---

[34] Ibid.

[35] Ibid., 13–23; Marie-Christine Heinze, "Yemen's War as Seen from the Local Level," in *Politics, Governance, and Reconstruction in Yemen* (Washington, DC: Project on Middle East Political Science, January 2018), 34. https://pomeps.org/2018/01/10/politics-governance-and-reconstruction-in-yemen

[36] Knights, "Air War."

[37] Yemen Data Project, "Yemen Data Project Air Raids Summary for August 2019," September 13, 2019. https://mailchi.mp/7c6cd4284d06/september2019-yemen-data-project-update-563155?e=b95b4d66d8

[38] UNOHCR, "Situation of Human Rights in Yemen (A/HRC/39/43)," August 17, 2018, 39–40. https://ohchr.org/_layouts/15/WopiFrame.aspx?sourcedoc=/Documents/Countries/YE/A_HRC_39_43_EN.docx&action=default&DefaultItemOpen=1

[39] Taimur Khan, "Yemen War Threatens to Spill into International Arena as Maritime Risks Grow," *The National*, March 23, 2017. www.thenational.ae/world/yemen-war-threatens-to-spill-into-international-arena-as-maritime-risks-grow-1.14432

mines, extended-range rockets, and drones, many of which featured designs or components that traced back to Iran.[40]

As time passed and the promise of a rapid victory receded, Saudi Arabia and the UAE increasingly sponsored different proxies and pursued divergent agendas in Yemen. Riyadh continued to back Hadi, supported Islah, a mainstream Islamist party with ties to the Muslim Brotherhood, and remained fixated on rolling back Houthi influence in the north. The UAE, meanwhile, distrusted the Muslim Brotherhood so partnered with secessionist forces and harder line Salafist groups in its management of the war in the south, where it also sought to stamp out Al-Qaeda in the Arabian Peninsula and carve out a separate sphere of influence.[41] The effects of this misalignment became strategically significant as the war dragged on with the two states' respective proxies often working at cross-purposes and eventually coming to blows.[42] Commanding little credibility of his own, Hadi steadily lost agency over the anti-Houthi forces fighting in his name and sporadically acted out to reassert himself.[43]

The marriage of convenience between the Houthis and Saleh lasted much longer than most observers predicted but finally collapsed in late 2017 under rumors that Saleh was preparing to reconcile with Riyadh. Saleh's desertion was short-lived – he was killed by Houthi fighters during interfactional clashes in the capital only days later.[44] Hopes that Saleh's departure might accelerate an end to the conflict soon gave way to a realization that his death only further complicated the path to peace.[45] Most knowledgeable observers judged the chances as near zero that either side would soon achieve a decisive win and reassert centralized control over Yemen. Rather, most deemed it likely that the country would subsist

---

[40] Jonathan Saul, Parisa Hafezi, and Michael Georgy "Iran Steps Up Support for Houthis in Yemen's War," *Reuters*, March 21, 2017. www.reuters.com/article/us-yemen-iran-houthis-idUSKBN16S22R

[41] Kristian Coates Ulrichsen, "Endgames for Saudi Arabia and the United Arab Emirates in Yemen," in *Politics, Governance, and Reconstruction in Yemen*, 32–33; ICG, "Yemen: Averting a Destructive Battle for Hodeida," June 2018, 3. https://crisisgroup.org/middle-east-north-africa/gulf-and-arabian-peninsula/yemen/b59-yemen-averting-destructive-battle-hodeida

[42] Salisbury, "National Chaos," 16; ICG, "Destructive Battle," 9.

[43] Ibid., 18; Charles Schmitz, "Hadi's Political Chaos May Hamper Yemen Talks," *Middle East Institute*, May 10, 2018. www.mei.edu/content/article/yemens-ray-hope

[44] Shuaib Almosawa and Ben Hubbard, "Yemen's Ex-President Killed as Mayhem Convulses Capital," *New York Times*, December 4, 2017. www.nytimes.com/2017/12/04/world/middleeast/saleh-yemen-houthis.html

[45] Ibid.; Anthony H. Cordesman, "Saleh and the War in Yemen," Center for Strategic and International Studies, December 4, 2017. www.csis.org/analysis/saleh-and-war-yemen; Michael Horton, "The Poetic Demise of Yemen's Most Powerful Man," *The American Conservative*, December 6, 2017. www.theamericanconservative.com/articles/the-poetic-demise-of-yemens-most-powerful-man

for the foreseeable future in a condition of violent internal competition that one expert has characterized as a "chaos state."[46]

## A Dynamic Beginning

As with other protracted wars, the nature of the contest in Yemen changed over time in ways that affect the consideration of air power's role. The analysis that follows therefore organizes the conflict into two major phases. This first section examines the conduct and impact of coalition actions during the eighteen months from the start of the intervention in March 2015 until the onset of UN-brokered negotiations in Kuwait in mid-2016. This period witnessed conspicuous adjustments in warfighting strategy and territorial control. The first two subsections evaluate the limited effectiveness achieved by the air-only Decisive Storm/Restoring Hope bombing efforts, dissecting punishment and denial operations separately. The third subsection then reviews the coalition's more successful combined-arms operations after Golden Arrow.

Using the Kuwait talks as an inflection point, the second section focuses on developments from mid-2016 through late 2019. This phase featured fewer discernible changes in battlefield fortunes. Instead, the coalition's decision to persist with a controversial blockade, and an intensified decapitation campaign, appear to have only exacerbated the conditions in Yemen for little-to-no strategic gain. The final subsection discusses the Emirati-led 2018 Red Sea advance on Hudaydah, its aftermath, and the trajectory of the war in late 2019.

### Punishing from Above

Early coalition bombing featured parallel but distinct punishment efforts to coerce both Saleh and the Houthis. Seeing Saleh as an opportunist, the Saudis applied direct pressure for the express purpose of compelling him to abandon his expedient alliance with the more ideologically motivated Houthis.[47] Air operations against Saleh and his loyalists included early political decapitation strikes targeting the person of the former president himself.[48] Saleh survived, however, and remained defiant well into 2017.

---

[46] Salisbury, "Stemming the Rise."

[47] April Longley Alley, "Collapse of the Houthi-Saleh Alliance and the Future of Yemen's War," in *Politics, Governance, and Reconstruction in Yemen*, 12, footnote 19.

[48] "Saudi-Led Air Strikes Hit Yemen for Third Straight Day," *Al Jazeera*, March 28, 2015. www.aljazeera.com/news/2015/03/yemen-aden-saudi-arabia-150327174924579.html; Reuters in Cairo, "Saudi Airstrikes in Yemen Target House of Ex-President Saleh," *The Guardian*, May 10, 2015. www.theguardian.com/world/2015/may/10/saudi-air-strikes-in-yemen-target-house-of-ex-president-saleh

When Saleh met his end late that year, it was at the hands of his Houthi co-conspirators rather than as a slain Saudi high-value target. Whether intended to actually take his life or simply to intimidate him, there is no evidence that the coalition's unsuccessful decapitation strikes in spring 2015 or thereafter stirred in Saleh any change of heart.

The Saudis' punishment attacks against the Houthis also included attempted decapitation. Initial air strikes missed the group's commander, Abdul-Malik al-Houthi, but killed three of his subordinates and injured a fourth.[49] There were no further decapitation kills before the opening of the mid-2016 Kuwait talks, though, suggesting that the Saudi coalition struggled to locate and track individual human targets.[50] In light of the time elapsed since the March strikes, and the absence of perceivable pressure in the interim, it would be hard to attribute the improvement in the Houthis' willingness to negotiate in April 2016 to leadership fears about their personal safety. Despite initial success, decapitation efforts against Abdul-Malik and his contemporaries proved no more effective than those versus Saleh.

On a grander scale, the coalition also conducted deliberate and widespread air strikes against civilian, economic, and infrastructure targets. This was part of a clear, if unacknowledged, collective punishment strategy.[51] Nonmilitary objects damaged or destroyed included residential blocks, markets, mosques, schools, clinics, wells, factories, electrical stations, and government facilities countrywide.[52] Utilities like water, power, and food storage and distribution were particularly hard hit.[53] Saudi bombing levied its harshest punishment on the Houthi heartland of

---

[49] Michael Pizzi, "Saudis Launch Air Campaign to Defend Yemen Government," *Al Jazeera*, March 25, 2015. http://america.aljazeera.com/articles/2015/3/25/houthi-aden.html

[50] The next notable Houthi leadership death by air strike occurred June 8, 2016. Ali Oweida, "Top Houthi Commander Killed in Yemen Airstrike," *Anadolu Agency*, June 8, 2016. http://aa.com.tr/en/middle-east/top-houthi-commander-killed-in-yemen-airstrike/586404

[51] Merat, "'The Saudis"; Knights, "Air War"; Knights and Mello, "Air Campaign."

[52] Ibid.; Human Rights Watch (HRW), "Joint Letter to HRC: Create an International Investigating Mechanism for Yemen," February 23, 2016. www.hrw.org/news/2016/02/23/joint-letter-hrc-create-international-investigating-mechanism-yemen; Asa Fitch and Mohammed Al-Kibsi, "Heavy Toll in Yemen Conflict Draws Scrutiny," *Wall Street Journal*, December 10, 2015. www.wsj.com/articles/heavy-toll-in-yemen-conflict-draws-scrutiny-1449743401

[53] Iona Craig, "Bombed into Famine: How Saudi Air Campaign Targets Yemen's Food Supplies," *Guardian*, December 12, 2017. www.theguardian.com/world/2017/dec/12/bombed-into-famine-how-saudi-air-campaign-targets-yemens-food-supplies; Jason Fritz interview with Charles Schmitz, "The Costs of the War in Yemen," *Warcast*, podcast audio, June 13, 2018. https://warontherocks.com/podcast/warcast

Sa'dah.[54] By August 2015, Sa'dah City exhibited the worst devastation to civilian infrastructure of any urban center in Yemen despite hosting no ground fighting.[55] The scale, placement, and timing of these attacks conveyed a plain intention to strong-arm the Houthis by raising the human costs of continued resistance.

But the suffering of the Yemeni people and the focused ruin wrought on Sa'dah failed to bring the Houthis to heel. Instead, they escalated horizontally, lashing out with cross-border strikes of their own into southern Saudi Arabia. Rather than compelling their adversary to compromise or capitulate, the coalition's two-tiered punishment strategy – attacking both the general population and the Houthi homeland – only intensified the conflict.

A closer examination of the assumptions underpinning this strategy suggests that the chances for Saudi Arabia to prevail through collective punishment were never good. An acutely underdeveloped country, Yemen lacked adequate targetable infrastructure to hold at-risk for useful effect.[56] The paucity of physical pressure points was attested to by reports that fixed-target lists were exhausted in the first days of Decisive Storm.[57] Having only recently seized power, the Houthis also harbored little stake in the economic viability of the now-dismembered Yemeni state. Nor was strategic bombing ever likely to trigger a revolt against Houthi rule. The Yemeni population was socially diverse, politically disempowered, and badly fragmented by decades of divide-and-rule elite politics.[58] Neither attacks on the national means of production or on the other inhabitants of Yemen offered much, then, by way of leverage.

Although the Houthis would seem naturally more inclined to empathize with their northern countrymen, the strategic premise of the air onslaught against Sa'dah was similarly flawed. Sa'dah boasted even less physical capital to hold at risk – its neglect and impoverishment were one

---

[54] HRW, "Targeting Saada: Unlawful Coalition Airstrikes on Saada City in Yemen," June 30, 2015. www.hrw.org/report/2015/06/30/targeting-saada/unlawful-coalition-airstrikes-saada-city-yemen

[55] UN Security Council, "Final Report of the Panel of Experts on Yemen Established Pursuant to Security Council Resolution 2140 (2014)," January 22, 2016, 163–65. https://digitallibrary.un.org/record/819771

[56] For parallels in Somalia (1992–93) and Afghanistan (2001) see Daniel Byman, Matthew Waxman, and Eric V. Larson, *Airpower as a Coercive Instrument* (Santa Monica: RAND, 1999), 115; Ward Thomas, "Victory by Duress: Civilian Infrastructure as a Target in Air Campaigns," *Security Studies* 15:1 (January–March 2006): 9.

[57] Binnie and O'Connor, "Indecisive Storm"; Knights and Mello, "Air Campaign."

[58] Gerald M. Feierstein, "Yemen: The 60-Year War," Middle East Institute, February 2019. https://mei.edu/sites/default/files/2019-02/Yemen%20The%2060%20Year%20War.pdf

of the original motivators of the Houthi movement. Moreover, its inhabitants had endured near-constant warfare with the central government over the course of the past decade. The six conflicts between 2004 and 2011 all predated any Houthi aspirations to overthrow Sanaa but nonetheless entailed brutal and indiscriminate attacks on civilians and civil infrastructure. Saudi Arabia was an active participant in the last of these, with the RSAF bombing on behalf of then-President Saleh.[59] As a result, the Houthis and their fellow northern tribesmen were both acclimated to hardship and conditioned to perceive the coalition's counterpopulation campaign as only the latest phase of an existential contest for survival.

*Denial by Air Interdiction*

Concurrent with leadership and population punishment bombing, the Saudi air campaign also involved denial actions to foil the Houthis' military strategy. After quickly securing its own freedom of action in the skies, the coalition mounted a considerable interdiction blitz to freeze the movement of Houthi and Saleh–loyalist forces countrywide. Attacks hit roads, bridges, assembly areas, supply points, garrisons, and fuel stations.[60] Saudi airdrops, meanwhile, upgraded the ground threat that pro-government militias posed by supplying them with advanced antitank weapons.[61]

Beginning in April 2015, the coalition concentrated on isolating Aden to relieve pressure on pro-Hadi elements holding out in the besieged port city.[62] Critically, an eight-man team of Emirati forward air controllers was inserted to better direct defensive air strikes and naval gunfire support.[63] And here again, air-supplied arms, ammunition, and communications equipment helped sustain embattled and outnumbered government resistance forces.[64]

Nevertheless, the curtain of fire laid down from above failed to completely insulate Aden or to halt Houthi expansion nationwide. Albeit at a lesser rate, enemy forces continued to flow south, and Hadi-aligned forces were unable

[59] Salmoni et al., *Regime and Periphery*, 129–57.
[60] SUSRIS translations of coalition press briefings for Days 3, 4, 6, 9, and 17. http://susris.com/special-sections/turmoil-in-yemen-2015
[61] SUSRIS transcripts for Days 19, 20, and 2; Michael Horton, "Houthis Stand Firm against Airstrikes in Yemen," *Jane's Intelligence Review*, June 1, 2015.
[62] SUSRIS transcripts for Days 4, 6, 7, 8, 11, 12, 14, 15, 17, and 21.
[63] William Maclean, Noah Browning, and Yara Bayoumy, "Yemen Counter-Terrorism Mission Shows UAE Military Ambition," *Reuters*, June 28, 2016. www.reuters.com/article/us-yemen-security-emirates-idUSKCN0ZE1EA
[64] Mohammad Mukhashaf, "Yemeni Fighters Repel Houthis in Aden after Arms Drop," *Reuters*, April 3, 2015. www.reuters.com/article/us-yemen-security-aden-houthis-idUSKBN0MU0KU20150403

to convert to the offensive.[65] The Houthis still held the majority of the country and managed to continue modest ground gains.[66] Though "hybridized" with the addition of Saleh's Republican Guard, the Houthis were still at core a light guerrilla force and so better able to reduce their exposure to air attack than a conventional army.[67] They abandoned convoy movements, reverted to stricter use of civilian camouflage, and adopted a much lower force-to-space profile during behind-the-lines movement.[68]

The early air effort, then, returned disappointing results. Airborne firepower and ground-based terminal attack control broke Houthi momentum, preventing a state takeover and preserving the government's toehold in Aden. But neither collective punishment nor air interdiction could induce surrender or any other sought-for modification of adversary behavior. The coalition's objectives could not be achieved exclusively from the air.

### The Air-Ground Offensive

Standoff air strikes against Houthi fielded forces were insufficient in and of themselves to turn the tide of the ground war. Air power was essential, however, to enable the air-ground offensive that finally did. The July 2015 Golden Arrow operation in Aden would not have been possible without ground-directed suppressive firepower. The Emirati-led amphibious landing was ambitious and ably executed, and air's portion of the supporting fires task was significant, comprising 136 strikes during the first 36 hours.[69] The subsequent breakout received similarly heavy fixed-wing air support. Air strike frequency reportedly reached nearly 150 sorties per day in September 2015, its peak rate for the war.[70]

[65] AFP, "Situation in Yemen Unchanged Weeks into Air War," *Defense News*, May 4, 2015. www.defensenews.com/story/defense/international/mideast-africa/2015/05/04/reality-ground-yemen-unchanged-weeks-air-war/26897097
[66] Sarah Almukhtar et al., "Mapping Chaos in Yemen: Houthi Fighters Continue Steady Advance," *New York Times*, June 17, 2015. www.nytimes.com/interactive/2015/03/26/world/middleeast/geography-of-chaos-in-yemen-maps.html?_r=0
[67] Lucas Winter, "The Adaptive Transformation of Yemen's Republican Guard," *Small Wars Journal*, 7 (March 2017). http://smallwarsjournal.com/jrnl/art/the-adaptive-transformation-of-yemen%E2%80%99s-republican-guard
[68] Alexandre Mello and Michael Knights, "The Hodeida Campaign (Part 2): Can Yemen Recapture Major Ports from the Houthi Rebels?" Washington Institute, May 15, 2018. www.washingtoninstitute.org/policy-analysis/view/the-hodeida-campaign-part-2-can-yemen-recapture-hodeida-from-the-houthi-reb; Michael Knights, "The Houthi War Machine: From Guerilla War to State Capture," *Combating Terrorism Center* 11:8 (September 2018). www.ctc.usma.edu/houthi-war-machine-guerilla-war-state-capture
[69] Mazzetti and Schmitt, "Quiet Support for Saudis"; Mello and Knights, "Golden Arrow."
[70] Knights, "Air War." Figures for sortie rates drawn from Knights due to his unique access. General trend analysis is based on more granular data furnished by the Yemen Data Project (YDP). Although YDP does not match Knights' 150 per day statistic it does

Once established ashore, helicopter gunships proved essential to the ground advances that followed.[71] Both the post-Aden breakthroughs and the thrusts through Ma'rib were executed under air cover provided by AH-64D Apache and Bell 407 MRH attack helicopters.[72] The coalition appears to have depended heavily on these low-flying, longer-loiter aircraft for dedicated close air support (CAS) services due to operating altitude and air-ground coordination issues that impaired the use of its faster jet fighter-bombers in that role.[73] Soon after, the UAE also began to deploy into theater the AT-802, a light turboprop specifically modified for the CAS mission.[74] Public details on sortie type tallies and munitions expenditures are sparse, but the UAE's May 2016 request for a substantial restock of 4,000 air-launched Hellfire missiles verified that the Apaches, Bells, and AT-802s were energetically engaged in a combat role.[75]

In addition to introducing mission-suitable CAS assets, Golden Arrow also marked an improvement in the quality of the supported ground force component. The reinforcement at Aden brought tanks, up-armored vehicles, professional Emirati and Saudi soldiers, and a core of additional Yemeni fighters trained and outfitted abroad.[76] These coalition-led armored columns remained susceptible to the kind of hit-and-run ambushes that the Houthis employed to good effect in the earlier Sa'dah wars.[77] They also confronted a Houthi adversary that fought with undiminished intensity, despite early setbacks and squeezed supply lines. In late 2015, for instance, the Houthis mounted a multi-prong counteroffensive that threatened to recapture al Anad airbase.[78] And despite more than a year of bombing and blockade, the Houthis managed

register a wartime high in September 2015. YDP's total air raid estimate – a more conservative category – is 920 for that month.

[71] Jeremy Binnie, "Apaches Deployed to Yemen," *Jane's Defence Weekly*, August 12, 2015; Jeremy Binnie, "Analysis: Saudi-led Coalition Opens New Front in Yemen," *IHS Defence Weekly*, September 3, 2015.

[72] Knights and Mello, "Escalating Northern Front."

[73] Mazzetti and Schmitt, "Quiet Support for Saudis"; Angus McDowall, Phil Stewart, and David Rohde, "Yemen's Guerrilla War Tests Military Ambitions of Big-Spending Saudis," *Reuters*, April 20, 2016. www.reuters.com/investigates/special-report/saudi-military

[74] Jeremy Binnie, "Yemeni Pilots Carry Out Airstrikes with AT-802 Turboprops," *Jane's Defence Weekly*, October 28, 2015.

[75] Jeremy Binnie, "UAE Set to Get 4,000 More Hellfire Missiles," *IHS Jane's 360*, May 18, 2016. www.janes.com/article/60428/uae-set-to-get-4-000-more-hellfire-missiles

[76] Mello and Knights, "Ground War"; Hokayem and Roberts, "The War in Yemen," 173–74.

[77] Knights and Mello, "Northern Front"; Salmoni et al., *Regime and Periphery*, 143–57.

[78] Michael Horton, "The Houthis' Counter-Offensive in Yemen: Strategy, Aims, and Outcomes," *Terrorism Monitor* 13:22 (November 13, 2015). https://jamestown.org/program/the-houthis-counter-offensive-in-yemen-strategy-aims-and-outcomes

to maintain their siege on the hotly contested city of Taizz. Yet on balance, Saudi- and Emirati-backed forces made steady if uneven progress against a foe that often enjoyed the advantages of superior numbers and the opportunity to choose and prepare defended terrain. That the coalition was able to persist without sustaining heavy casualties is to the credit of airborne fire preparation and armed overwatch.

Aerial bombing saved Aden but wasn't sufficient to flip the battlefield equation against an adaptive and resilient Houthi enemy. The addition of effective air power fire support, though, enabled the insertion of a more credible ground force at Aden and the reclamation of considerable real estate in the combined-arms ground offensives that followed. This dramatically shrunk the Houthis' zone of control and foreclosed the possibility that they could conquer the country.

## Slow-Burn Strategies

The more stagnant three years of conflict that followed the failed Kuwait talks temper the previous findings. Dramatic as the impact of air-ground synergy was to the early war turnabout, coalition gains soon reached their natural limit. The Emirati-led ground force was critically hamstrung by disunity of effort – once it had retaken much of the south, its progress had largely outrun the shared interests of its various, and often competing, components. Troop ceilings and casualty concerns, meanwhile, prevented either the UAE or Saudi Arabia from summoning the requisite manpower from their own ranks to pursue a more ambitious invasion and occupation strategy.[79] Lacking the resources to escalate further but unwilling to concede or radically revise their demands, the coalition opted to maintain punitive pressure in hopes that the cumulative effects of embargo or attrition would eventually change conditions in their favor.[80]

### Prolonged Blockade

A review of the longer duration impacts of the coalition's blockade is useful in evaluating its utility as a coercive instrument in a chaos state. As a tool to target enemy military capability, the blockade has been unsuccessful in starving the Houthis of outside material support. Indeed, external aid from Iran, once obscure and uncertain, appears to have increased

---

[79] Hokayem and Roberts, "The War in Yemen," 166, 174, 177–79.
[80] Jeremy Binnie, "Saudi Prince Says Time Is on Coalition's Side in Yemen War," *Jane's Defence Weekly*, May 3, 2017.

over the long run.[81] Visible evidence of this assistance abounds. Key indicators include the appearance of imported weapons and tactics and an upswing in foreign-fighter participation and casualties.[82]

The evolution of Houthi missile and drone capabilities over the course of the war is a particularly compelling example. Courtesy of continued weapons smuggling via sea and overland through Oman, the Houthis acquired Iranian surface-to-surface missiles of increasingly longer range. These missile systems lacked the necessary accuracy for discriminate military effect but nonetheless extended the Houthis' reach from the sparsely populated cross-border provinces of Jizan and Najran all the way to Riyadh. This afforded the Houthis the capability to counter-escalate in much more spectacular fashion, threatening high-visibility attacks on distant critical infrastructure targets like major airports and oil facilities.[83]

The Houthis also have a growing stable of Iranian-origin remotely piloted aircraft (RPA). Although advertised as indigenously designed, the Houthis' Qasef RPA, for instance, is a copy of Iran's Ababil III. These systems lack the payload to inflict substantial damage but serve as low-cost substitutes for missiles, allowing the Houthis to continue embarrassing and difficult-to-counter attacks on some of the same strategic targets. On account of their superior accuracy, RPAs have also proven effective in a tactical role within Yemen. The Houthis have deployed them in a reconnaissance mode for artillery spotting, as a stand-off delivery system for improvised explosive attacks, and as a defense suppression tool by crashing them into Patriot missile battery radars.[84]

Though much less dramatic, a similar situation developed in the surface-to-air realm. Rather than a diminution of residual capability, as might be expected, the threat to coalition aircraft over Yemen increased after imposition of the blockade. Hostile fire losses and near-misses ticked

[81] Yara Bayoumy and Phil Stewart, "Iran Steps Up Weapons Supply to Yemen's Houthis Via Oman," *Reuters*, October 20, 2016. www.reuters.com/article/us-yemen-security-iran -idUSKCN12K0CX; Saul et al., "Iran Steps Up Support."

[82] Jeremy Binnie, "Saudi Coalition Says Iran Smuggling SAMS to Yemen," *Jane's Defence Weekly*, March 28, 2018; Joshua Koontz, "Iran's Growing Casualty Count in Yemen," *War on the Rocks*, June 1, 2017. https://warontherocks.com/2017/06/irans-growing-casualty-count-in-yemen; see also note 30.

[83] Lisa Barrington and Aziz El Yakoobi, "Yemen Houthi Drones, Missiles Defy Years of Saudi Air Strikes," *Reuters*, September 17, 2019. https://reuters.com/article/us-saudi-aramco-houthis/yemen-houthi-drones-missiles-defy-years-of-saudi-air-strikes-idUSKBN1W22F4; Dhia Muhsin, "Houthi Use of Drones Delivers Potent Message in Yemen War," *IISS*, August 27, 2019. https://iiss.org/blogs/analysis/2019/08/houthi-uav-strategy-in-yemen

[84] Ibid.; Ludovico Carlino and Columb Strack, "Houthi Militants Change UAV Tactics in Yemen Conflict," *Jane's Intelligence Review*, March 20, 2019; Barrington and El Yakoobi, "Yemen Houthi Drones."

upward in 2017–19 as the Houthis restored surviving one-off SA-6 and SA-9 systems to operation, converted air-to-air missiles for ground launch, and fielded new Iranian-made MANPADS (man-portable air defense systems).[85] Again, Saudi spokesmen were cagey about disclosing losses, but videos show Saudi F-15s and Emirati F-16s narrowly dodging exploding missiles, and three US MQ-9 Reapers were downed by Houthi fire, one while operating at medium altitude, and fatal helicopter crashes attributed to unspecified "technical problems" continued to mount.[86]

As a component of the collective punishment campaign, on the other hand, the blockade unquestionably amplified the anguish of the Yemeni people. It has proven much more effective in this regard than in enfeebling Houthi-Saleh military capability. In concert with the deliberate aerial bombing of nonmilitary targets and the Houthis' own economic disruptions, the Saudi-led embargo destroyed an anemic pre-war economy, disrupted licit trade, and deprived portions of the country of essential services for years on end. It incurred rampant disease, massive displacement, and brought Yemen to the brink of nationwide famine.[87] But even this orchestrated disaster failed to precipitate an internal uprising to throw off the yoke of Houthi rule.[88] To the contrary, blockade-induced scarcity drove up commodity prices, produced perverse profit motives, and corrupted local actor interests in ways that have had the reverse effect.[89] By creating the kind of war economy conditions that incentivize sustaining

---

[85] Cooper, "Air Defenses (Part Two)"; Tom Cooper, "The Houthis' Do-It-Yourself Air Defenses (Part Three)," *War Is Boring*, January 23, 2018. https://warisboring.com/the-houthis-do-it-yourself-air-defenses-3; C. J. Chivers and Robert F. Worth, "Seizure of Antiaircraft Missiles in Yemen Raises Fears that Iran Is Arming Rebels There," *New York Times*, February 8, 2013. https://nytimes.com/2013/02/09/world/middleeast/weapons-seizure-in-yemen-raises-worries-of-irans-influence.html

[86] Jeremy Binnie, "Saudi Arabia Says F-15 Survived SAM Hit Over Yemen," *Jane's Defence Weekly*, March 22, 2018; Jeremy Binnie and Neil Gibson, "US Reaper Shot Down over Sanaa," *Jane's Defence Weekly*, October 5, 2017; Unattributed, "CENTCOM: MQ-9 Reaper Shot Down over Yemen Last Week," *Military Times*, June 16, 2019. https://militarytimes.com/news/your-military/2019/06/16/centcom-mq-9-reaper-shot-down-over-yemen-last-week; Idrees Ali, "US Drone Shot Down over Yemen: Officials," *Reuters*, August 21, 2019. https://reuters.com/article/us-yemen-security-usa-drone/u-s-military-drone-shot-down-over-yemen-officials-idUSKCN1VB180; Arnaud Delalande, "Air War in Yemen," *AirForces Monthly* 354 (September 2017): 97; Aziz El Yaakoubi, "Two Saudi Pilots Killed in Helicopter Crash: State Media," *Reuters*, September 14, 2018. https://reuters.com/article/us-yemen-security-saudi/two-saudi-pilots-killed-in-helicopter-crash-state-media-idUSKCN1LU1VT

[87] Craig, "Bombed into Famine"; ICG, "Instruments of Pain: Conflict and Famine in Yemen," April 13, 2017. www.crisisgroup.org/middle-east-north-africa/gulf-and-arabian-peninsula/yemen/b052-instruments-pain-i-conflict-and-famine-yemen; Fritz and Schmitz.

[88] "Hadi Officials Acknowledge Off-the-Record that Overthrow Is an Implicit Objective of the Blockade." See ICG, "Instruments," 3.

[89] Salisbury, "National Chaos," 20, 24–29; Salem et al., "Battle."

the status quo, the combination of blockade and civilian infrastructure bombing may have helped to entrench the conflict and consolidate Houthi control in the north.[90] Whether intended to serve as a tool of strategic interdiction for counter-military purposes or as a means to trade civilian pain for strategic leverage, then, the blockade appears to have delivered little by way of benefit.[91]

### Late-Game Decapitations

Coalition strikes did not kill Saleh or split the Houthi-Saleh alliance in the first phase of the war. Both of those outcomes eventually came to pass, however, and it is at least possible that the continuing Saudi-led decapitation campaign played some indirect role in bringing this about. In October 2016 a coalition air strike on a high-profile funeral at the Al Kubra Hall in Sanaa killed two of Saleh's key senior lieutenants. The well-publicized attack – which also killed more than 150 other mourners and shocked many foreign observers for its blatant disregard for collateral casualties[92] – has been credited with weakening Saleh's ability to command and control his affiliated forces.[93] Conceivably this may have exacerbated the tensions between Saleh and the Houthis that ultimately collapsed their alliance. If the October air strike was a contributing factor toward unravelling the partnership, however, that development was a very delayed-onset consequence – more than a year would pass after the Al Kubra funeral strike before the breakdown. Limited insight to intra-alliance dynamics restricts what can be reliably inferred about cause and effect, but it seems doubtful that this single strike's effect was sufficient to induce the break – it appears more likely that it interacted with other less scrutable variables to produce that outcome.[94]

Turning from causality to consequences, the Houthi-Saleh split also failed to trigger the expected windfall in follow-on defections. The Houthis had progressively cross-pollinated or co-opted lower-level leadership, such that much of the combat power of the Republican Guard units once loyal to Saleh had been leeched away by the time of the

---

[90] Salisbury, "National Chaos," 20, 24–29; Alley, "Collapse," 13.
[91] Regarding unintended and counterproductive effects in air strategy execution, see Barry D. Watts, "Ignoring Reality: Problems of Theory and Evidence in Security Studies," *Security Studies* 7:2 (Winter 1997/98): 115–71.
[92] HRW, "Yemen: Saudi-Led Funeral Attack Apparent War Crime," October 13, 2016. www.hrw.org/news/2016/10/13/yemen-saudi-led-funeral-attack-apparent-war-crime
[93] Salisbury, "National Chaos," 14.
[94] A combination of the Republican Guard's higher susceptibility to direct attack early in the war and this midcourse decapitation may have conspired to play a role in the split. See Alley, "Collapse," 9–12; Salisbury, "National Chaos," 14–15.

divorce.[95] As a result, when the Houthi-Saleh pact finally fell apart the infighting between the two organizations was short, less fierce than anticipated, and ultimately nonfatal for the Houthis.[96] With the notable exception of his nephew, Tareq Saleh, a former Republican Guard commander, few of Saleh's subordinates were eager or able to realign with the foreign-led forces that had been relentlessly bombing them.[97] The down-echelon loyalty decisions of many of his holdover commanders and tribal allies were ultimately driven more by a pragmatic assessment of local conditions and prospects than any straightforward fealty to the former president.[98] Saleh's prompt demise at the Houthis' hands further dampened the strategic fallout from the disintegrated alliance, confirming for many fence-sitters the wisdom of a wait-and-see policy.

Saleh aside, a string of subsequent air strike assassinations of senior Houthi personalities illustrates the improved performance of the coalition's continued strategy of leadership pursuit. Refining their employment of Reaper-class Wing Loong II RPAs recently acquired from China, the Emiratis and Saudis appear to have developed a more effective process for tracking and killing Houthi principals over the course of the conflict.[99] The most prominent victim of this renewed effort was Saleh al Sammad, the Houthis' highest-ranking political officer.[100] The real impact of these late-game successes, though, remains to be determined.

In the short term these killings may have rendered the possibility of a negotiated settlement more remote. By creating vacancies often filled by ascendant hardliners, air strike assassinations may be further radicalizing Houthi top-tier leadership – that certainly appears to have been the case for the al Sammad killing.[101] If so, the effects in this regard are not

[95] Winter, "Republican Guard"; Alley, "Collapse," 11.

[96] Ibid.; Salisbury, "National Chaos," 13–15.

[97] Ben Hubbard and Nour Youssef, "Yemen's War Enters a Dark Stage as Rebels Squeeze the Capital," *New York Times*, December 23, 2017. www.nytimes.com/2017/12/23/wo rld/middleeast/yemen-sana-houthis-saudi-arabia.html; Jeremy Binnie, "Saleh's Nephew Joins UAE-Backed Offensive in Yemen," *Jane's Defence Weekly*, April 24, 2018.

[98] Salisbury, "National Chaos," 14; Salem et al., "Battle."

[99] Jeremy Binnie and Neil Gibson, "Saudi Air Force Credited with Killing Yemeni Rebel Leader," *Jane's Defence Weekly*, April 25, 2018; Rawan Shaif and JackWatling, "How the UAE's Chinese-Made Drone Is Changing the War in Yemen," *Foreign Policy*, April 27, 2018. https://foreignpolicy.com/2018/04/27/drone-wars-how-the-uaes-chinese-made-drone-is-changing-the-war-in-yemen

[100] Binnie and Gibson, "Saudi Air Force."

[101] Unattributed, "What Does the Death of Saleh Al-Sammad Mean for Yemen's Houthis?" *Al Jazeera*, April 24, 2018. www.aljazeera.com/indepth/features/saleh-al-sammad-yemen-houthis-180424170317613.html; "'Death of Political Solution': Yemen's Houthis Vow to Avenge Death of Top Leader," *Middle East Eye*, April 23, 2018. www.middleeasteye.net/news/yemens-houthis-pledge-revenge-death-leader-saleh-al-samad-2077843753

dissimilar to those of targeted killing campaigns conducted by the United States or Israel.[102] There are, however, crucial differences between the Saudi-led effort in Yemen and these analogues. Long-term American and Israeli counterterrorism killing programs are sustained for limited and negative objectives. Specifically, these programs are maintained to disrupt or degrade persistent and irreconcilable nonstate threats at minimal cost and risk.[103] The indefinite maintenance of a similarly open-ended attrition effort in Yemen would be a decidedly suboptimal outcome for the Saudis, who undertook the intervention for the much more ambitious and positive purpose of restoring a pre-war political order.

## The Hudaydah Epilogue

In 2018 the coalition reenergized its ground campaign with an Emirati-led push northward along the Red Sea coast, advancing with the aid of air strikes and Apache gunship fire support toward the last major Houthi-controlled port at Hudaydah.[104] Hudaydah was a seaborne smuggling access point and a source of substantial revenue for the Houthis. It was also the conduit through which humanitarian aid reached the majority of the country's population. The disruption of this lifeline during a bitter battle to secure the city was anticipated to have disastrous consequences for millions of already struggling and food-insecure Yemenis.[105] Ultimately the specter of an even greater crisis in Yemen spurred the United States to pressure the coalition to postpone their final assault in favor of a new round of UN-brokered negotiations in Stockholm. The Houthis, on the verge of what was shaping up to be a painful loss, acceded to talks despite serious trust concerns.[106]

[102] Keith Patrick Dear, "Beheading the Hydra? Does Killing Terrorist or Insurgent Leaders Work?" *Defence Studies* 13:3 (2013): 312–14.
[103] Daniel Byman, "Targeted Killing, American Style," *Brookings Institution*, January 20, 2006. www.brookings.edu/opinions/targeted-killing-american-style; Gal Luft, "The Logic of Israel's Targeted Killing?" *Middle East Quarterly* 10:1 (Winter 2003). www.meforum.org/articles/other/the-logic-of-israel-s-targeted-killing
[104] Mohammed Ghobari, "Arab Coalition Bombs Houthis around Hodeidah Airport, Urges Them to Withdraw," *Reuters*, June 18, 2018. www.reuters.com/article/us-yemen-security/arab-aircraft-hammer-houthis-around-airport-of-major-yemen-port-hodeidah-idUSKBN1JE0P4?feedType=RSS&feedName=topNews.
[105] ICG, "How to Halt Yemen's Slide into Famine," November 21, 2018. www.crisisgroup.org/middle-east-north-africa/gulf-and-arabian-peninsula/yemen/193-how-halt-yemens-slide-famine
[106] ICG, "Saving the Stockholm Agreement and Averting a Regional Conflagration in Yemen," July 18, 2019. https://crisisgroup.org/middle-east-north-africa/gulf-and-arabian-peninsula/yemen/203-saving-stockholm-agreement-and-averting-regional-conflagration-yemen

As this book goes to print most of the aspects of the resulting ceasefire accord, the Stockholm Agreement, have yet to be realized, but a cataclysmic battle for Hudaydah has been averted. The accord is modest in scope and terms and represents only a first halting step toward what would need to be much wider negotiations to wind down the conflict. Hudaydah notwithstanding, fighting continued, having only shifted from the Red Sea coast to fronts further inland.[107]

Still, the Hudaydah epilogue underscores the value of frontline air support in generating combat outcomes and coercive leverage. Though they understandably deny it, there seems to be little doubt that the Houthis' concessions – including withdrawal to allow UN administration of the port – were the product of the coalition's impending air-ground assault. And like Golden Arrow before it, the Hudaydah offensive appeared to benefit more from well-directed air support than from a weakening in Houthi resolve or readiness owed to the supply constriction and decapitation campaigns detailed here.[108]

Though the Saudis framed the push on Hudaydah as a prelude to the long-promised march on Sanaa, the UAE itself expressly dismissed this probability, characterizing even the successful capture of the port city as an effort to press the Houthis to return to negotiations on more favorable terms.[109] The Emirati position was a tacit acknowledgment that the coalition's odds of retaking the capital, much less the Houthis' mountain strongholds in Sa'dah, were exceedingly dim. After international pressure preempted the Hudaydah assault, Abu Dhabi used the Stockholm Agreement as a strategic off-ramp, initiating a significant drawdown of its forces in the summer of 2019 and publicly prioritizing a diplomatic solution over further military action.[110]

[107] ICG, "Crisis Group Yemen Update #11," May 16, 2019. www.crisisgroup.org/middle-east-north-africa/gulf-and-arabian-peninsula/yemen/crisis-group-yemen-update-11

[108] Air raids in Hodeidah increased fourfold with the initiation of the offensive. YDP, "Monthly Yemen Data Project Update," January 5, 2018. https://us16.campaign-archive.com/?u=1912a1b11cab332fa977d3a6a&id=5570d2d2b9; Michael Knights, "The Challenges of Urban Fighting in Hodeida," Washington Institute, January 15, 2019. www.washingtoninstitute.org/policy-analysis/view/the-challenges-of-urban-fighting-in-hodeida

[109] ICG, "Destructive Battle"; Patrick Tucker, "Houthis 'Softening,' But UAE Minister Says Yemen Security Could Still Require Foreign Troops," *Defense One*, May 21, 2018. www.defenseone.com/threats/2018/05/houthis-softening-uae-minister-says-yemen-security-could-still-require-foreign-troops/148380/?oref=d-river

[110] Elana DeLozier, "UAE Drawdown May Isolate Saudi Arabia in Yemen," Washington Institute, July 2, 2019. https://washingtoninstitute.org/policy-analysis/view/uae-drawdown-in-yemen-may-isolate-saudi-arabia

Persistent interfactional frictions, meanwhile, had only magnified as the agendas of the coalition's local allies-of-convenience continued to deviate. In the security vacuum that emerged in the wake of Emirati withdrawal from the south, these tensions finally erupted into full-blown combat. In August 2019 Emirati-backed forces aligned with the southern separatists and Saudi-backed forces aligned with Hadi's government clashed in Aden. Infighting quickly expanded into the surrounding governorates as the two sides struggled to dominate the south. Interfactional violence was only contained through the intervention of the factions' respective patrons in Riyadh and Abu Dhabi.[111] The incident dispelled any lingering hopes of completely expunging the Houthi insurgency through proxy warfare and combined-arms support.

### Implications

As a brute force strategy, the light-footprint formula had failed. Yet domestic constraints still precluded the coalition from escalating to a point where they might pursue a brute force solution independent of their fractious and unreliable Yemeni proxies.[112] Moving forward, all indicators pointed to a high probability of further fragmentation and campaign stall. The Saudi-led intervention, then, can only be described as successful if defined as a coercive denial campaign. This being the case, the campaign's progress to date is best viewed as hard-bought bargaining space within which to find a meaningful compromise with the Houthis, rather than proof that their ultimate defeat is within reach.

As an exercise in coercion, Yemen revalidates the case for targeting the enemy's military capability and suggests that this holds as true for third-party interventions in civil wars as it does for state-on-state conflict. Beyond this, the conflict also provides insight on the comparative value of different methods of air attack. Here the combined-arms air-ground combat of Golden Arrow and the 2018 Red Sea offensive clearly swung the balance, dramatically altering the martial prospects of an adversary that proved resilient to aerial bombardment and supply constrictions. The Saudi air campaign reinforces the argument made elsewhere that

---

[111] ICG, "After Aden: Navigating Yemen's New Political Landscape," August 30, 2019. https://crisisgroup.org/middle-east-north-africa/gulf-and-arabian-peninsula/yemen/07 1-after-aden-navigating-yemens-new-political-landscape

[112] Jeremy Binnie, "Sudan Has 'Largest Force' in Arab Coalition," *Jane's Defence Weekly*, June 26, 2019.

forward edge battlefield attrition, vice strategic interdiction, is often the more potent employment of air power.[113]

The coalition's introduction of a combat-credible ground force served as a catalyst that obliged Houthi- and Saleh-loyalist forces to either concentrate, and thereby render themselves vulnerable to airborne fire-power, or disperse and in doing so sacrifice combat power and potentially cede territory. In this, the Saudi experience in Yemen appears to confirm the dynamics that others have argued explain America's difficulties in Kosovo and early success in Afghanistan (see Chapters 4 and 5).[114] Yemen also, however, supports the judgment that America's post–Cold War air power successes are less replicable than it might seem at first blush.[115] Despite the engagement of cutting-edge aircraft, copious quantities of guided munitions, and generous western enabler support, the Saudis were unable to emulate America's precision strike proficiency. The RSAF paid steep penalties in dynamic targeting due to deficiencies in doctrine, pilot training, and combat experience.[116] The coalition's progress in Yemen depended more heavily on the introduction of Emirati tactical air control expertise and CAS-capable attack helicopters and turboprops than on the employment of sophisticated weapons and sensors.

## Conclusion

Enough evidence is now available on the war in Yemen to draw some preliminary inferences about what the Saudi experience portends for structurally similar scenarios elsewhere. First, Yemen suggests that air power is most effective when used to directly attack the enemy's fielded forces. Air support to a conventionally reinforced proxy enabled the coalition to claw back key terrain and attrit enemy combat strength, denying Houthi victory. This development obliged a stubborn but stymied adversary to explore the possibility of a compromise. Yemen, then, adds another case to the ledger in favor of denial over punishment,

---

[113] Phil Haun and Colin Jackson, "Breaker of Armies: Air Power in the Easter Offensive and the Myth of Linebacker I and II in the Vietnam War," *International Security* 40:3 (Winter 2015/16): 139–78.

[114] Bruce R. Pirnie et al., *Beyond Close Air Support: Forging a New Air-Ground Partnership* (Santa Monica: RAND, 2005), 38–60.

[115] Stephen Biddle, "Afghanistan and the Future of Warfare," *Foreign Affairs*, March/April 2003. www.foreignaffairs.com/articles/afghanistan/2003-03-01/afghanistan-and-future-warfare

[116] Larry Lewis, "Promoting Civilian Protection during Security Assistance: Learning from Yemen," CNA, May 2019, 15–18. https://cna.org/CNA_files/PDF/IRM-2019-U-019749-Final.pdf

cautions that the era of close combat is far from over, and commends the deployment of mission-suitable close air support capabilities to roll back irregular threats.

Second, Yemen casts further doubt on the efficacy of punishment bombing, blockade, or decapitation for coercing opponents in an internal conflict. Collective punishment and blockade generated little leverage on a substate Houthi adversary that lacked an exploitable stake in either averting humanitarian catastrophe or preserving the country's scant economic infrastructure. The slow progress and dubious returns of Saudi-targeted killing efforts, meanwhile, reflect the often prohibitively high intelligence demands and unpredictable downstream consequences of decapitating an unconventional adversary.[117]

Third, regardless of strategy, an unequal power relationship is no recipe for sure coercive success. Overconfident in its material superiority, Saudi Arabia fell into a now-familiar cognitive trap. Riyadh's maximalist objectives in Yemen were hopelessly ambitious and a deeply flawed predicate by which to define an acceptable win-set for the slugfest of a civil war. As twentieth-century history testifies, wartime compellence is a difficult endeavor, and even an effective counter-military campaign can rarely compel an adversary to submit to an outcome indistinguishable from battlefield defeat.[118] Albeit on a different scale, Yemen hints that the inverse relationship that others have drawn between power asymmetry and the probability of coercive success is not a uniquely American phenomenon.[119]

The fourth and final finding regards the viability of using air power and local proxies as a low-cost, low-risk formula for brute force victory. Yemen is the latest in a series of twenty-first-century conflicts where this so-called light footprint approach has been tried. The indeterminate status of interventions in Libya, Somalia, and Syria testify to the difficulty of attaining positive outcomes when applying a limited-means blueprint in a splintered society, especially one subject to competing foreign interference. In Yemen, the technique has been productive as a coercive denial strategy but has foundered as a brute force solution. The Saudis and their allies have been handicapped by poor proxy cohesion, self-imposed escalation constraints, critical training deficiencies, and hostile state-sponsor support. They

---

[117] Robert Pape, *Bombing to Win* (Ithaca: Cornell University Press, 1996).    [118] Ibid.
[119] Phil Haun, *Coercion, Survival, and War: Why Weak States Resist the United States* (Stanford: Stanford University Press, 2015); Todd S. Sechser, "Goliath's Curse: Coercive Threats and Asymmetric Power," *International Organizations* 64:4 (Fall 2010): 627–60.

have been able to perpetuate instability – an outcome they see as politically preferable to the consolidation of a potentially hostile regime – but cannot deliver a constructive end-state. Yemen and these other contemporary test cases, then, confirm that the air power-and-proxy formula is highly sensitive to conditions and context and often a suitable strategy for the achievement of only modest or negative objectives.

# 10    Russia's Air War Win in Syria
## A Kinetic Approach to Counterinsurgency

*Ralph Shield**

## Introduction

Russia's surprise intervention in the Syrian Civil War was a rare excursion beyond Moscow's post-Soviet sphere of interest and its first serious foray in the Middle East since the end of the Cold War. Highly relevant to this volume, it was an air-centric operation incongruent with prior Russian and Soviet military practice but similar in many respects to the contemporary Western-model air campaigns described in the preceding chapters. Once engaged, moreover, Russia's military demonstrated poise and capabilities that appeared to far exceed outside expectations.

Two concurrent but conceptually inconsistent narratives emerged from early impressions of Russia's air war in Syria. One sprang from extensive devastation of contested cities like Aleppo. This conversation drew comparisons to Moscow's brutal response to previous uprisings in Afghanistan and Chechnya, implying a stubborn attachment to blunt-force methods.[1]

* The views expressed by the author do not reflect those of the US government, the Department of Defense, or any of its organizations. This chapter is an updated and re-edited version of the author's article "Russian Airpower's Success in Syria: Assessing Evolution in Kinetic Counterinsurgency," *Journal of Slavic Military Studies* 31:2 (2018): 227–32. It is reproduced here with permission from Taylor and Francis Group. www.tandfonline.com
1 Mark Galeotti, "Putin Is Playing by Grozny Rules in Aleppo," *Foreign Policy*, September 29, 2016. http://foreignpolicy.com/2016/09/29/putin-is-playing-by-chechen-rules-in-aleppo-syria-russia; Editorial staff, "Grozny Rules in Aleppo," *The Economist*, October 1, 2016. https://economist.com/news/leaders/21707929-why-west-must-protect-people-syria-and-stand-up-vladimir-putin-grozny-rules; Michael Kimmelman, "Berlin, 1945; Grozny, 2000; Aleppo, 2016," *New York Times*, October 14, 2016. https://nytimes.com/2016/10/15/world/middleeast/aleppo-destruction-drone-video.html?mcubz=0; Alistair Bell and Tom Perry, "Obama Warns Russia's Putin of 'Quagmire' in Syria," *Reuters*, October 2, 2015. http://reuters.com/article/us-mideast-crisis-syria-airstrikes/obama-warns-russias-putin-of-quagmire-in-syria-idUSKCN0RW0W220151003; Pavel Baev, "Unfriended: How Russia's Syria Quagmire Is Costing It Middle Eastern Allies," *Brookings*, January 7, 2016. https://brookings.edu/blog/order-from-chaos/2016/01/07/unfriended-how-russias-syria-quagmire-is-costing-it-middle-eastern-allies; Muhammad Mansour, "Is Syria Russia's New Afghanistan?" Washington Institute for Near East Policy, October 16, 2015. http://washingtoninstitute.org/fikraforum/view/is-syria-russias-new-afghanistan

The other narrative centered on Russia's employment of sophisticated new targeting technologies in Syria, citing these advancements as confirmation of significant progress in military modernization and reform.[2] Few analyses reconciled these divergent narratives to render a supported judgment about how recent capability enhancements have – or have not – meaningfully influenced Russia's effort to shore up the Syrian regime.[3] Acknowledging that data limitations, conflicting accounts, and the fact that the war is ongoing constrain what can be reasonably accomplished toward this end, the ensuing analysis seeks to address the gap, particularly regarding the air aspects of the Russian intervention.[4]

This chapter investigates whether Russia's air war in Syria reveals evidence of conceptual evolution since its earlier counterinsurgency engagements in Afghanistan and Chechnya. It acknowledges that the

---

[2] Ruslan Pukhov and Michael Kofman, CSIS podcast, "Russia's Intervention in Syria: Lessons Learned," January 13, 2017. https://csis.org/events/russias-intervention-syria-lessons-learned; Interview with Michael Kofman, hosted by Jeffrey Mankoff, CSIS podcast series *Russian Roulette*, "Of Ceasefires and Successions – Russian Roulette Episode #13," September 23, 2016. https://csis.org/podcasts/russian-roulette?page=2); Mark Galeotti, Edward W. Walker, and Fred H. Lawson, University of California, Berkeley, Center for Middle Eastern Studies podcast, "Russia's Military Intervention in Syria: A Panel Discussion," December 4, 2015. http://cmes.berkeley.edu/russias-military-intervention-in-syria-a-panel-discussion-2; Paul McLeary, "Putin's Smart Bombs Aren't All That Smart," *Foreign Policy*, October 4, 2015. http://foreignpolicy.com/2015/10/14/putin-smart-bombs-arent-all-that-smart; Kim Sengupta, "Russia's 'Rustbucket' Military Delivers a Hi-Tech Shock to West and Israel," *Independent*, January 29, 2016. http://independent.co.uk/news/world/middle-east/war-in-syria-russia-s-rustbucket-military-delivers-a-hi-tech-shock-to-west-and-israel-a6842711.html

[3] Gustav Gressel, "Lessons from Russia's Intervention in Syria," *European Council on Foreign Relations*, February 5, 2016. http://ecfr.eu/article/commentary_lessons_from_russias_intervention_in_syria5085; Dmitry Gorenburg, "What Russia's Military Operations in Syria Can Tell Us about Advances in its Capabilities (PONARS Eurasia Policy Memo No. 424)," *PONARS Eurasia*, March 2016. http://ponarseurasia.org/memo/advances-russian-military-operations; Nikolai Sokov, "Russia's New Conventional Capability: Implications for Eurasia and Beyond (PONARS Eurasia Policy Memo No. 472)," *PONARS Eurasia*, April 2017. http://ponarseurasia.org/memo/russias-new-conventional-capability-implications-eurasia-and-beyond; Kier Giles, "Assessing Russia's Reorganized and Rearmed Military," Carnegie Endowment for International Peace, May 3, 2017. http://carnegieendowment.org/2017/05/03/assessing-russia-s-reorganized-and-rearmed-military-pub-69853

[4] This chapter leverages the collected insights of close observers of the conflict about belligerent behavior, supplemented by verifiable reporting on force disposition and munitions use, to draw inferences about RuAF operating concepts and battlefield effectiveness. The assessment is based exclusively on English-language source material but contains secondhand reflections of native language reporting via the summaries and analyses of recognized Russian- and Arabic-speaking regional experts. In terms of scope and time horizon, this treatment focuses on the first eighteen to twenty months of the intervention and mirrors the RuAF's weight-of-effort in concentrating on the western portions of populated and "useful" Syria.

introduction of advanced technologies and adjusted tactics have yielded real improvements in Russian Air Force (RuAF) battlefield lethality and survivability but argues these have not yet precipitated a fundamental shift in Russia's doctrine for employing air power to kill insurgents. Evolution in military capabilities cannot fully explain the RuAF's superior performance in Syria. Rather, structural and strategic differences between the Syria case and its precursors offer more compelling explanations for Russia's ability to secure more favorable short-run outcomes in its latest adventure.

Moreover, a close reading of the Syria case reveals that Russia subscribes to a different theory of influence for the use of air power in small wars. The Russian model not only discounts civilian casualty concerns but deliberately targets civilians to facilitate local offensive operations. In combination with Moscow's narrowed political aims, this model allows Russia to eschew certain higher risk missions and reduces its dependence on reconnaissance and precision. As a result, the Russian approach is cheaper to resource and may prove readily exportable to other conflicts.

A refined understanding of the instrumentality of Russian air power advancements to recent ground gains in Syria is useful for a number of reasons. Most immediately, it informs efforts to forecast the future of Syria's civil war, a matter of obvious and continuing interest. Insight into the drivers of the RuAF's achievements in Syria is also relevant for predicting the possibility and course of Russian interventions into similar low-intensity conflicts elsewhere, as Syria appears to be a harbinger of Russian activism in the greater Middle East.[5] And more generally, the Russian experience in Syria offers a counterpoint case, like those of Israel and Saudi Arabia in Chapters 7 and 9, for examining the employment of air power by non-Western states. In this regard, it highlights how different strategic cultures and constraints may impact foreign development and application of the air weapon.

This chapter proceeds in six parts. The first section sketches the Syrian conflict for background and context (see Figure 10.1). The second measures the impact of new precision munitions and reconnaissance platforms in Syria on the RuAF's operational paradigm. The third gauges the RuAF's related improvement in air-ground integration and dynamic

[5] Anna Borshchevskaya and Jeremy Vaughan, "How the Russian Military Reestablished Itself in the Middle East (Policy Watch 2709)," Washington Institute for Near East Policy, October 17, 2016. http://washingtoninstitute.org/policy-analysis/view/how-the-russian-military-reestablished-itself-in-the-middle-east; Tim Ripley, "Russia Learns Military Lessons in Syria," *Jane's Intelligence Review*, April 20, 2017; Sokov, "Russia's New Conventional Capability."

Figure 10.1  Map of Syria

targeting. The fourth section proposes alternative explanations for the RuAF's better showing in Syria, exploring the impact of strategic context and narrow military and political objectives. The fifth examines Russia's very different approach to air strike-inflicted civilian casualties and suffering. Finally, the conclusion considers the implications of these findings for Russian doctrine development, force design, and ambitions abroad.

## Syria's Civil War

Syria's civil war grew out of the Arab Spring uprisings that swept across North Africa and the Middle East in early 2011. In line with the repressive strong-arm tactics employed by his father Hafez, Syrian President Bashar al-Assad responded to spontaneous popular protests with a brutal crack-down. The resulting confrontation steadily intensified as more Syrians clamored for Assad's ouster and the regime stubbornly refused to brook any meaningful compromise with antigovernment elements, characteriz-ing them instead as a conspiracy of foreign agents and jihadist terrorists. Because the crisis grew more slowly, and Assad was less hyperbolic in his immediate response than his counterpart Muammar Qaddafi, the situ-ation did not trigger an urgent international intervention like Libya. Nevertheless, regime atrocities touched off an escalating action-reaction cycle.[6] Rather than intimidating the resistance, a campaign of mass arrests, torture, and disappearances by the secret police exacerbated public outrage. By fall 2011 Syria had deployed its army and air force against restive sections of the populace.[7] When this failed to quell dis-turbances, and instead accelerated a transition to armed insurgency, Assad increased his use of force still further, eventually employing ballis-tic missiles, barrel bombs, and chemical weapons against his own citizens.[8] In a cynical effort to discourage foreign intervention and delegitimize the opposition, the regime worked to radicalize and sectar-ianize the growing insurgency, releasing true jihadist terrorists from prison and massacring Sunni civilians.

Still, the regime lost ground. The shocking cruelty of the government's response alienated wide swathes of the population, triggering large-scale defections and sending more and more communities over to the oppos-ition. The opposition, however, remained splintered, lacking a central organizing leader, agenda, or outside benefactor.[9] But by late 2015 the areas under Assad's control had shrunk to a fifth of the country. Despite the arrival of pro-regime Iranian military advisers, and then Iranian-sponsored proxy militias in 2012 and 2013, rebel advances threatened the capital and coastal strongholds. Suffering a critical manpower crisis, a pariah on the world stage, and kept barely afloat by slim financial lifelines from Tehran and Moscow, experts saw no path for Assad to reclaim the fractured Syrian state.[10]

Until this point the Kremlin had offered crucial but limited material, monetary, and diplomatic aid. Moscow interjected itself during the chem-ical weapons redline fiasco in 2013, proposing a deal that helped to preserve Assad in power and short-circuit a looming US-led punitive

---

[6] Marc Lynch, *The New Arab Wars: Uprisings and Anarchy in the Middle East* (New York: Public Affairs, 2016), 109.
[7] Robin Yassin-Kassab and Leila al-Shami, *Burning Country: Syrians in Revolution and War* (London: Pluto Press, 2016), 99.
[8] Ibid., 148–49.    [9] Ibid., 87, 96, 188–91; Lynch, *The New Arab Wars*, 131.
[10] Yassin-Kattab and al-Shami, *Burning Country*, 224.

strike that looked like the first step toward regime change by humanitarian intervention. Then, in summer 2015, fearing Assad was on his last legs, Islamic Revolutionary Guard Corps – Quds Force commander Qassem Soleimani proposed to Putin a plan to combine forces with Iranian-provided ground power.[11] Russia's subsequent direct military involvement reversed the trajectory of the war.

Russian naval vessels, foreign cargo ships, and an RuAF airbridge of near daily An-124 and Il-76 transport flights moved Russian forces to Hmeimim (formerly Bassel al-Assad) airbase and delivered new arms and equipment to the battered Syrian military.[12] The RuAF deployed various strike aircraft, some with precision bombing capability, as well as transport and attack helicopters. Artillery and rocket forces also arrived and joined the frontlines to augment Syria's surface fires for major engagements. The Russian personnel footprint in Syria eventually grew to nearly 5,000.

A grinding series of Russian- and Iranian-reinforced Syrian army offensives over the next months and years re-extended regime control in the western portions of Syria. Using a combination of bombardment-backed advances, negotiated evacuations, and violable "de-escalation zone" cease-fires, the Syrians and their allies methodically recaptured key urban centers and strategic terrain. By leveraging air power and a mixed and modest ground force, the pro-regime coalition sequentially isolated and retook opposition holdouts in Homs, Aleppo, and Eastern Ghouta, as well as Islamic State strongholds further east in Palmyra and Dayr az Zawr.

## The Irrelevance of Reconnaissance Strike

The most noted achievement of Russia's air war in Syria was the expanded fielding of precision-strike technologies.[13] The deployment of a combination of guided weapons and advanced sensors marked the belated emergence of a Russian "reconnaissance-strike complex," a late Soviet-era operating concept based on the integrated employment of precision munitions, area reconnaissance platforms, and tactical

---

[11] Samuel Charap, Elina Treyger, and Edward Geist, "Understanding Russia's Intervention in Syria," *RAND Research Report* (2019), 3–4; Tim Ripley, *Operation Aleppo: Russia's War in Syria* (Lancaster, UK: Telic-Herrick Publications, 2018), 24–26.

[12] Ripley, *Operation Aleppo*, 27–28.

[13] Vladimir Isachenkov, "New Russian Military Might on Full Display in Syria," *San Diego Union Tribune*, October 24, 2015. http://sandiegouniontribune.com/sdut-syria-mission-demonstrates-russias-new-prowess-2015oct24-story.html; Robert Lee, "Russian Military Operations in Syria," *Moscow Defense Brief* 1:51 (2016): 11.

command and control networks.[14] Material limitations prevented the Soviet Union from making the investments necessary to operationalize this warfighting construct, but the American military eventually embraced and to a large extent realized this vision.[15] If the RuAF actualized a "reconnaissance-strike complex" in Syria, this represents a significant transition from Russia's historical application of air power in counterinsurgency. Indeed, a deficiency in exactly these functions has been cited by others as the driving rationale for Russia's resort to the liberal use of indiscriminate, mass fires to put down past insurrections.[16]

Hard data remains scarce but there is little doubt that RuAF operations in Syria featured a greater utilization of precision-guided munitions (PGM) than Chechnya, Afghanistan, or the air service's brief conventional engagement in Georgia.[17] PGM use included the expanded deployment of legacy laser and electro-optically guided missiles as well as the introduction of new satellite-guided, coordinate-seeking weapons in substantial quantities.[18] And although the majority of the munitions expended by the RuAF over Syria were unguided bombs,[19] a significant

[14] J. Hawk, Daniel Deiss, and Edwin Watson, "Electronic Ears over Aleppo," *SouthFront*, September 10, 2016. https://southfront.org/russia-defense-report-electronic-ears-over-aleppo; Roger McDermott, "Russia Tests Network-Centric Air Operations in Syria," *Eurasia Daily Monitor* 12:184 (October 13, 2013). https://jamestown.org/program/russia-tests-network-centric-air-operations-in-syria; Sokov, "Russia's New Conventional Capability." For an explanation of Soviet doctrine, see Milan Vego, "Recce-Strike Complexes in Soviet Theory and Practice," Soviet Army Studies Office, Fort Leavenworth, Kansas (June 1990). http://dtic.mil/dtic/tr/fulltext/u2/a231900.pdf
[15] Dima Adamsky, *The Culture of Military Innovation* (Stanford: Stanford University Press, 2010).
[16] Robert H. Scales, *Future Warfare: Anthology* (Carlisle, PA: Strategic Studies Institute, 2000), 225–26.
[17] Guy Plopsky, "Russian Airpower in Syria: An Emphasis on Precision Strike?" *Eurasia Review*, October 15, 2015. http://eurasiareview.com/15102015-russian-airpower-in-syria-an-emphasis-on-precision-strike-analysis; Lee, "Russian Military Operations in Syria," 11. Per Plopsky, PGMs accounted for 3 and 1.5 percent of munitions dropped in the First and Second Chechen Wars, respectively, and only 0.5 percent of those dropped in the Five Day War with Georgia. By comparison, early estimates approximated PGM use in Syria at about 20 percent of Russia's expended ordnance totals. Notable unguided weapons in use include the BETAB-500 bunker-busting bombs, RBK-500-SPE-D cluster munitions, and various caliber rocket pods.
[18] Plopsky, "Russian Airpower in Syria"; Michael Kofman, "Russia's Arsenal in Syria: What Do We Know?" *War on the Rocks*, October 18, 2015. https://warontherocks.com/2015/10/russias-arsenal-in-syria-what-do-we-know; David Cenciotti, "These Photos of Everyday Life at Hmeymim Say a Lot about the Russian Air Force Operations in Syria," *Aviationist*, December 22, 2015. https://theaviationist.com/2015/12/22/everyday-life-at-latakia-airbase-photos; Dave Majumdar, "The Russian Air Force Is Back: Stealth, Su-35s and Syria," *The National Interest*, July 21, 2016. http://nationalinterest.org/blog/the-buzz/the-russian-air-force-back-stealth-su-35s-syria-17059?page=2
[19] Plopsky, "Russian Airpower in Syria"; McDermott, "Russia Tests Network-Centric Air Operations in Syria"; Roger McDermott, "Russia's Application of Military Power in Syria," *Eurasia Daily Monitor* 13:41 (March 1, 2016). https://jamestown.org/program/r

portion of these were delivered using new computer-controlled bomb release technology that allegedly compares to the accuracy of PGMs themselves.[20]

Battle damage verification against fielded forces remains notoriously difficult, particularly against an irregular enemy, and even more so in the midst of an active conflict. Nevertheless, enough anecdotal evidence for Syria exists to surmise that the RuAF has achieved a qualified success in the employment of precision and near-precision technology. Although officially released materials present a charitably filtered view, verified RuAF weapon seeker and targeting system videos showing munitions successfully striking fixed targets and stationary vehicles demonstrate solid operational competence and improved per-sortie kill rates over Russia's past conflicts.[21] This is corroborated by participant interviews and the judgments of third-party conflict observers that correlate the onset of Russian bombardment with improvement in air strike lethality.[22] In Aleppo, for example, Russian air strikes were characterized by those subject to their effects as consistently accurate when deployed against identifiable targets.[23] The fact that its fighter-bombers have been

ussias-application-of-military-power-in-syria; Douglas Barrie and Joseph Dempsey, "Something Old, Something New – Russian Air-Delivered Weapons in Syria," IISS Manama Dialogue, November 1, 2015. https://iiss.org/en/manama%20voices/blogsec tions/2015-f60f/russian-weapons-in-syria-5916; Anton Lavrov, "Russia's GLONASS Satellite Constellation," *Moscow Defense Brief* 4:60 (2017). http://mdb.cast.ru/mdb/4-2 017/item2/article3

[20] Hadi Gholami Nohouj, "Cost-Effective Aerial Campaign: Russian Airstrikes in Syria and the SVP-24," *Southfront*, September 1, 2017. https://southfront.org/cost-effective-aerial-campaign-russian-airstrikes-syria-svp-24; Michael Peck, "Did Russia Really Build a Smarter Smart Bomb?" *The National Interest*, March 14, 2016. http://nationalinterest .org/feature/did-russia-really-build-smarter-smart-bomb-15484

[21] Eliott Higgins, "Geolocation and Analysis of Russian Ministry of Defence Airstrike Videos," Bellingcat.org, October 5, 2015. https://bellingcat.checkdesk.org/en/story/736 ; Margarita Antidze and Jack Stubbs, "Before Syria, Russia Struggled to Land Air Strikes on Target," *Reuters*, October 26, 2015. http://reuters.com/article/us-mideast-crisis-syria-russia-bombing/before-syria-russia-struggled-to-land-air-strikes-on-target-idUSKCN0SK1WF20151026; Matthew Bodner, "Russia Shows Early Success, New Capabilities in Syria," *Defense News*, October 18, 2015. https://defensenews.com/home/ 2015/10/18/russia-shows-early-success-new-capabilities-in-syria; Thomas Gibbons-Neff, "Anatomy of a Russian Airstrike in Syria," *Washington Post*, September 30, 2015. https://washingtonpost.com/news/checkpoint/wp/2015/09/30/anatomy-of-a-russian-air strike-in-syria/?utm_term=.b1e723f1272d

[22] Author interview with Genevieve Casagrande, Institute for the Study of War (ISW), August 2, 2017; Alexander Corbeil, "Russia Is Learning about Syria," Carnegie Endowment for International Peace, January 11, 2017. http://carnegieendowment.org/ sada/67651

[23] Suleiman Al-Khalidi and Humeyra Pamuk, "Russian Firepower Helps Syrian Forces Edge toward Turkey Border," *Reuters*, February 8, 2016. http://reuters.com/article/us-mideast-crisis-syria-turkey/russian-firepower-helps-syrian-forces-edge-toward-turkey-b order-idUSKCN0VH0SH; Faysal Itani, "Aleppo's Fate Is No Surprise," Atlantic

able to obtain this result while operating almost exclusively from medium altitude signals the RuAF's new proficiency in the air delivery of guided and unguided ordnance.

A related departure from Russia's past record was the RuAF's drastically diminished aircraft attrition in Syria.[24] For the fixed-wing fleet this was explicable by adherence to a medium-altitude flight profile – Russian strike fighters simply operated above the effective altitude of the anti-air systems available to their insurgent adversaries.[25] The ability to do so and remain relevant to the fight below was a result of the adoption of guided munitions and munition delivery systems. As the United States discovered during the 1991 war against Iraq, Operation Desert Storm, higher combat elevation detracts from the accuracy of computer-aided dumb-bomb delivery, but this was not a particularly costly trade-off in light of Russia's relative insensitivity to noncombatant casualties and damage.[26]

Less frequently, Russia employed its Long-Range Aviation (LRA) strategic bombers to deliver precision weapons in a ground support role. This included dramatic appearances by Tu-160 Blackjack and Tu-95MS Bear heavy bombers flying circuitous routes from Russian airbases to deploy GLONASS coordinate-seeking munitions versus fixed facility targets. The volley-launching of these long-range cruise missiles may have contributed to battlefield outcomes by adding supplemental stand-off fires. More often, though, their rationale appears to have been theatrical, intended to demonstrate Russia's long-reach power-projection weapons for an international audience.[27] Although unquestionably imprecise, carpet-bombing raids by LRA Tu-22 M3s against Islamic State targets in the eastern deserts appear to have been more combat relevant, especially in the latter stages of the eastern offensives.[28] Understandably, in light of Russia's shorter engagement in Syria, RuAF strategic bombers were not

Council, November 29, 2016. http://atlanticcouncil.org/blogs/syriasource/aleppo-s-fate-is-no-surprise

[24] Pukhov, "A Proving Ground of the Future."

[25] The downing of an Su-25 over Idlib province during a rare low-level attack run on February 3, 2018, was Russia's first fixed-wing loss to ground fire. Tim Ripley, "First Russian Jet Shot Down in Syria," *Jane's Defence Weekly*, February 6, 2018. An increased share of RuAF night flights may have also played a role in suppressing fixed-wing losses. Ben Cenciotti, "Russian Air Force Su-34s and Su-24s Night Operations at Latakia Air Base," *Aviationist*, October 23, 2015. https://theaviationist.com/2015/10/23/photos-of-ruaf-night-launch

[26] Barry Watts, *Six Decades of Guided Munitions and Battle Networks: Progress and Prospects* (Washington, DC: CSBA, 2007), 196–97. For altitude's effects on Russia's GLONASS-based bomb-delivery system, see Tomislav Mesaric, "Su-25SM Prepares for Flight," *AirForces Monthly* 349 (April 2017): 96–97.

[27] Ripley, *Operation Aleppo*, 50–51, 89, 122.

[28] Ripley, *Operation Aleppo*, 47, 50–51, 79–80, 145, 184–85.

adapted as loitering, large-capacity, precision-bomb arsenal planes for the close-support mission the way that re-roled USAF B-1B and B-52 "heavies" had been in Afghanistan and Iraq.[29] The RuAF's tactical platforms represented the more relevant yardstick for measuring Russian precision performance.

Though better guidance technology and operator competence yielded an enhanced single-shot probability of kill, this did not necessarily demonstrate transition to a new concept for force employment. To discern if this represents a meaningful shift toward adoption of the reconnaissance-strike operational paradigm, as originally conceived, it is necessary to investigate what share of these more accurate strikes were (1) reconnaissance driven and (2) directed at depth against second-echelon forces.[30] These criteria generate considerable cause for skepticism.

The first order issue regards reconnaissance resources. In proportion to strike activity, Russia's allocation of dedicated intelligence, surveillance, and reconnaissance (ISR) assets to Syria is small by Western standards for a contemporary air campaign. A rough comparison with the ratio of ISR-to-strike assets deployed by US and allied air forces under Operation Inherent Resolve (OIR) in Syria and Iraq since 2014 highlights the contrast in reconnaissance dependence and approach. The OIR coalition drew on a wide assortment of manned ISR platforms and sensors to support its air strike operations in Iraq and Syria, including E-8C JSTARS, RAF Sentinel R1s, RC-135V/W Rivet Joints, EP-3E Aries II, RC-12X Guardrails, and U-2s. These specialized aircraft were supplemented by a deep bench of reconnaissance- and targeting-pod-equipped strike fighters.[31] In contrast, the only dedicated airborne ISR assets the

[29] Wesley Morgan, "B-1 Bomber: The Underappreciated Workhorse of America's Air Wars," *Stars and Stripes*, December 30, 2015. https://stripes.com/news/us/b-1-bomber-the-underappreciated-workhorse-of-america-s-air-wars-1.386570; Oriana Pawlyk, "B-1B Lancer's Evolving Mission Includes More Close-Air Support," *Military.com*, January 14, 2018. https://military.com/daily-news/2018/01/14/b-1b-lancers-evolving-mission-take-more-close-air-support.html; Joseph Trevithick, "B-52s Are Back in the Skies of Afghanistan Dropping Bombs once Again," *The Drive*, September 13, 2017. https://thedrive.com/the-war-zone/14304/b-52s-are-back-in-the-skies-of-afghanistan-dropping-bombs-once-again

[30] Vego, "Recce-Strike Complexes," 8–10; Ruslan Pukhov, "A Proving Ground of the Future," *Russia in Global Affairs* (online), March 30, 2016. http://eng.globalaffairs.ru/number/A-Proving-Ground-of-the-Future-18075

[31] Unattributed, "Intel Briefing – Inherent Resolve: A Long Haul," *AirForces Monthly* 348 (March 2017): 72–85; Sydney J. Freeberg Jr., "Airstrikes Up in Iraq and Syria, Afghanistan Easts ISR: CENTCOM," *Breaking Defense* (online), July 20, 2016. http://breakingdefense.com/2016/07/airstrikes-up-in-iraq-syria-afghanistan-eats-isr-centcom-data; Benjamin Lambeth, "The US Is Squandering Its Airpower," *Washington Post* (online), March 5, 2015. https://washingtonpost.com/opinions/stop-squandering-our-airpower-advantage/2015/03/05/193d65ca-bf88-11e4-bdfa-b8e8f594e6ee_story.html?tid=a_inl&utm_term=.518a1e497674; Scott A. Vickery, "Operation Inherent Resolve:

RuAF maintained in Syria were two IL-20 Coots and the intermittent presence of one of Russia's two new Tu-214 R ISR testbed aircraft.[32] The RuAF air group's pool of potential intelligence collectors was further thinned by a shortage of targeting pods that impaired the ability of Russian strike fighters to provide the kind of nontraditional ISR common to their Western counterparts.[33]

Tail count alone suggests the RuAF never matched the 1:2 ISR-to-strike sortie ratio reportedly maintained by US and coalition air forces in Iraq and Syria, much less the 4:1 ratio that NATO executed in a roughly analogous effort supporting a beleaguered ground force partner in Afghanistan.[34] Reports that the RuAF pressured the Syrian Arab Air Force (SyAAF) to provide tactical reconnaissance services seem to confirm a critical shortfall.[35] Yet RuAF strike sortie counts regularly equaled or exceeded those of the US and allied campaign in Syria and Iraq, begging the question whether the majority of these attacks were truly "targeted" in any meaningful way.[36]

Nor did the RuAF manifest a pattern of systemic attack against insurgent second-order forces. The combination of new Tu-214Rs, legacy Il-20 Coots, and a constellation of UAVs proved insufficient to provide the air group reliable warning of significant enemy movements.

An Interim Assessment (PolicyWatch 2354)," Washington Institute for Near East Policy (online), January 13, 2015. http://washingtoninstitute.org/policy-analysis/view/oper ation-inherent-resolve-an-interim-assessment

[32] Hawk et al., "Ears above Aleppo"; Tim Ripley, "Russia Deploys Its Most Capable ISTAR Platform to Syria," *Jane's Defense Weekly*, February 17, 2016; Caitlin Patterson, "Russia's Surging Electronic Warfare Capabilities," *The Diplomat* (online), April 19, 2016. http://thediplomat.com/2016/04/russias-surging-electronic-warfare-capabilities

[33] Barrie and Dempsey, "Something Old, Something New"; Pukhov, "A Proving Ground of the Future." Regarding nontraditional ISR, see "Annex C: Multi-Role Aircraft with an ISR Mission" to "Appendix 2–0: Global Integrated Intelligence, Surveillance, and Reconnaissance Operations," Curtis E. LeMay Center for Doctrine Development and Education (online), January 29, 2015, 61–61. https://doctrine.af.mil/download.jsp?filen ame=2-0-Annex-GLOBAL-INTEGRATED-ISR.pdf

[34] See Freeberg, "Airstrikes Up in Iraq and Syria."

[35] Tom Cooper, "Does the Russian Air Force Even Know What Is Going on in Syria?" *War Is Boring* (online), November 5, 2016. https://medium.com/war-is-boring/does-the-russian-air-force-even-know-what-is-going-on-in-syria-82333eadca31

[36] David Axe, "Russia Is Launching Twice as Many Airstrikes as the US in Syria," *Daily Beast* (online), February 23, 2016. http://thedailybeast.com/russia-is-launching-twice-as-many-airstrikes-as-the-us-in-syria; Steven Lee Myers and Eric Schmitt, "Russia Military Uses Syria as Proving Ground, and West Takes Notice," *New York Times* (online), October 14, 2015. https://nytimes.com/2015/10/15/world/middleeast/russian-military-uses-syria-as-pr oving-ground-and-west-takes-notice.html?mcubz=0; Genevieve Casagrande, "Russian Airstrikes in Syria (September 30, 2015 – September 19, 2016)," Institute for the Study of War (ISW), September 2016. http://understandingwar.org/sites/default/files/Russian% 20Airstrikes%20Maps%20SEPT%202015-SEPT%202016.pdf; Sengupta, "Russia's 'Rustbucket.'"

The most dramatic demonstration of this was the RuAF's failure to detect and interdict the massing of ISIS forces before their assault and re-conquest of Palmyra, despite the benefit of austere and uncluttered surrounding terrain.[37] But the RuAF also failed to notice or disrupt other major opposition movements, including the advance of the Free Syrian Army's Central Division on Idlib in late October 2015 and the movement of a mounted ISIS formation along the Khan Nassir-Aleppo corridor in February 2016.[38]

In a similar vein, Russia's execution of the types of surface attacks typical of intelligence-driven campaigns – like decapitation strikes against leadership personalities and command facilities – were rare and RuAF deep interdiction bombing of distant supply lines episodic at best.[39] Russia's air strike assassinations of rebel leaders looked to be accidents or outliers rather than indicative of a determined targeted killing program. And though air operations to isolate opposition-held areas from external assistance expanded in scale with Russia's arrival, the focus generally remained on local ground-maneuver objectives rather than independent and systemic air attack on rebel sources of supply.[40] Acknowledging that the identification of irregular insurgents is substantially more difficult than the heavy conventional forces that reconnaissance-strike was conceived to combat, Russia apparently lacked the requisite deep-look ISR resources to implement the concept.[41]

[37] Chris Kozak, "Russian Air Strikes in Syria: November 21 – December 19, 2016," ISW (online), December 21, 2016; Pavel Flegenhauer, "Russian Mission in Syria Beset by Problems Despite Victory in Aleppo," *Eurasia Daily Monitor* 13:197 (December 15, 2016). https://jamestown.org/program/russian-mission-syria-beset-problems-despite-victory-aleppo

[38] Cooper, "Does the Russian Air Force Even Know What Is Going on in Syria?"

[39] Ibid.; author interview with Casagrande; Genevieve Casagrande and Jodi Brignola, "Russian Strikes in Syria: November 9–19, 2015," ISW (online), November 20, 2015. http://iswresearch.blogspot.com/2015/11/russian-strikes-in-syria-november-9-19.html; Tim Ripley, *Operation Aleppo: Russia's War in Syria* (Lancaster, UK: Telic-Herrick Publications, 2018), 64.

[40] RuAF support to pro-regime ground advances that cut lines of communications to opposition hubs in Jarjisa, Nubl, al-Zahraa, and Aleppo are typical of the trend. Sam Heller, "The Regime Is Close to a Victory that Could Turn the War," *Vice News* (online), February 4, 2016. https://news.vice.com/article/the-syrian-regime-is-close-to-a-victory-that-could-turn-the-war; Jodi Brignola and Genevieve Casagrande, "Russian Airstrikes in Syria: January 8–14, 2016," ISW (online), January 26, 2016. http://iswresearch.blogspot.com/2016/01/russian-airstrikes-in-syria-january-8.html

[41] For a counterpoint, see Eric Schmitt, "Aboard a US Eye in the Sky, Staring Down ISIS in Iraq and Syria," *New York Times* (online), December 25, 2016. https://nytimes.com/2016/12/25/world/middleeast/aboard-a-us-eye-in-the-sky-staring-down-isis-in-iraq-and-syria.html?_r=0

### Evaluating Air-Ground Synergy

In light of this ISR deficiency, a quorum of onlookers and analysts concluded that the RuAF receives much of its targeting data from Russian forward observers, its Hezbollah and Iranian ground-force partners, or the Syrian regime's pervasive intelligence apparatus.[42] These sources, supplemented by Russian UAVs that were ill-equipped for broad area search but well suited to near-front surveillance, could conceivably provide enough information to substitute for the RuAF's shortfall in deep-look airborne ISR. Due to the nature of its sensors, the effective range of such an alternative system would be necessarily shallower than that of a reconnaissance-strike complex, but the RuAF may still have attained significant kill-chain compression absent Western-standard ISR density, particularly in support of close combat.

In the RuAF's campaign, the difficulty of distinguishing opposition from noncombatant targets was alleviated to some extent by Russia's lesser concern over collateral damage and civilian casualties. This presumably eliminated some of the decision delay that often slows US air strike response to emergent targets as Russia's higher collateral damage tolerances reduced the time required to adjudicate positive identification and weapon selection.[43] Although not a reconnaissance-strike complex as originally envisioned, such a process might nonetheless represent a shortcut conceptual segue toward the kind of dynamic targeting model that carried the United States to a rapid and inexpensive early victory over the Taliban in 2001.

Circumstantial evidence supports this hypothesis. The critical role of embedded forward air controllers was a lesson learned from Russia's past counterinsurgency engagements, and frequent references to their presence in Syria illustrated that the lesson was not lost in this conflict.[44]

---

[42] Gressel, "Lessons from Russia's Intervention"; Paul Bucala and Genevieve Casagrande, "How Iran Is Learning from Russia in Syria," ISW (online), February 3, 2017. http://understandingwar.org/backgrounder/how-iran-learning-russia-syria; Jesse Rosenfeld, "Russia Is Arming Hezbollah, Say Two of the Group's Commanders," *The Daily Beast* (online), January 11, 2016. http://thedailybeast.com/russia-is-arming-hezbollah-say-two-of-the-groups-field-commanders

[43] "Dynamic Targeting and the Tasking Process" and "Appendix A: Targeting and Legal Considerations," in "Annex 3–60: Targeting," Curtis E. LeMay Center for Doctrine Development and Education, February14, 2017. https://doctrine.af.mil/download.jsp?filename=3-60-D17-Target-Dynamic-Task.pdf

[44] Ripley, "Russia Learns Military Lessons in Syria"; Edward B. Westermann, "The Limits of Soviet Airpower: The Failure of Military Coercion in Afghanistan, 1979–89," *Journal of Conflict Studies* 19:2 (1999): 6; Pavel K. Baev, "Russia's Airpower in the Chechen War: Denial, Punishment and Defeat," *Journal of Slavic Military Studies* 10:2 (June 1997): 9; Marcel de Haass, "Russian Airpower over Chechnya: Lessons Learned Applied," *The Officer Magazine*, 18.

Further, battlefield reconnaissance was reportedly one of the principal duties charged to Russian special operations and Spetsnaz forces deployed in-country, suggesting a heavier reliance on more qualified operators to perform target identification and air strike control.[45] This constituted an overdue adaptation from Chechnya and Afghanistan, where deficient expertise was a recurring problem.[46] Observers in Syria also enjoyed the benefit of new equipment specially designed for rapidly and reliably passing target location data from observer teams to overhead aircraft.[47] The deaths of multiple special operations forward observers, including at least one during an *in-extremis* close air support (CAS) call, verified, moreover, that these personnel were deployed to the bleeding edge of the battlefield.[48]

Hezbollah and Quds Force partners also affirmed that Russian advisors trained them to call in air strikes, an initiative that may have compensated for the limited numbers of Russian observers in Syria's geographically dispersed, multifront battlespace.[49] Beyond the forward line of troops, Russia has acknowledged employing its new UAVs for frontline observation, artillery spotting, and post-strike damage assessment.[50] Indeed,

---

[45] Aleksey Nikolsky, "Russian Special Forces in Syria," *Moscow Defense Brief* 2:58 (2017): 8; Mark Galeotti, "The Three Faces of Russian Spetsnaz in Syria," *War on the Rocks* (online), March 20, 2016. https://warontherocks.com/2016/03/the-three-faces-of-russian-spetsnaz-in-syria; Agence France Presse, "Russia Admits Special Forces 'Directing Warplanes' in Syria," *Times of Israel* (online), March 23, 2016. http://time sofisrael.com/russia-admits-special-forces-directing-warplanes-in-syria; Thomas Grove, "Russian Special Forces Seen as Key to Aleppo Victory," *Wall Street Journal* (online), December 16. 2016. https://wsj.com/articles/russian-special-forces-seen-as-key-to-aleppo-victory-1481884200

[46] Timothy L. Thomas, "Air Operations in Low Intensity Conflict: The Case of Chechnya," *Airpower Journal* (Winter 1997): 58. http://airpower.maxwell.af.mil/airchro nicles/apj/apj97/win97/thomas.pdf; de Haass, "Russian Airpower over Chechnya," 20; Westermann, "The Limits of Soviet Airpower," note 46.

[47] See descriptions of Metronome system laser range-finding binoculars and radio tablet in Mesaric, "Su-25SM Prepares for Flight." See also references to the GLONASS-enabled Strelets reconnaissance and command and control system in Aleksey Ramm, "Operational Reconnaissance in the Russian Armed Forces," *Moscow Defense Brief* 2:58 (2017): 16.

[48] Unattributed, "The Hero of Palmyra," *Southfront* (online), April 1, 2016. https://youtube .com/watch?v=px9b2kAAcAE; Nikolsky, "Russian Special Forces in Syria," 9.

[49] Nicholas Blanford, "OSINT Summary: Reports of Hizbullah Armoured Brigade Underline Its Combat Evolution in Syria," *IHS Jane's Terrorism and Insurgency Monitor*, November 1, 2015; Max Fisher, "In Syrian War, Russia Has Yet to Fulfill Superpower Ambitions," *New York Times* (online), September 24 2016. https://nytimes .com/2016/09/25/world/middleeast/russia-syria-ambitions.html?mcubz=0

[50] Anton Lavrov, "Russian UAVs in Syria," *Moscow Defense Brief* 60:4 (2017). http://mdb .cast.ru/mdb/2-2017/item3/article4; Alexey Nikolsky, "Glonass" and "Special Operations Forces – The Causes of Russia's Military Success in Syria," *Vedomosti* (online), March 1, 2017. http://vedomosti.ru/politics/articles/2017/03/01/679434-glonass-spetsoperatsii; McDermott, "Russia's Application of Military Power in Syria";

a rare glimpse inside a pro-regime command and control facility confirmed that streaming video from these assets was available to those directing ground maneuver, certifying some degree of air-ground integration.[51]

With little insight to the actual mechanics of tactical coordination between co-belligerents, the task of measuring the cross-cueing between RuAF air strike operations and this assemblage of UAVs, foreign ground forces, and forward air controllers is challenging. If the simple transfer of real estate is used as a performance metric the slow initial progress of the Syrian ground war suggests rather poor air-ground synergy.[52] Syria featured few of the lightning-speed, lop-sided breakthroughs that defined Operation Enduring Freedom (see Chapter 5). But the effectiveness of the so-called "Afghan model" was acutely sensitive to ground-force skill disparity and inhibited by complex terrain and astute enemy use of cover and concealment, and such factors also pertained to the competition in Syria.[53] Battle lines in western Syria were frequently drawn across or around built-up cities and suburbs, the insurgents made extensive use of subterranean tunnels to evade bombardment and circumvent siege blockades, and regime progress was highly dependent on an elite subset of Syrian Arab Army, Hezbollah, and Quds Force cadres.[54] It would thus

Diana Mihailova and J. Hawk, "Orlan-10 UAVs in Action against Ukrainian Artillery," *Southfront* (online), July 9, 2016. https://southfront.org/orlan-10-uavs-in-action-against-ukrainian-artillery; Unattributed, "Combat Usage of Russian Drones in Syrian War," *Southfront* (online), December 23, 2016. https://southfront.org/combat-usage-of-russian-drones-in-syrian-war; David Axe and Patrick Hilsman, "Russia Is Flying Israeli Drones against Anti-Assad Rebels in Syria," *Daily Beast* (online), March 24, 2016. http://thedailybeast.com/articles/2016/03/24/russia-is-flying-israeli-drones-against-anti-assad-rebels-in-syria.html; Tara Copp, "Ukraine, Syria Giving US Glimpse into Russian Tactics," *Stars and Stripes* (online), December 9, 2015. https://stripes.com/news/ukraine-syria-giving-us-glimpse-into-russian-tactics-1.383024#.WNVP0zZMRE_
[51] Tim Ripley, "OSINT Helps Uncover Details of Aleppo Battle," *Jane's Intelligence Review*, January 31, 2017.
[52] Neil Hauer, "Russia's Attempts to Intervene in the Syrian War Have Fallen Flat," *National Post* (online), November 30, 2015. http://nationalpost.com/opinion/neil-hauer-russias-attempts-to-intervene-in-the-syrian-war-have-fallen-flat; Aron Lund, "Evaluating the Russian Intervention in Syria," Diwan – Middle Insights from Carnegie (online), December 7, 2015. http://carnegie-mec.org/diwan/62207?lang=en; Pukhov, "A Proving Ground of the Future."
[53] Stephen Biddle, "Allies, Airpower, and Modern Warfare: The Afghan Model in Afghanistan and Iraq," *International Security* 30:3 (Winter 2005/06): 161–76.
[54] Carter Center, Syria Conflict Mapping Project, https://d3svb6mundity5.cloudfront.net/dashboard/index.html; Aron Lund, "Into the Tunnels: The Rise and Fall of Syria's Rebel Enclave in the Eastern Ghouta," The Century Foundation (online), December 21, 2016; Elliot Carter, "Syrian Rebels Shift to Tunnel Warfare," *War Is Boring* (online), March 15, 2015. https://warisboring.com/syrian-rebels-shift-to-tunnel-warfare; Lucas Winter, "The Emergence of Syria's Tunnel Bombs," *OE Watch* 4:7 (July 2014): 62–69; Christopher Kozak, "An Army in All Corners: Assad's Campaign Strategy in

be problematic to base an audit of RuAF air support entirely on the trading of territory.

A finer measure for air-ground integration is effective performance of close air support (CAS). The RuAF's record with CAS in Syria, as it turns out, is mixed but improving. The onset of Russian air strikes was marred by a string of early fratricide events that incurred Hezbollah casualties in the vicinity of Aleppo, after which Russian fixed-wing assets reportedly ceased servicing targets near the front lines.[55] This inauspicious start and the subsequent withdrawal from theater of all Russian Su-25 Frogfoots – the CAS workhorse of the Afghan and Chechen wars – in March 2016[56] implied a reluctance to use fast jets for close support, a disturbing echo of Russia's air-ground synchronization woes in Chechnya.[57]

Regime elements also suffered a number of setbacks in their quest to retake key terrain despite heavy RuAF assistance, such as ISIS's late October assault on the regime's main supply route to Aleppo and pro-regime reverses in Maheen and Hawareen during the initial stages of the push toward Palmyra in early December 2015.[58] Thereafter, though, reports of fratricides subsided despite a substantial escalation in air strike

Syria (Middle East Security Report 26)," ISW (online), April 2015. http://understanding war.org/report/army-all-corners-assads-campaign-strategy-syria

[55] Unattributed, "Errant Russia Airstrike Kills Hezbollah Fighters: Report," *Now* (online), October 30, 2015; Unattributed, "Russia Jets Accidentally Target Syria Regime Troops," *Now* (online), October 16, 2015; Tom Cooper, "Syrian Regime Bombs Eastern Aleppo while Russia Focuses Its Bloody Strikes Elsewhere," *War Is Boring* (online), November 22, 2016. https://warisboring.com/syrian-regime-bombs-eastern-aleppo-while-russia-focuses-its-bloody-strikes-elsewhere

[56] Dmitry Gorenburg and Michael Kofman, "There Is No Russian Withdrawal from Syria," *War on the Rocks* (online), March 18, 2016. https://warontherocks.com/2016/03/there-is-no-russian-withdrawal-from-syria; Dario Leone, "Russian Air Force Su-25 Frogfoot Attack Aircraft Dropped 6,000 (Mostly Unguided) Bombs over Syria," *Aviationist* (online), March 19, 2016. https://theaviationist.com/2016/03/19/russian-air-force-su-25-frogfoot-attack-aircraft-dropped-6000-mostly-unguided-bombs-over-syria

[57] Timothy L. Thomas, "Grozny 2000: Urban Combat Lessons Learned," *Military Review* (July–August 2000): 55, 57. http://fmso.leavenworth.army.mil/documents/grozny2000/grozny2000.htm; de Haas, "Russian Airpower over Chechnya," 16, 18; The Frogfoots' share of CAS duties presumably fell to helicopter gunships until a new variant of the type was reintroduced in 2017. Andrey Frolov, "Mi Attack Helicopters: Use in Recent Conflicts and Export Potential," *Moscow Defense Brief* 6:56 (2016): 9; James Miller, "Putin's Attack Helicopters and Mercenaries Are Winning the War for Assad," *Foreign Policy* (online), March 30, 2016; Unattributed, "Russia's Su-25SM3 Fighter Jets to Be Dispatched to Syrian Hmeymim Airbase," *Southfront* (online), January 31, 2017. https://southfront.org/russias-su-25sm3-fighter-jets-to-be-dispatched-to-syrian-hmeymim-airbase

[58] Christopher Kozak, "ISIS Contests Regime Supply Line to Aleppo City," ISW (online), October 28, 2015. http://iswresearch.blogspot.com/2015/10/isis-contests-regime-supply-line-to.html; Genevieve Casagrande and Jared Ferris, "Russian Strikes in Syria: December 3–12, 2015," ISW (online), December 13, 2015. http://iswresearch.blogspot.com/2015/12/russian-strikes-in-syria-december-3-12.html

tempo. Many of these strikes continued to fall in proximity to the front lines with no recurrence of the costly errors of the early intervention, demonstrating the RuAF's improvements in close fire support to foreign forces.[59] This is a significant achievement in light of the stubborn inter-service challenges the Russian armed forces had only recently overcome.[60]

The RuAF's continuing difficulties with urgent and defensive CAS, the more demanding subset of the type, however, undermines the thesis that Russia realized a leap in air-ground integration. Consider how failures in defensive CAS contributed to the loss of Palmyra. Despite generating an impressive overall bomb total, the RuAF was unable to save an embattled outpost from being overrun by ISIS on what would appear to be CAS-conducive desert terrain.[61] The fall of Palmyra was dismissed by some as a consequence of the regime's commitment of a particularly weak hold-force, but other examples with more equitable ground-force comparisons corroborate the point. At Khan Touman in May 2016, for instance, a capable formation of Iranian Quds Force and allied Shiite militias lost the city, incurred significant casualties, and suffered a humiliating setback that Iranian sources specifically ascribed to weak Russian air support.[62] Similarly, RuAF air strike assistance was unable to save Syrian military, Hezbollah, and Afghan Shiite militia forces from being overrun by Islamist rebels at the Artillery College in southern Aleppo in early August 2016.[63]

Observers note other trends that appear to substantiate the case. Those focused on ground combat reported that the RuAF is slow to engage opposition anti-armor teams,[64] that support to troops-in-contact makes

---

[59] Hiba Dlewati, "Burning Tires in Aleppo: A Desperate People Try to Fend Off Warplanes," *Syria Deeply* (online), August 5, 2016. https://newsdeeply.com/syria/art icles/2016/08/05/burning-tires-in-aleppo-a-desperate-people-try-to-fend-off-warplanes

[60] Benjamin Lambeth, *Russia's Air Power in Crisis* (Washington, DC: Smithsonian, 1999), 141; Olga Oliker, *Russia's Chechen Wars 1994 – 2000: Lessons from Urban Combat* (Santa Monica: RAND, 2001), 33, 51; Lee, "Russia Military," 11.

[61] Pavel Flegenhauer, "Russian Mission in Syria Beset by Problems Despite Victory in Aleppo," *Eurasia Daily Monitor* 13:197 (December 15, 2016). https://jamestown.org/pr ogram/russian-mission-syria-beset-problems-despite-victory-aleppo

[62] Tom Perry and Babak Dehghanpisheh, "For Iran and Hezbollah, a Costly Week in Syria," *Reuters* (online), May 13, 2016. http://reuters.com/article/us-mideast-crisis-syria-insight/for-iran-and-hezbollah-a-costly-week-in-syria-idUSKCN0Y42FZ;     Paul Bucala, "What the Khan Tuman Defeat Means for Iran," *Critical Threats* (online), May 12, 2016. https://criticalthreats.org/analysis/what-the-khan-tuman-defeat-means-for-iran

[63] Jeremy Binnie, "Rebels Take Key Base in Southern Aleppo," *Jane's Defence Weekly*, August 12, 2016.

[64] Type 63 (online pseudonym), "Airpower in Syria: Words Have Meaning, Airstrike or CAS?" Type 63: A Collection of Musings on Middle East Conflict (online blog),

up only a small portion of the RuAF's overall sortie count, and that lost territory tends to go uncontested for twelve to twenty-four hours before Russian bombing responds.[65] In the air, meanwhile, the RuAF's short-duration, out-and-back flight profiles confirm that pilots are not loitering above the battlefield in CAS stacks or otherwise responding to in-flight, off-board retasking.[66]

The sum of available evidence suggests that although air-ground integration benefited from interwar and intrawar adaptation, the overwhelming majority of Russian jet sorties in Syria were still deliberately planned missions. The RuAF does not appear to have operationalized the processes necessary to react on-the-fly to battlefield emergencies and failed to take full advantage of its precision-technology platform improvements. The service's progress thus remains incomplete in its doctrinal migration toward a more agile operational paradigm.[67] Essentially, Russia cannot yet emulate the ground-directed dynamic targeting construct that defines twenty-first-century American counterinsurgency air support.[68]

This does not imply that air power has been immaterial to ground gains or the overall course of the conflict. To the contrary, air-delivered firepower and combined arms maneuver have been key enablers to Assad's siege-and-starve strategy and essential to reversing the tide of the war.[69] Credible experts cite Russian bombing as a decisive contributor to the regime's recovery in Latakia, its successful push to Palmyra, and its conquest of Aleppo following years of fallback and stalemate.[70] This involves the RuAF's notable – if not revolutionary – improvement in CAS capability. But the lion's share of Russian ground attack operations has emphasized volume and density of fire over speed or accuracy of

October 8, 2015. http://type63.com/2015/10/airpower-in-syria-words-have-meaning.html

[65] Author interview with Casagrande.

[66] Cooper, "Does the Russian Air Force Even Know What Is Going on in Syria?"

[67] Ibid.

[68] Mike Benitez, "How Afghanistan Distorted Close Air Support and Why It Matters," *War on the Rocks* (online), June 29, 2016. https://warontherocks.com/2016/06/how-afghanistan-distorted-close-air-support-and-why-it-matters

[69] Kozak, "An Army in All Corners."

[70] Christopher Kozak, "Control of Terrain in Syria," ISW (online), December 23, 2015. http://understandingwar.org/backgrounder/control-terrain-syria-december-23-2015; Sam Heller, "Russia Is in Charge in Syria: How Moscow Took Control of the Battlefield and Negotiating Table," *War on the Rocks* (online), June 28, 2016. https://warontherocks.com/2016/06/russia-is-in-charge-in-syria-how-moscow-took-control-of-the-battlefield-and-negotiating-table; Jodi Brignola, "Russian Airstrikes in Syria: January 20 – 25, 2016," ISW (online), January 26, 2016. http://iswresearch.blogspot.com/2016/01/russian-airstrikes-in-syria-january-20.html; James Miller, "Syrian Rebel Group Cites Assad Regime's 'Absolute Reliance' on Russian Air Power," *The Interpreter* (online), January 27, 2016. http://interpretermag.com/just-how-effective-are-russian-airstrikes-in-syria

delivery. Most of the RuAF's support materialized as behind-the-lines barrage bombardment, consisting of either months-long sustained saturation bombing as in Salma and Aleppo or suppressive air assaults surged in anticipation of pro-regime ground advances.[71] On balance, the use of air power in Syria bears less similarity to dynamic targeting than to the fire preparation of industrial-style warfare, little distinguished conceptually from the frontal aviation air support of past Soviet and Russian conflicts stretching back to World War II.[72]

### Beyond Evolution – An Allied Air Force and a Minimal Objective

If new technology and tactics delivered only modest evolution then what explains the discontinuity between the RuAF's painful past acquaintance with counterinsurgency and its surprise low-cost success in Syria? The SyAAF played some role in Russia's success. The existence of an allied host-country air arm in the Syrian war was fundamentally different from Chechnya and easily overlooked in comparisons with Afghanistan, where the Soviet Air Force overshadowed and distrusted its Afghan counterpart.[73] Steeled by crucial Russian infusions of ammunition, spare parts, and maintenance assistance, the rejuvenated SyAAF remained a critical contributor to an air war whose execution did not depend much on operational subtlety or technical sophistication.[74] It both burden-shared the daily bombing task load and retained responsibility for certain more dangerous low-level mission sets.[75] SyAAF's role in rotary-wing troop transport appears to have been particularly relevant to reducing Russia's helicopter losses but was not the sole example.[76] Leveraging a new night-flight proficiency provided courtesy of Russian pilot training, the SyAAF also mounted a semi-effective armed reconnaissance campaign against opposition supply routes. Syrian highway hunter-killer sorties used

---

[71] Author interview with Casagrande; author review of ISW's "Russian Airstrikes in Syria" online reports dated from September 30, 2015, through January 27, 2017.

[72] Kenneth R. Whiting, "Soviet Air-Ground Coordination, 1941–1945," in *Case Studies in the Development of Close Air Support*, ed. Benjamin Franklin Cooling (Washington, DC: Office of Air Force History, 1990), 143.

[73] Olga Oliker, *Building Afghanistan's Security Forces in Wartime: The Soviet Experience* (Santa Monica: RAND, 2011), 41–42, 50–51.

[74] C. J. Chivers, "Syrian Leader's Arms under Strain as Conflict Continues," *New York Times* (online), August 2, 2012. http://nytimes.com/2012/08/03/world/middleeast/as-conflict-continues-in-syria-assads-arms-face-strain.html; Cooper, "What's Left of the Syrian Arab Air Force?"

[75] Cooper, "Syrian Arab Air Force: Air Power in Decline," 58–62.

[76] Shield, "Russian Airpower's Success in Syria: Assessing Evolution in Kinetic Counterinsurgency," 227–32.

combat-converted, elder-generation L-39 Albatross training jets that operated below the Russian hard deck, conducting a deep interdiction mission that the Russian fixed-wing force had generally forsaken.[77]

The reason Russia could afford the risk associated with neglecting these missions related to a second and more influential variable behind its success in Syria – Moscow's more modest strategic ambitions. Unlike its prior operations to reverse a satellite state's coup or a Soviet republic's secession, Russia's objectives in Syria were relatively limited. Putin dispatched Russian military force to preserve the Assad regime but remained uncommitted to the more formidable task of reestablishing Damascus's sovereignty over the ante bellum Syrian state. Having saved Assad's western bastion from collapse, secured its own access to the Eastern Mediterranean, and changed the geopolitical equation to its favor, Moscow was satisfied with incremental, and occasionally reversible, progress in further expanding regime control.[78] By modulating its military effort Russia also insulated itself from casualty exposure and maintained leverage over its Syrian, Iranian, and Hezbollah partners.

The strategic costs of Russia's inability or unwillingness to execute a more comprehensive, countrywide air campaign in Syria were much more manageable than they were either when Cold War insecurity drove the Soviet Union to invade Afghanistan or during Moscow's desperate attempts to reassert federal authority over the breakaway republic of Chechnya. Hence, Russian forces could abdicate responsibility for sealing Syria's borders against rebel resupply, defending isolated hinterland outposts, or patrolling reclaimed territory in support of regime garrison troops.

The political complexity that discouraged deeper US engagement in the Syrian civil war also accrued to Russia's favor. Russia reaped the benefit of the collateral American-led campaign against ISIS, engaging Islamists only when tactically necessary or strategically convenient, and negotiating a series of expedient cease-fires to shift and conserve combat power as it neutralized various rebel factions in turn.[79] Some of these

---

[77] Tom Cooper, "Al Assad's Nighttime Killers," *War Is Boring* (online), December 26, 2016. https://warisboring.com/al-assads-nighttime-killers; Tim Ripley, "Syrian L-39ZA Lost over Aleppo," *Jane's Defence Weekly*, December 5, 2016.

[78] Michael Kofman, "A Comparative Guide to Russia's Use of Force: Measure Twice, Invade Once," *War on the Rocks* (online), February 16, 2017. https://warontherocks.com/2017/02/a-comparative-guide-to-russias-use-of-force-measure-twice-invade-once

[79] Ellen Stockert, "Russian Maneuvers in Syria: May 1 – June 7, 2017," ISW (online), June 8, 2017. http://iswresearch.blogspot.com/2017/06/russias-maneuvers-in-syria-may-1-june-7.html; Genevieve Casagrande and Ellen Stockert, "Russian Airstrikes in Syria: Pre- and Post-Ceasefire," ISW (online), July 20, 2017. http://iswresearch.blogspot.com/2017/07/russian-airstrikes-in-syria-pre-and.html; Maksymilian Czuperski, et al.,

cease-fires apparently contradicted the wishes of the Damascus regime, illustrating Russia's pursuit of its own narrow national interests and disregard of Syrian priorities.[80] With the advantage of a unilateral calculus uncluttered by many of the considerations that weighed on its Western counterparts, Moscow plucked opportunity from chaos in Syria. The failure of many US pundits and policy makers to appreciate in advance Russia's ability to do so is a phenomenon at least one astute Russia watcher has attributed to subconscious cultural bias.[81]

### Controlling for Coercive Intent

Just as a prejudiced perspective might have obscured the possibility of a geostrategic win for Putin in Syria, estimates of the RuAF's precision-strike aptitude may be skewed by misconceptions about the relationship between collateral damage and Russian strategy. Stunning scenes of urban ruin in places like Aleppo graphically illustrate the humanitarian impact of Russian bombardment on civilian populations and infrastructure. Due to the high premium that Western-model "hearts and minds" counterinsurgency doctrine places on limiting these consequences, their occurrence is generally interpreted as an indication of inaccuracy. The implicit assumption is that if Russia had the ability to wage a more discriminate air campaign, it would do so. This dangerous misunderstanding, however, underappreciates the coercive philosophy behind Russia's contemporary approach to counterinsurgency and thus threatens to distort assessments of its evolving warfighting competence. It is also an assumption that in the Syrian case can be definitively disproven.

In spite of its wider deployment of more selective weapons, Russia's entry into the air war in Syria did not reduce human suffering. To the contrary, there is substantial evidence the RuAF's arrival increased civilian costs. Some portion of this effect results from increased conflict intensity that could have little to do with RuAF behavior – Russian bombing added to that of the SyAAF rather than substituted for it and so had no mitigating effect on the regime's ruthless barrel-bombing.[82] But

"Breaking Aleppo," The Atlantic Council (online), February 2017, 16–18. http://publi cations.atlanticcouncil.org/breakingaleppo

[80] Dmitri Trenin, *What Is Russia Up To in the Middle East?* (Cambridge, UK: Polity Press, 2018), 72–74.

[81] Michael Kofman, "The Russian Quagmire in Syria and Other Washington Fairy Tales," *War on the Rocks* (online), February 16, 2016. https://warontherocks.com/2016/02/the-russian-quagmire-in-syria-and-other-washington-fairy-tales

[82] Unattributed, "More Than 3173 Barrel Bombs Dropped on Syria since the Russian Military Intervention," Syrian Network for Human Rights (online), December 8, 2015. http://sn4hr.org/blog/2015/12/08/15312

the Russian intervention also directly coincided with the increased utilization of inherently indiscriminate area weapons, including thermobaric, incendiary, and cluster munitions, some of which were not previously in the SyAAF arsenal.[83] Many of these weapons, furthermore, were deployed from RuAF aircraft, confirming that Russia was actively engaged in their use rather than merely complicit through the transfer of this ordnance to its Syrian partners.[84] The infliction of civilian harm in these cases was both purposive and consistent with the Assad regime's strategy to depopulate opposition-controlled areas and thus deprive the insurgency of material support and perceived legitimacy.[85]

Indeed, Russia regularly leveraged improved weapon accuracy to amplify – rather than minimize – civilian suffering. The efficiency of conscious attacks against civilian infrastructure, including food, water, sanitation, and school facilities, bore this out.[86] The starkest illustration, though, was the RuAF's systematic attacks on hospitals, medical staff, and ambulances.

Attacks on civilian medical infrastructure and personnel pre-dated the RuAF's arrival.[87] The SyAAF adopted this tactic relatively early on as part of Assad's self-declared scorched-earth strategy.[88] But Russia's entrance saw the rate of such attacks increase by nearly 90 percent.[89] The most compelling evidence of RuAF participation was the adroit

[83] Unattributed, "Russia/Syria: Extensive Recent Use of Cluster Munitions," Human Rights Watch (online), December 20, 2015. https://hrw.org/news/2015/12/20/russia/syr ia-extensive-recent-use-cluster-munitions; Mary Wareghan, "Incendiary Weapons Burn again in Syria," Human Rights Watch (online), April 12, 2017. https://hrw.org/ne ws/2017/04/12/incendiary-weapons-burn-again-syria

[84] Unattributed, "Russian Forces Are Worse than the Syrian Regime in Terms of Cluster Munitions Use," Syrian Network for Human Rights (online), March 23, 2017 http://s n4hr.org/blog/2017/03/24/36449; Unattributed, "Dataset of Russian Attacks against Syria's Civilians," May 13, 2016. https://bellingcat.com/resources/articles/2016/05/13/ dataset-of-russian-attacks-against-syrias-civilians

[85] David Ignatius, "Surrender and You Can Eat Again: Aleppo on the Brink," *Washington Post* (online), October 4, 2016. https://washingtonpost.com/opinions/global-opinions/s urrender-and-you-can-eat-again-aleppo-on-the-brink/2016/10/04/fff6ecd0-8a6f-11e6-8 75e-2c1bfe943b66_story.html?utm_term=.d0819aab9e27; Aron Lund, "The Slow Violent Fall of East Aleppo," The Century Foundation (online), October 7, 2016. http s://tcf.org/content/commentary/slow-violent-fall-eastern-aleppo

[86] Genevieve Casagrande and Ellen Stockert, "Russia's Unrelenting Attacks in Syrian Civilians," ISW (online), April 29, 2017. http://understandingwar.org/backgrounder/ru ssias-unrelenting-attacks-syrian-civilians; Tom Miles, "Syria Committed War Crime by Bombing Damascus Water Supply: UN," *Reuters* (online), March 14, 2017. https://reu ters.com/article/us-mideast-crisis-syria-water/syria-committed-war-crime-by-bombing- damascus-water-supply-u-n-idUSKBN16L0W5

[87] Fouad M. Fouad et al., "Health Workers and the Weaponisation of Health Care in Syria: A Preliminary Inquiry for The Lancet – American University of Beirut Commission on Syria," *Lancet* 390 (2017): 2517–18.

[88] Yassin-Kassab and Al-Shami, *Burning Country,* 106.

[89] Fouad M. Fouad et al., "Heath Workers," 2518.

employment of advanced bunker-busting munitions against hospitals driven deep underground by repetitive Russian and regime air strikes.[90] Standard efforts to reduce the rate of attacks by providing the Russians and their regime allies a list of coordinates of hospitals only facilitated their targeting.[91] So-called "double-tap attacks" on ambulances and first responders, meanwhile, became so common as to be routine.[92]

Rather than spelling relief, the advent of advanced Russian weapons, guidance, and navigation systems intensified civilian suffering. The RuAF's behavior in Syria contradicts the theory that the misery it inflicts while battling rebellions is the overkill by-product of an enemy-centric strategy and a deficit in more discriminate tools.[93] The incidence of civilian harm in Syria was intentional and targeted. For Russia, violence against noncombatants is a feature, not a bug, of its counterinsurgency doctrine. Moscow finds this type of despair-inducing punishment coercively useful. As with other aspects of RuAF force employment philosophy, the Russians subscribe to a fundamentally different concept of warfare and air power's role in it. In addition to clarifying Moscow's mercilessly coercive logic, this realization provides a tragic but useful corrective to diagnoses that would dismiss Russian progress toward integrating precision technology on the basis of widespread collateral damage alone.[94] In short, general devastation is an unreliable indicator, in and of itself, of the RuAF's ability to hit what they are aiming at.

[90] Alaa Nassar, Bahira al-Zarier, and Justin Schuster, "'Bunker Busters' Destroy Idlib Cave Hospital: 'Bombing a Hospital Is Just Commonplace Now,'" *Syria Direct* (online), April 23, 2017. http://syriadirect.org/news/'bunker-busters'-destroy-idlib-cave-hospital-'bombing-a-hospital-is-just-commonplace-now'; Unattributed, "Syrian and Russian Forces Targeting Hospitals as a Strategy of War," Amnesty International (online), March 3, 2016. https://amnesty.org/en/press-releases/2016/03/syrian-and-russian-forces-targeting-hospitals-as-a-strategy-of-war; Osama Abu Zeid, Noura Hourani, and Justin Schuster, "Airstrikes Take Out 3 North Syrian Hospitals in Less than 24 Hours: 'A Systematic Tactic of Destroying Medical Infrastructure,'" *Syria Direct* (online), April 27, 2017. http://syriadirect.org/news/airstrikes-take-out-3-north-syrian-hospitals-'a-system atic-tactic-of-destroying-medical-infrastructure.' The rate at which medical facilities are targeted by air strike in Syria is tenfold the rate in contemporary air campaigns like the Saudi-led war in Yemen, strongly suggesting that these are not execution errors. Evan Hill and Christiaan Triebert, "12 Hours. 4 Syrian Hospitals Bombed. One Culprit: Russia," *New York Times* (online), October 13, 2019. https://nytimes.com/2019/10/13/world/middleeast/russia-bombing-syrian-hospitals.html
[91] Aaron Lund, "The UN Made a List of Hospitals on Syria. Now They're Being Bombed," *The Century Foundation (online)*, June 13, 2019. https://tcf.org/content/report/un-made-list-hospitals-syria-now-theyre-bombed/?agreed=1
[92] C. Hayes Wong and Christine Yen-Ting Chen, "Ambulances under Siege in Syria," *BMJ Global Health* 3:6 (November 2018): 2, 4–5.
[93] Scales, *Future Warfare*; de Haass, "Russian Airpower," 19.
[94] David Axe, "Unguided Disaster: Russia Is Using Old, Dumb Bombs, Making Syria Air War Even More Brutal," *The Daily Beast* (online), October 2, 2015. http://thedailybeast.com/russia-is-using-old-dumb-bombs-making-syria-air-war-even-more-brutal

## Conclusion

The conclusions drawn here have real implications for Russian war preparation and force planning. Given the vicious logic underlying Russia's counterinsurgency strategy, the RuAF's operational demand for PGMs is likely to be smaller than that of Western air forces. Russian commanders would naturally desire precision weapons to minimize fratricide or improve their probability-of-kill against high-value targets.[95] But absolved of concern about noncombatant casualties and collateral damage, they will likely continue to employ indiscriminate dumb munitions in volume for other purposes. Syria, then, will probably reinforce the impression that Russian military leaders reportedly took from Chechnya that massive aerial bombardment can be used to avert or minimize the costs of urban ground combat in a low-intensity conflict.[96]

By the same token, Russia's success in Syria may dampen the urge to spend scarce capital to close the reconnaissance gap. Expensive, high-fidelity sensors designed to discern individual enemy combatants from busy backgrounds – of the kind that claimed a significant share of US defense spending over the past decade – seem less salient to their chosen strategy and likely promise a poor return on investment. Faced with finite discretionary funding, productive capacity, and innovative attention, Russia may feel no need to divert resources from the acquisition of higher-end anti-access/area-denial (A2AD) weapon systems to prepare for new deployments against insurgent adversaries.[97] The possibility of future similar expeditionary adventures presents few opportunity costs. Moscow seems likely to conclude from Syria that the solution to foreign insurgencies lies in the setting of modest political and military objectives, an unconstrained application of conventional combat power, and selective employment of precision weapons against whatever targets are

---

[95] David Majumdar, "Russia's Half-Baked Air War in Syria," *The National Interest* (online), October 6, 2015. http://nationalinterest.org/blog/the-buzz/russias-half-baked-air-war-syria-14022

[96] Quentin Hodgson, "Is the Bear Learning? An Operational and Tactical Analysis of the Second Chechen War, 1999–2002," *Journal of Strategic Studies* 26:2 (June 2003): 72; de Haass, "Russian Airpower," 8–9, 18.

[97] Indeed, some A2AD systems have proven their value even in the subconventional Syria scenario. Advanced surface-to-air missile systems like the S-300 and S-400, for example, though immaterial to the incumbent-insurgent competition, have been arguably essential to delimiting adverse foreign interference in the conflict. Karen DeYoung, "Russian Air Defense Raises Stakes of US Confrontation in Syria," *Washington Post* (online), October 17, 2016. https://washingtonpost.com/world/national-security/russian-air-defense-raises-stakes-of-us-confrontation-in-syria/2016/10/17/85c89220-948c-11e6-bb29-bf2701dbe0a3_story.html?utm_term=.54d20ed67141

most coercively useful.[98] Counterintuitively from the contemporary American perspective, Syria may then neither discourage Russia from additional counterinsurgency commitments abroad nor spur new capability investments in lower-end warfighting.

In Syria, in addition to attacking insurgents directly, Russia employed air power to amplify civilian suffering, accelerate conflict fatigue, and further disabuse an exhausted populace of any hope that further atrocities would prod outside powers to intervene on its behalf. Because Russia resists ambitious Western-style nation-building projects, it can ignore concerns about the kind of blowback such tactics might incur were it seeking to create or rehabilitate a more inclusive and democratic state. Instead the RuAF enjoyed license from its authoritarian hosts in Damascus to destroy much of the country and disaffect large swathes of its citizens. For its part, Russia's limited and selfish objectives are served nearly as well – and perhaps better – by a dysfunctional and perpetually dependent Syria than they would be by a more stable and self-sufficient country. After all, besides being a much more expensive and risky undertaking, a less crippled Syria might be more inclined to behave in ways at odds with Moscow's druthers.

Russia's involvement in Syria extended beyond the air domain. The Kremlin's ground-force train-and-equip effort was also influential in shifting the momentum to Assad's favor. Moreover, the "fact of" Russia's involvement altered the strategic landscape in ways that had cascading effects on regional actor alignment and conflict dynamics not addressed earlier.[99] The analysis presented here instead measures key elements of Russia's air war execution and operating concepts. Russian air operations exhibited progressive evolution but not a paradigmatic change. The RuAF's performance against the Syrian insurgency was a startling improvement over its past outings, but this turnabout was not due exclusively, or even principally, to its facility with new technology and tactics or training. Rather, the conflict environment in Syria was less

---

[98] Eugene Miakinkov, "The Agency of Force in Asymmetrical Warfare and Counterinsurgency: The Case of Chechnya," *Journal of Strategic Studies* 34:5 (October 2011): 647–80.

[99] J. Hawk, Daniel Deiss, and Edwin Watson, "Russian Military Advisers in Syria," *Southfront* (online), February 27, 2016. https://southfront.org/russia-defense-report-feb -27-2016-russian-military-advisers-in-syria; McDermott, "Russia's Asymmetric Military Power"; Pavel Felgenhauer, "Russian Mission in Syria Beset by Problems Despite Victory in Aleppo," *Eurasia Daily Monitor* 13:197 (December 15, 2016). http s://jamestown.org/program/russian-mission-syria-beset-problems-despite-victory-alepp o; Tim Ripley, "Tipping the Balance – Russia's Intervention in Syria Six Months On," *Jane's Defence Weekly*, March 8, 2016; Faysal Itani, "Aleppo's Fate Is No Surprise," Atlantic Council (online), November 29, 2016. http://atlanticcouncil.org/blogs/syria source/aleppo-s-fate-is-no-surprise

demanding in certain respects relative to previous Russian campaigns, and Russia's more limited objectives and participation allowed it to reduce operational risk by abjuring some of the most hazardous missions. Unfortunately, however, the fact that Moscow's success was highly situation dependent offers only scant consolation to concerned Western observers as Russia may still feel encouraged to reexport the Syria model to other destabilized states. More troubling still, events in Syria confirm worst-case assumptions about Russia's coercive campaign design and to vindicate those who argue the viability of an authoritarian solution to civil conflict.[100]

---

[100] Baev, "Russia's Airpower in the Chechen War," 13–14; Thanassis Cambanis, "Putin's Crushing Strategy for Syria," *Boston Globe* (online), November 20, 2015; Zach Abels, "What's Behind the Effectiveness of Russia's Syria Strategy," *The National Interest* (online), March 3, 2016. http://nationalinterest.org/blog/the-buzz/behind-the-effectiveness-russias-syria-strategy-15394; see also Jacqueline L. Hazelton, "The 'Hearts and Minds' Fallacy: Violence, Coercion, and Success in Counterinsurgency Warfare," *International Security* (Summer 2017). https://belfercenter.org/publication/hearts-and-minds-fallacy-violence-c oercion-and-success-counterinsurgency-warfare; Daniel Byman, "'Death Solves All Problems': The Authoritarian Model of Counterinsurgency," *Journal of Strategic Studies* 39:1 (2016): 62–93.

# 11    Air Power in the Battle of Mosul

*Stephen Renner**

On July 4, 2014, Abu Bakr al-Baghdadi stepped into the pulpit of
Mosul's al-Nuri mosque to deliver the Friday sermon. He called himself
"Caliph Ibrahim" and praised "the mujahidin brothers" upon whom
"Allah has bestowed the grace of victory and conquest."[1] That conquest
culminated with the capture of Mosul, Iraq's second largest city and
home to two million people (see Figure 11.1). Al-Baghdadi's fighters
swept into Mosul in early June 2014 from the western deserts in Toyota
trucks and easily defeated the Iraqi Security Forces, armed with
advanced American weaponry but unready or unwilling to engage in
close combat against the highly motivated Salafist militants. "The city
fell like a plane without an engine," one fleeing resident told a Western
journalist.[2] The Islamic State in Iraq and Syria would hold and fortify
Mosul for the next three years.

Three years later, on June 21, 2017, the Islamic State occupiers blew up
the al-Nuri mosque as Iraqi forces pressed on all sides. Of the famous
minaret, leaning east since at least the fourteenth century, only the pedi-
ment remained. The mosque's dome and gates stood intact, but the rest of
the complex was indistinguishable from the surrounding rubble. The
destruction was deeply symbolic. Iraqi Prime Minister Haider al-Abadi
called it the Islamic State's "formal declaration of defeat."[3] The Islamic
State's Amaq press agency countered with its own release: "American
warplane destroys the Great Mosque of al-Nuri and al-Hadba Minaret in

---

* The views expressed by the author do not reflect those of the US government, the
Department of Defense, or any of its organizations.
[1] "Abu Bakr Al-Baghdadi Appears in Video, Delivers Sermon in Mosul," Site Intel Group,
July 5, 2014. https://news.siteintelgroup.com/Jihadist-News/abu-bakr-al-baghdadi-appe
ars-in-video-delivers-sermon-in-mosul.html
[2] Martin Chulov, "Isis Insurgents Seize Control of Iraqi City of Mosul," *The Guardian*,
June 10, 2014. www.theguardian.com/world/2014/jun/10/iraq-sunni-insurgents-islamic-
militants-seize-control-mosul
[3] Samuel Osborne, "Isis Blowing Up Grand al-Nuri Mosque 'A Declaration of Defeat,' says
Iraqi PM," *The Independent*, July 22, 2017. www.independent.co.uk/news/world/middle-
east/isis-defeat-grand-al-nuri-mosque-mosul-blown-up-iraqi-prime-minister-haider-al-a
badi-islamic-state-a7802056.html

255

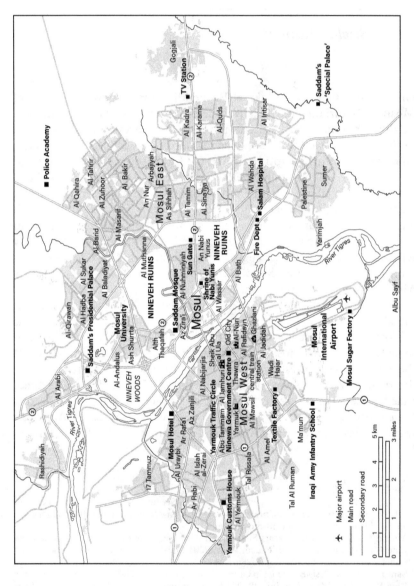

Figure 11.1  Map of Mosul, Iraq

#Mosul."[4] Coalition reconnaissance video that showed the simultaneous detonation of explosive charges placed directly on the minaret refuted this particular claim of destruction from the air. Amaq's propagandists might, however, be excused for thinking that audiences could find their attribution plausible. American-led air power had devastated the ancient city.

Photographs of Mosul after the battle bring to mind pictures of other cities ravaged in war. The empty lots, wrecked buildings, and debris-filled streets resemble Manila, Caen, Budapest, Sarajevo, and Grozny. Based solely on the photographic evidence one could conclude that the use of air power in the Battle of Mosul had been indiscriminate, inaccurate, and ineffective. Such a comparison, although plausible on the level of visual analogy, would be deeply misleading. The coalition air campaign to defeat the Islamic State in Mosul was the most tightly controlled, specifically targeted, and precise in history. It permitted Iraqi ground forces to reclaim the city they had abandoned three years earlier and repudiated the most dire predictions about the utility of air power in dense urban areas.

The campaign to liberate Mosul from ISIS may be the purest expression yet of twenty-first-century warfare. It was highly politicized, ideologically charged, fought in a fractured state among civilians by a coalition of the willing, with great power involvement on all sides, and exposed to the world on social media. The air war, too, represented an intensification of operational trends over the past two decades: enhanced command and control measures, universal employment of precision munitions, increased intelligence, surveillance, and reconnaissance capabilities, ubiquity of remotely piloted aircraft, and decreased tolerance for civilian casualties. None of these factors was new in 2016, but each of them was manifested over Mosul to a degree not previously seen.

## The Roots and Rise of the Islamic State in Iraq and Syria

The Islamic State in Iraq and Syria (ISIS) grew out of the Al-Qaeda (AQ) franchise in Iraq led by Abu Musab al-Zarqawi.[5] Osama bin Laden and Ayman Zawahiri, cofounders of AQ, declined to admit Zarqawi to the core group in 1999 because they disagreed with his militancy toward Shia Islam, but they did agree to support his efforts to establish a Mesopotamian jihadist group, Jamaat al-Tawhid wal-Jihad (JTJ), and

[4] Screenshot from Amaq news agency release June 21, 2017. www.themantle.com/international-affairs/battle-narratives
[5] The Islamic State is also known as ISIS (the Islamic State in Iraq and al-Sham), ISIL (the Islamic State in Iraq and the Levant), and Daish/Da'esh (al-Dawla al-Islamiya fi al-Iraq wa al-Sham).

allowed him to build a training camp in western Afghanistan.[6] JTJ thrived in the disorganized Sunni resistance that sprung up in the year following the US-led invasion. Zarqawi soon became known for his brutality; he personally beheaded hostages and targeted religious Shias as well as US forces.[7]

Bin Laden's desire to enhance Al-Qaeda's influence over the Sunni insurgency in Iraq proved stronger than his antipathy toward Zarqawi's slaughter of Shias, and in October 2004 the two jihadists agreed that JTJ would become an affiliate known as Al-Qaeda in Iraq (AQI). AQI continued to enforce sharia law ruthlessly, an approach Zawahiri considered unnecessarily divisive, and both he and bin Laden counseled against excessively violent suppression of fellow Muslims. Zarqawi ignored their injunctions, preferring instead to build his own parallel jihadist movement. This movement survived Zarqawi's death in June 2006 from a US air strike and proclaimed its existence as the Islamic State of Iraq (ISI) on October 15, 2006. Zarqawi's successor as leader of AQI, Abu Ayyub al-Masri, pledged his loyalty to ISI's leader, Abu Omar al-Baghdadi.[8]

The unrelenting violence and pitiless authoritarianism in areas under ISI dominance alienated many of the sheikhs in the Anbar region, leading them to take up American arms against the jihadis. As a result of the Anbar Awakening and the Bush administration's 2007 surge of US forces, ISI was "routed from most of Iraq ... [and] withdrew into a limited terrorist campaign in northern Iraq."[9] ISI's flight led to a steady decline in the level of violence in Iraq, and the deaths of both al-Masri and Omar al-Baghdadi in a joint US-Iraqi raid in April 2010 gave hope that the seven-year wave of terror had truly ended.[10]

The Islamic State named its new leader the next month. Ibrahim Awad al-Badari, an Islamic scholar before the 2003 invasion, became a low-level insurgent sometime after and was imprisoned by US forces in 2004. He joined the military council of ISI after his release and rose to become

---

[6] William McCants, *The ISIS Apocalypse: The History, Strategy, and Doomsday Vision of the Islamic State* (New York: St Martin's Press, 2015), 7–9.

[7] Aaron Zelin, "The War between ISIS and al-Qaeda for Supremacy of the Global Jihadist Movement," Washington Institute for Near East Policy, June 2014. www.washingtonin stitute.org/uploads/Documents/pubs/ResearchNote_20_Zelin.pdf

[8] Zelin, "The War between ISIS and al-Qaeda."

[9] Patrick Johnston et al., *Foundations of the Islamic State: Management, Money, and Terror in Iraq, 2005–2010* (Santa Monica: RAND Corporation, 2016), 2.

[10] Waleed Ibrahim, "Al Qaeda's Two Top Iraq Leaders Killed in Raid," *Reuters*, April 19, 2010. https://reuters.com/article/us-iraq-violence-alqaeda/al-qaedas-two-top-iraq-lead ers-killed-in-raid-idUSTRE63I3CL20100419; declining violence: *The Economist*, "Iraq: Still Bloody," January 5, 2013. www.economist.com/middle-east-and-africa/201 3/01/05/still-bloody

a close advisor to Omar al-Baghdadi. Perhaps in homage to his predecessor, he took the nom de guerre Abu Bakr al-Baghdadi. The Islamic State's strategy changed little with the succession. Still under intense pressure from US and Iraqi security forces, Abu Bakr al-Baghdadi's ISI relied on suicide bombers wearing vests or driving explosive-laden cars (also known as vehicle-borne improvised explosive devices, or VBIEDs) to keep the central government off balance and to stoke the fires of sectarianism. The most spectacular bombings were coordinated attacks that began in Mosul on August 15, 2011, in which 64 civilians were killed and 287 wounded.[11] At nearly the same moment, al-Baghdadi decided ISI should become involved in the emerging Syrian civil war.

Al-Baghdadi appointed Abu Muhammed al-Jawlani, an experienced AQI jihadi, to lead the ISI cell later known as the Jabhat al-Nusra (JN). This faction proved to be "the most effective rebel fighting force in Syria, something which brought it to the forefront of the war."[12] JN gained and maintained control of substantial areas in northern Syria only after it learned to moderate its violence and cooperate with other insurgent groups. Al-Baghdadi tried to capitalize on JN's success without compromising ISI's insistence on its own supremacy in governance of occupied towns.[13] In April 2013, he announced via audio message that ISI and JN had merged into a group called the Islamic State in Iraq and Syria.[14]

The Syrian civil war provided al-Baghdadi with the opportunity to seize, hold, and govern territory at the expense of the weakened government in Damascus. This opportunity had been denied him in Iraq in large part because of US troops, whose presence served to not only strengthen and mentor the Iraqi Security Forces, but also as a check on excessive sectarianism within the Iraqi government. The withdrawal of American forces in December 2011 offered ISIS an opening: It "removed a counterweight to Iranian influence, halted professionalization of the Iraqi Army, and reduced American visibility into those forces as they were progressively weakened by the Shia dominated regime in Baghdad."[15]

---

[11] US State Department, "Terrorist Designation of Ibrahim Awwad Ibrahim Ali al-Badri," Media Note, October 4, 2011. The designation had al-Baghdadi's birth name correct but had not yet correlated al-Badri/AQI with al-Baghdadi/ISI. https://2009-2017.state.gov/r/pa/prs/ps/2011/10/174971.htm

[12] Erin Marie Saltman and Charlie Winter, *Islamic State: The Changing Face of Modern Jihadism* (Quilliam Foundation, 2014), 30.

[13] McCants, *ISIS Apocalypse*, 85.

[14] "Iraqi al-Qaeda and Syrian Group 'Merge,'" *Al Jazeera*, April 9, 2013. www.aljazeera.com/news/middleeast/2013/04/201349194856244589.html

[15] Seth Jones et al., *Rolling Back the Islamic State* (Santa Monica: RAND Corporation, 2017), xi.

In July 2012 ISI launched a year-long campaign of VBIED attacks and jailbreaks. The attacks climaxed with the infamous Abu Ghraib prison break that freed 500, many of whom were AQI veterans. In addition to providing ISI with an injection of hardened fighters, the Abu Ghraib attack, which lasted for several hours and cost the ISF 68 fatalities, demonstrated the capability of the jihadis to best the ISF in a localized conventional engagement. As for the VBIED operations, the large number of vehicles used in the clustered attacks suggested centralized manufacture, and the sophisticated coordination demonstrated meticulous planning and close control.[16] The campaign swelled ISI's ranks, created chaos in the cities, and undermined the Maliki government. Perhaps most important was the psychological effect on the Sunnis. One careful analyst observed at the time that the Sunnis were "teetering on the edge of an uprising."[17]

In April 2013, the murder of a Sunni soldier in Hawija led to a government raid and the deaths of forty-four protestors.[18] Less bloody but more consequential was a December incident in Ramadi, Anbar's provincial capital. A firefight broke out in a Sunni dissident tent city that left thirteen dead, and in response, forty Sunni members of parliament submitted their resignations.[19] The army withdrew in confusion, and ISIS capitalized on the temporary power vacuum and spike in anti-government sentiment by launching sustained attacks on both Ramadi and Fallujah. A combination of tribal and government troops reclaimed Ramadi, but by January 4, 2014, ISIS fighters controlled Fallujah.[20]

The Islamic State's January offensive ushered in a new wave of terror in Baghdad and its surrounding provinces. More than a thousand civilians died that month across the country; the grim count ticked up steadily to 2,500 by June.[21] Through the spring, ISIS attacked the ISF in Anbar, ambushing isolated outposts and military columns and staging raids into towns in the Euphrates valley, before withdrawing to avoid suffering

[16] Jessica Lewis, *Al-Qaeda in Iraq Resurgent: The Breaking the Walls Campaign, Part I* (Washington, DC: Institute for the Study of War, 2013), 20. http://understandingwar.org/sites/default/files/AQI-Resurgent-10Sept_0.pdf

[17] Ibid., 33.

[18] Kirk Sowell, "Maliki's Anbar Blunder," *Foreign Policy*, January 15, 2014. https://foreignpolicy.com/2014/01/15/malikis-anbar-blunder

[19] Kamal Namaa, "Fighting Erupts as Iraq Police Break Up Sunni Protest Camp," *Reuters*, December 30, 2013. www.reuters.com/article/us-iraq-violence-idUSBRE9BT0620 13120

[20] "Iraq Government Loses Control of Fallujah," *Al Jazeera*, January 4, 2014. www.aljazeera.com/news/middleeast/2014/01/iraq-government-loses-control-fallujah-20141414625597514.html

[21] "Iraq 2014: Civilian Deaths Almost Doubling Year on Year," Iraq Body Count, January 1, 2015. www.iraqbodycount.org/analysis/numbers/2014

significant casualties. Despite early losses, the ISF launched its own limited counteroffensive in March, and by May had captured the villages surrounding Fallujah and established control of the roads going into the city.[22] But ISIS, strengthened by the consolidation of its position in Syria and claiming the city of Raqqa as its capital, struck back in June. Attacking first in Samarra, jihadis occupied the university and police stations before being driven out. On June 6, they turned toward Mosul, and after only three days captured the city, including former US military installations and a prison from which they released 3,000 prisoners.[23] Within days, ISIS captured Hawija, Baiji, and Tikrit. At an Iraqi military academy outside Tikrit, the Islamists executed more than 1,500 ISF recruits and staff.[24]

When ISIS reached its high-water mark in the fall of 2014, it controlled more than 40,000 square miles and 10 million people, an area and population slightly larger than Virginia.[25]

## The United States Responds

By August 2014, the United States no longer expected that the Iraqi government could stop ISIS. The jihadis were poised to attack the Kurdish capital of Erbil, where the United States had a substantial diplomatic and commercial presence. ISIS also threatened to commit genocide against the Yazidis, an ethnic minority isolated in the Sinjar Mountains. The Obama administration had been "deeply concerned about the events that have transpired in Mosul," but its "strong, coordinated response to push back this aggression" had not included direct military engagement.[26] On the evening of August 7, the president announced a change in his policy of nonintervention: "Today I authorized two operations in Iraq: targeted air strikes to protect our American personnel, and a humanitarian effort to help save thousands of Iraqi civilians who are trapped on a mountain without food and water and facing almost certain

[22] Patrick Martin, "Iraq Situation Report, May 11–24, 2014," Institute for the Study of War. www.understandingwar.org/backgrounder/iraq-situation-report-may-11–24–2016
[23] Jessica Lewis, "The Islamic State of Iraq and al-Sham Captures Mosul and Advances toward Baghdad," Institute for the Study of War, June 11, 2014. www.understanding war.org/backgrounder/islamic-state-iraq-and-al-sham-captures-mosul-and-advances-to ward-baghdad
[24] "Iraq to Hang 27 for IS Camp Speicher Massacre," BBC News, August 8, 2017. www .bbc.com/news/world-middle-east-40866081
[25] ISIS extent: Jones et al., Rolling Back the Islamic State, 20; US comparison: www.cen sus.gov
[26] US State Department spokesman Jen Psaki, quoted in Suadad Al-Salhy and Tim Arango, "Sunni Militants Drive Iraqi Army out of Mosul," New York Times, June 10, 2014. www .nytimes.com/2014/06/11/world/middleeast/militants-in-mosul.html

death." He acknowledged the contradiction with his earlier stance regarding ISIS, but, he said, "when the lives of American citizens are at risk, we will take action ... And when many thousands of innocent civilians are faced with the danger of being wiped out, and we have the capacity to do something about it, we will take action."[27] Subsequently US Air Force C-17s and C-130s parachuted food, water, and medical supplies to the besieged Yazidis on Mount Sinjar, and US Navy F/A-18s dropped 500-pound laser-guided bombs (GBU-12s) on ISIS artillery positions and support convoys near Erbil.[28] After three days, Kurdish Peshmerga troops counterattacked ISIS and secured towns thirty miles southwest of Erbil. Thousands of Yazidis also escaped the Islamists owing to the airdrops and four air strikes in the Sinjar area. These small victories notwithstanding, a spokesman for the Joint Chiefs reminded journalists of the administration's line: "This is a focused effort, not a wider air campaign."[29] And so it remained for several months.

The next crisis that demanded US attention was the siege of Kobani, a Kurdish town on the Syrian-Turkish border. ISIS had gathered its forces in the area in mid-September, and within three weeks Kobani's capture appeared possible. US aircraft began striking ISIS targets in the area even as the Department of Defense (DoD) spokesman tried to manage press expectations about success. "This is going to be a long struggle. This group will adapt, and we're going to have to adapt right along with them. And air strikes alone, you're just not going to bomb them away. It's not going to happen like that."[30] Rear Admiral John Kirby was certainly correct on the last point. Even though Kurdish troops cleared the city on January 27, 2015, ISIS forces in the Kobani area were regular targets for air strikes until early May.[31]

[27] "Statement by the President," August 7, 2014. https://obamawhitehouse.archives.gov/the-press-office/2014/08/07/statement-president
[28] US Department of Defense News Releases NR-419–14, NR-420–14, and NR-421–14, August 8, 2014. https://dod.defense.gov/News/Releases/Year/2014/Month/8/?Page=2
[29] Rod Nordland and Helene Cooper, "Capitalizing on US Bombing, Kurds Retake Iraqi Towns," *New York Times*, August 10, 2014. www.nytimes.com/2014/08/11/world/middleeast/iraq.html
[30] "Department of Defense Press Briefing by Rear Adm. Kirby in the Pentagon Briefing Room," September 30, 2014. https://dod.defense.gov/News/Transcripts/Transcript-View/Article/606936/department-of-defense-press-briefing-by-rear-adm-kirby-in-the-pentagon-briefing
[31] Kobani cleared: "US General Says Syrian Town of Kobani Taken from Islamic State," *Reuters*, January 31, 2015. https://uk.reuters.com/article/uk-mideast-crisis-syria-kobani/u-s-general-says-syrian-town-of-kobani-taken-from-islamic-state-idUKKBN0L40U820150131?rpc=401; ISIS targeted: Operation Inherent Resolve headquarters released daily strike summaries from January 1, 2015. Not until May 4, 2015, was there more than a single day with no air strikes in the Kobani area. www.inherentresolve.mil/Media-Library/Strike-Releases

Haider al-Abadi, who after a contentious political struggle replaced Nouri al-Maliki as Iraq's prime minister in September 2014, directed the ISF to conduct a broad offensive in the summer of 2015 to reassert government control of Anbar. Sixteen months after ISIS's first failed attempt to seize Ramadi, the jihadis succeeded in May 2015 by launching a wave of suicide attacks under the cover of a sandstorm that hindered US air operations. Iraqi forces retreated under the onslaught of VBIEDs, allowing ISIS to capture the provincial capital and more than 100 US-provided vehicles, including a half-dozen tanks.[32] Government troops set out to retake Ramadi on July 13 but were unable to breach the ISIS defenses despite twenty-nine air strikes in support.[33] In December, the Iraqi army began a well-provisioned, three-axis, armor-supported advance into Ramadi and by the end of the year Prime Minister al-Abadi raised the Iraqi flag over the city.[34]

After a period to rest and rebuild, the ISF planned to recapture Fallujah. Elements of five divisions of the Iraqi army, augmented by the elite US special forces–trained Counter Terrorism Service (CTS), 20,000 members of the Federal Police (FEDPOL), and substantial units of the Shiite militia known as the Popular Mobilization Forces (PMF), took up positions around the city in May 2016.[35] Prime Minister al-Abadi announced the beginning of "Operation Breaking Terrorism" in a television address on May 23, but the ISF did not immediately enter the city, preferring instead to degrade ISIS strength through air and artillery strikes.[36] When the ISF did move into the city, it evicted ISIS from Fallujah in just one month.

For the remainder of the summer, the ISF focused on securing the approaches to Mosul, capturing two crucial airfields around Qayyarah and reaching the western bank of the Tigris in mid-July. Qayyarah itself fell to the ISF in late August, and the stage was set for the Battle of Mosul.[37]

[32] Richard Sisk, "ISIS Captures Hundreds of US Vehicles and Tanks in Ramadi from Iraqis," Military.com, May 20, 2015. https://military.com/daily-news/2015/05/20/isis-captures-hundreds-of-us-vehicles-and-tanks-in-ramadi-from-i.html

[33] OIR Strike Release, July 13, 2015. www.inherentresolve.mil/Portals/14/Documents/Strike%20Releases/2015/07July/20150713%20Strike%20Release%20final.pdf?ver=2017-01-13-131142-967

[34] Ahmed Rasheed and Stephen Kalin, "Iraq's Abadi Plants Flag in Ramadi to Mark Islamic State Defeat," Reuters, December 29, 2015. www.reuters.com/article/us-mideast-crisis-iraq-ramadi-idUSKBN0UC0UP20151229

[35] Patrick Martin, "The Campaign for Fallujah: May 26, 2016," Institute for the Study of War. www.understandingwar.org/backgrounder/campaign-fallujah-may-26–2016

[36] Falih Hassan and Tim Arango, "Iraqi Forces Try to Retake Falluja from ISIS," New York Times, May 23, 2016. www.nytimes.com/2016/05/24/world/middleeast/iraq-falluja-isis.html

[37] Emily Anagnostos, "Iraq Control of Terrain: July 14, 2016" and "Iraq Control of Terrain: August 25, 2016." www.understandingwar.org/backgrounder/iraq-control-terrain-july-14–2016 and www.understandingwar.org/backgrounder/iraq-control-terrain-map-august-25–2016

### The Fight for Mosul

That battle was officially joined on October 16, 2016. In an operation called Eagle Strike by the international coalition and We Are Coming, Nineveh, by Prime Minister al-Abadi, approximately 100,000 Iraqi troops faced an ISIS force estimated at 5,000 fighters. The Iraqi forces included 40,000 Peshmerga, which had been critical in stopping the ISIS advance in northern Iraq and isolating Mosul from the northern and eastern approaches. Owing to an agreement between the national and regional governments in Baghdad and Erbil, however, the Peshmerga would not be used in combat in the city itself. Of the remaining 60,000 troops, 15,000 were PMF militia (largely confined to operations in the desert southwest of Mosul), and 500 were US advisors, logisticians, and JTACs (joint terminal attack controllers).[38] The balance were soldiers of regular Iraqi army formations – primarily the 1st, 9th, 15th, and 16th Divisions – paramilitary policemen of the FEDPOL, or CTS operators. Opposing the ISF were 5,000 ISIS fighters backed by twice that many support personnel. Well armed, the ISIS force had also "constructed an elaborate series of defensive works inside the city, fortifying buildings, blocking avenues of approach, creating obstacles, and constructing underground shelters and tunnels."[39]

The Iraqi plan reflected the lessons learned in the battles of Ramadi and Fallujah as well as the political realities of the fractured ISF. Great effort was given to mustering sufficient logistical support. Each major component of the ISF would advance on its own axis, which minimized the requirement for close coordination among ground units. In the first weeks of the campaign, movement was confined to securing the Tigris's southern banks and Mosul's eastern hemisphere. As in the earlier urban fighting, the Counter Terrorism Service proved to be the most effective ISF formation. It was CTS that breached the city on November 1, and by mid-December it had captured twenty neighborhoods in northeastern

---

[38] Operation We Are Coming: Charlie Winter, "How the Islamic State Is Spinning the Mosul Battle," *Atlantic*, October 20, 2016. www.theatlantic.com/international/archive/2016/10/isis-mosul-propaganda-iraq-kurds-peshmerga/504854; ISF and ISIS forces: Numbers for ISF vary from 94,000 to 108,500; ISIS estimates ranged from 3,000 to 10,000. I have taken the round middle ground in both cases. See Tim Hume, "Battle for Mosul: How ISIS Is Fighting to Keep Its Iraqi Stronghold," CNN, October 25, 2016. www.cnn.com/2016/10/24/middleeast/iraq-mosul-isis-tactics; US Army Mosul Study Group, *What the Battle for Mosul Teaches the Force*, Study No 17-24U, September 2017, 6. www.armyupress.army.mil/Portals/7/Primer-on-Urban-Operation/Documents/Mosul-Public-Release1.pdf; Thomas D. Arnold and Nicolas Fiore, "Five Operational Lessons from the Battle for Mosul," *Military Review*, January–February 2019. https://armyupress.army.mil/Journals/Military-Review/English-Edition-Archives/Jan-Feb-2019/Arnold-Mosul

[39] Mosul Study Group, *What the Battle for Mosul Teaches*, 5.

Mosul while the Iraqi army units struggled on their southeast attack axis.[40]

That struggle was in part the result of a brutal fight around the Al Salam hospital in early December. Armor from the 9th Division had made a dash for the Tigris, reaching the hospital located 1,200 meters from the river, on the afternoon of December 6. Having captured their object-ive with relative ease, the company's leaders disregarded basic security tasks. They did not disperse their vehicles, failed to clear adjacent build-ings, and did not post pickets or obstacles on access roads. In the evening, ISIS fighters initiated a fierce counterattack from tunnels and the sur-rounding residential areas. The assault began with a suicide car bomb that managed to drive into the midst of the parked armor, one of 15 VBIEDs detonated near the hospital in the ensuing 24 hours. The first blast disabled several of the tanks and infantry fighting vehicles and blocked the exit so ISIS could easily destroy those that remained.[41] Celebratory ISIS videos released after the fighting clearly show more than a dozen wrecked or burned BMP-1s and HMMWVs.[42] Coalition air strikes through the night, including very close support from an AC-130, kept most of the 100 ISF soldiers alive, although few escaped unwounded and more than 20 Iraqi soldiers died in the action.[43] The battle of Al Salam hospital was a clarifying event for the ISF in Mosul, forcing Iraqi generals to confront two basic facts: ISIS fighters were ruthless, clever, and deter-mined to make the ISF pay dearly for every city block; and air power was essential for maneuvering in the dense urban terrain. The hospital remained in ISIS hands for another month, finally falling to the ISF on January 10, 2017, only two weeks before the end of combat operations in east Mosul. Twenty-five aerial attacks on the hospital complex eased the

[40] Emily Anagnostos, "Iraq Control of Terrain: December 15, 2016," Institute for the Study of War. www.understandingwar.org/backgrounder/iraq-control-terrain-decem ber-15-2016

[41] Ahmed Rasheed, Saif Hameed, and Isabel Coles, "Iraqi Troops Pull Out from Mosul Hospital after Fierce Battle," *Reuters*, December 7, 2016. https://reuters.com/article/us-mideast-crisis-iraq/iraqi-troops-pull-out-from-mosul-hospital-after-fierce-battle-idUSK BN13X1EI; "Daesh Launches Overnight Attack against Iraqi Troops in Mosul," *Gulf News*, December 7, 2016. https://gulfnews.com/world/mena/daesh-launches-overnight-attack-against-iraqi-troops-in-mosul-1.1941577; "Fierce Battles Leave Hospital in Iraqi City of Mosul Gutted," *Associated Press*, January 11, 2017. https://foxnews.com/world/fierce-battles-leave-hospital-in-iraqi-city-of-mosul-gutted

[42] "Battle for Mosul's Hospital Was a Bloodbath. Here's the Footage." https://funker530 .com/mosul-hospital

[43] Susannah George, "A Lethal Mistake Leads to a Harrowing Ambush in Iraq's Mosul," *Associated Press*, December 8, 2016. https://bostonglobe.com/news/world/2016/12/08/le thal-mistake-leads-harrowing-ambush-iraq-mosul/4UeHrvZdRSct0ITQIJ4PVK/story .html

task: "Honestly, the battle was 75 percent fought from the air," said an Iraqi sergeant major.[44]

That pattern continued when the fight moved across the Tigris in spring 2017. After a month of rest and reconstitution during which air and artillery strikes focused on interdicting ISIS supply routes and demolishing prepared defensive positions, the ISF advanced on west Mosul. The Iraqis stepped off on the morning of February 23, making substantial gains in the south, as ISIS ceded the area around Mosul airport.[45] Two weeks into the campaign, CTS seized the Ghazlani military base west of the airport, and FEDPOL reached the government center on the edge of the Old City. The police divisions were unwilling to enter the ancient streets without mutual support and so held their line for two months. CTS, however, continued to clear city blocks north, moving clockwise through the industrial areas and suburbs outside the Old City. The regular formations, 9th and 15th Divisions, advanced sluggishly from the west along Highway 1 and through the Yarmuk power plant.[46] By the end of April, the 15th Division held the ground that CTS had captured up to the defunct rail line that forms a distinct curve around the Thawra neighborhood. Meanwhile, the 16th Division crossed the Tigris north of the city, and the 9th finally blocked Highway 1 and was advancing southwest. At the beginning of Operation Eagle Strike, ISIS controlled almost 100 square miles around Mosul; on May 1, 2017, that area had been reduced to 10 square miles. Ten days later, when the 16th Division cleared the suburban sprawl north of the city in the Tigris bend, ISIS territory was cut in half. The final month of the battle of Mosul was waged over an area just twice the size of New York City's Central Park.

The ferocity of the fighting increased as ISIS's control zone diminished. The jihadis inflicted nearly half of all ISF casualties after government forces had closed within 1 kilometer of the al-Nuri mosque.[47] As in east Mosul, a hospital figured heavily in the last battles – this time it was the al-Jamhuri medical center, a seventy-five-acre complex on the right bank of the Tigris where one of the two pockets of ISIS resistance remained. ISIS established military headquarters at the medical complex, which featured an extensive tunnel system connecting the various buildings. Isolated

[44] "Fierce Battles Leave Hospital in Iraqi City of Mosul Gutted," *Associated Press*, January 11, 2017.
[45] Emily Anagnostos, "Mosul City Campaign: February 22–24, 2017," Institute for the Study of War. www.understandingwar.org/sites/default/files/Mosul%20City%20Camp aign%20FEB22-24%20UPDATE%20reduced.pdf
[46] Emily Anagnostos, "Mosul City Campaign: March 9–16, 2017," Institute for the Study of War. www.understandingwar.org/sites/default/files/Mosul%20City%20Campaign% 20March%209–16%20reduced.pdf
[47] Arnold and Fiore, "Five Operational Lessons."

there, ISIS resorted to shooting fleeing civilians from the hospital's heights and sending female suicide bombers into the advancing ISF formations.[48]

## Air Operations

The air operation over Mosul was part of a joint, combined arms campaign to "defeat ISIS as a military force on the battlefield in Iraq and Syria . . . destroy their equipment, and kill their fighters."[49] The objective echoed President Obama's language, which itself demonstrated a recognition that ISIS's ideological moorings left them impervious to coercion. After the first month of US air strikes, Obama gave a prime-time address to describe his plan "to degrade and ultimately destroy" ISIS. Notably absent were any references to sanctions, messaging, or restrictions. Instead, he highlighted the jihadis' brutality and counseled patience because "it will take time to eradicate a cancer like ISIL."[50] Although observers frustrated by the desultory pace of Operation Inherent Resolve might dispute the characterization, the operation, focused on attrition of the enemy's capability, was a brute force campaign. And it was conducted as a combined arms team within a coalition. If measured by the number of ISIS fighters killed and the amount of equipment destroyed, the assessment of Iraqi sergeant major Hassan Ali Jalil cited earlier – that 75 percent of the battle was fought from the air – is undoubtedly correct. But ISIS's claim to legitimacy was rooted in its establishment of a physical state, and by 2014 to defeat that claim meant that a ground force would have to reoccupy and readminister areas captured by the jihadis. Air power, therefore, was the primary killing mechanism, but on its own it was insufficient to accomplish the coalition's mission.

### Command and Control

The US Central Command (CENTCOM) established Combined Joint Task Force Operation Inherent Resolve in October 2014 to serve as the

---

[48] Civilians: "Mosul Battle: IS Kills 230 Fleeing Civilians, Says UN," *BBC*, June 8, 2017. www.bbc.com/news/world-middle-east-40200008; suicide bombers: Stephen Kalin, "Iraqi Prime Minister Congratulates Armed Forces for Mosul 'Victory,'" *Reuters*, July 9, 2017. www.reuters.com/article/us-mideast-crisis-iraq/iraqi-prime-minister-con gratulates-armed-forces-for-mosul-victory-idUSKBN19U0CT

[49] CJTF-OIR Fact Sheet. www.inherentresolve.mil/Portals/14/Documents/Mission/2017 0717-%20Updated%20Mission%20Statement%20Fact%20Sheet.pdf?ver=2017-07-1 7-093803-770

[50] Statement by the president on ISIL, September 10, 2104. https://obamawhitehouse.arc hives.gov/the-press-office/2014/09/10/statement-president-isil-1

headquarters for all coalition operations against ISIS. From August 2016, and for the entirety of the Battle of Mosul, CJTF-OIR was led by the commander of the XVIII Airborne Corps, Lieutenant General Stephen Townsend. Responsibility for coalition operations in Iraq was delegated to rotating divisional headquarters, which would staff the Combined Joint Forces Land Component Command (CJFLCC). The 1st Infantry Division with Major General Joseph Martin in command succeeded the 101st Airborne Division in November 2016 as Headquarters CJFLCC-OIR.[51]

From its inception airmen and analysts opposed this ground-centric command arrangement. They felt that a great opportunity had been lost to attack ISIS's sources of strength from the air while the ISF was still reeling from defeat.[52] It is certain that ISIS stole the march on the entire world by capturing Fallujah, Mosul, Hawija, Tikrit, and Baiji in the summer of 2014 and that the Iraqi forces were unable to mount a counteroffensive for nearly a year. It is less clear, given the Obama administration's determination to avoid civilian casualties, its insistence on working through indigenous ground forces, and the US air component's "atrophied target-development muscles," that placing an Air Force lieutenant general at the head of CJTF-OIR in 2014 would have yielded dramatically different results.[53]

By the time that Operation Eagle Strike commenced in October 2016, the political-military context had evolved. Widespread coverage of ISIS atrocities along with a broader international coalition eroded some of the Obama administration's tentativeness in prosecuting the war. And in the Pentagon there had been considerable turnover in personnel, with the new team generally exhibiting a more hawkish approach to OIR. Most notable was the change in the secretary of defense, as Ash Carter, who had opposed the 2011 withdrawal of US forces from Iraq, replaced Chuck Hagel as the secretary of defense. Carter described his sense, after meeting with CENTCOM leaders in early 2015, that the United States "lacked a comprehensive, achievable plan for success."[54]

One way to trace the trend toward aggressive action is to examine the gradual loosening of the aerial rules of engagement (ROE) and expansion of target engagement authority (TEA). For more than a year after

---

[51] Combined Joint Task Force Inherent Resolve History. www.inherentresolve.mil/Portals/ 14/Documents/Mission/HISTORY_17OCT2014-JUL2017.pdf?ver=2017-07-22-095 806-793

[52] For a full accounting of this frustration, see Benjamin Lambeth, *America's Air War Against ISIS* (Annapolis, MD: Naval Institute Press, March 2021).

[53] Lambeth, *America's Air War against ISIS*.

[54] Ash Carter, *A Lasting Defeat: The Campaign to Destroy ISIS*, Belfer Center Special Report, 2017. www.belfercenter.org/LastingDefeat

commencing air strikes against ISIS in August 2014, authority to approve strikes that could cause civilian casualties had been held at CENTCOM headquarters in Tampa. In September 2015 that authority was delegated to the CJTF-OIR commander, Lieutenant General Sean MacFarland. MacFarland pushed TEA on to his subordinate brigadier generals who ran the strike cells in the Combined Joint Operation Centers in Baghdad and Erbil (CJOC-B and -E). After XVIII Corps relieved III Corps in August 2016, Lieutenant General Townsend further delegated TEA to colonels serving in the CJOCs.[55] These incremental changes in the rules governing target engagement authority increased the number of senior officers who could approve strikes, thereby ensuring a twenty-four-hour TEA presence in the CJOCs and putting an end to the "don't wake the general" strike delays that occurred earlier in OIR.[56] In late December 2016, following the intense urban combat in east Mosul and the al-Salam hospital debacle, Townsend extended TEA for defensive purposes to the lieutenant colonel battalion commanders serving as advisors to ISF generals.[57]

Target engagement authority remained constrained, however, by Pentagon rules governing a "sliding scale of allowable civilian casualties, based on the value of the target and the location."[58] That scale is known as the "noncombatant casualty cut-off value," or NCV. The NCV for particular operations and locations is classified but according to 2016 reporting was set at ten for OIR.[59] Calculating the NCV for a particular strike request was a complicated task that involved weapons experts, targeting technicians, and operational lawyers. These specialties, along with intelligence analysts and JTACs, formed the core of the CJOC strike cells. Each member had a particular role to play, from recommending

[55] Personal experience. Author served from January to July 2017 in CJOC-E as deputy Joint Air Component Coordinating Element with target engagement authority.
[56] Lambeth, *America's Air War against ISIS.*
[57] Susannah George and Balint Szlanko, "US Changes Rules of Engagement for Mosul Fight in Iraq," *Associated Press*, February 24, 2017. www.military.com/daily-news/2017/02/24/us-changes-rules-engagement-mosul-fight-iraq.html; Maj Gen Joseph Martin, "Commander's Perspective: CJFLCC in Iraq," Center for Army Lessons Learned, October 2017. https://usacac.army.mil/sites/default/files/publications/17567.pdf
[58] Tom Vanden Brook, "New Rules Allow More Civilian Casualties in Air War against ISIS," *Military Times*, April 19, 2016. www.militarytimes.com/flashpoints/2016/04/19/new-rules-allow-more-civilian-casualties-in-air-war-against-isis
[59] Nick McDonell, "Civilian Casualties Are Not Inevitable. The Military Sets an Acceptable Number in Advance," *Los Angeles Times*, March 31, 2017. www.latimes.com/opinion/op-ed/la-oe-mcdonell-civilian-casualties-ncv-20170331-story.html; Lolita C. Baldor, "New War Rules Emphasize Need to Avoid Civilian Casualties," *Associated Press*, December 13, 2016. www.militarytimes.com/news/your-military/2016/12/14/new-war-rules-emphasize-need-to-avoid-civilian-casualties

a particular weapon, to choosing the most advantageous aim point, to verifying that the strike would meet the ROE requirements.

The CJOC strike cells were an extra-doctrinal arrangement designed early in 2014 to slow down the strike process and ensure that tactical expediency did not overtake the administration's strategic imperative to avoid civilian casualties. But just as the TEA delegation signaled comfort with a more aggressive attitude toward targeting ISIS, the CJOCs developed techniques to expedite attacks. The introduction of airmen as strike directors in CJOC-E also added a level of sophistication in air power expertise. For the first half of the Battle of Mosul, both CJOC-E strike directors were armor officers. As the battle continued and those officers' deployments ended, CJFLCC's senior airman ensured two fighter crewmen (one USAF F-16 pilot and one USMC F-18 weapons system officer and forward air controller) took on those roles. The strike cells evolved to match the increasing intensity of the air war against ISIS.[60]

### Employment and Management of Precision Munitions

The use of air-delivered precision guided munitions (PGMs) has been steadily increasing since their first significant employment in Operation Desert Storm. Air Forces Central (AFCENT) headquarters has not yet released a munitions breakdown for the 117,000 weapon releases in Operation Inherent Resolve, but a joint staff officer estimated 99.5 percent had been PGMs.[61] For the coalition, the Battle of Mosul was a PGM-only affair.[62]

Coalition aircraft used their full range of PGMs against a large array of targets in Mosul. The most common target-weapon combination was a GBU-38v1 dropped on an ISIS fighting position in a building. The GBU-38v1 is a 500-pound GPS-guided Joint Direct Attack Munition (JDAM) built with a standard Mk-82 bomb body (300-pound warhead, 192 pounds of explosive) that could be carried by all fixed-wing coalition aircraft. The low-blast GBU-38v4, whose warhead contained less than 30 pounds of explosive, minimized collateral damage in Mosul's dense urban terrain and was often used for strikes on or near mosques and schools. The 250-pound GBU-39 Small Diameter Bomb was effective

---

[60] Author's personal experience.

[61] Total number: AFCENT Airpower Summaries. www.afcent.af.mil/About/Airpower-S ummaries; percentage: Paul D. Shinkman, "ISIS War Drains US Bomb Supply," *US News and World Report*, February 17, 2017. www.usnews.com/news/world/articles/2017–02–17/us-raiding-foreign-weapons-stockpiles-to-support-war-against-the-islamic-state-group

[62] AC-130 and A-10 cannon rounds, although not precision guided, are considered precise weapons owing to the accuracy of their direct fire.

against nearly all ISIS positions, as was the dual laser- and GPS-guided GBU-54. The 2,000-pound JDAM (GBU-31) was used primarily for overnight terrain denial missions. These missions, in which a dozen bombs might be dropped at intersections in front of ISF lines to complicate ISIS's suicide VBIED attacks, were unpopular with some aircrews who viewed them as a waste of ordnance.[63] They were, however, popular with the ISF soldiers for whom the suicide vehicle was the most feared ISIS weapon.[64]

The jihadis turned car bomb construction into a macabre art form, with "Mad Max" vehicles featuring steel plates welded over critical components. Production of car bombs became a cottage industry, and finding neighborhood VBIED factories was a high priority for coalition airborne- and ground-based reconnaissance assets. Once identified and vetted, those facilities rose to the top of deliberate target strike lists. Coalition remotely piloted aircraft (RPAs) or AH-64 helicopters armed with highly maneuverable laser-guided AGM-114 Hellfire missiles were the preferred airborne weapons system for destroying VBIEDs on the move.[65] Even when car bombs escaped attack from the air, intelligence analysts frequently traced their routes back to the point of origin, which would then be surveilled for possible targeting.

The fight for Mosul witnessed the first combat use of a precision rocket to complement the Hellfire at one-third the cost. The Advanced Precision Kill Weapon System consists of a laser-guidance kit inserted between the motor and warhead of the 2.75-inch rockets already used by a wide variety of strike aircraft. Crews began loading them on A-10s in 2016 and more than 60 had been employed in Mosul by February 2017.[66] The very small (9-pound) warhead demands precise laser aiming, but it also permits strikes to be conducted safely very close to friendly forces or noncombatants.[67]

From the beginning of anti-ISIS air strikes in August 2014 until the Battle of Mosul got underway in October 2016, AFCENT recorded more than 57,000 weapons deliveries. The months October 2016 to July 2017

[63] Lambeth, *America's Air War against ISIS.*
[64] Mike Giglio, "This Is How Ground Troops in Mosul Are Calling US Airstrikes on ISIS," Buzzfeednews.com, November 19, 2016. www.buzzfeednews.com/article/mikegiglio/th is-is-how-ground-troops-in-mosul-are-calling-us-airstrikes
[65] Mad Max: Mosul Study Group, *What the Battle for Mosul Teaches*, 36–37. One ISF soldier famously stopped a VBIED attack with his bulldozer, and survived. https://m.youtube .com/watch?v=WZUoSyEzeeU
[66] Matthew Cox, "US Forces Bank on New Weapon to Protect Civilians in Next Mosul Battle," Military.com, February 1, 2017. www.military.com/daily-news/2017/02/01/us-forces-bank-new-weapon-protect-civilians-next-mosul-battle.html?ESRC=todayinmil .sm
[67] Author's personal experience.

added 36,000 more.[68] This rate of munition expenditure was wholly unexpected in the budget programming cycle that preceded the rise of ISIS, which meant that PGM stocks quickly ran low. The Air Force chief of staff admitted as early as 2015 that PGMs were being dropped "faster than we can replenish them."[69] The shortfalls meant that allies' purchases were delayed, and other combatant commands' magazines were raided.[70] Although the AFCENT commander's insistence in September 2016 that "We've got plenty of weapons" might have been true, by spring 2017 strike directors and TEAs were acutely aware that certain weapons – particularly low-collateral bombs, Hellfire missiles, and GPS-guided artillery rounds – were limited resources that needed to be husbanded carefully.[71]

### Critical Mass: Remotely Piloted Aircraft

Without accurate targeting information, precision guidance is a useless extravagance. Although electronic and human intelligence played critical roles in the fight for Mosul, the key surveillance asset was the fleet of RPAs orbiting the city.

At any one time during the battle more than a dozen RPAs orbited over Mosul, in addition to perhaps six fixed-wing strike aircraft, four attack helicopters, and two manned reconnaissance aircraft.[72] The JTACs would have a "stack" of aircraft from 2,000 to 30,000 feet. This embarrassment of ISR riches enabled an unprecedented view of a contemporary battlefield, but it also was difficult to manage, often inefficient and duplicative, and actually impeded air strikes in some cases. The multiplicity of RPA platforms induced a large deconfliction burden on the airspace management team. A typical Mosul stack might have looked like this: in the highest altitude band, a USAF MQ-9 Reaper armed with AGM-114s

[68] AFCENT Airpower Summaries.
[69] Gen Mark Welsh, cited in John Tirpak, "Empty Rack," *Air Force Magazine*, December 2016. www.airforcemag.com/MagazineArchive/Pages/2016/December%202016/Empty-Racks.aspx
[70] Ibid.; Jack Heretik, "US Running Low on Bombs due to Strikes against ISIS," *Washington Free Beacon*, May 1, 2017. https://freebeacon.com/national-security/u-s-running-low-bombs-due-to-strikes-against-isis
[71] Quote: Lt Gen Jeffrey Harrigian, "Department of Defense Press Briefing by Lt. Gen. Harrigian via Teleconference from Al Udeid Air Base, Qatar," September 13, 2016. https://dod.defense.gov/News/Transcripts/Transcript-View/Article/943264/department-of-defense-press-briefing-by-lt-gen-harrigian-via-teleconference-fro: husbanded carefully: Author's personal experience.
[72] Campell MacDiarmid, "The Battle to Retake Mosul Is Stalemated," *Foreign Policy*, December 22, 2016. https://foreignpolicy.com/2016/12/22/the-battle-to-retake-mosul-is-stalemated; MacDiarmid cites forty-three strike aircraft, a number that would have encompassed all the strike assets airborne in the entire area of operations.

and 500-pound GBUs; below that would be a pair of USAF MQ-1B Predators; below them another pair of MQ-1C Gray Eagles, one operated by US Army crews and one by special operations crews. Below the armed RPAs would be up to eight tactical unmanned aerial systems (TUASs), small enough to be launched from a local field or even by hand. The CJOCs would be able to view any of the video feeds (as well as the targeting-pod video from the fixed-wing strike aircraft also in the stack). The variation in look angles and altitudes helped with the problems of tracking targets through urban canyons but could not completely mitigate them.

Early in the campaign, JTACs and strike directors tried to ensure no RPAs could possibly fly through the bomb fall line during an air strike. As the battle continued and RPA coverage thickened even as the intensity of strikes increased, concern for the "robots" diminished, and the CJOC accepted the risk that a TUAS might be hit by a falling weapon. The deconfliction problem in the other direction – how to keep manned aircraft from hitting an RPA – dogged the strike cell through the end of battle. The sheer number of TUASs, their crews' limited communications links with the CJOC, and their slow speeds made it difficult to move them out of the way of a diving fighter. This restricted the number of A-10 AGR-20 rocket or 30mm strafe deliveries that could be accomplished.[73]

ISIS also employed its own remotely piloted aircraft to good effect. The first known use of drones by ISIS came in August 2014, when jihadis uploaded video of a captured Syrian army base. Later videos featured drones conducting pre-attack reconnaissance, and by April 2015, ISIS propaganda footage showed what it claimed to be a drone operations center through which senior commanders could direct ground combat. At the end of the year drones were being used to command suicide car bombers as well as record their attacks. Multiple videos released early in Operation Eagle Strike show that ISIS leaders had a robust remotely piloted aircraft ISR enterprise of their own, which by this time consisted largely of Chinese-manufactured and commercially available DJI quadcopters.[74] In January 2017 came the first reports from the ISF of grenade-dropping drones; the ISIS propaganda video predictably followed.[75] The number of attacks reached 60 to 100 per month at the peak of the ISIS drone campaign in spring 2017. The commander of US

---

[73] Author's personal experience.
[74] Steven Stalinsky and R. Sosnow, "A Decade of Jihadi Organizations' Use of Drones," Middle East Media Research Institute, February 21, 2017. www.memri.org/reports/dec ade-jihadi-organizations-use-drones–early-experiments-hizbullah-hamas-and-al-qaed a#ISIS%20Anchor
[75] www.funker530.com/abrams-tank-commander

Special Operations Command later testified, "There was a day when the Iraqi effort nearly came to a screeching halt, where literally over 24 hours there were 70 drones in the air ... and our only available response was small arms fire."[76]

American forces explored a number of countermeasures that together degraded the ISIS drone threat and helped reorient ISF toward the offensive. Radio and GPS jamming devices of all sizes were rushed to Iraq to deny the quadcopters access to ISF formations. Coalition intelligence and signals analysts began to focus on finding the human operators, and computer exploitation teams became more practiced at extracting the data chips from crashed drones to discover the launch sites, which subsequently became targets. Iraqi Security Forces were quick to adopt their enemy's technology. Some units bought DJI Phantom quadcopters of their own to supplement coalition RPA feeds. They used these drones to harass ISIS snipers and were even able to fly them through buildings to perform post-strike battle damage assessments.[77]

### Civilian Casualties

The imperative to avoid civilian casualties was a part of OIR from its inception. Substantial criticism was leveled at the Obama administration for what was seen as excessive fastidiousness in this regard that permitted ISIS to target civilians deliberately. Noted defense analyst Anthony Cordesman expressed this concern as early as October 2014: "If an air campaign is too limited, or is too restricted in targeting and rules of engagement, minimizing immediate casualties can mean a massive cumulative rise in total casualties, displaced persons, refugees, and atrocities over time."[78] The fear of inflicting civilian casualties was one reason the authority to approve air strikes was held at the four-star level for more than a year after the air war commenced. CJTF-OIR's first deputy for air operations understood in 2014 that "there was a requirement for zero civilian casualties."[79] As late as 2018 the senior USAF officer in Iraq

[76] Gen Raymond Thomas, quoted in Don Rassler, "The Islamic State and Drones," Combating Terrorism Center, July 2018. https://ctc.usma.edu/app/uploads/2018/07/Islamic-State-and-Drones-Release-Version.pdf

[77] "Iraqis Use Drones to Turn Tables on ISIS," Military.com. www.military.com/dodbuzz/2017/04/27/iraqis-use-drones-turn-tables-isis; post-strike BDA: Author's personal experience.

[78] Anthony Cordesman, "The Air War against the Islamic State: The Need for an 'Adequacy of Resources,'" Center for Strategic and International Studies, October 29, 2014, 7. www.csis.org/analysis/air-war-against-islamic-state-need-%E2%80%9Cadequacy-resources%E2%80%9D

[79] Maj Gen Jeffrey Lofgren, quoted in Lambeth, *America's Air War against ISIS*.

stated that OIR had always "had zero civilian casualties as [its] goal."[80] A cumbersome strike process was constructed that required both a US general officer and government of Iraq approval before execution. Even as the war intensified, the Trump administration did not repeal President Obama's ROE. Secretary of Defense James Mattis told a journalist there would be "no relaxation in the intention to protect the innocent."[81] Furthermore, coalition partners in the air campaign had their own national representatives ("red card holders") in the CAOC who could veto any strike request that did not meet their own governments' restrictions. Inherent Resolve was doctrinally, structurally, and technologically designed to avoid civilian casualties. How did it do?

The coalition's official figure for civilian fatalities caused by its forces in the Battle of Mosul is 352. Airwars.org, a nonprofit air campaign watchdog group, "conservatively estimated that between 1,066 and 1,579 civilians likely died from coalition air and artillery strikes during the 9-month battle."[82] Part of the disparity can be explained by fundamental assumptions and methodology. The coalition civilian casualty teams assume its aircrews and analysts followed the ROE; Airwars investigators assume survivors are both correct and truthful. Further, each side is in possession of information not initially held by the other: extensive pre- and post-strike surveillance footage for the CJTF, and local insight and access for Airwars.

It is of course possible that both are correct because the coalition does not account for ISF helicopter attacks and artillery strikes. Iraqi artillery equipment, particularly the Iranian-supplied Improvised Rocket-Assisted Munition (IRAM), was notoriously inaccurate, and its crews, particularly the Iranian-supplied Federal Police, were notoriously unconcerned about inflicting casualties in the Sunni city that, as they saw it, welcomed ISIS. A Counter Terrorism Service general described FEDPOL's tactic: "The method was shelling each neighborhood with artillery and rockets consistently and then attacking with Humvees. They are acting with recklessness and madness."[83]

A single tragic civilian casualty event seemed to threaten the operation's success. On March 17, 2017, as CTS was fighting through the al-Jadidah neighborhood a kilometer west of the central train station, an

[80] Brig Gen Andrew Croft, quoted in Lambeth, *America's Air War against ISIS.*

[81] Quoted in Lambeth, *America's Air War against ISIS.*

[82] Samuel Oakford, "Counting the Dead in Mosul," *Atlantic*, April 5, 2018. www.theatlantic.com/international/archive/2018/04/counting-the-dead-in-mosul/556466

[83] Mustafa Salim and Loveday Morris, "In Mosul, Iraqi Forces Struggle to Hang On to Government Complex Days after Retaking It," *Washington Post*, March 10, 2017. www.washingtonpost.com/world/middle_east/in-mosul-iraqi-forces-struggle-to-hang-on-to-government-compound-days-after-retaking-it/2017/03/10/9080acec-0369-11e7-9d14-9724d48f5666_story.html?utm_term=.b23b532604ee

Iraqi forward air controller (IFAC) requested a strike on a sniper position on the second floor of a house. CJOC-E approved the strike with a single GBU-38v1. The weapon hit the desired aim point, the IFAC called it a successful strike, and CTS advanced. A week later Iraqi civil defense workers digging through the rubble discovered that the entire building had collapsed, killing 101 Iraqis harbored in the basement and 4 in an adjacent house.[84]

When these reports were found to be credible, there was a near cessation of air and artillery strikes. Iraqi forces were "under orders to request US-led coalition air strikes only when absolutely necessary," and the Erbil strike cell was given to understand that General Townsend thought the air campaign would not survive another catastrophic air strike.[85] CJTF-OIR's investigation showed that the large amount of explosives ISIS had stored in the building had detonated at bomb impact, causing the walls to collapse and the floors to pancake into the basement. After a few tentative weeks, the pace of air strike requests began to increase, as did visual evidence of ISIS's brutality. ISR platforms recorded ISIS fighters herding civilians into houses prepared as fighting positions in attempts to incite coalition strikes. Weapons releases, the most precise measurement of air strike intensity, which declined nearly 20 percent from March to April 2017, increased significantly in May (+13 percent) and June (+25 percent) as the battle reached its end stages.[86] In August, after Mosul was back in Iraqi hands, General Townsend responded directly to an Airwars report denigrating CJTF's mitigation of civilian casualties. The Coalition, he wrote, did "everything within its power to limit harm to non-combatants and civilian infrastructure," while ISIS "tortured, beheaded, and burned those that did not agree with them."[87]

---

[84] Maj Gen Joseph Martin and Brig Gen Matthew Isler, "Department of Defense News Briefing on the Findings of an Investigation into a March 17 Coalition Air Strike in West Mosul," May 25, 2017. https://dod.defense.gov/News/Transcripts/Transcript-View/Art icle/1194694/department-of-defense-news-briefing-on-the-findings-of-an-investiga tion-into-a

[85] Loveday Morris, "Iraqi Forces Open New Front in Mosul Offensive, Gearing Up for a Final Showdown," *Washington Post*, May 5, 2017. www.washingtonpost.com/world/ middle_east/iraqi-forces-open-new-front-in-mosul-offensive-gearing-up-for-a-final-sho wdown/2017/05/04/a2fd1596-30c7-11e7-a335-fa0ae1940305_story.html?utm_ter m=.2642e8ee9977; Gen Townsend: Author's personal experience.

[86] AFCENT Airpower Summary, June 30, 2017. https://www.afcent.af.mil/Portals/82/Do cuments/Airpower%20summary/Airpower%20Summary%20-%20June%202017.pdf?v er=2017-07-10-040401-420

[87] Lt Gen Stephen J. Townsend, "Response to Samuel Oakford on ForeignPolicy.com." https://airwars.org/news-and-investigations/former-coalition-commander-lt-gen-town send-responds-to-airwars-article-on-raqqa

### Air Power Effectiveness

Coalition air forces exhibited high levels of military effectiveness in the Battle of Mosul. At the tactical level, maintenance crews generated the required number of aircraft sorties to prosecute the campaign, and aircrew from all participating nations were able to execute ISR, close air support, and battlefield interdiction missions in a challenging (if low threat) urban environment. Joint terminal attack controllers both nominated targets for destruction and approved final weapons release. If analyzed as a single engagement, an air strike in Mosul in 2016–17 might look much like any other strike in Iraq or Afghanistan since 2002. But in aggregate the scale, intensity, and complexity of the air campaign demanded more tactical proficiency than Western air forces had demonstrated since the end of major combat operations in 2003.

At the operational level of warfare, coordination was adequate at the outset and became more efficient as the campaign progressed. In addition to the command and control adjustments in the combined joint operational centers described earlier, coalition air forces (predominantly the USAF) demonstrated the ability to process, exploit, and disseminate intelligence data to operational-level targeteers and planners. Although years of striving toward a common operational and intelligence picture of the battlefield have not yet yielded absolute success, there has been steady incremental progress in eliminating the worst information stovepipes, at least within the Anglosphere forces.

The effectiveness of air power over Mosul enabled what must be judged a political success. If it may be argued that Western and Iraqi missteps created the conditions for the rise of ISIS in 2014, it must also be conceded that, once committed, the coalition, and particularly Western air power, destroyed in Mosul the last hopes for al-Baghdadi's caliphate to become a fully realized state.

### Conclusion

Operation Inherent Resolve did not produce any major combat aviation milestones – no game-changing technologies, no shock and awe decapitation strikes. It was, instead, part of the continuing maturation of existing weaponry, systems, and ideas. Critics who point to the anemic pace of attacks when compared to Desert Storm and the early days of Enduring Freedom and Iraqi Freedom are correct, of course, but one wonders if those are useful analogies. The strategic context – substantial political uncertainty, significant angst about the strength of the coalition, tremendous concern about civilian casualties – seems more closely aligned with that of the Kosovo or Libya campaigns. In any case, the careful application of air power enabled a fractured proxy ground force to capture an ancient city well fortified and defended by fanatical fighters.

# 12 Retrospect and Prospect: Air Power in the Age of Primacy and Beyond

*Colin F. Jackson**

The chapters in this volume chronicle the influence of air power on war making and peacemaking in the age of primacy. Although the episodes were not exclusively American, they were almost universally contests between unequals. The defining characteristic of all the cases examined is the profound asymmetries in power, interest, and technology. The possession of uncontested air superiority transformed such wars from wrestling matches or duels into acts of dominant powers imposing their will from the air.[1]

This chapter first explores the inferences that might be drawn from the wars of the age of primacy. How did dominant powers seek to use air power to accomplish a range of political ends? How successful were such strategies in military and political terms? What innovations emerged in the process of war making? How did asymmetries in power and technology influence civilian attitudes toward the use of air power? Second, it examines which elements of the age of primacy might endure the transition to an age of great power rivalry. Once air superiority is a goal and not a given, will air forces be able to exert influence in the same ways or will the strategies of air power and their effectiveness shift dramatically? Which innovations will survive and which are likely to succumb in war between great powers? And how will the allure of air power change as the costs of the instrument and its promise shift in response to a changing security environment?

## Air Power in the Age of Primacy

The natural temptation in such a review of the preceding chapters is to search for simple and universal lessons from the age of primacy. It would

---

* The views expressed by the author do not reflect those of the US government, the Department of Defense, or any of its organizations.
[1] The term "dominant power" is shorthand for states and militaries that enjoy outsized military and technological advantages over their opponents. This includes cases in which the United States fought with weaker regional powers or militants; it also includes cases in which regional or great powers such as Israel and Russia fought against weaker opponents.

be comforting to assume that the frequent application of air power would validate or falsify longstanding theories about the promise and the limits of air power. Seldom have modern air forces been so frequently engaged in conflict, and the history of the age of primacy is at least as rich as the preceding Cold War. From Desert Storm to present, the United States has employed air power, first episodically and now almost continuously, across a number of theaters.

The greatest obstacles to generalization are variation in ends, ways, and context across these wars. In certain cases, the ambitions of the dominant powers were limited, involving cost imposition or some form of coercion; in other cases, air power was used to overthrow regimes and reimpose order in shattered societies. The variation in ways is equally confounding. The range and mix of air strategies employed varied from case to case, and this constrains our ability to extract hard and fast conclusions about the efficacy of various strategies. Finally, the contexts of each specific campaign frustrate attempts to draw sweeping conclusions. As Kosovo highlights, air power can compel concessions without the aid of ground forces. Still, the nearly complete isolation of Serbia reminds us that political context may be the critical intervening variable in explaining the outsized success of air power. For all these reasons, we are left with a set of plausible propositions and open questions about our understanding of causality within and across cases.

## Political Ambitions and Air Power

Not surprisingly, the efficacy of air power in political and military terms varied with the ambitions of the sender and the characteristics of the target. Most dominant powers were fully capable of using air power to secure modest political goals. In the cases of Lebanon, Syria, and Mosul, as well as the scattered engagements of the war on terror, strong states used air power to disrupt weak states and militant groups and impose substantial costs. This was easier when the target state or organization presented visible and valuable targets for air forces to strike. Militant organizations offered the opposite. Lacking heavy vehicles and valuable targets, such organizations hid within civilian populations and compelled air forces to use a mix of manned and unmanned intelligence platforms to identify targets amid social clutter. The emphasis placed on reducing civilian casualties led air forces to devote more intelligence assets and time to the targeting, engagement, and assessment process. The indeterminate outcomes of various sustained aerial attrition campaigns in Iraq, Afghanistan, Yemen, Syria, Lebanon, and elsewhere point to the military and political resilience of militant organizations in the face of heavy and sustained blows.

Several of the campaigns in this volume involved attempts by dominant powers to compel their adversaries to accept some political demand short of regime change. The political successes of air power in Bosnia and Kosovo would appear to challenge post-Vietnam arguments about the limits of air power.[2] In both instances, air power tipped the balance in civil wars and forced Serbia to make substantial territorial concessions. On closer examination, however, these claims appear less absolute. In Bosnia, as Hughes points out in Chapter 3, successful ground offensives by Croat and Bosnian forces meant that the Serbs were, by the end of the Dayton talks, being asked to accept facts on the ground rather than concede territory still in their control. In Kosovo (Chapter 4), Russia's decision to desert its Serbian ally left the Milosevic regime diplomatically isolated. This undoubtedly influenced Milosevic's decision to concede to US and NATO demands. In either case, a change in the contextual variables – ground offensives or third-party support – might have turned successful compellence into open-ended stalemate.

More ambitious attempts to compel enemy concessions in Lebanon and Yemen ended in failure. Israeli attempts to compel Hezbollah to release hostages and cease its rocket attacks by striking its forces, its command and control, leaders, and supporters failed. Hezbollah continued its rocket attacks until the last day of the war. Even less successful was Israel's attempt at extended compellence – the notion that punishing the Lebanese state would force it to crack down on Hezbollah. Neither the embargo nor the Israeli deep strikes into Beirut compelled the Lebanese government to force Hezbollah into submission. The Saudi campaign in Yemen came to grief along similar lines. The early Saudi bid to force the Houthi regime to return Yemeni President Hadi to power failed as did a parallel effort to roll back or even contain Iranian influence in Yemen. Both in Lebanon and Yemen, embattled regimes that enjoyed the material and diplomatic backing of powerful third parties, chose to absorb punishment rather than concede in the face of sustained air attack.

The track record of coercing nonstate or quasi-state actors such as Hezbollah or the Taliban has been even less impressive. Militant organizations that aspire to become full-fledged states seem even less likely to respond to a sender's calculus of coercion and more inclined to accept the risks and possible rewards of protracted defiance.

[2] Mark Clodfelter, *The Limits of Airpower: The American Bombing of North Vietnam* (Lincoln: University of Nebraska Press, 2006); Robert A. Pape, *Bombing to Win: Air Power and Coercion in War* (Ithaca: Cornell University Press, 1996).

The Second Lebanon War (Chapter 7) offers a glimpse into the related question of postwar general deterrence. Though it is clear that Israel's military performance was decidedly mixed, and its political demands of Lebanon and Hezbollah were not satisfied, the absence of any subsequent wars with Hezbollah raises the possibility that Israel achieved the broader purpose of the war – the restoration of deterrence. There is no definitive way to prove that Israeli actions in 2006 explain Hezbollah's decision to forgo subsequent military action.[3] Still, this may be a case in which a dominant power fell well short of its operational goals, failed to compel its enemy to submit, and yet somehow managed to restore a measure of security and stability. This may support Schelling's basic observation that compellence is considerably more difficult than deterrence. Or it may indicate that Hezbollah, while unwilling to accept the reputational costs of overt submission, was nevertheless sufficiently chastened by the punishment it received to forgo future military action against Israel.[4]

Paradoxically, the more ambitious political aim of regime overthrow may be simpler to achieve with modern air power. Whereas coercion is by nature a process of violent persuasion in which the object is a shrouded enemy decision-making process, regime change by brute force does not require the enemy's assent.[5] In Afghanistan, Saddam's Iraq, Libya, and ISIS-occupied Syria and Iraq, brute force air campaigns were sufficient to shatter existing regimes and expose them to overthrow by domestic factions. In most instances, this involved the coordination of great power air attacks with ground campaigns. In Libya, what began as a Western bid to protect the population from Qaddafi's crackdown ultimately precipitated the overthrow of a weakened regime by local parties. With the exception of the Saudi campaign in Yemen and the US invasion of Iraq, the air instrument gave dominant powers the ability to break weak states without committing large numbers of ground troops.

Where air power proved less decisive was in the aftermath of regime change. As outside patrons and their domestic clients sought to rebuild political orders in Iraq, Afghanistan, and Syria, the air instrument provided a ready tool to suppress but not to extinguish political resistance. As Schultz notes in Chapter 2, air power, usually in the form of some constellation of manned and unmanned ISR (intelligence, surveillance,

[3] Thomas Schelling, *Arms and Influence* (New Haven: Yale University Press, 1966), 70–91; Lawrence Freedman, *Deterrence* (Cambridge: Polity Press, 2004), 109–15.

[4] Ibid., Schelling, 124–25; Robert Art and Kelly Greenhill, eds., "Coercion: An Analytical Overview," in *Coercion: The Power to Hurt in International Politics*, eds. Kelly Greenhill and Peter Krause (New York: Oxford University Press, 2018), 18.

[5] Ibid., Freedman, 39; Alexander Downes, "Step Aside or Face the Consequences: Explaining the Success and Failure of Compellent Threats to Remove Foreign Leaders," in *Coercion: The Power to Hurt*, eds. Greenhill and Krause, 95–97.

and reconnaissance) and strike platforms, gave the dominant powers the ability to "mow the grass" against militant organizations such as Al-Qaeda, ISIS, Hezbollah, Hamas, and others. What air power could not do was trace a path from the suppression of resistance to collaboration with the new regimes. On one level, this points to the limits of instrumental violence of any stripe in restoring organized obedience or authority in shattered states. In civil war, the restoration of order becomes a problem of chained compellence; the state builder and his patrons must first compel insurgents to desist and then compel a large fraction of the population to obey the new regime. On a narrower front, however, what is striking was the gap between air power's ability to shatter states and its inability to influence state restoration. An instrument that could reliably promise the rapid overthrow of regimes offered no real answer to the inevitable sequels.

In almost every case, proponents of air power offered plausible strategies to achieve ambitious goals in rapid fashion. In many cases, however, the inability to deliver quick, decisive victories led air forces to lower their sights from war termination to attrition. Israeli military leaders opened the war with plans to rapidly impose their will on Hezbollah. When these plans failed to deliver military victory, and tactical results failed to translate into the desired political actions (Lebanese in-group policing or Hezbollah submission), Israeli leaders shifted from pursuit of a decisive outcome into a cumulative campaign of punishment. Something quite similar emerges from the Saudi campaign in Yemen. Having failed to overthrow the Houthis, restore the old regime, and expel Iran, the Saudis embarked on collective punishment of the Houthis and local preemption against Iran. We may ask whether these are anomalies or the presumptive fallback in instances of overreach. Confronted with the failure to achieve the desired ends, air forces may be primed to revise their aims downward and simultaneously demand wider target sets and more liberal authorities in a search to demonstrate success or stave off failure.

### Strategies of Air Power in the Age of Primacy

If the ends pursued by dominant powers varied considerably in the age of primacy, so too did the ways in which states sought to use air power to achieve them. Under most circumstances, strategy is the art of choice under scarcity and uncertainty. Scarcity and uncertainty force the strategist to assess alternative courses of action, carefully weighing their respective costs, benefits, and risks, lest an errant choice fatally compromise the pursuit of the desired political ends or preclude a later exploration of alternatives.

The age of primacy was in this respect an anomaly. The ease of achieving and maintaining air superiority made it possible for air planners to explore the full menu of air strategies at limited cost and risk. The absence of opposition in the air or robust air defenses meant that the marginal costs, human and financial, of waging war from the air were remarkably low by historical standards.[6]

As the cases in this volume reveal, choice without scarcity typically ended in the reflexive application of existing strategies in order of institutional preference. The strategies that held the promise of rapid and independent victory through the air were most appealing. This tended to privilege strategic attack, whether in the form of attack on leadership or the enemy's high-value economic or material assets. Only after such early bids failed to deliver the knockout blow or compel submission did air forces shift to attack on the enemy's fielded forces.[7]

Where traditional operational constraints on air planners were absent, strategic attack was the first card played. In Kosovo, it was the failure of the first week's attacks on Serbian air defenses and strategic targets to force an early political decision that led to a broadening of the target set to include Serbian ground forces. Much to the frustration of CIA officers on the ground, the early weeks of the 2001 air campaign in Afghanistan focused on leadership targets, training camps, and "high-value" targets in Kabul and Kandahar. Only after three weeks of inconclusive strategic attack did the air campaign shift to direct attack on the Taliban's ground forces. The opening moves of Operation Iraqi Freedom featured the unsuccessful attempt to kill Saddam Hussein at Dora Farms and the "shock and awe" attacks on regime command and control in Baghdad. In Lebanon, the Israeli Chief of Staff lobbied unsuccessfully for strategic attacks on Hezbollah and the Lebanese state to force a quick decision. The failure of early strikes against Hezbollah leadership forced the Israeli Air Force to shift from its preferred strategies of strategic attack and interdiction into the realms of missile hunting and close air support.

---

[6] Only the Royal Air Force in its "air policing" operations against rebels in Iraq, Palestine, and the Northwest Frontier Province of India in the early interwar period enjoyed comparable freedom of action and immunity from ground fire. It would not be a stretch to refer to the age of primacy as the second age of air policing. For an account of air policing, see Charles Townshend, "Civilization and Frightfulness: Air Control in the Middle East between the Wars" in *Warfare, Diplomacy, and Politics: Essays in Honor of A. J.P. Taylor*, ed. Chris Wrigley (London: Hamish Hamilton, 1987).
[7] In the Cold War, strategic interdiction was a close second in institutional preference order. For an array of reasons – enemy prepositioning, speed of campaigns, irregular opponents – concentrated and sustained attacks on enemy logistical systems were not as prominent in the age of primacy as they were in the Cold War.

The Libyan and Bosnian campaigns offer an important contrast born of explicit political constraints. In Libya, the Obama administration's overarching desire to avoid postwar entanglement led to an indirect approach; in Obama's judgment, the best way to limit US involvement was to destroy the regime's air defenses and stop Qaddafi's ground offensive. By design, the United States would then leave NATO allies to impose a no-fly zone and local forces to overthrow Qaddafi.[8] In Bosnia, it was Lieutenant General Ryan who imposed strict limits on US targeting, focusing narrowly on Serbian forces surrounding designated safe areas. It is telling, as Hughes points out, that the Air Force official history of the Bosnian campaign devoted a chapter to exploring alternatives to the air campaign as executed; this post hoc examination highlighted the potential advantages of and institutional preferences for directly striking Serbian strategic centers rather than fielded forces.[9]

In none of the cases examined here did strategic attack, either in the form of leadership strikes or countervalue targeting, deliver rapid, decisive results. Decapitation strikes were throws of the dice. In Afghanistan, Iraq, Lebanon, and Yemen, first strikes missed, enemy leaders went to ground, and the bolts from the blue were replaced by protracted manhunts.

Paradoxically, attacking the enemy's fielded forces was the strategy of last resort and highest payout. Proponents of strategic attack were generally reluctant to forgo independent bids for victory through direct attack on the opposing state because that would necessitate the introduction of ground forces. In the vast majority of cases, it was the failure of strategic attack that opened the door to targeting enemy armies. It was in these campaigns against the enemies' ground forces that air forces had their most profound military and political impact.

The destruction of the enemy's armed forces had three distinct effects. First, by weakening the enemy armies on the attack, air power could deny them the objects of their offensives. Whether in Desert Storm, Bosnia, or Kosovo, the attack on fielded forces brought enemy offensives to a halt. Second, air attacks weakened enemy armies on the defense. The prolonged air campaign softened up the Iraqi units in Kuwait and left them vulnerable to breakthroughs by US ground forces; in Yemen, Saudi and Emirati attacks on fielded forces enabled the modest counteroffensive by

---

[8] Robert Gates, *Duty: Memoirs of a Secretary at War* (New York: Knopf, 2014), 518–20; Barack Obama, "Remarks by the President in Address to the Nation on Libya," National Defense University, March 28, 2011.

[9] Lieutenant Colonel Robert Pollock, "Roads Not Taken: Theoretical Approaches to Operation Deliberate Force," in *Deliberate Force: A Case Study in Effective Air Campaigning* (Maxwell Air Force Base: Air University Press, 2000), 431–53.

allied forces against the Houthis. Finally, the destruction of a state's armed forces exposed it to threats from within. Battered armies might face coup attempts or bids by armed factions to usurp power.

The military and political effectiveness of attacks on enemy armies varied along several dimensions. Air attacks were easiest against conventional armies; it was far simpler to attack large concentrations of vehicles, artillery pieces, and infantry than dispersed, irregular forces operating within civilian populations. Equally important, air attack was most successful when combined with pressure on the ground. In the absence of ground action, an enemy could hunker down and hope to endure the aerial siege; in the face of a ground offensive, the enemy was forced to confront two threats simultaneously. Even militia armies such as the Northern Alliance and the Libyan anti-government forces were capable of mounting offensives once air forces struck the opposing forces directly.

### Innovations of the Age of Primacy: Air Power Takes on New Targets and New Partners

While the shortcomings of strategic attack drove air forces into direct attack on enemy ground forces, the methods of the late Cold War and Desert Storm were an imperfect answer to the problems of the age of primacy. Existing strategies were built on the assumptions of conventionally equipped enemies and first-world allies. By contrast, air forces in the age of primacy confronted irregular opponents and had to rely on semi-skilled partners. To make air power effective in this new milieu, militaries had to develop ways to bring old tools to bear on a new class of enemies. Counter-network operations and the new advisory model emerged as the answers to these functional challenges, and these innovations bridged the gap between the tools of air power and the particular operational problems of the age of primacy.

### *Counter-Network Operations: Attacking a Different Enemy*

The success of regime change in Afghanistan and Iraq and the failures of political reconstruction set the stage for the new problem of insurgency. The question for senior military leaders was how to suppress rebellion and restore political order using the tools at hand.

One answer was to scale up existing counterterrorism strategies and combine them with more extensive use of airborne ISR and strike. Though the progenitors of the new strategies came from the ground branches of the special operations community, their ideas could not be implemented without air power. What emerged was a killing machine built around a targeting algorithm and drawing on a mix of intelligence inputs and an array of ground and air assets. By the peak of the wars in Iraq and Afghanistan, the joint special operations task forces had become the strategic reserve for commanders in both theaters – they were the fire brigade commanders and politicians used to focus violence on groups and areas of acute need.

The new theory of victory was present in miniature as early as the 1990s. The special operations community entered these wars with experience in small-scale counterterrorism operations in Colombia and Bosnia.[10] The problem they faced was how to defeat criminal or insurgent networks in the context of civil wars. Israel had developed similar ideas with intelligence-led operations against Hamas in the late 1990s.[11] General Stanley McChrystal, the commander of Joint Special Operations Command (JSOC) and the father of the counter-network operations revolution, consciously drew on even earlier models such as the French counterterrorism campaign in the Battle of Algiers.[12]

Although the theory of victory evolved over time, the core idea of US leaders was to use small numbers of special operations forces, intelligence collectors, and air power to dismantle clandestine, militant organizations. In some periods, the logic of counter-network operations centered on decapitation; by killing or capturing a movement's senior leaders, the attacker sought to induce organizational collapse.[13] In other instances, counter-network operations appeared to be an attrition campaign to locate and remove enough militants to degrade or disrupt the movement. In the later phases of the campaigns in Iraq and Afghanistan, counter-network operations sought to fracture militant organizations and alliances by focusing violence on irreconcilable elements and persuading reconcilable factions to exit the fight or switch sides.

[10] Mark Bowden, *Killing Pablo: The Hunt for the World's Greatest Outlaw* (New York: Atlantic Monthly Press, 2001), 72–74, 147–53, 259–60; Sean Naylor, *Relentless Strike: The Secret History of Joint Special Operations Command* (New York: St. Martin's Press, 2015), 56–57, 64–66.
[11] Ronan Bergman, *Rise and Kill First: The Secret History of Israel's Targeted Assassinations* (New York: Random House, 2018), 385–97, 480–82, 503.
[12] General Stanley McChrystal, *My Share of the Task: A Memoir* (New York: Penguin, 2014), 123–24; Gillo Pontecorvo, "The Battle of Algiers" (Rizzoli, Rialto Pictures, 1966); Jean Lartéguy, *The Centurions* (New York: Penguin Books, 2015; Paul Aussaresses, *The Battle of the Casbah: Counter-Terrorism and Torture* (New York: Enigma Books, 2006); Ted Morgan, *My Battle of Algiers: A Memoir* (New York: Smithsonian Books, 2005); Général Maurice Schmitt, *Alger – Été 1957: Une victoire sure le terrorisme* (Paris: L'Harmattan, 2002).
[13] Richard Shultz, *Military Innovation in War: It Takes a Learning Organization, A Case Study of Task Force 714 in Iraq (JSOU Report 16–6)* (MacDill Air Force Base: Joint Special Operations University Press, 2016), 16.

In all variants, counter-network operations revolved around the target-ing process. McChrystal, echoing earlier counterterrorist operators, saw the new campaigns as a "fight for intelligence."[14] Intelligence drove targeted raids and strikes; the intelligence captured on those raids – detainees, documents, computers, cell phones – provided the raw mater-ial for follow-on operations. Ground raids and air strikes caused insur-gents to react; their subsequent movement and communications further illuminated their organization. The French had used ground raids and prisoner interrogations to feed the targeting cycle and cripple a terrorist network in the 1957 Battle of Algiers. McChrystal's ambition was to combine these ideas with new tools and apply them on unprecedented scale to break insurgent networks.[15]

The acronym F3EA – find, fix, finish, exploit, analyze – encapsulated this targeting process. McChrystal's insight was that his ground oper-ators, like air force pilots, were most adept at the finish portion of the targeting cycle – the delivery of violence on an identified target. He sought to improve exploitation and analysis of intelligence as a way to feed follow-on operations and increase pressure on the insurgent groups. If the joint task forces could accelerate the targeting cycle and dramatically increase the tempo of targeted operations, then they might break the back of the militant groups.[16]

Air power played an indispensable role in McChrystal's model. On the operational level, helicopters enabled operators to execute raids and air strikes and offered an alternative means to finish fleeting targets. Equally important, manned and unmanned aircraft provided the signals and imagery intelligence necessary to find and fix insurgent targets. Insurgent use of cell phones, for example, gave the task forces a way to find and track targets; the expanding fleet of RPAs provided full-motion video coverage to track and in some cases "finish" insurgent targets. The increased tempo of operations would not have been possible without the exponential growth in the task force's organic aircraft fleet and their disproportionate share of theater-level ISR. By adding these key ingredi-ents, the task force vastly increased its speed of response and its ability to acquire and develop new targets.[17]

---

[14] Mark Mazzetti, *The Way of the Knife: The CIA, a Secret Army, and a War at the Ends of the Earth* (New York: Penguin, 2013), 130; Frank Kiston, *Low Intensity Operations: Subversion, Insurgency & Peacekeeping* (New Dehli: Natraj Publishers, 1992), 99–101; Frank Kiston, *Bunch of Five* (London: Faber and Faber, 1977), 29–30; Roger Trinquier, *Modern Warfare: A French View of Counterinsurgency* (Leavenworth: Command and General Staff College, 1985), 37, 43–46.

[15] Ibid., Mazzetti, 130; ibid., McChrystal, 198–99.     [16] Ibid., Shultz, 41–44.

[17] Ibid., McChrystal, 137, 157–58, 177–78; ibid., Shultz, 48–51; ibid., Naylor, 262–64; Colonel Joel Rayburn and Colonel Frank Sobchak, eds., *The US Army in the Iraq War,*

The final element of the model was the fusion of intelligence and operations. As Schultz and Renner highlight in Chapters 2 and 11, the emergence of new technologies such as Rover and chat created the manned and unmanned kill web that connected operators in the air and on the ground with intelligence officers. The Americans, like the Israelis several years earlier, streamlined the targeting process by putting operators and intelligence officers of all agencies in the same physical location. The full integration of rival intelligence agencies into the task force required overcoming longstanding traditions of compartmentalization and parochial competition for control of information.[18] By forcing a critical mass of analysts and operators into a room and connecting them virtually with a still larger universe of collaborators in the global surveillance-strike architecture, the task force tore down institutional barriers to cooperation, combined human, imagery, and signals intelligence, and compressed the targeting cycle dramatically.[19]

The question is the extent to which counter-network operations were effective either militarily or politically. Most observers agree that the striking increase in the tempo of special operations transformed the military fight against the insurgent organizations in Iraq between 2004 and 2010 and in similar fashion in Afghanistan between 2009 and 2012.[20] McChrystal later wrote the number of operations in Iraq grew from 10 in April 2004 to 300 a month just two years later.[21] By capturing or killing thousands of Al-Qaeda in Iraq and Sunni and Shia militants, the task force disrupted the enemies' operations, depleted their leadership, and forced them onto the defensive.[22] It remains an open debate how much causal weight should be assigned to the task force's counter-network operations, relative to competing explanations such as the troop surge, changes in counterinsurgency doctrine and posture, the Sunni Awakening, and ethnic cleansing in turning the tide of the war in Iraq between 2006 and 2010.[23]

*Volume 1: Invasion, Insurgency, Civil War, 2003–2006* (Carlisle: United States Army War College Press, 2019), 463.
[18] Ibid., Shultz, 26–27.    [19] Ibid., McChrystal, 149–54.
[20] Michael Gordon and General Bernard Trainor, *Endgame: The Inside Story of the Struggle for Iraq, From George W. Bush to Barack Obama* (New York: Pantheon Books, 2012); Bob Woodward, *The War Within: A Secret White House History, 2006–2008* (New York: Simon and Schuster, 2008), 380–81; ibid., Shultz, 65–71; ibid., Gates, 254.
[21] Ibid., McChrystal, 145.
[22] Thomas Ricks, *The Gamble: General Petraeus and the American Military Adventure in Iraq* (New York: Penguin, 2010), 186; ibid., Rayburn and Sobchak, eds., *The US Army in the Iraq War, Volume 1*, 433; ibid., Naylor, 309–10.
[23] Austin Long and John Lindsay, "Correspondence: Assessing the Synergy Thesis in Iraq," *International Security* 37:4 (Spring 2013): 181–89.

What is less clear is the lasting political effect of these operations. The counter-network campaign began in 2003 in the hope that the elimination of senior leaders might cause insurgent organizations to unravel.[24] Over time, tactical successes in eliminating former regime elements and terrorist leaders such as Abu Musab al-Zarqawi revealed this to be overly optimistic.[25] Though successors might be less experienced or effective, decapitation against irregular organizations was if anything less decisive than decapitation strategies against traditional states. The fallback position of the special operations task forces in Iraq and Afghanistan, and of their Israeli peers in the fight against Hamas, was to target the mid-level leaders – what the Israelis referred to as the "supreme operational echelon."[26] Echoing the French in the 1950s and American commanders in the later phases of Vietnam, the modern special operators argued that neither the titular leaders nor the foot soldiers were the centers of gravity of the militant organizations; the greatest vulnerability was the array of facilitators – recruiters, propagandists, financiers, bomb makers, and planners – who stood behind the foot soldiers.[27]

In practice, targeting oscillated between focused hunts for very senior leaders and the cumulative pursuit of a far larger set of mid-level leaders. As the tempo of operations increased, the line between strategy and rationalization often blurred; it was sometimes unclear whether the focus on mid-level leaders reflected their intrinsic importance or simply the greater ease of finding and finishing this larger category of targets. The overarching risk was that the targeting cycle could take on a life of its own – that the autocatalytic process of operations feeding future operations could become detached from a sober assessment of the political effects, current and lasting, on the enemy organization, the surrounding populations, and the political competition for power. Tactical virtuosity and tempo were at best measures of performance that could easily blot out the consideration of the links between tactical success and the political objects of suppressing rebellion and restoring organized obedience.[28]

Late in the Iraq war and again in the waning phases of the Afghan counterinsurgency, leaders sought to rectify this by tying the killing machine more directly to the political competition for power. At one level this was an admission of the limits of attrition whatever its scale or

---

[24] Ibid., Naylor, 230–32; ibid., Rayburn and Sobchak, eds., Volume 1, 123.

[25] Ibid., McChrystal, 235.

[26] Ibid., Bergman 499–500, 581; ibid., Shultz, 4, 8, 17, 52–53, 66–67.

[27] David Galula, *Counterinsurgency Warfare: Theory and Practice* (St. Petersburg: Hailer Publishing, 2005), 77, 123–27; ibid., Trinquier, 8–9, 44–45; Mark Moyar, *Phoenix and the Birds of Prey: Counterinsurgency and Counterterrorism in Vietnam* (Nebraska: Bison Books, 2007), 59–64.

[28] Ibid., Bergman, 629–30; ibid., Moyar, *Oppose Any Foe*, 306–7; ibid., Shultz, 67–68.

focus. As Colonel John Christian, a long-time operator in Iraq acknowledged, "I've done the math and it's going to take us two hundred and forty-seven years to kill them all." Faced with the impossibility of killing their way to political settlement, coalition leaders sought to divide Sunni and Shia militants into reconcilable and irreconcilable categories. By striking irreconcilables and passing over or in some cases coopting or releasing reconcilables, military leaders hoped to fracture the insurgent coalition and promote side switching by reconcilable factions.[29]

Integrating military operations and political logic proved far more difficult. Connecting counter-network operations to Iraqi politics introduced new players and new considerations. The task force and reconciliation team found themselves embroiled in the violent bargaining of a multiplayer civil war. Just as the counter-network operations had imposed greater intelligence demands than attacks on conventional armies, the manipulation of insurgent alliances proved far more demanding than finding and striking mid-level insurgent leaders.[30] The line between tactical virtuosity and political blowback was never finer than in the peak of the Iraqi civil war as coalition leaders weighed simultaneous operations against Sunni and Shia militants while seeking the buy-in of the fragile and biased Iraqi government.[31]

On balance, counter-network operations were a powerful new tool to disrupt, degrade, and displace militant organizations. The strategy was a vast improvement on past denial strategies in that it moved beyond the targeting of massed formations and vehicles to attack the structure of militant organizations. But it was at best a tool to clear and not to hold or build; as the return of Al-Qaeda in Iraq, rebranded as ISIS, in 2014 demonstrated, militant organizations could survive and reemerge once the killing machine moved on to different targets.[32] At the peak of the Iraq surge, the reconciliation push was a noble attempt to connect the killing machine to the political aims of the war. It remains unclear the extent to which the selective application of violence against irreconcilables and targeted prisoner releases added to the sea changes underway in 2007–8.[33] What is clear is that connecting military operations to political ends

---

[29] Ibid., McChrystal, 259, 242–46, 264; ibid., Trainor and Gordon, 261–63.
[30] Major General Michael Flynn, Captain Matt Pottinger and Paul Batchelor, *Fixing Intel: A Blueprint for Making Intelligence Relevant in Afghanistan* (Washington: Center for New American Security, January 2010), 7–9.
[31] Emma Sky, *The Unraveling: High Hopes and Missed Opportunities in Iraq* (New York: Public Affairs, 2016), 221–22; ibid., Trainor and Gordon, 191, 220–25, 320–28, 439–43; ibid., McChrystal, 266–69.
[32] Daniel Byman, *Road Warriors: Foreign Fighters in the Army of Jihad* (New York: Oxford University Press, 2019), 167; ibid., Shultz, 68–71.
[33] Ibid., Trainor and Gordon, 419–20.

required a much more detailed understanding of the underlying political competition. It was no longer enough to generate targets; to manipulate the course of a civil war, the Coalition would need to understand Iraqi politics at the micro level in near real time. In the end, as in the Israeli experience with Hamas, the counter-network theory of victory and the vast expansion in the killing machine were more effective at removing leaders, imposing costs, and disrupting militants than at manipulating factions, exterminating movements, or restoring obedience.

### *Amplifying Allies: Air Power and the New Advisory Model*

If counter-network operations sought to refashion an old strategy to fit a new target, the second major innovation was an attempt to discover the best way to apply air power in support of allies on the ground – how to "win without (our own) troops." The greatest selling points of air strategies were low human cost and limited entanglement from the sender's point of view. By providing air support only and partnering with someone else's ground forces, a dominant power could in theory wage a joint campaign without absorbing casualties and sidestep the uncertainties of postwar reconstruction. Cynically, dominant powers reserved the option to withdraw air support at any time – a luxury they did not enjoy in campaigns where large numbers of their own ground forces were engaged.

To make this division of labor effective, dominant powers employed a small number of advisors to coordinate air operations and partner ground operations. This was far from a new idea. In the 1972 Easter Offensive, small numbers of American advisors, working with frontline units and manning a tactical air control system, provided South Vietnamese units the air support to stop and partially roll back a massive North Vietnamese conventional invasion.[34] As detailed in Chapter 5, US special forces and tactical air control parties brought similar capabilities to bear in support of the Northern Alliance in the opening stages of the Afghan campaign. These advisors operated on the front lines, employing laser designators and satellite communications to control attacks on battlefield targets under direct observation.[35] This

[34] Phil Haun and Colin Jackson, "Breaker of Armies: Air Power in the Easter Offensive and the Myth of Linebacker 1 and 2 in the Vietnam War," *International Security* 40:3 (Winter 2015/2016): 139–78.
[35] Gary Schroen, *First In: An Insider's Account of How the CIA Spearheaded the War on Terror in Afghanistan* (New York: Random House, 2005), 233, 240–41, 248, 293, 331–33; Gary Berntsen and Ralph Pezzullo, *Jawbreaker: The Attack on Bin Laden and Al-Qaeda* (New York: Crown Publishers, 2005), 266–69; Steve Call, *Danger Close: Tactical Air Controllers in Afghanistan and Iraq* (College Station: Texas A&M University Press, 2007).

"Afghan Model," which combined special forces, tactical air control parties (TACPs), and Afghan forces and whose greatest offensive weapon was close air support, was the key to Northern Alliance breakthroughs in 2001–2 and the swift collapse of the Taliban army and regime.[36] Toward the end of the campaign, the limits of the Afghan Model emerged. At Tora Bora, Afghan partner forces supported by US special operators and air power failed to defeat enemy forces in the mountains along the Pakistani border and lost a fleeting opportunity to capture or kill senior Al-Qaeda leaders. Three months later in Operation Anaconda, even the introduction of large numbers of US conventional forces was insufficient to produce a dramatically different outcome; once again, problems with Afghan partners and the limits of air-ground coordination allowed Al-Qaeda and Taliban forces to escape into Pakistan.[37]

Over the course of the long wars in Afghanistan, Iraq, and Syria, the United States moved from the original Afghan Model to a new advisory model in which advisors directed air support from a tactical operations center. Instead of sitting on the forward line of troops and putting eyes on the target and the aircraft, the air controllers frequently used RPAs and manned aircraft to observe and strike targets remotely.[38]

Three forces drove this shift from frontline advising to advisory support from the rear. The first was the expanding supply of tools that made remote observation possible. Once RPAs became more readily available and a functioning kill web connecting pilots, collectors, analysts, and ground operators was in place, advisors could control air strikes effectively from a position behind the forward line of troops.[39] Second, the surge in demand for air controllers forced commands to decide where to allocate these critical assets. Once it was feasible to pull observers back without losing the means to observe targets remotely, it was more efficient

---

[36] Stephen Biddle, *Afghanistan and the Future of Warfare: Implications for Army and Defense Policy* (Carlisle: Strategic Studies Institute, 2002), 23–26.

[37] Peter Krause, "The Last Good Chance: A Reassessment of US Operations at Tora Bora," *Security Studies* 17, 644–84; Sean Naylor, *Not a Good Day to Die: The Untold Story of Operation Anaconda* (New York: Berkley Publishing Group, 2005); ibid., Berntsen, 274–77; Steve Coll, *Directorate S: The CIA and America's Secret Wars in Afghanistan and Pakistan* (New York: Penguin Press, 2018), 103–8, 125–27.

[38] The doctrinal distinction here is between Type 1 (direct observation) and Type 2 (indirect or remote observation) close air support. For a detailed discussion, see Joint Publication 3–09–03 *Close Air Support*, November 25, 2014, III-42–45; Call, *Danger Close*, 147, 206–8.

[39] Ibid., Rayburn and Sobchak, 1, 463–64; Colonel Joel Rayburn and Colonel Frank Sobchak, eds., *The US Army in the Iraq War, Volume 2: Surge and Withdrawal* (Carlisle: United States Army War College Press, January 2019), 315–16, 505, 507; ibid., Coll, 388–91; ibid., Naylor, *Relentless Strike*, 355–57, 423–24; ibid., Gates, 126–33.

to put the finite number of CAS experts in a tactical operations center rather than scattering them across a series of frontline units.

Accompanying partner forces brought a third set of risks and complexities inherent in the relationship between advisors and partner forces. If advisors routinely accompanied partner forces, then those forces might be reluctant to operate aggressively without advisors present. Because long-term independence was the ultimate objective, routinely accompanying forces might undermine the long-term success of the mission. Second, the commanders of partner forces seldom delegated authority for the release of fires to junior, frontline leaders. If only a senior Iraqi or Afghan commander could clear fires, then there was no point in pushing JTACs forward when the point of decision was in a US or partner operations center behind the front. Third, if US advisors were injured or killed while accompanying partner forces, then the evacuation of those advisors would become the main effort at the cost of interrupting the ongoing partnered operation. Fourth, remote CAS offered advisors a way to set partnered forces up for success. By attacking the main line of resistance from the air, US advisors could open the way for partner forces to break through and occupy the objective without Americans present. Success in the absence of US advisors improved the morale and confidence of partner forces and local populations.

This new advisory model was the foundation for the small-footprint, military successes of post–2014 Syria, Iraq, and Afghanistan. In the absence of advisors on the ground, air forces struggled to identify and engage targets in cluttered environments. The new advisory model addressed this problem, making possible the elegant division of labor civilian leaders sought: Politicians could have the benefits of joint, air-ground operations against an enemy's armies without the human costs and entanglement of sending their own troops.

Notwithstanding the military successes in the later phases of the wars in Iraq, Syria, and Afghanistan, the new advisory model had its own limits. As in previous wars, the efficacy of air power depended upon some minimal level of competence and will to fight by partner forces. Similarly, the quality of advisors mattered. It is hard to overlook the contrast between US late war successes in Iraq, Syria, and Afghanistan (2014–20) and the stalemate that emerged in the Saudi/Emirati–partnered operations in Yemen (Chapter 9).

But the most striking feature of the new advisory model was its high financial cost. As one American general put it, "we have found a model that saves blood but not treasure." As Schultz and Renner observe in Chapters 2 and 11, the move from frontline to remote CAS meant heavy reliance on RPAs. Parallel concerns with minimizing civilian casualties meant that US advisors routinely "soaked" areas with multiple RPAs for hours before approving air strikes. This very deliberate, very slow, and very capital-intensive way of war ensured that the cost of fighting primitive enemies was exceptionally high relative to the tactical and political effects achieved.

Although the desire to avoid collateral damage was laudable, the extent to which this exquisite care and cost translated into goodwill in the local or international environment remained unclear. As Schultz notes in Chapter 2, it stood to reason that collateral damage could inflame rebellion and suppress collaboration with the client regime; similarly, the United States expected that reductions in civilian casualty rates would demonstrate sincerity and earn reciprocal understanding or goodwill among NGO and international audiences. But as Schultz points out, local reactions to civilian casualties varied widely. In some instances, it no doubt fueled resentment and resistance; in other instances, locals were either more inured to human suffering than Western audiences might expect or accepted this as the cost of uprooting the militants in their midst.[40]

Though the United States went to great lengths and great costs to reduce civilian casualties, the cases in this volume suggest that there was no one, natural equilibrium between pursuing enemies and sparing innocents. Russian forces in Syria and Saudi and Emirati forces in Yemen were largely indifferent to civilian casualties; in many instances, they moved from indifference to deliberate terror bombing of civilians as illustrated in Chapters 9 and 10. Even the United States set very different thresholds for acceptable civilian casualties (expressed in terms of "non-combatant casualty cutoff value" (NCV) or the maximum number of expected civilian casualties in a given strike military commanders could independently authorize) across contemporary theaters. According to published reports, the NCV in Afghanistan was set at zero while the corresponding NCV during the same period in Iraq and Syria was ten (Chapter 11).[41]

---

[40] See Schultz, Chapter 2, for contending views on drone blowback. See also Michael Waltz, *Warrior Diplomat: A Green Beret's Battles from Washington to Afghanistan* (Nebraska: Potomac Books, 2014), 1–26.

[41] Nick McDonnell, "Civilian Casualties Are Not Inevitable. The Military Sets an Acceptable Number in Advance," March 31, 2017. https://latimes.com/opinion/op-ed/la-oe-mcdonell-civilian-casualties-ncv-20170331-story.html (accessed May 1, 2020); Samuel Moyne, "A War without Civilian Deaths?" *The New Republic*, October 23, 2018. https://newrepublic.com/article/151560/damage-control-book-review-nick-mcdonell-bodies-person (accessed May 1, 2020); Scott Graham, "The Non-Combatant Casualty Cut-Off Value: Assessment of a Novel Targeting Technique in Operation Inherent Resolve," *International Criminal Law Review* 18:4 (July 2018):

This vast difference in sensitivity to civilian casualties reflected per-ceived risks to friendly forces and the mission. In higher intensity fights, the United States was willing to accept higher civilian casualties to protect its advisors and allies and accomplish the mission. It also reflected a basic difference in political aims. In Iraq and Syria, the United States sought to destroy ISIS but had no intention of administering the territory or popu-lation; the political costs of collateral damage were lower than they might have been had the United States anticipated a postwar role in restoring order. In Afghanistan, by contrast, the war was fought within the context of a political reconstruction of the Afghan state. In this context, the penalties for striking the innocent in the course of striking the guilty were much higher because the overarching objective was to promote collaboration with the Afghan government. What was indisputable was the relationship between speed and cost on the one hand and legal authorities on the other. The more restrictive the rules of engagement, and the lower the acceptable level of civilian casualties, the slower and more expensive the prosecution of the war on militants became.

### Lessons of the Age of Primacy?

At what may be the end of the age of primacy, it is fair to ask what conclusions can be drawn about the military and political efficacy of air power. On a strictly military level, unchallenged air superiority meant that the risk to air forces had never been lower. Aircraft were more or less free to roam at medium altitude in search of targets, and the combination of precision weapons, ground observers, and targeting pods enabled airmen to strike with unparalleled precision. The greatest obstacle to striking targets and avoiding casualties was intelligence. Here the counter-network operations revolution looms large. The urgency of attacking militant organizations after 2003 led to an organizational fusion of intelli-gence and operations whose scale, scope, and tactical virtuosity were unprecedented. The US military exits the age of primacy with a killing machine designed to destroy militant networks across a range of theaters.

The impressive military accomplishments of air power in this period can easily obscure the challenges of connecting tactical success with political effects. As in the Cold War, the success or failure of compellence hinged on the demands made and the capabilities, resolve, and alliance support of the enemy rather than the absolute capability of the attacker. The unusually propitious circumstances of the air campaigns in Bosnia

655–85; Sarah Sewall, *Chasing Success: Air Force Efforts to Reduce Civilian Harm* (Maxwell Air Force Base: Air University Press, March 2016).

and Kosovo should not blind us to the uncertainties of coercion even under the most favorable operational conditions.

Toppling weak regimes by brute force proved eminently achievable. What proved more elusive were the suppression of rebellion and the restoration of friendly regimes in the aftermath of these catastrophic successes. Even with unchallenged air supremacy, and abundant intelligence assets, air forces could at best contribute tactical successes in open-ended counterinsurgency and counterterrorism campaigns.

It should come as little surprise that air power became the weapon of first resort during the age of primacy. The risks to air forces had never been lower and the independent influence of air power, at least under certain circumstances, had never been higher. Yet in many instances victory from the air brought a winner's curse. As Chapter 8 highlights, nowhere was that clearer than in the aftermath of regime change in Libya. Air power, at least in an independent form, offered few answers to the unavoidable sequels of victories it had delivered.

In many respects, the age of primacy was a natural experiment in the potential of air power. Under the most permissive military conditions, and in possession of overwhelming advantages in technology and power, air forces rediscovered that coercion was as much a question of political circumstance as military power; few participants emerged from the near-run successes in the Balkans convinced that coercion would prove straightforward in the future. And an instrument billed as an independent means of achieving inexpensive, political victories remained maddeningly shackled to events and complexities on the ground. Even with uncontested air dominance, air forces generally had to attack enemy ground forces directly to accomplish the stated political goals. To attack those armies, air forces needed partners on the ground and advisors to control and focus air power.

### A Return to Battle: Air Power in the Age of Great Power Rivalry

The question at the end of the age of primacy is what will survive the transition to great power rivalry. How will the emergence of peer competitors with robust offensive and defensive strike capabilities affect the ambitions and the effectiveness of air power? Which lessons and innovations of the age of primacy are likely to carry over into the age of great power rivalry and which will be made extinct by these environmental changes? How will changes in the environment and the efficacy of air power change the relationships between the instrument and civilian decision makers?

What may be easiest to miss in this transition is the stubborn persistence of old problems. While dominant powers, particularly the United States, may have soured on open-ended engagements in small wars, the problems of rebellion and militancy are unlikely to disappear. There are few signs that Islamist militancy is on the wane so great powers will have to manage the threats it poses to regional interests and homelands. Rebellions remain far cheaper to foment and sustain than to extinguish, and this may make them attractive tools in the new great power rivalries. Iran's use of Shia groups in Iraq, Syria, Yemen, Lebanon, and Palestine and Pakistan's use of Sunni militants in its rivalry with India demonstrate the strategic utility of proxy war. Proxy war offers rivals an inexpensive, sufficiently deniable, and highly effective means to impose disproportionate costs on stronger rivals.[42]

If irregular wars persist, then great powers will need to devise more cost-efficient ways to wage them. How can great powers squarely focused on the prospect of high-end warfighting manage peripheral challenges at acceptable human and financial cost? As many of the chapters in this volume demonstrate, dominant powers have developed ways to disrupt their enemies but appear to be on the wrong side of the cost-exchange ratio.[43] Even with very deep pockets, dominant powers eventually sour on open-ended campaigns whose running costs dwarf those borne by the militants and their patrons. Even the recent small-footprint campaigns against ISIS in Iraq and Syria and against the Taliban and ISIS-K in Afghanistan conceal the substantial manpower costs of the kill web that supports forces in the air and on the ground. The holy grail remains the development of a management strategy that saves blood and treasure.

One answer might be a high-low equipment mix. The running costs of the postwar air campaigns in Iraq, Syria, and Afghanistan have been driven by the operating costs of high-end aircraft and the ISR and precision-strike demands of civilian casualty reduction. The cost per flight hour of fourth- and fifth-generation aircraft tells the first story. The A-10, F-16, and F-15 costs per flight hour are $20,000, $23,000, and $40,000, respectively; the F-22 cost approaches $70,000/hour. By comparison, the A-29 Super Tucano turboprop currently in use with Afghan forces costs $1,000 per flight hour and can deliver dumb bombs

---

[42] Eli Berman and David Lake, eds., *Proxy Wars: Suppressing Violence through Local Agents* (Ithaca: Cornell University Press, 2019), 1–26; C. Christine Fair, *Fighting to the End: The Pakistan Army's Way of War* (New York: Oxford University Press, 2014), 259–60.

[43] As outlined in Chapters 3 and 4, the prominent exceptions to this are Bosnia and Kosovo. In both cases, the short duration and finality of the campaigns kept the costs of intervention low.

with practical accuracy sufficient for most strike missions.[44] For a time, the US Air Force seemed intent on purchasing 300 light attack aircraft under the observation attack replacement (OA-X) program to lower the cost of close air support in small wars. The February 2020 decision to pull back from this buy in favor of a single-minded focus on great power war means that few cost savings are likely to be found in the short run.[45]

The second if more controversial way to address the costs of air power in small wars is to revisit the impact of rules of engagement on financial cost. As long as small wars were the primary focus, rich countries could rationalize the use of high-end aircraft and munitions against low-end opponents. The emergence of great power rivalry may force a more hard-headed reappraisal of the costs and benefits of this approach. Political choices on status- versus conduct-based targeting and the NCV value effectively drive the investment of ISR and precision munitions to a point where the marginal cost of avoiding civilian casualties may exceed the benefit in local and international goodwill. As it stands, the United States pays a very high price for a clean conscience in small wars; the question is whether the recent drive to minimize civilian casualties will eventually price some great powers out of this category of operations.

Third, great powers can reexamine their reliance on exquisite munitions. If great powers must husband precision munitions for high-end contingencies, they may need to explore the use of less expensive solutions to achieve acceptable outcomes in secondary theaters. Combining smart platforms and dumb munitions is one possible solution. Russian vendors are currently promoting an onboard targeting system with an accuracy of 3–5 meters that is similar to recent claims by other light attack manufacturers.[46] A complementary approach would be to drive the cost

[44] Sebastien Roblin, "The Duel of the Light Attack Planes: Tucano vs. Texan vs. Scorpion," *The National Interest*, July 10, 2017. https://nationalinterest.org/blog/the-buzz/duel-the-light-attack-planes-tucano-vs-texan-vs-scorpion-21470 (accessed May 10, 2020)
[45] Gareth Jennings, "Pentagon Budget 2021: US Light Attack Aircraft Requirement Moves from USAF to USSOCOM," *Jane's Defence Weekly*, February 12, 2020. https://janes-ihs-com.usnwc.idm.oclc.org/Janes/Display/FG_2698267-JDW (accessed May 10, 2020); Valerie Insinnia, "Sorry Sierra Nevada Corp and Textron: The US Air Force Isn't Buying Light Attack Planes," *Defense News*, February 10, 2020. https://defensenews.com/smr/federal-budget/2020/02/10/sorry-sierra-nevada-corp-and-textron-the-us-air-force-isnt-buying-light-attack-planes (accessed May 10, 2020)
[46] Michael Peck, "Look Out America: Russia Is Claiming to Have Smarter 'Smart Bombs,'" *The National Interest*, November 8, 2019. https://nationalinterest.org/blog/buzz/look-out-america-russias-claiming-have-smarter-smart-bombs-95166 (accessed May 10, 2020); Joseph Trevithick, "Here Is What Each of the Pentagon's Air-Launched Missiles and Bombs Actually Cost: Arming America's Combat Aircraft, Drones, and Helicopters Is an Extremely Expensive Business," February 18, 2020. www.thedrive.com/the-war-zone/32277/here-is-what-each-of-the-pentagons-air-launched-missiles-and-bombs-actually-cost (accessed May 10, 2020)

of precision munitions down. Bulk purchases of legacy precision-guided munitions such as Hellfire missiles, GPS-guided bombs, and Paveway laser-guided bomb kits and the ensuing learning curve effects have already reduced the unit cost of these weapons dramatically. Another path is the procurement of lower-cost precision munitions. The recent introduction of weapons such as the laser-guided 70mm rocket Advanced Precision Kill Weapons System (APKWS) signals a move to reduce cost at the point of design.[47]

None of these drives for economy will come naturally. As recent policy debates have shown, statesmen and military leaders alike may prefer to close peripheral theaters rather than balance the demands of great power rivalry and lesser threats. Second, the political decision to separate out from the base defense budget the costs of the wars in Iraq and Afghanistan under the heading of "overseas contingency operations" (OCO) removed many of the incentives for Congress and the services to assess the costs of operations. Third, air forces are generally designed to maximize effectiveness rather than efficiency. However sensible the proposition that cost savings in one arena may free up resources for another, the old habits of cost insensitivity are likely to endure.

While great powers are unlikely to divest entirely from small wars, the greatest changes in the age of great power rivalry will be the return of symmetry and strategic interaction. China and Russia are adversaries that have the defenses to hold opponents at arm's length; they are also powers with the means to look and strike deep at fixed bases and moving naval targets. In China and Russia, the United States and its allies face rivals intent on revising the liberal international order in their favor. Both possess the technological base necessary to compete with the United States, and both have spent the past twenty years designing around the US capabilities developed during the age of primacy. The emergence of two near-peer competitors will transform any clash of arms from a matter of dictation by the strong to the weak into a wrestling match.

All the things that were easy in the age of primacy – most important, the ease of maintaining unchallenged air superiority – will become hard and costly again. In this new world, the consequences of errant strategic choice will be far higher. In the age of primacy, dominant powers could afford to test a series of strategies in the hopes that one would have the desired political effect. In the age of great power rivalry, the presence of

---

[47] APKWS II brings the cost of a 2-meter CEP laser-guided weapon down to $22,500 in comparison with the $70,000 cost of a Hellfire missile. For a more complete breakdown of the relative costs of precision munitions, see John R. Hoehn, "Precision-Guided Munitions: Background and Issues for Congress (R45996)," *Congressional Research Service*, April 15, 2020.

animate, focused, and powerful opponents will make the early choices more consequential and rapid adaptation paramount.

Two shifts have occurred that will make the use of air power more difficult in future clashes with China or Russia. The first is the development of increasingly capable integrated air defense systems (IADS).[48] The deployment of layered sensor networks and double-digit surface-to-air missile systems will make it increasingly difficult for aircraft to penetrate defenses and deliver weapons at close range. If air forces in the age of primacy could reasonably expect to take down air defenses as a prelude to free-roving operations, air forces of the future will face far more costly and protracted rollback campaigns and the troublesome prospect of repetitive raiding against resilient defensive systems. A regional war in this new environment may impose costs and risks on air forces not seen since the US campaigns over North Vietnam or the allied air offensives over Europe in 1943–44.[49]

The second major change is the fielding of large numbers of highly accurate conventional ballistic missiles and cruise missiles and over-the-horizon targeting systems. If rivals can see and strike fixed bases and moving naval targets reliably, then many of the foundations of the US security model will be at risk. The death of sanctuary, on land and at sea, will make the problem of projecting power in Europe and Asia far more difficult.[50]

The offensive air strategies of the age of primacy all rested on an implicit foundation of what Barry Posen referred to as "command of the commons."[51] Unchallenged air superiority at medium altitude gave great powers the ability to loiter over the battle space with limited risk. This simplified intelligence gathering and made great powers accustomed to the unblinking eye and unsleeping ear of imagery and signals collection. This sanctuary extended to the space domain where the United States

[48] Sean O'Connor and Mark Cazalet, "Analyzing Russia's SAM Capabilities: Deployments, Capabilities, Future Prospects," *Jane's Intelligence Briefing*, March 9, 2020; Richard Fisher and Sean O'Connor, "China Bolsters Anti-Missile Capabilities with Russian SAMs," *Jane's Intelligence Review*, June 3, 2019.

[49] Noble Frankland, *Bomber Offensive: The Devastation of Europe* (New York: Ballantine Books, 1970).

[50] Mark Gunzinger, Carl Rehberg, Jacob Cohn, Timothy Walton, and Lukas Autenried, *An Air Force for an Era of Great Power Competition* (Center for Strategic and Budgetary Analysis, 2019), 69–90; Andrew Tate, "China's Growing Missile Arsenal Challenges US Freedom of Operation," *Jane's Defence Weekly*, October 2, 2019; Andrew Tate, "China Touts Capabilities of DF-26 as ASBM," *Jane's Defence Weekly*, January 28, 2019; Andrew Erickson, "Showtime: China Reveals Two 'Carrier-Killer' Missiles," *The National Interest*, September 3, 2015. https://nationalinterest.org/feature/showtime-china-reveals-two-carrier-killer-missiles-13769 (accessed June 10, 2020)

[51] Barry Posen, "Command of the Commons: The Military Foundation of US Hegemony," *International Security* 28:1 (Summer 2003): 5–46.

and to a lesser extent Russia and China were able to collect intelligence without interference and constrained only by competing demands on scarce assets. Command of the commons also enabled air forces to deliver strikes at close range, observe effects, and reengage as needed. Elaborate tactics and procedures emerged to apply fires to targets within visual range of either ground observers or aircraft. It is easy to forget how much the achievements of air power in the age of primacy depended on proximity. The pillars of air war in the age of primacy have been short-range aircraft, short-range munitions, and short-range ISR platforms.[52] If air forces try to achieve similar ends at longer range, they are far less likely to be militarily effective.[53]

As the risks from enemy IADS mount, operational concepts that rely on loitering are likely to be rendered obsolete. If airborne platforms cannot afford to loiter, and space assets are at risk from a range of antisatellite weapons, then air forces may lose the insights into enemy dispositions they have enjoyed for the past three decades. The fog of war will thicken as levels of uncertainty rise in targeting and the post-strike assessment of effects. Similarly, the close air support missions of the age of primacy may be prohibitively costly in an environment of robust and resilient IADS. It is hard to imagine circumstances in which ground controllers and orbiting aircraft will be able to orchestrate air support in the face of layered sensor networks and mobile surface-to-air missiles.

The presence of robust IADS will instead force air forces to fight to get to their targets. Aircraft, particularly those lacking stealth characteristics, will struggle to penetrate modern IADS.[54] Even fifth-generation, stealth aircraft will likely labor to locate and engage targets without revealing their presence to air defense networks. If the bomber seldom gets through, then the weight may shift to long-range, penetrating munitions such as cruise missiles, ballistic missiles, and hypersonic weapons. As reliance on such munitions mounts, so too will the relative importance of munitions inventories vis-à-vis aircraft numbers. The operational balance in future conflicts may hinge not just on the first salvo but the last.

---

[52] Mark Gunzinger and Bryan Clark, *Sustaining America's Precision Strike Advantage* (Washington: Center for Strategic and Budgetary Analysis, 2015), 18–19.
[53] As air forces seek to engage targets at longer range, they will pay substantial penalties in terms of weapons load and aerial refueling requirements. The lag between the identification of distant targets and the delivery of weapons will increase the chances they will miss those targets. Finally, long-range engagements will deprive air forces of direct battle damage assessment.
[54] Lt Gen David Deptula, Mg Gen Lawrence Stutzriem, and Heather Penny, "Ensuring the Common Defense: The Case for Fifth Generation Airpower," *Mitchell Institute Policy Papers* 20, April 2019, 9–10; ibid., Gunzinger et. al., *An Air Force for an Era of Great Power Competition*, v–vi, 42–46.

The side with the last munitions may hold important advantages over opponents who have expended certain classes of weapons and lack the ability to replenish them rapidly.[55]

These changes will also force a reassessment of the defense. As the Iranian attacks on Saudi Arabian oil facilities in 2019 and a US air base in Iraq in 2020 demonstrated, the proliferation of cruise missiles and drones have brought long-range precision strike capabilities within the reach of regional powers and militant proxies. If China and Russia can use more advanced conventional ballistic and cruise missiles to attack key assets such as fixed bases and naval surface ships, and such weapons prove very hard and expensive to attack directly, then the United States will face a choice between pulling back out of range of such systems or developing new ways to operate within their envelopes.[56] Pulling back may under-mine the credibility of US deterrent threats and assurances to regional allies; staying forward may expose US assets to unacceptable risk of loss in a high-end war fight. The growing lethality of long-range precision strike also means the revisionist powers need not overcome the US advantages in fifth-generation air-to-air capability. Missile warfare may in this sense bypass the air-to-air construct on which US defensive doctrine has been built since World War II.

The counter-air fight may be transformed into a counter-missile fight on three dimensions. The first involves the struggle to find and kill the metaphorical archer. The poor performance of the US and Israeli air forces in mobile missile hunting in Desert Storm (Chapter 6) and the Second Lebanon War (Chapter 7) highlights the challenges of finding and killing this category of targets even under permissive conditions.[57] The second approach is the attempt to shoot the arrows down. Here again, decades of competitive research and development suggest that ballistic and even cruise missile defense is considerably more challenging and costly than the offensive missile employment.[58] The third option would be to blind the archer by attacking his sensor network. As in the

---

[55] Mark Gunzinger and Bryan Clark, *Winning the Salvo Competition: Rebalancing America's Air and Missile Defenses* (Washington: Center for Strategic and Budgetary Analysis, 2016), 2–4; Jacob Cohn, Timothy Walton, Adam Lemon and Toshi Yoshihara, *Leveling the Playing Field: Reintroducing Theater Range Missiles in a Post-INF World* (Washington: Center for Strategic and Budgetary Analysis, 2019), 3–16.

[56] Ibid., Gunzinger et al., *Winning the Salvo Competition*, 12–13; ibid., Cohn et al., *Leveling the Playing Field*, 6–10.

[57] Col Herbert Kemp, "Countering Mobile Missiles: Holding the Entire Launch Cycle at Risk," *Mitchell Institute Policy Papers* 27, September 2019; ibid., Gunzinger et al., *Winning the Salvo Competition*, iv.

[58] Theodore Postol, "Why Missile Defense Won't Work," *MIT Technology Review*, April 1, 2002. www.technologyreview.com/2002/04/01/235142/why-missile-defense-wont-work (accessed June 10, 2020); ibid., Gunzinger et al., *Winning the Salvo Competition*, 8.

Cold War, aggressive attack on enemy sensor networks and command and control networks could easily end in inadvertent nuclear escalation if the target countries fear the loss of their nuclear forces or command and control.[59] What is clear is that defeating the enemy air threat will have more to do with countering enemy missiles than shooting down enemy aircraft. This will force the United States in particular to develop new forces and capabilities to address the threat of enemy conventional ballistic missiles, cruise missiles, and hypersonic weapons.

One logical response may be imitation. By investing in long-range conventional precision strike, the United States and other Western powers may be able to project power at range and bypass an increasingly challenging counter-IADS fight. Three obstacles loom large. If the past is any predictor, the cost and time of developing new classes of long-range munitions will be substantial. Second, such munitions will be useless unless they are paired with survivable, over-the-horizon targeting systems. These investments will compete for the same dollars being invested in expanding the fifth-generation fighter and bomber inventories. Third, long-range missiles raise thorny basing questions in Europe and Asia. Even if post-INF conventional missiles can be produced, allies may be reluctant to accept the risk of hosting them.[60]

What then is the role of air power in a world where the commons is contested or even denied? The first sobering conclusion is that the age of primacy may well have been the high-water mark in the independent influence of air power on political outcomes. In wars between equals, great powers are unlikely to be able to compel their adversaries to concede using air power alone. Strategies that rely on the ability to roam and loiter over the battle space may be obsolete in a high-intensity fight; the strategies and tactics surrounding persistent air-breathing ISR, close air support, and missile hunting look particularly vulnerable in wars against countries with robust IADS and offensive precision strike capabilities. While other approaches such as strategic attack, interdiction, and leadership targeting remain militarily plausible, such strategies have seldom achieved their political aims even under permissive conditions. Air forces will face far longer odds in great power war as they struggle to penetrate more lethal and resilient defensive networks without the luxury of an unblinking eye of overhead intelligence. Fixed targets, whether military or economic, will be the most vulnerable to air attack by either side;

---

[59] Caitlin Talmadge, "Would China Go Nuclear? Assessing the Risk of Chinese Nuclear Escalation in a Conventional War with the US," *International Security* 41:4 (Spring 2017): 53–55; Barry Posen, *Inadvertent Escalation: Conventional War and Nuclear Risks* (Ithaca: Cornell University Press, 1991), 1–4, 28–35, 205–6.

[60] Ibid., Cohn et al., *Leveling the Playing Field*, 17–32.

mobile targets hiding in clutter and protected by air defenses will likely be more survivable. For these reasons, countervalue campaigns and punishment strategies may become more appealing as the challenges of attacking peer military forces become more tactically and technologically difficult and costly.

If there is a silver lining for air forces, it is that no other instrument currently available is likely to depose it as the weapon of first political resort. The high cost, slow speed, and prospective entanglements associated with the use of ground forces in high-intensity wars will limit their appeal. Naval forces, particularly large surface combatants, will face very real threats from enemy long-range strike assets. Though some point to cyber warfare as a potentially influential low-cost tool, the effects of offensive cyber warfare remain far from clear. All these things leave air forces as a necessary tool in any future war of salvoes. Even if air power cannot accomplish its most ambitious independent aims in peer contests, air forces, particularly those equipped with long-range munitions, will provide the most reliable means to deliver precision strikes against a host of targets. The rising significance of long-range strike may provoke considerable competition within air forces as bomber and missile forces offer more compelling answers to the leading threats than the short-range fighters that have held sway since the second half of the Cold War. The greatest risk to air power's pride of place may emerge from an interservice competition to deliver long-range missile fires. The US Army, Marine Corps, and Navy are all engaged in the development of long-range strike systems. Over the long run, there is no reason why traditional air forces will enjoy a natural monopoly over land-based or sea-based missile systems.

The appeal of air power to civilian statesmen may wane. Whether this change comes through educated foresight or through the shock of high aircraft losses in the opening phases of a war of equals, the mystique of air power is likely to be the first casualty of great power war. As in the opening stages of World War II, enthusiasm for limited-liability strategies and the air arm in particular are likely to be replaced by a realization that ambitious political aims against nuclear-armed rivals can only be accomplished at great cost and great risk. If this gives statesmen a new incentive for strategic prudence, it may be one of the few unintended benefits of the return to great power rivalry.

# Index

306

CPSIA information can be obtained
at www.ICGtesting.com
Printed in the USA
BVHW011653150322
631538BV00007B/55

9 781108 984751